MEMOIRS

OF

RICHARD CUMBERLAND,

WRITTEN BY HIMSELF.

CONTAINING

AN ACCOUNT OF HIS LIFE AND WRITINGS,

INTERSPERSED WITH

ANECDOTES AND CHARACTERS

OF

SEVERAL OF THE MOST DISTINGUISHED PERSONS OF HIS TIME, WITH WHOM HE HAS HAD INTERCOURSE AND CONNECTION.

WITH ILLUSTRATIVE NOTES.

BY

HENRY FLANDERS,

AUTHOR OF "THE LIVES AND TIMES OF THE CHIEF JUSTICES."

PHILADELPHIA:

PARRY AND McMILLAN.

1856.

PHILADELPHIA:
T. K. AND P. G. COLLINS, PRINTERS.

EDITOR'S PREFACE.

THE author of the following pages held a conspicuous place in London literary society; and was on familiar terms with many of the most eminent men of his time and country. "The sketches and anecdotes which he has introduced into his *Memoirs* are in the highest degree interesting; whilst his habits of observing and discriminating character give to his delineations an authority, and consequently a value, which it is difficult to over-estimate."[1]

The career of Cumberland in Spain is a curious episode in his life; and, in connection with Jay's mission to that country, of especial interest to the student of American history.

The Editor has divided the narrative into chapters, and added notes, illustrative of the text, which he ventures to hope has enhanced the value and interest of the work.

PHILADELPHIA, March, 1856.

[1] Encyclopædia Britannica.

CONTENTS.

CHAPTER I.

CHAPTER II.

CHAPTER III.

CHAPTER IV.

CHAPTER V.

CHAPTER VI.

CHAPTER VII.

CHAPTER VIII.

CHAPTER IX.

CHAPTER X.

CHAPTER XI.

CHAPTER XII.

CHAPTER XIII.

MEMOIRS

OF

RICHARD CUMBERLAND.

CHAPTER I.

Author's Preface—His ancestors—Doctor Richard Cumberland—Doctor Richard Bentley—Swift's Battle of the Books—Anecdotes of Bentley—Collins—His controversy with Bentley—Roger Cotes—Character of Bentley—Mrs. Bentley—Richard Bentley, the younger—His connection with Horace Walpole—Character of Walpole—Elizabeth Bentley—Joanna Bentley, Cumberland's mother—Author's reflections—His boyhood—His teacher, Arthur Kinsman—Anecdote of—Cumberland at school—Joshua Barnes—Warburton—Death of Dr. Bentley—Cumberland's success in his studies—Attempts English verse—His home—His mother forms his taste in poetry—Goes to Westminster—Vincent Bourne—Warren Hastings—Colman—Hinchliffe, Smith, and Vincent—Dr. Nichols—Execution of Lords Kilmarnock and Balmerino—Anecdote of Selwyn—Progress of the rebels—Westminster school—Eton school—Edmund Ashby—Cumberland goes to the play—Garrick—Death of Cumberland's sister—Enters Trinity College.

At the close of the year 1804, whilst I am still in possession of my faculties, though full of years, I sit down to give a history of my life and writings. I do not undertake the task lightly, and without deliberation; for I have weighed the difficulties, and am prepared to meet them. I have lived so long in this world, mixed so generally with mankind, and written so voluminously and so variously, that I trust my motives cannot be greatly misunderstood, if, with strict attention to truth, and in simplicity of style, I pursue my narrative, saying nothing more of the immediate object of these memoirs, than in honor and in conscience I am warranted to say.

I shall use so little embellishment in this narrative that, if the reader is naturally candid he will not be disgusted; if he is easily amused he will not be disappointed.

2

As I have been through life a negligent recorder of dates and events relating to myself, it is very possible I may fall into errors of memory as to the order and arrangement of certain facts and occurrences; but whilst I adhere to veracity in the relation of them, the trespass, I presume, will be readily overlooked.

Of many persons with whom I have had intercourse and connection, I shall speak freely and impartially. I know myself incapable of wantonly aspersing the characters of the living or the dead; but, though I will not indulge myself in conjectures, I will not turn aside from facts, and neither from affectation of candor, nor dread of recrimination, waive the privilege, which I claim for myself in every page of this history, of speaking the truth from my heart. I may not always say all that I could; but I will never knowingly say of any man what I should not.

As I am descended from ancestors illustrious for their piety, benevolence, and erudition, I will not say I am not vain of that distinction; but I will confess it would be a vanity, serving only to expose my degeneracy, were it accompanied with the inspiration of no worthier passion.

Doctor Richard Cumberland, who was consecrated Bishop of Peterborough in the year 1691, was my great grandfather. He was author of that excellent work entitled 'De Legibus Naturæ,' in which he effectually refutes the impious tenets of Hobbes; and whilst he was unambitiously fulfilling the simple functions of a parish priest in the town of Stamford, the revolution having taken place, search was made after the ablest Protestant divines to fill up vacancies in the hierarchy, and rally round their late endangered church. Without interest, and without a wish to emerge from his obscurity and retirement, this excellent man, the vindicator of the insulted laws of nature, received the first intelligence of his promotion from a paragraph in the public papers, and, being then sixty years old, was with difficulty persuaded to accept the offer when it came to him from authority. The persuasion of his friends, particularly Sir Orlando Bridgeman, at length overcame his repugnance; and to that see, though very moderately endowed, he forever after devoted himself, and resisted every offer of translation, though repeatedly made, and earnestly recommended. To such of his friends who pressed an exchange upon him, he was accustomed to reply that Peterborough was his first espoused, and should be his only one; and, in fact, according to his principles, no church revenue could enrich him, for I have heard my father say that, at the end of every year, whatever overplus he found, upon a minute inspection of his accounts, was by him distributed to the poor, reserving only one small deposit of twenty-five pounds in cash, found at his death in his bureau, with directions to employ it for the discharge of his funeral expenses; a sum, in his modest calculation, fully sufficient to commit his body to the earth.

Such was the humility of this truly Christian prelate, and such his disinterested sentiments as to the appropriation of his episcopal revenue. The wealthiest see could not have tempted him to accumulate, the poorest sufficed for his expenses, and of those he had to spare for the poor; yet he was hospitable in his plain and primitive style of living, and had a table ever open to his clergy and his friends. He had a sweetness and placidity of temper that nothing ever ruffled or disturbed. I know it cannot be the lot of human creature to attain perfection; yet so wonderfully near did this good man approach to consummate rectitude, that, unless benevolence may be carried to excess, no other failing was ever known to have been discovered in his character. His chaplain, Archdeacon Payne, who married one of his daughters, and whom I am old enough to remember, makes this observation in the short sketch of the bishop's life which he has prefixed to his edition of 'The Sanchoniatho.' This and his other works are in the hands of the learned, and cannot need any effort on my part to elucidate what they so clearly display, the vast erudition and patient investigation of the author.

The death of this venerable prelate was, like his life, serene and undisturbed: at the extended age of eighty-six years and some months, as he was sitting in his library, he expired without a struggle, for he was found in the attitude of one asleep, with his cap fallen over his eyes, and a book in his hand, in which he had been reading. Thus, without the ordinary visitations of pain or sickness, it pleased God to terminate the existence of this exemplary man.

He possessed his faculties to the last, verifying the only claim he was ever heard to make as to mental endowments; for whilst he acknowledged himself to be gifted by nature with good wearing parts, he made no pretensions to quick and brilliant talents; and in that respect he seems to have estimated himself very truly, as we rarely find such meek and modest qualities as he possessed in men of warmer imaginations and a brighter glow of genius, with less solidity of understanding, and, of course, more liable to the influences of their passions.

Bishop Cumberland was the son of a respectable citizen of London, and educated at St. Paul's school, from whence he was admitted of Magdalen College in Cambridge, where he pursued his studies, and was elected fellow of that society, to which I had the honor to present a copy of that portrait from which the print hereunto annexed was taken.[1]

In the oriental languages, in mathematics, and even in anatomy, he was deeply learned; in short, his mind was fitted for elaborate and profound researches, as his works more fully testify. It is to be lamented that his famous work, 'De Legibus Naturæ,' was allowed to come before the public with so many and such glaring errors of the press, which his absence and considerable distance from London disabled him from correcting. I had a copy interleaved and corrected and amended throughout by Doctor Bentley, who, being on a visit to my father at his parsonage-house in Northamptonshire, undertook that kind office, and completed it most effectually. This book I gave, when last at Cambridge, to the library of Trinity College; and if by those means it shall find a passport to the University press, I shall have cause to congratulate myself for having so happily bestowed it.

Of Doctor Richard Bentley, my maternal grandfather, I shall next take leave to speak. Of him I have perfect recollection. His person, his dignity, his language, and his love, fixed my early attention, and stamped both his image and his words upon my memory. His literary works are known to all, his private character is still misunderstood by many; to that I shall confine myself, and, putting aside the enthusiasm of a descendant, I can assert, with the veracity of a biographer, that he was neither cynical, as some have represented him, nor overbearing and fastidious in the degree, as he has been described by many. Swift, when he foisted him into his vulgar 'Battle of the Books,' neither lowers Bentley's fame nor elevates his own; and the petulant poet, who thought he had hit his manner when he made him haughtily call to Walker for his hat, gave a copy as little like the character of Bentley as his translation is like the original of Homer. That Dr. Walker, vice-master of Trinity College, was the friend of my grandfather, and a frequent guest at his table, is true; but it was not in Doctor Bentley's nature to treat him with contempt, nor did his harmless character inspire it. As for the hat, I must acknowledge it was of formidable dimensions,

[1] Cumberland's pleasing sketch of his paternal ancestor is justified by his contemporary reputation. He was a man of varied and profound learning, elevated moral sentiments, and unaffected humility. From the year 1658, memorable for the death of Cromwell, until he was raised to the Bishopric, in 1791, he discharged the duties of a parish priest with zeal and unpretending piety. In addition to the Treatise 'De Legibus Naturæ,' he was the author of 'An Essay on the Jewish Weights and Measures;' 'Sanchoniathon's Phœnician History,' translated from Eusebius; and 'Origines Gentium Antiquissima.'

yet I was accustomed to treat it with great familiarity, and, if it had ever been further from the hand of its owner than the peg upon the back of his great arm-chair, I might have been dispatched to fetch it, for he was disabled by the palsy in his latter days; but the hat never strayed from its place, and Pope found an office for Walker that I can well believe he was never commissioned to in his life.[1]

I had a sister somewhat elder than myself. Had there been any of that sternness in my grandfather, which is so falsely imputed to him, it may well be supposed we should have been awed into silence in his presence, to which we were admitted every day. Nothing can be further from the truth; he was the unwearied patron and promoter of all our childish sports and sallies; at all times ready to detach himself from any topic of

[1] The essay of Sir William Temple, upon the subject of ancient and modern learning, was the occasion of a famous controversy between Dr. Bentley and Charles Boyle, afterwards Earl of Orrery. Sir William, in his essay, had highly commended the Greek epistles of Phalaris; and Boyle subsequently published a new edition of them. The essay of Temple was answered by W. Wotton, B. D., with an appendix by Dr. Bentley. 'In that appendix,' such is the account prefixed to Swift's 'Battle of the Books,' 'the doctor falls hard upon a new edition of Phalaris just out, by the Honorable Charles Boyle, to which Mr. Boyle replied at large with great learning and wit; and the doctor voluminously rejoined.' Bentley was opposed by the most celebrated wits and critics of his time; but it has long been conceded that he was victorious. The spuriousness of the epistles was successfully demonstrated. Swift's motive in attacking Bentley is apparent. He wished to vindicate the literary judgment of his patron, Sir William Temple, who had not escaped unscathed in the controversy. 'Day being far spent,' such is Swift's description of the progress of the battle, and Bentley's appearance on the field, 'and the numerous forces of the moderns half inclining to a retreat, there issued forth from a squadron of their *heavy-armed foot* a captain, whose name was Bentley, the most deformed of all the moderns; tall, but without strength or proportion. His armor was patched up of a thousand incoherent pieces; and the sound of it, as he marched, was loud and dry, like that made by the fall of a sheet of lead, which an *etesian* wind blows suddenly down from the roof of some steeple. His helmet was of old rusty iron, but the vizor was brass, which, tainted by his breath, corrupted into copperas, nor wanted gall from the same fountain; so that, whenever provoked by anger or labor, an atramentous quality of most malignant nature was seen to distil from his lips. In his right hand he grasped a flail, and (that he might never be unprovided of an *offensive* weapon) a vessel full of ordure in his left. Thus completely armed, he advanced with a slow and heavy pace, where the modern chiefs were holding a consult upon the sum of things; who, as he came onwards, laughed to behold his crooked leg and hump shoulder, which his boot and armor vainly endeavored to hide, were forced to comply with and expose.'

The 'Battle of the Books,' like all Swift's works, abounds with wit, satire, and coarseness.

Bentley's arrogance made him many enemies. The poets, especially, seemed to owe him a grudge. Pope introduced him into 'The Dunciad,' and Dr. Garth thus assailed him in his Dispensary:—

'So diamonds owe a lustre to their foil,
And to a Bentley 'tis we owe a Boyle.'

conversation, to take an interest and bear his part in our amusements. The eager curiosity natural to our age, and the questions it gave birth to, so teasing to many parents, he, on the contrary, attended to and encouraged, as the claims of infant reason never to be evaded or abused; strongly recommending that to all such inquiries answer should be given according to the strictest truth, and information dealt to us in the clearest terms, as a sacred duty never to be departed from. I have broken in upon him many a time in his hours of study, when he would put his book aside, ring his hand-bell for his servant, and be led to his shelves to take down a picture-book for my amusement. I do not say that his good nature always gained its object, as the pictures which his books generally supplied me with were anatomical drawings of dissected bodies, very little calculated to communicate delight; but he had nothing better to produce; and, surely, such an effort on his part, however unsuccessful, was no feature of a cynic: a cynic should be made of sterner stuff. I have had from him, at times, whilst standing at his elbow, a complete and entertaining narrative of his schoolboy days, with the characters of his different masters very humorously displayed, and the punishments described which they at times would wrongfully inflict upon him for seeming to be idle and regardless of his task, 'when the dunces,' he would say, 'could not discover that I was pondering it in my mind, and fixing it more firmly in my memory than if I had been bawling it out amongst the rest of my school-fellows.'

Once, and only once, I recollect his giving me a gentle rebuke for making a most outrageous noise in the room over his library and disturbing him in his studies; I had no apprehension of anger from him, and confidently answered that I could not help it, as I had been at battledore and shuttlecock with Master Gooch, the Bishop of Ely's son. 'And I have been at this sport with his father,' he replied; 'but thine has been the more amusing game, so there is no harm done.'

These are puerile anecdotes, but my history itself is only in its nonage; and even these will serve in some degree to establish what I affirmed, and present his character in those mild and unimposing lights, which may prevail with those who know him only as a critic and controversialist—

> As slashing Bentley with his desperate hook,

to reform and soften their opinions of him.

He recommended it as a very essential duty in parents to be particularly attentive to the first dawnings of reason in their children; and his own practice was the best illustration of his doctrine; for he was the most patient hearer and most favorable interpreter of first attempts at argument and meaning that I ever knew. When I was rallied by my mother, for roundly asserting that I never slept, I remember full well his calling on me to account for it; and when I explained it by saying I never knew myself to be asleep, and therefore supposed I never slept at all, he gave me credit for my defence, and said to my mother, 'Leave your boy in the possession of his opinion; he has as clear a conception of sleep, and at least as comfortable an one, as the philosophers who puzzle their brains about it, and do not rest so well.'

Though Bishop Lowth, in the flippancy of controversy called the author of 'The Philoleutherus Lipsiensis' and detector of Phalaris, *aut Caprimulgus aut fossor*, his genius has produced those living witnesses, that must for ever put that charge to shame and silence. Against such idle inconsiderate words, now dead as the language they were conveyed in, the appeal is near at hand; it lies no further off than to his works, and they are upon every reading man's shelves; but those, who would have looked into his heart, should have stepped into his house, and seen him in his private and domestic hours; therefore it is that I adduce these little anecdotes and trifling incidents, which describe the man, but leave the author to defend himself.

His ordinary style of conversation was naturally lofty, and his frequent use of *thou* and *thee* with his familiars carried with it a kind of dictatorial tone, that savored more of the closet than the court; this is readily admitted, and this on first approaches might mislead a stranger; but the native candor and inherent tenderness of his heart could not long be veiled from observation, for his feelings and affections were at once too impulsive to be long repressed, and he too careless of concealment to attempt at qualifying them. Such was his sensibility towards human sufferings, that it became a duty with his family to divert the conversation from all topics of that sort; and if he touched upon them himself he was betrayed into agitations, which if the reader ascribes to paralytic weakness, he will very greatly mistake a man who, to the last hour of his life, possessed his faculties firm and in their fullest vigor: I therefore bar all such misinterpretations as may attempt to set the mark of infirmity upon those emotions, which had no other source and origin but in the natural and pure benevolence of his heart.

He was communicative to all without distinction that sought information, or resorted to him for assistance; fond of his college almost to enthusiasm, and ever zealous for the honor of the purple gown of Trinity. When he held examinations for fellowships, and the modest candidate exhibited marks of agitation and alarm, he never failed to interpret candidly of such symptoms; and on those occasions he was never known to press the hesitating and embarrassed examinant, but oftentimes, on the contrary, would take all the pains of expounding on himself, and credit the exonerated candidate for answers and interpretations of his own suggesting. If this was not rigid justice, it was, at least in my conception of it, something better and more amiable; and how liable he was to deviate from the strict line of justice, by his partiality to the side of mercy, appears from the anecdote of the thief, who robbed him of his plate, and was seized and brought before him with the very articles upon him: the natural process in this man's case pointed out the road to prison; my grandfather's process was more summary, but not quite so legal. While commissary Greaves, who was then present, and of counsel for the college *ex officio*, was expatiating on the crime, and prescribing the measures obviously to be taken with the offender, Doctor Bentley interposed, saying, 'Why tell the man he is a thief? he knows that well enough, without thy information, Greaves.—Harkye, fellow, thou seest the trade which thou hast taken up is an unprofitable trade, therefore, get thee gone, lay aside an occupation by which thou canst gain nothing but a halter, and follow that by which thou mayst earn an honest livelihood.' Having said this, he ordered him to be set at liberty against the remonstrances of the by-standers, and insisting upon it that the fellow was duly penitent for his offence, bade him go his way, and never steal again.

I leave it with those, who consider mercy as one of man's best attributes, to suggest a plea for the informality of this proceeding, and to such I will communicate one other anecdote, which I do not deliver upon my own knowledge, though from unexceptionable authority, and this is, that when Collins had fallen into decay of circumstances, Dr. Bentley, suspecting he had written him out of credit by his 'Philoleutherus Lipsiensis,' secretly contrived to administer to the necessities of his baffled opponent, in a manner that did no less credit to his delicacy than to his liberality.[1]

[1] Anthony Collins was a gentleman of ample estate, who devoted his leisure to literature and philosophical inquiries. As a metaphysician, he discovered no mean ability, and displayed equal candor and courage in avowing the conclusions to which his studies conducted him. In 1713 he published 'A Discourse on Free-thinking.' The object of the work was to vindicate the unlimited freedom of inquiry, and to expose the tyranny exercised by the abettors of priestcraft, under paganism, Popery, or any other corrupt form of

A morose and overbearing man will find himself a solitary being in creation; Dr. Bentley, on the contrary, had many intimates; judicious in forming his friendships, he was faithful in adhering to them. With Sir Isaac Newton, Doctor Mead, Doctor Wallis of Stamford, Baron Spanheim, the lamented Roger Cotes,[1] and several other distinguished and illustrious contemporaries, he lived on terms of uninterrupted harmony, and I have good authority for saying, that it is to his interest and importunity with Sir Isaac Newton, that the inestimable publication of the 'Principia' was ever resolved upon by that truly great and luminous philosopher. Newton's portrait by Sir James Thornhill, and those of Baron Spanheim and my grandfather by the same hand, now hanging in the Master's lodge of Trinity, were the bequest of Dr. Bentley. I was possessed of letters in Sir Isaac's own hand to my grandfather, which, together with the corrected volume of Bishop Cumberland's 'Laws of Nature,' I lately gave to the library of that flourishing and illustrious college.

The irreparable loss of Roger Cotes in early life, of whom Newton had pronounced, 'Now the world will know something,' Doctor Bentley never mentioned but with the deepest regret; he had formed the highest expectations of new lights and discoveries in philosophy from the penetrating force of his extraordinary genius, and on the tablet devoted to his memory, in the chapel of Trinity College, Doctor Bentley has recorded his sorrows and those of the whole learned world in the following beautiful and pathetic epitaph:—

H. S. E.
Rogerus Roberti filius Cotes,
Hujus Collegii S. Trinitatis Socius,
Et Astronomiæ et experimentalis

---

religion. Collins, though distinguished both for moral and intellectual elevation, was nevertheless a disbeliever in Revelation. In his Discourse, he seemingly intended to attack Revealed Religion generally. This called forth Bentley, whose reply was entitled 'A Letter to F. H. (Francis Hare), D. D., by Philoleutherus Lipsiensis.'

Cumberland, I suspect, has fallen into an error, when he speaks of Collins' circumstances. I find no mention, in the biographical works I have consulted, of his suffering from pecuniary difficulties. He was born in 1676, and died in 1729.

[1] This celebrated philosopher and mathematician, who died at the early age of thirty-four, inspired all men of science with the highest opinion of his abilities. He died too soon to fulfil the promise of his youth; but what nobler eulogy could he covet, than Newton's exclamation, on hearing of his death:— 'If Mr. Cotes had lived, we should have known something.' He was born in 1682, and died in 1716.

'Delivering early to the voice of fame
The promise of a great immortal name.'

Philosophiæ Professor Plumianus;
Qui immatura Morte præreptus,
Pauca quidem ingenii Sui
Pignora reliquit,
Sed egregia, sed admiranda,
Ex intimis Matheseôs penetralibus,
Felici Solertiâ tum primum eruta;
Post magnum illum Newtonum
Societatis hujus spes altera
Et decus gemellum;
Cui ad summam Doctrinæ laudem,
Omnes morum virtutumque dotes
In cumulum accesserunt;
Eo magis spectabiles amabilesque,
Quod in formoso corpore
Gratiores venirent.
Natus Burbagii
In agro Leicestriensi.
Jul. x. MDCLXXXII.
Obiit. Jun. v. MDCCXVI.

His domestic habits, when I knew him, were still those of unabated study: he slept in the room adjoining to his library, and was never with his family till the hour of dinner; at these times he seemed to have detached himself most completely from his studies; never appearing thoughtful and abstracted, but social, gay, and possessing perfect serenity of mind and equability of temper. He never dictated topics of conversation to the company he was with, but took them up as they came in his way, and was a patient listener to other people's discourse, however trivial or uninteresting it might be. When 'The Spectators' were in publication, I have heard my mother say he took great delight in hearing them read to him, and was so particularly amused by the character of Sir Roger de Coverley, that he took his literary decease most seriously to heart. She also told me, that, when in conversation with him on the subject of his works, she found occasion to lament that he had bestowed so great a portion of his time and talents upon criticism instead of employing them upon original composition, he acknowledged the justice of her regret with extreme sensibility, and remained for a considerable time thoughtful and seemingly embarrassed by the nature of her remark; at last recollecting himself, he said: 'Child, I am sensible I have not always turned my talents to the proper use for which I should presume they were given to me; yet I have done something for the honor of my God and the edification of my fellow creatures; but the wit and genius of those old heathens beguiled me, and as I despaired of raising myself up to their standard upon fair ground, I thought the only chance I had of looking over their heads was to get upon their shoulders.'[1]

Of his pecuniary affairs he took no account; he had no use for money, and dismissed it entirely from his thoughts; his establishment in the mean time was respectable, and his table affluently and hospitably served. All these matters were conducted and arranged in the best manner possible by one of the best women living; for such, by the testimony of all who knew her, was Mrs. Bentley, daughter of Sir John Bernard, of Brampton, in Huntingdonshire, a family of great opulence and respectability, allied to the Cromwells and Saint Johns, and by intermarriages connected with other great and noble houses. I have perfect recollection of the person of my grandmother, and a full impression of her manners and habits, which, though in some degree tinctured with hereditary reserve and the primitive cast of character, were entirely free from the hypocritical cant and affected sanctity of the Oliverians. Her whole life was modelled on the purest principle of piety, benevolence, and Christian charity; and in her dying moments, my mother being present and voucher of the fact, she breathed out her soul in a kind of beatific vision, exclaiming in rapture as she expired, 'It is all bright, it is all glorious!'

I was frequently called upon by her to repeat certain scriptural texts and passages which she had taught me, and for which I seldom failed to be rewarded, but by which I was also frequently most completely puzzled and bewildered; so that I much doubt if the good effects of this practice upon immature and infantine understandings, will be found to keep pace with the good intentions of those who adopt it. One of these holy apothegms, viz: 'The eyes of the Lord are in every place, beholding the evil and the good,' I remember to have cost me many a struggle to interpret, and the result of my construction was directly opposite to the spirit and meaning of the text. I was also occasionally summoned to attend upon the readings of

[1] Bentley was born on the 27th January, 1662. Thomas Bentley, his father, is said to have been a blacksmith, and his mother, the daughter of a stonemason. To those, however, who value merit, in some measure according to its pedigree, it may be well to mention that his ancestors, in the ascending degrees, belonged to the higher class of English yeomen. What Shakspeare is among poets, and Bacon among philosophers, such is Bentley among critics. As a man, however, we cannot join Cumberland in speaking his praise. Learned, arrogant, rapacious and oppressive, he seemed to be actuated by no higher motives than power and interest. 'His government of Trinity College,' says the 'Encyclopedia Britannica,' 'was that of an unprincipled despot.' The particulars of his life are too well known, or too easily referred to, to be repeated here. He died, July 14th, 1742.

long sermons and homilies of Baxter, as I believe, and others of his period; neither by these was I edified, but, on the contrary, so effectually wearied, that by noises and interruptions I seldom failed to render myself obnoxious, and obtain my dismission before the reading was over.

The death of this exemplary lady preceded that of my grandfather by a few years only, and by her he had one son, Richard, and two daughters, Elizabeth and Joanna. Richard was a man of various and considerable accomplishments; he had a fine genius, great wit, and a brilliant imagination; he had also the manners and address of a perfect gentleman, but there was a certain eccentricity, and want of worldly prudence in my uncle's character, that involved him in distresses, and reduced him to situations uncongenial with his feelings, and unpropitious to the cultivation and encouragement of his talents. His connection with Mr. Horace Walpole, the late Lord Orford, had too much of the bitter of dependence in it to be gratifying to the taste of a man of his spirit and sensibility; the one could not be abject, and the other, I suspect, was not by nature very liberal and large minded. They carried on, for a long time, a sickly kind of friendship, which had its hot fits and its cold; was suspended and renewed, but I believe never totally broken and avowedly laid aside. Walpole had by nature a propensity, and by constitution a plea, for being captious and querulential, for he was a martyr to the gout. He wrote prose and published it; he composed verses and circulated them, and was an author, who seemed to play at hide-and-seek with the public. There was a mysterious air of consequence in his private establishment of a domestic printing press, that seemed to augur great things, but performed little. Walpole was already an author with no great claims to excellence, Bentley had those powers in embryo, that would have enabled him to excel, but submitted to be the projector of Gothic establishments for Strawberry Hill, and humble designer of drawings to ornament a thin folio of a meagre collection of odes by Gray, the most costive of poets, edited at the Walpolian press. In one of these designs Bentley has personified himself as a monkey, sitting under a withered tree with his pallet in his hand, while Gray reposes under the shade of a flourishing laurel in all the dignity of learned ease. Such a design with figures so contrasted might flatter Gray, and gratify the trivial taste of Walpole; but, in my poor opinion, it is a satire in copper-plate, and my uncle has most completely libelled both his poet and his patron without intending so to do.

Let this suffice at present for the son of Doctor Bentley; in the course of these memoirs I shall take occasion to recall the attention of my readers to what I have further to relate of him.[1]

Elizabeth Bentley, eldest daughter of her father, first married Humphry Ridge, Esq., and, after his decease, the Rev. Dr. Favell, fellow of Trinity College, and after his marriage with my aunt, Rector of Witton, near Huntingdon, in the gift of Sir John Bernard, of Brampton. She was an honorable and excellent lady; I had cause to love her, and lament her death. She

[1] Bentley, the younger, possessed excellent talents, which, however, raised him to no particular eminence. He was the friend of Gray, and, at one time, of Walpole. The Gothic villa of Strawberry Hill owed much of its fame to his taste and designs. He had a natural turn for architecture, but never gave to the art any special study. Walpole, in one of his letters, styles him 'a true treasure of taste and drawing.' The temper of Walpole was capricious, and his friendship precarious. He quarrelled with Bentley, as with Gray, and 'the good-humored, laughing George Montague.' Cumberland, however, has unjustly disparaged his genius. 'It is the fashion,' said Byron, 'to underrate Horace Walpole; firstly, because he was a nobleman, and, secondly, because he was a gentleman; but to say nothing of the composition of his incomparable letters, and of 'The Castle of Otranto,' he is the *ultimus Romanorum*, the author of the 'Mysterious Mother,' a tragedy of the highest order, and not a puling love-play. He is the father of the first romance, and of the last tragedy in our language, and surely worthy of a higher place than any living author, be he who he may.'—*Preface to 'Marino Faliero.'*

Such is Byron's estimate of his literary labors; Macaulay thus portrays his character. 'He was,' says the brilliant essayist and historian, 'unless we have formed a very erroneous judgment of his character, the most eccentric, the most artificial, the most fastidious, the most capricious of men. His mind was a bundle of inconsistent whims and affectations. His features were covered by mask within mask. When the outer disguise of obvious affectation was removed, you were still as far as ever from seeing the real man. He played innumerable parts, and overacted them all. When he talked misanthropy, he out-Timoned Timon. When he talked philanthropy, he left Howard at an immeasurable distance. He scoffed at courts, and kept a chronicle of their most trifling scandal; at society, and was blown about by its slightest veerings of opinion; at literary fame, and left fair copies of his private letters, with copious notes to be published after his decease; at rank, and never for a moment forgot that he was an honorable; at the practice of entail, and tasked the ingenuity of conveyancers to tie up his villa in the strictest settlement. The conformation of his mind was such, that whatever was little seemed to him great, and whatever was great seemed to him little. Serious business was a trifle to him, and trifles were his serious business. To chat with blue stockings; to write little copies of complimentary verses on little occasions; to superintend a private press; to preserve from natural decay the perishable topics of Ranelagh and White's; to record divorces and bets, Miss Chudleigh's absurdities and George Selwyn's good sayings; to decorate a grotesque house with pie-crust battlements; to procure rare engravings and antique chimney-boards; to match odd gauntlets; to lay out a maze of walks within five acres of ground—these were the grave employments of his long life. From these he turned to politics as an amusement. After the labors of the print-shop and the auction-room, he unbent his mind in the House of Commons. And, having indulged in the recreation of making laws and voting millions, he returned to more important pursuits—to researches after Queen Mary's comb, Wolsey's red hat, the pipe which Van Tromp smoked during his last seafight, and the spur which King William struck into the flank of sorrel.'

inherited the virtues and benignity of her mother, with habits more adapted to the fashions of the world.

Joanna, the younger of Doctor Bentley's daughters, and the Phœbe of Byrom's pastoral, was my mother.[1] I will not violate the allegiance I have vowed to truth in giving any other character of her than what in conscience I regard as just and faithful. She had a vivacity of fancy and a strength of intellect in which few were her superiors: she read much, remembered well, and discerned acutely: I never knew the person who could better embellish any subject she was upon, or render common incidents more entertaining by the happy art of relating them; her invention was so fertile, her ideas so original, and the points of humor so ingeniously and unexpectedly taken up in the progress of her narrative, that she never failed to accomplish all the purposes which the gayety of her imagination could lay itself out for: she had a quick intuition into characters, and a faculty of marking out the ridiculous, when it came within her view, which of force I must confess she made rather too frequent use of. Her social powers were brilliant, but not uniform, for on some occasions she would persist in a determined taciturnity, to the regret of the company present, and at other times would lead off in her best manner, when perhaps none were present who could taste the spirit and amenity of her humor. There hardly passed a day in which she failed to devote a portion of her time to the reading of the Bible; and her comments and expositions might have merited the attention of the wise and learned. Though strictly pious, there was no gloom in her religion, but, on the contrary, such was the happy faculty which she possessed of making every doctrine pleasant, every duty sweet, that what some instructors would have represented as a burden and a yoke, she contrived to recommend as a recreation and delight. All that son can owe to parent, or disciple to his teacher, I owe to her.

My paternal grandfather, Richard, only son of Bishop Cumberland, was rector of Peakirk, in the diocese of Peterborough, and Archdeacon of Northampton. He had two sons and one daughter, who was married to Waring Ashby, Esquire, of Quenby Hall, in the county of Leicester, and died in childbirth of her only son, George Ashby, Esquire, late of Haselbeach, in Northamptonshire. Richard, the eldest son of Archdeacon Cumberland, died unmarried, at the age of twenty-nine, and the younger, Denison, so named from his mother, was my father. He was educated at Westminster School, and from that admitted fellow-

[1] Dr. Byrom's Pastoral was printed in No. 603 of the 'Spectator.'

commoner of Trinity College, in Cambridge. He married at the age of twenty-two, and though in possession of an independent fortune, was readily prevailed upon by his father-in-law, Doctor Bentley, to take the rectory of Stanwick, in the county of Northampton, given to him by Lord Chancellor King, as soon as he was of age to hold it. From this period, he fixed his constant residence in that retired and tranquil spot, and sedulously devoted himself to the duties of his function. When I contemplate the character of this amiable man, I declare to truth I never yet knew one so happily endowed with those engaging qualities which are formed to attract and fix the love and esteem of mankind. It seemed as if the whole spirit of his grandfather's benevolence had been transfused into his heart, and that he bore as perfect a resemblance of him in goodness, as he did in person: in moral purity he was truly a Christian, in generosity and honor he was perfectly a gentleman.

On the nineteenth day of February, 1732, I was born, in the Master's Lodge of Trinity College, *inter silvas Academi*, under the roof of my grandfather Bentley, in what is called the Judge's Chamber. Having therefore prefaced my history with these few faint sketches of the great and good men whom I have the honor to number amongst my ancestors, I must solicit the condescension of my readers to a much humbler topic, and proceed to speak professedly of myself.

Here, then, for a while, I pause for self-examination, and to weigh the task I am about to undertake. I look into my heart; I search my understanding; I review my life, my labors, the talents I have been endowed with, and the uses I have put them to, and it shall be my serious study not to be found guilty of any partial estimates, any false appreciations of that self, either as author or man, which of necessity must be made to fill so large a portion of the following pages. When, from the date at which my history now pauses, I look forward through a period of more than seventy and two years, I discover nothing within my horizon of which to be vain-glorious; no sudden heights to turn me giddy, no dazzling gleams of fortune's sunshine to bewilder me; nothing but one long, laborious track, not often strewed with roses, and thorny, cold, and barren, towards the conclusion of it, where weariness wants repose, and age has need of comfort. I see myself unfortunately cast upon a lot in life neither congenial with my character, nor friendly to my peace; combating with dependence, disappointment, and disgusts, of various sorts, transplanted from a college, within whose walls I had devoted myself to studies, which I pursued with ardent passion and a rising reputation, and what to obtain? What, but the experience of difficulties, and the credit of overcoming them; the useful chastisement which unkindness has inflicted, and the conscious satisfaction of not having merited, nor, in any instance of my life, revenged it?

If I do not know myself I am not fit to be my own biographer; and if I do know myself I am sure I never took delight in egotisms, and now behold! I am self-devoted to deal in little else. Be it so! I will abide the consequences; I will not tell untruths to set myself out for better than I have been, but as I have not been overpaid by my contemporaries, I will not scruple to exact what is due to me from posterity.—*Ipse de me scribam.* (Cic.)

I have said that I was born on the 19th of February, 1732; I was not the eldest child, though the only son, of my mother; my sister Joanna was more than two years older than I, and more than twice two years before me in apprehension, for whilst she profited very rapidly by her mother's teaching, I by no means trod in her steps, but, on the contrary, after a few unpromising efforts, peremptorily gave up the cause, and persisted in a stubborn repugnance to all instruction. My mother's good sense and my grandfather's good advice concurred in the measures to be taken with me in this state of mutiny against all the powers of the alphabet; my book was put before me, my lesson pointed out, and though I never articulated a single word, I conned it over in silence to myself. I have traces of my sensations at this period still in my mind, and perfectly recollect the revolt I received from reading of the Heathen Idols, described in the 115th psalm as having eyes and not seeing, ears, and not hearing, with other contrarieties, which between positive and negative so completely overset my small stock of ideas, that I obstinately stood fast upon the halt, dumb and insensible to instruction as the images in question. Of this circumstance, exactly as I relate it, with those sensations, which it impressed upon my infantine mind, I now retain, as I have already said, distinct recollection.

If there is any moral in this small incident, which can impart a cautionary hint to the teachers of children, my readers will forgive me for treating them with a story of the nursery. I have only to add, that when I at length took to my business, I have my mother's testimony for saying that I repaid her patience.

My family divided their time between Cambridge and Stanwick so long as my grandfather lived, and when I was turned of six years I was sent to the school at Bury Saint Edmund's, then under the mastership of the Reverend Arthur Kinsman, who formed his scholars upon the system of Westminster, and was a Trinity College man, much esteemed by my grandfather.

This school, when I came to it, was in high reputation, and numbered a hundred and fifty boys. Kinsman was an excellent master, a very sufficient scholar, and had all the professional requisites of voice, air and aspect, that marked him out at first sight as a personage decidedly made on purpose—*habere imperium in pueros.* In his hands I can truly witness the reins of empire never slackened, but we did not murmur against his authority, for with all his warmth of temper he was kind, cordial, open-hearted, and an impartial administrator of punishments and praises, as they were respectively deserved. His name was high in the counties of Suffolk and Norfolk, and the chief families in those parts were present with him in the persons of their representatives, and some yet living can bear witness to the vigor of his arm. He was fiery zealous for the honor of his school, which by the terms of his establishment was subject to the visitation of those who were in the government of it, and I remember, upon a certain occasion, when these gentlemen entered the school-room, in the execution of their office (I being then in the rostrum in the act of construing Juvenal), he ordered me to proceed without noticing their appearance, and something having passed to give him offence against one of their number in particular, taking up the passage then under immediate recitation, he echoed forth, in a loud and pointed tone of voice—

—— Nos, nostraque lividus odit.

It must be confessed that my good old master had a vaunting kind of style in setting forth his school, and once in conversation with my grandfather in Trinity Lodge, he was so unaccountably misled by the spirit of false prophecy, as to venture to say, in a rallying kind of way—'Master, I will make your grandson as good a scholar as yourself.'—To this Doctor Bentley, in the like vein of raillery, replied—'Pshaw, Arthur, how can that be, when I have forgot more than thou ever knew'st?' Certain it is that my inauspicious beginnings augured very ill for the bold prediction, thus improvidently hazarded; for so supremely idle was I, and so far from being animated by the charms of the Latin grammar, that the labor of instruction was but labor lost, and it seemed a chance if I was destined to arrive at any other acquirement but *the art of sinking*, in which I regularly proceeded till I found my proper station at the very bottom of my class, which, as far as idleness could be my security, I was likely to take lasting possession of.

I am persuaded, however, that the tranquillity of my ignorance would have suffered no interruption from the remonstrances of

3

the worthy usher of the under-school, who sat in a plaid night-gown and let things take their course, had not the penetrating eye of old Kinsman discovered the grandson of his friend far in the rear of the line of honor, and in a fair train to give the flattest contradiction to his prophecy. Whereupon, one day, which by me can never be forgotten, calling me up to him in his chair at the head of the school, he began with much solemnity and in a loud voice to lecture me very sharply, whilst all eyes were upon me, all ears open, and a dead silence, horrible to my feelings, did not leave a hope that a single word had escaped the notice of my schoolfellows. I well remember his demanding of me what report I could expect him to make of me to my grandfather Bentley. I shuddered at the name, even at that early age so loved and so revered. I made no defence—I had none to make—and he went thundering on, further perhaps than he need to have gone, had he given less scope to his zeal, and trusted more to his intuition, for the keenness of his reproof had sunk into my heart; I was covered with shame and confusion. I retired abashed to my seat, which was the lowest in my class, and that class the lowest save one in the under-school. I hid my face between my hands, resting my head upon the desk before me, and gave myself up to tears and contrition; when I raised my eyes and looked about me, I thought I discovered contempt in the countenances of the boys. At that moment the spirit of emulation, which had not yet awaked in my heart, was thoroughly roused; but whilst I was thus resolving upon a reform I fell ill, whether from agitation of mind or from cause more natural I know not. I was, however, laid up in a sick bed for a considerable time, and in that piteous situation visited by my mother, who came from Cambridge on the alarm, and under her tender care I at length regained both my spirits and my health.

My mother now returned to Cambridge, and I was taken into Kinsman's own house as a boarder, where, being associated with boys of a better description, and more immediately under the eye of my most timely admonisher, I took all the pains that my years would admit of to deserve his better opinion and regain my lost ground. My diligence was soon followed by success, and success encouraged me to fresh exertions.

I presume the teachers of grammar do not expect boys of a very early age to understand it as a body of rules, but merely as an exercise of memory; yet it is well to imprint it on their memories, that they may more readily apply to it as they advance in their acquaintance with the language. I had naturally a good memory, and practice added such a facility of getting by heart, that in my repetitions, when we challenged for places, I entered the lists with all possible advantages, and soon found myself able to break a lance with the very best of my competitors. The good man in the plaid gown now began to regard me with less than his usual indifference, and my early star was evidently in the ascendant. Such were to me the happy consequences of my worthy master's seasonable admonition.

After the decease of Mrs. Bentley, my mother, whose devotion to her father was returned by the warmest affection on his part, passed much of her time, as my father did of his, at Cambridge; there I also passed my holidays, and the undescribable gratification those delightful seasons gave me hath left traces of the times long past and the persons now dead, that can only be effaced by death, and of their surviving even that I should be loth to lose the hope. I was become capable of understanding my grandfather to be the great man he really was, and began to listen to him with attention, and treasure up his sayings in my mind. I was admitted to dine at his table, had my seat next to his chair, served him in many little offices, and went upon his errands with a promptitude and alacrity that showed what pride I took in such commissions, and tempted his good nature to invent occasions for employing me.

One day, I full well remember, my old master Kinsman walked into the room, and was welcomed by my grandfather with the cordiality natural to him. In the mean time my heart fluttered with alarm and dread of that report which he had once threatened to prefer against me: nothing could be further from his generous thoughts, and as soon as ever he was at leisure to notice such an insignificant little being, it was with the affection and caresses of a father; when I looked in his face, there was no longer any feature of the schoolmaster in it, the terrors of the ferula and the rod were vanished out of sight, and that upright strutting little person, which in authority was so awful, had now relaxed from its rigidity, and no longer strove to swell itself into importance. Arthur, notwithstanding, was a great man on his own ground, and though he venerated the master of Trinity College, he did not renounce a proper self-esteem for the master of Bury School, and the dignity appertaining to that office, which he filled, and to which Bentley himself had once stooped for instruction. He was a gay social fellow, who loved his friend and had no antipathy to his bottle; he had then a kind of dashing discourse, savoring somewhat of the shop, which trifles did not check and contradiction could not daunt. He had at this very time been recreating his spirit with the company in the combination room, and was fairly primed with priestly port. My grandfather, I dare say, discovered nothing of this, and Walker, who accompanied Kinsman to the lodge, was exactly in that state when silence is the best resort. Arthur, in the mean time, whose tongue conviviality had by no means tied up, began to open his school books upon Bentley, and had drawn him into Homer; Greek now rolled in torrents from the lips of Bentley, and the most learned of moderns chanted forth the inspired rhapsodies of the most illustrious of ancients in a strain delectable indeed to the ear, but not very edifying to poor little me and the ladies; nay, I should even doubt if the master of Bury School understood all that he heard, but that the worthy vice-master of Trinity was innocent of all apprehension, and clear of the plot, if treason was wrapped up in it, I can, upon my knowledge of him, confidently vouch. This, however, I remember, and my mother has frequently, in time past, refreshed my recollection of it, that Joshua Barnes, in the course of this conversation, being quoted by Kinsman, as a man understanding Greek, and speaking it almost like his mother tongue—'Yes,' replied Bentley, 'I do believe that Barnes had as much Greek, and understood it about as well, as an Athenian blacksmith.'[1] Of Pope's Homer he said he had read it; it was an elegant poem, but no translation. Of the learned Warburton, then in the outset of his fame, he remarked that there seemed to be in him a voracious appetite for knowledge; he doubted if there was a good digestion. This is an anecdote I refer to those who are competent to make or reject the application.[2]

[1] Joshua Barnes was born at London, on the 10th of January, 1654, and died the 3d of August 1712. Notwithstanding Bentley's disparaging comment on his attainments, Barnes was considered one of the most learned Greek scholars of his day. He was Greek professor at Cambridge, and published an edition of Anacreon and Homer. He is said to have been more remarkable for the quickness of his wit, and the happiness of his memory, than for the solidity of his judgment. As a theologian, he maintained that spiritual sins, such as pride, defamation, &c., were more offensive to God than those which spring from too great an indulgence of the senses.

[2] If we judge of Warburton's abilities from the terms in which Dr. Johnson speaks of them, in his edition of Shakspeare, we shall rate them highly. Others of his contemporaries, however, distrusted his learning, and despised his talents. The pride, not to say, the insolence of his manners, made him many enemies. He was once addressed in a pamphlet, 'To the most impudent man alive.'

Warburton was thus referred to in Johnson's celebrated interview with George III. The king said, 'that he heard Dr. Warburton was a man of such general knowledge, that you could scarce talk with him on any subject on which he was not qualified to speak, and that his learning resembled Garrick's acting, in its universality.' His Majesty then talked of the controversy between Warburton and Lowth, which he seemed to have read, and asked Johnson what he thought of it. Johnson answered, 'Warburton has most general, most scholastic learning; Lowth is the more correct scholar. I do not know which of them calls names best.' The king was pleased to say he was of the same opinion; adding, 'You do not think then, Dr. Johnson, that there was

At no great distance of time from this period, which I have been now recording, Doctor Bentley died, and was buried in Trinity College chapel, by the side of the altar table, where a square, black stone records his name, and nothing more. It remains with the munificence of that rich society to award him other monumental honors, whenever they may think it right to grace his memory with a tablet. He was seized with a complaint that, in his opinion, seemed to indicate a necessity of immediate bleeding; Dr. Heberden, then a young physician, practising in Cambridge, was of a contrary opinion, and the patient acquiesced. His friend, Dr. Wallis, in whose skilful practice and experience he so justly placed his confidence, was, unfortunately, absent from Stamford, and never came upon the summons for any purpose but to share in the sorrows of his family, and lament the non-compliance with the process he had recommended, which, according to his judgment of the case, was the very measure he should himself have taken.

I believe I felt as much affliction as my age was capable of when my master Kinsman imparted the intelligence of my grandfather's death to me, taking me into his private chamber, and lamenting the event with great agitation. Whilst I gave vent to my tears, he pressed me tenderly in his arms, and encouraging me to persist in my diligence, assured me of his favor and protection. He kept me out of school for a few days, gave me private instruction, and then sent me forth, ardently resolved to acquit myself to his satisfaction. From this time, I may truly say my task was my delight. I rose rapidly to the head of my class, and, in the whole course of my progress through the upper school, never once lost my place of head boy, though daily challenged by those who were as anxious to dislodge me from my post as I was to maintain myself in it. As I have the honor to name both Bishop Warren and his brother Richard, the physician, as two amongst the most formidable of my form-fellows, I may venture to say, that school-boy must have been more than commonly alert whom they could not overtake and depose; but the exertion of my competitors was such a spur to my industry and ambition, that my mind was perpetually in its business. Had I, in any careless moment, suffered a discomfiture, my mortification would have been most poignant; but the dread I had of that event caused me always to be prepared against it, and I held possession of my post under a suspended sword, that hourly menaced me without ever dropping.

much argument in the case.' Johnson said he did not think there was. 'Why truly,' said the king, 'when once it comes to calling names, argument is pretty well at an end.'—*Boswell's Johnson*, vol. ii. p. 39.

Whilst I dwell on the detail of anecdotes like the above, I must refer myself to the candor of the reader, but though it behoves me to study brevity, where I cannot furnish amusement, it would be totally inconsistent with the plan I have laid down, to pass over in total silence this period of my life; an era in the history of every man's mind and character, only to be omitted when it is not to be obtained; a plea which those, who are their own biographers, are not privileged to make.

My good old master was a hospitable man, and every Wednesday held a kind of public day, to which his friends and neighbors used to resort. On that day he drank his bottle of port and played his game of back-gammon, after which he came in gayety of heart to evening-school for one hour only. It was a gala day for all the boys, and for me in particular, as I was sure on all those occasions to be ordered up to the rostrum to recite and expound Juvenal, and he seldom failed to keep me so employed through the whole time. He had a great partiality for that nervous author, and I remember his reciting the following passage in a kind of rapturous enthusiasm in the ears of all the school, crying out that he defied the writers of the Augustan age to produce one equal to it. The classical reader very probably will not second his opinion, but I dare say he will not fail to anticipate the passage, which is as follows:—

> Esto bonus miles, tutor bonus, arbiter idem
> Integer; ambiguæ siquando citabere causæ,
> Incertæque rei, Phalaris licet imperet ut sis
> Falsus, et admoto dictet perjuria Tauro,
> Summum crede nefas animam preferre padori,
> Et propter vitam vivendi perdere causas.

This is unquestionably a fine passage and a sublime moral, but I rather suspect there is a quaintness, and something of what the Italians call *concetto*, in the concluding line, that is not quite in the style and cast of the purer age.

The tasks of a school-boy are of three descriptions: he is to give the construction of his author, to study his repetitions, and to write what are called his exercises, whether in verse or prose. In the former two, the tasks of construing and saying by heart, it was the usage of our school to challenge for places: in this province my good fortune was unclouded; in my exercises I did not succeed so well, for, by aiming at something like fancy and invention, I was too frequently betrayed into grammatical errors, whilst my rivals presented exercises with fewer faults, and, by attempting scarcely anything, hazarded little. These premature and imperfect sallies, which I gave way to, did me no credit with my master, and once in particular, upon my giving in a copy of Latin verses, unpardonably incorrect, though not entirely void of imagination, he commented upon my blunders with great severity, and in the hearing of my form-fellows threatened to degrade me from my station at their head. I had earned that station by hard labor and unceasing assiduity; I had maintained it against their united efforts for some years, and the dread of being at once deprived of what they had not been able to take from me, had such an effect on my sensibility, that I never perfectly recovered it, and probably should at no time after have gained any credit in that branch of my school business, had I not been transplanted to Westminster.

The exercise, for which I was reprehended, I well remember was a copy of verses upon Phalaris's bull, which bull I confess led me into some blunders, that my master might have observed upon with more temper. I stood in need of instruction, and he inflicted discouragement.

Though I love the memory of my good old master, and am under infinite obligations to his care and kindness, yet having severely experienced how poignant are the inflictions of discouragement to the feelings, and how repulsive to the efforts of the unformed embryo genius, I cannot state this circumstance in any better light than as an oversight in point of education, which, though well-intentioned on his part, could only operate to destroy what it was his object to improve.

When the talents of a young and rising author shall be found to profit by the denunciations and browbeatings of his hypercritical contemporaries, then, and not till then, it will be right to train up our children according to this system, and discouragement be the best model for education, which the conductors of it can adopt.

As our master had lately discontinued his custom of letting his boys act a play of Terence before the Christmas holidays, after the example of Westminster, some of us undertook without his leave, though probably not without his knowledge and connivance, to get up the tragedy of Cato at one of the boarding-houses, and invite the gentry of the town to be present at our childish exhibition. We escaped from school one evening, and climbed the wall that intercepted us from the scene of action, to prepare ourselves for this goodly show. A full-bottomed periwig for Cato, and female attire for Portia and Marcia, borrowed from the maids of the lodging house, were the chief articles of our scanty wardrobe, and of a piece with the wretchedness of our property was the wretchedness of our performance. Our audience, however, which was not very select, endured us, and we slept upon our laurels, till the next morning being made to turn out for the amusement of the whole school, and go through a scene or two of our evening's entertainment, we acquitted ourselves so little to the satisfaction of Mr. Kinsman, that after bestowing some hearty buffets upon the virtuous Marcia, who had towered above her sex in the person of a most ill-favored wry-necked boy, the rest of our *dramatis personæ* were sentenced to the fine of an imposition, and dismissed. The part of Juba had been my cast, and the tenth satire of Juvenal was my portion of the fine inflicted.

It was about this time I made my first attempt in English verse, and took for my subject an excursion I had made with my family in the summer holidays to visit a relation in Hampshire, which engaged me in a description of the docks at Portsmouth, and of the races of Winchester, where I had been present. I believe my poem was not short of a hundred lines, and was written at such times as I could snatch a few minutes from my business or amusements. I did not like to risk the consequences of confiding it to my school-fellows, but kept it closely secret till the next breaking up, when I exhibited it to my father, who received it after his gracious manner with unreserved commendation, and persisted in reciting it to his intimates, when I had gained experience enough to wish he had consigned it to oblivion.

Though I have no copy of this childish performance, I bear in my remembrance two introductory couplets, which were the first English lines I every wrote, and are as follows:—

> Since every scribbler claims his share of fame,
> And every Cibber boasts a Dryden's name,
> Permit an infant Muse her chance to try;
> All have a right to that, and why not I?

One other lame and miserable couplet just now occurs to me, as being quoted frequently upon me by my mother as an instance in the art of sinking, and it is clear I had stumbled upon it in my description of the dock-yard, viz:—

> 'Here they weave cables, there they main-masts form,
> Here they forge anchors—useful in a storm.'

My good father, however, was not to be put by from his defences by trifles, and stoutly stood by my anchors, contending that as they were unquestionably useful in a storm, I had said no more of them than was true, and why should I be ashamed of having spoken the truth? Yet ashamed I was some short time after, not indeed for having violated the truth, but for suppressing it, and my dilemma was occasioned by the following circumstance. I had picked up an epigram amongst my school-fellows, which struck my fancy, and without naming the author (for I knew him not), I repeated it to my father—it was this—

Poets of old did Argus prize
Because he had an hundred eyes,
But sure more praise to him is due,
Who looks an hundred ways with two.

In repeating this epigram, which perhaps the reader can find an author for, I did not give it out as my own, but it was so understood by my father, and he circulated it as mine, and took pleasure in repeating it as such amongst his friends and intimates. In this state of the mistake, when his credit had been affixed to it, I had not courage to disavow it, and the time being once gone by for saving my honor, I suffered him to persist in his error under the continual terror of detection. The dread of thus forfeiting his good opinion hung upon my spirits for a length of time; it passed, however, undiscovered to the end of his life, and I now implore pardon of his memory for the only fallacy I ever put upon him to the conviction of my conscience.

After the death of Doctor Bentley, my family resided in the parsonage house of Stanwick near Higham Ferrers in Northamptonshire; it had been newly built from the ground by my father's predecessor, Doctor Needham, from a plan of Mr. Burroughs, of Caius College, an architect of no small reputation; it was a handsome square of four equal fronts, built of stone, containing four rooms on a floor, with a gallery running through the centre; it was seated on the declivity of a gentle hill, with the village to the south, amongst trees and pasture grounds in view, and a small stream in the valley between; on the north, west and south were gardens, on the east the church at some little distance, and in the intermediate space an excellent range of stables and coach houses, built by my father, and forming one side of a square court laid out for the approach of carriages to the house. The spire of Stanwick Church is esteemed one of the most beautiful models in that style of architecture in the kingdom; my father added a very handsome clock and ornamented the chancel with a railing, screen and entablature upon three-quarter columns, with a singing gallery at the west end, and spared no expense to keep his church not only in that neatness and decorum which befits the house of prayer, but also in a perfect state of good and permanent repair.

Here in the hearts of his parishioners, and the esteem of his neighbors, my good father lived tranquil and unambitious, never soliciting other preferment than this for the space of thirty years, holding only a small prebend in the church of Lincoln, given to him by his uncle, Bishop Reynolds. He was in the commission of the peace, and a very active magistrate in the reconcilement of parties, rather than in the commitment of persons: in those quiet parts offences were in general trivial, and the differences merely such as an attorney could contrive to hook a suit upon, so that with a very little legal knowledge, and a very hospitable generous disposition, my father rarely failed to put contentious spirits to peace by reference to the kitchen and the cellar. In the mean time, his popularity rose in proportion as his beer-barrels sunk, and as often as he made peace he made friends, till, I may say without exaggeration, he had all men's good word in his favor and their services at his command. In the mean time, such was the orderly behavior and good discipline of his own immediate flock, that I have frequently heard him say he never once had occasion during his long residence amongst them to issue his warrant within the precincts of his own happy village, which being seated between the more populous and less correct parishes of Raunds and Higham-Ferrers, he used appositely to call Little Zoar, but made no further allusions to the evil neighborhood of Zoar.

In this peaceful spot, with parents so affectionate, I was the happiest of beings in my breakings-up from school. Those delightful scenes are fresh in my remembrance, and when I have occasionally revisited them, since the decease of objects ever so dear to me, the sensations they have excited are not for me to describe. I had inherited an excellent constitution, and, though not robust in make, was more than commonly adroit in my athletic exercises. In swiftness of foot for a short distance no boy in Bury School could match me, and, when at Cambridge, I gave a general challenge to the collegians, which was decided in Trinity Walks in my favor.

Those field sports, of which the young and active are naturally so fond, I enjoyed by my father's favor, in perfection, and in my winter holidays constantly went out with him upon his hunting days, and was always admirably mounted. He was light and elegant in his person, and had in his early youth kept horses and rode matches at Newmarket after the example of his elder brother; but though his profession had now put a stop to those levities, he shared in a pack of hariers with a neighboring gentleman, and was a bold and excellent rider. In my first attendances upon him to the field, the joys of hunting scarcely compensated for the terrors I sometimes felt in following him against my will upon a racing galloway, which he had purchased of old Panton, and whose attachment to her leader was such as left me no option as to the pace I would wish to go, or the leaps I would avoid to take. At length, when age added strength and practice gave address, falls became familiar to me, and I left both fear and prudence behind me in the pleasures of the chase.

It was in these intervals from school that my mother began to form both my taste and my ear for poetry, by employing me every evening to read to her, of which art she was a very able mistress. Our readings were, with very few exceptions, confined to the chosen plays of Shakspeare, whom she both admired and understood in the true spirit and sense of the author. Under her instruction I became passionately fond of these our evening entertainments; in the mean time she was attentive to model my recitation, and correct my manner with exact precision. Her comments and illustrations were such aids and instructions to a pupil in poetry as few could have given. What I could not else have understood she could aptly explain, and what I ought to admire and feel nobody could more happily select and recommend. I well remember the care she took to mark out for my observation the peculiar excellence of that unrivalled poet in the consistency and preservation of his characters; and wherever instances occurred amongst the starts and sallies of his unfettered fancy of the extravagant and false sublime, her discernment oftentimes prevented me from being so dazzled by the glitter of the period as to misapply my admiration, and betray my want of taste. With all her father's critical acumen she could trace, and teach me to unravel, all the meanders of his metaphor, and point out where it illuminated, or where it only loaded and obscured the meaning; these were happy hours and interesting lectures to me, whilst my beloved father, ever placid and complacent, sate beside us, and took part in our amusement: his voice was never heard but in the tone of approbation; his countenance never marked but with the natural traces of his indelible and hereditary benevolence.

The effect of these readings was exactly that which was naturally to be foreseen. I began to try my strength in several slight attempts towards the drama, and as Shakspeare was most upon my tongue and nearest to my heart, I fitted and compiled a kind of cento, which I intitled 'Shakspeare in the Shades,' and formed into one act, selecting the characters of Hamlet and Ophelia, Romeo and Juliet, Lear and Cordelia, as the persons of my drama, and giving to Shakspeare, who is present throughout the piece, Ariel, as an attendant spirit, and taking for the motto to my title page—

Ast alii sex,
Et plures, uno conclamant ore—

I should premise that I was now at the head of Bury School, though only in my twelfth year, and not very slightly grounded in the Greek and Latin classics there taught.

The scene is laid in Elysium, where the poet is discovered, and opens the drama with the following address:—

'Most fair and equal hearers, know that whilst this soul inhabited its fleshly tabernacle, I was called Shakspeare; a greater name and more exalted honors have dignified its dissolution. Blest with a liberal portion of the divine spirit, as a tribute due to the bounty of the gods, I left behind me an immortal monument of my fame. Think not that I boast; the actions of departed beings may not be censured by any mortal wit, nor are accountable to any earthly tribunal. Let it suffice that in the grave—

When we have shuffled off this mortal coil—

all envy and detraction, all pride and vain-glory are no more; still, a grateful remembrance of humanity, and a tender regard for our posterity on earth follow us to this happy seat; and it is in this regard I deign once more to salute you with my favored presence, and am content to be again an actor for your sakes. I have been attentive to your sufferings at my mournful scenes; guardian of that virtue, which I left in distress, I come now, the instrument of Providence, to compose your sorrows, and restore to it the proportioned reward. Those bleeding characters, those martyred worthies, whom I have sent untimely to the shades, shall now, at length, and in your sight, be crowned with their beloved retribution, and the justice, which as their poet I withheld from them, as the arbiter and disposer of their fate, I will award to them; but for the villain and the adulterer—

The perjured and the simular man of virtue—

the proud, the ambitious, and the murderer, I shall

Leave such to heaven,
And to those thorns, that in their bosoms lodge
To prick and sting them.—

But soft! I see one coming, that often hath beguiled you of your tears—the fair Ophelia—'

The several parties now make their respective appeals, and Shakspeare finally summons them all before him by his agent Ariel, for whose introduction he prepares the audience by the following soliloquy—

'Now comes the period of my high commission:
All have been heard, and all shall be restor'd,
All errors blotted out and all obstructions,
Mortality entails, shall be remov'd,
And from the mental eye the film withdrawn,
Which in its corporal union had obscur'd
And clouded the pure virtue of its sight.
But to these purposes I must employ
My ready spirit, Ariel, some time minister
To Prospero, and the obsequious slave
Of his enchantments, from whose place preferr'd
He here attends to do me services,

And qualifies these beings for Elysium—
Hoa! Ariel, approach my dainty spirit!'

(Ariel *enters.*)

All hail, great master, grave sir, hail! I come
To answer thy best pleasure; be it to fly,
To swim, to dive into the fire, to ride
On the curled clouds—to thy strong-bidding task
Ariel and all his qualities—

Shakspeare.

'Know then, spirit,
Into this grove six shades consign'd to bliss
I've separately remov'd, of each sex three;
Unheard of one another and unseen
There they abide, yet each to each endear'd
By ties of strong affection: not the same
Their several objects, though the effects alike,
But husband, father, lover make the change.
Now though the body's perish'd, yet are they
Fresh from their sins and bleeding with their wrongs;
Therefore all sense of injury remove,
Heal up their wounded faculties anew,
And pluck affliction's arrow from their hearts;
Refine their passions, for gross sensual love
Let it become a pure and faultless friendship,
Raise and confirm their joys, let them exchange
Their fleeting pleasures for immortal peace:
This done, with speed conduct them each to other
So chang'd, and set the happy choir before me.'

I have the whole of this puerile production, written in a school-boy's hand, which by some chance has escaped the general wreck, in which I have lost some records, that I should now be glad to resort to. I am not quite sure that I act fairly by my readers when I give any part of it a place in these memoirs, yet as an instance of the impression, which my mother's lectures had made upon my youthful fancy, and perhaps as a sample of composition indicative of more thought and contrivance, than are commonly to be found in boys at so very early an age, I shall proceed to transcribe the concluding part of the scene, in which Romeo has his audience, and can truly affirm that the copy is faithful without the alteration or addition of a single word:—

Romeo.

'—O thou, the great disposer of my fate,
Judge of my actions, patron of my cause,
Tear not asunder such united hearts,
But give me up to love and my Juliet.

Shakspeare.

'Unthinking youth, thou dost forget thyself;
Rash inconsiderate boy, must I again
Remind thee of thy fate? What! know'st thou not
The man, whose desperate hand foredoes himself,

Is doom'd to wander on the Stygian shore
A restless shade, forlorn and comfortless,
For a whole age? Nor shall he hope to soothe
The callous ear of Charon, till he win
His passion by repentance and submission
At this my fixed tribunal, else be sure
The wretch shall hourly pace the lazy wharf
To view the beating of the Stygian wave,
And waste his irksome leisure.'

ROMEO.

Gracious powers,
Is this my doom, my torment—? Heaven is here
Where Juliet lives, and each unworthy thing
Lives here in heaven and may look on her,
But Romeo may not: more validity,
More honorable state, more worship lives
In carrion flies than Romeo; they may seize
On the white wonder of my love's dear hand,
And steal immortal blessings from her lips,
But Romeo may not; 'He is doom'd to bear
An age's pain and sigh in banishment,
To drag a restless being on the shore
Of gloomy Styx, and weep into the flood,
Till, with his tears made full, the briny stream'
Shall kiss the most exalted shores of all.

SHAKSPEARE.

'Now then dost thou repent thy follies past?

ROMEO.

'Oh, ask me if I feel my torments present,
Then judge if I repent my follies past.
Had I but powers to tell you what I feel,
A tongue to speak my heart's unfeign'd contrition,
Then might I lay the bleeding part before you;
But 'twill not be—something I yet would say
To extenuate my crime; I fain would plead
The merit of my love—but I have done—
However hard my sentence, I submit.
My faithless tongue turns traitor to my heart,
And will not utter what it fondly prompts;
A rising gust of passion drowns my voice,
And I'm most dumb when I've most need to sue.
(*Kneels.*)

SHAKSPEARE.

'Arise, young sir! before my mercy-seat
None kneel in vain; repentance never lost
The cause she pleaded. Mercy is the proof,
The test that marks a character divine;
Were ye like merciful to one another,
The earth would be a heaven and men the gods.
Withdraw awhile; I see thy heart is full;
Grief at a crime committed merits more
Than exultation for a duty done.
(ROMEO *withdraws.*)

SHAKSPEARE REMAINS AND SPEAKS—

'What rage is this, O man, that thou should'st dare
To turn unnatural butcher on thyself,
And thy presumptuous violent hand uplift
Against that fabric which the gods have rais'd?
Insolent wretch, did that presumptuous hand
Temper thy wond'rous frame? Did that bold spirit
Inspire the quicken'd clay with living breath?
Do not deceive thyself. Have the kind gods
Lent their own goodly image to thy use
For thee to break at pleasure?—
What are thy merits? Where is thy dominion?
If thou aspir'st to rule, rule thy desires.
Thou poorly turn'st upon thy helpless body,
And hast no heart to check thy growing sins:
Thou gain'st a mighty victory o'er thy life,
But art enslaved to thy basest passions,
And bowest to the anarchy within thee.
O! have a care
Lest at thy great account thou should'st be found
A thriftless steward of thy master's substance.
'Tis his to take away, or sink at will,
Thou but the tenant to a greater lord,
Nor maker, nor the monarch of thyself.'

I select these extracts because what is within hooks is of my own composing, whereas, in the preceding scenes, where the characters make their appeal, I perceive I had in general contrived to let them speak the language which their own poet had given to them. I presume to add that the passages I have extracted from their parts, as they stand in the originals of their great author, are ingeniously enough chosen, and appositely introduced. I likewise take the liberty to observe that where I have, in those scenes above alluded to, connected the extracts with my own dialogue, considering it as the work of so mere a novice, it is not contemptibly executed. As I have solemnly disavowed all deception or finesse in the whole conduct of these memoirs, so in this instance I have not sought to excite surprise by making my years fewer, or my verses better than they strictly and truly were, having faithfully attested the one, and correctly transcribed the other.

My worthy old master at Bury, now in the decline of life, intimated his purpose of retiring; and my father took the opportunity of transplanting me to Westminster, where he admitted me under Doctor Nichols, and lodged me in the boarding-house, then kept by Ludford, where he himself had been placed. He took me in his hand to the master, who seemed a good deal surprised to hear that I had passed through Bury school at the age of twelve, and immediately put a Homer before me, and after that an ode in Horace. I turned my eyes upon my father, and perceived him to be in considerable agitation. There happened to be no occasion for it, as the passages were familiar to me, and my amiable examiner seemed perfectly disposed to approve, cautioning me, however, not to read in too declamatory a style, 'which,' said he, 'my boys will call conceited.' It was highly gratifying to me to hear him say that he had found the boys who came out of Mr. Kinsman's hands generally better grounded in their business than those who came from other schools. The next day he gave me a short examination for form-sake at the table, and placed me in the Shell; as I was then only twelve years old, and small in stature for my years, my location in so high a class was regarded with some surprise by the corps into which I was so unexpectedly enrolled. Doctor Johnson, afterwards Bishop of Worcester, was then second master; Vincent Bourne,[1] well known to the literary world for his elegant Latin verses, was usher of the fifth form, and Lloyd, afterwards second master, was at the fourth. Cracherode, the learned collector and munificent benefactor to the Royal Museum, was in the head election, and at that time as grave, studious, and reserved as he was through life, but correct in morals and elegant in manners, not courting a promiscuous acquaintance, but pleasant to those who knew him, beloved by many, and esteemed by all. At the head of the town boys was the Earl of Huntingdon, whom I should not name as a boy; for he was even then the courtly and accomplished gentleman such as the world saw and acknowledged him to be. The late Earl of Bristol, the late Earl of Buckinghamshire, and the late Right Honorable Thomas Harley were my form-fellows; the present Duke of Richmond, then Lord March, Warren Hastings,[2] Colman,[3] and Lloyd were in the under school,

[1] Vincent Bourne was educated at Westminster School and Trinity College. The taste and elegance of his Latin compositions were his titles to distinction. For several years prior to his death, which occurred in 1747, he was under-master at Westminster. His character commanded the respect, but his habits and manners exposed him to the pleasantry of his pupils.

[2] The name of Warren Hastings involuntarily associates itself with one of the striking passages of British history. Eloquence has employed her most bewitching strains to assail or praise him; but when the influence of contemporary opinion shall cease to operate, history will sit in judgment on his career. Before that tribunal, the circumstances and motives that determined his conduct, in the great points of his life, will be weighed, and impartially pronounced on. It will be told that his abilities were ever equal to his power; that his most reprehensible acts were not committed in mere wantonness, but as subsidiary to the great purposes of his rule; that if he was rancorous in his hatreds, he was firm in his friendships; and that no sordid, mercenary motive, throughout his long career, was the impelling motive of his conduct. *Mens Æqua In Arduis*, is the inscription beneath his portrait in the Council-chamber of Calcutta; and justly expressive of his constancy and fortitude.

[3] Colman, the author of 'The Jealous Wife' and 'Clandestine Marriage,' was

and, what is a very extraordinary coincidence, there were then in school together three boys, Hinchliffe, Smith, and Vincent, who afterwards succeeded to be severally head masters of Westminster School, and not by the decease of any one of them.

Hinchliffe might well be called the child of fortune, for he was born in penury and obscurity, and was lifted into opulence and high station, not by the elasticity of his own genius, but by that lucky combination of opportunities, which merit has no share in making, and modesty no aptitude to seize. At Trinity College I knew him as an under-graduate below my standing; in the revolution of a few years I saw him in the station aforetime filled by my grandfather as master of the college, and holding with it the bishopric of Peterborough; thus doubly dignified with those preferments which had separately rewarded the learned labors of Cumberland and Bentley.

Smith labored longer and succeeded less, yet he wisely chose his time for relaxation and retirement, whilst he was yet unexhausted by his toils, sufficiently affluent to enjoy his independence, and, with the consciousness of having done his duty, to consult his ease, and to dismiss his cares.

Vincent, whom I love as a friend and honor as a scholar, has at length found that station in the deanery of Westminster, which, whilst it relieves him from the drudgery of the schoolmaster, keeps him still attached to the interests of the school, and eminently concerned in the superintendence and protection of it. As boy and man he made his passage twice through the forms of Westminster, rising step by step from the very last boy to the very captain of the school, and again from the junior usher through every gradation to that of second and ultimately of senior master; thus, with the interval of four years only devoted to his degree at Cambridge, Westminster has indeed kept possession of his person, but has let the world partake with her in the profit of his researches. Without deserting the laborious post, to which his duty fettered him, his excursive genius led him over seas and countries far remote, to follow and develop tracts, redeem authorities, and dig up evidences long buried in the grave of ages. This is the more to his honor, as his hours

born at Florence, in 1733. His father and Lord Bath, the great rival of Sir Robert Walpole, married sisters; and, by that nobleman's desire, he entered upon the study of the law, and was called to the bar. But Apollo and Littleton, says Wycherly, seldom meet in the same brain; the law proved an uncongenial pursuit, and he devoted himself to the muses and the belleslettres. He was connected for the greater part of his life with the drama, and though slightingly mentioned by Walpole, was justly distinguished as an author and critic.

of study were never taken but from his hours of relaxation, and he stole no moment from the instruction of the boy to enrich the understanding of the man. His last work, small in bulk, but great in matter, was an unanswerable defence of public education, by which, with an acuteness that reflects credit on his genius, and a candor that does honor to his heart, he demonstrates the advantages of that system, which had so well prospered under his care, and generously forbears to avail himself of those arguments which, in a controversy with such an opponent, some men would have resorted to. Let the mitred preacher against public schools rejoice in silence at his escape, but when the yet un-mitred master of the Temple, indisputably one of the first scholars and finest writers of his time, leaves the master of Westminster in possession of the field, it is not from want of courage, it less can be from want of capacity, to prolong the contest; it can only be from the operation of reason on a candid mind, and a clearer view of that system, which, whilst he was denouncing, he probably did not recollect that he was himself most unequivocally patronizing in the instance of his own son. Diversion of thought I well know is not uncommon with him, perversion never will be imputed to him.

When I found, upon coming into the Shell, that my station was to be quiescent, and that all challenging for places was at an end, I regretted it as an opportunity lost for turning out with new competitors, so much my seniors in age, and who seemed to regard me with an air of conscious superiority. I sat down, however, with ardor to my school business and also to my private studies, and I soon perceived that I had now no discouragements to contend with in my attempts at composition, for the very first exercise in Latin verse, which I gave in, gained the candid approbation of the master, and from that moment I acquired a degree of confidence in myself that gave vigor to my exertions; and though I bear all possible respect and gratitude to the memory of that kind friend of my youth, whose rigor was only the effect of anxiety for my well-doing, yet I cannot look back to this period of my education without acknowledging the advantages I experienced in being thus transplanted to Westminster, where to attempt was to succeed, and placed under a master, whose principle it evidently was to cherish every spark of genius which he could discover in his scholars, and who seemed determined so to exercise his authority, that our best motives for obeying him should spring from the affection that we entertained for him. Arthur Kinsman certainly knew how to make his boys scholars; Dr. Nichols had the art of making his scholars gentlemen; for there was a court of honor in that school, to whose unwritten laws every member of our community was amenable, and which, to transgress by any act of meanness that exposed the offender to public contempt, was a degree of punishment, compared to which the being sentenced to the rod would have been considered as an acquittal or reprieve.

Whilst I am making this remark, an instance occurs to me of a certain boy from the fifth, who was summoned before the seniors in the seventh, and convicted of an offence which, in the high spirit of that school, argued an abasement of principle and honor: Doctor Nichols having stated the case, demanded their opinion of the crime, and what degree of punishment they conceived it to deserve; their answer was unanimously—'The severest that could be inflicted'—'I can inflict none more severe than you have given him,' said the master, and dismissed him without any other chastisement.

It was not many days after my admission that I myself stood before him as a culprit, having been reported by the monitor for escaping out of the Abbey during divine service, and joining a party of my school-fellows for the unjustifiable purpose of intruding ourselves upon a meeting of quakers at their devotions. We had not been guilty of any gross impertinence, but the offence was highly reprehensible, and when my turn came to be called up to the master, I presume he saw my contrition, when, turning a mild look upon me he said aloud: 'Erubuit, salva est res,' and sent me back to my seat.

Was it possible not to love a character like this? Nichols certainly was a complete fine gentleman in his office, and entitled to the respect and affection of his scholars, who in his person found a master not only of the dead languages, but also of the living manners. As for me, who had experienced his lenity in the instance above related, it cannot be to my credit that I was destined to put his candor once more to the proof, yet so it was that in an idle moment I was disingenuous enough to give in an exercise in Latin verse, every line of which I had stolen out of Duport, if I rightly recollect. It passed inspection without discovery, and Doctor Nichols, after commending me for the composition, read my verses aloud to the seniors in the seventh form, and was proceeding to renew his praises, when, being touched with remorse for the disgraceful trick by which I had imposed upon him, I fairly confessed that I had pirated every syllable, and humbly begged his pardon. He paused a few moments and then replied: 'Child, I forgive you; go to your seat and say nothing of the matter. You have gained more credit with me by your ingenuous confession than you could have got by your verses, had they been your own.' I must be allowed to add, in palliation of this disreputable anecdote, that I had the grace to make the voluntary atonement next morning of an exercise as tolerable as my utmost pains and capacity could render it. I gave it in uncalled for; it was graciously received, and I took occasion to apprise the seniors in the seventh, that I had repented of my attempt.

About this time the victory of Culloden having given the death's-blow to the rebel cause, the Lords Kilmarnock and Balmerino were beheaded upon Tower Hill.[1] The elegant person of the former, and the intrepid deportment of the latter, when suffering on the scaffold, drew pity even from the most obdurate, and I believe it was at that time very generally lamented, that mercy, the best attribute of kings, was not, or could not be extended to embrace their melancholy case; every heart that felt compassion for their fate could find a plea for their offence; amongst us at school we had a great majority on the side of mercy, and not a few who, in the spirit of those times, divided in opinion with their party. In the mean while it seemed a point of honor with the boys neither to inflame nor insult each other's feelings on this occasion, and I must consider the decorum observed by such young partisans on such an occasion as a circumstance very highly to their credit. I don't doubt but respect and delicacy towards our kind and well-beloved master had a leading share in disposing them to that orderly and humane behavior.

When the rebels were in march and had advanced to Derby, appearances were very gloomy; there was a language held by some, who threw off all reserve, that menaced danger, and intimidated many of the best affected. In the height of this alarm, the Honorable Mrs. Wentworth, grandmother of the late Marquis of Rockingham, fearing that the distinguished loyalty of her noble house might expose her to pillage, secured her papers and buried her plate, flying to my father's house for refuge, where she remained an inmate during the immediate pressure of the danger she apprehended. Here I found her at my breaking up from school, a fugitive from her mansion at Harrowden, and residing in the parsonage house at Stanwick. She was a venerable and excellent lady, and retained her friendship for

[1] Selwyn, it is well known, had a morbid curiosity to witness criminal executions. He was present at the trials of Lords Kilmarnock and Balmerino—observing a Mrs. Bethel (a daughter of Lord Sandys, who was distinguished by what has been happily styled *a hatchet face*), looking wistfully at the rebel lords, 'What a shame it is,' he said, 'to turn her face to the prisoners till they are condemned.'—*Selwyn and his Contemporaries*, vol. i. p. 11.

my family to her death: she gave me a copy of the great Earl of Strafford's Letters in two folio volumes magnificently bound.

This was the time for my good father, who I verily think never knew fear, to stand forward in the exertion of that popularity, which was almost without example. He had been conspicuously active in assembling the people of the neighboring parishes, where his influence lay, and persuading them to enroll and turn out in the defence of their country. This he did in the very crisis of general despondency and alarm, whilst the disaffected in a near-neighboring quarter, abetted by a noble family, which I need not name, in the height of their exultation were burning him in effigy, as a person most obnoxious to their principles and most hostile to their cause. In a short time, at the expense merely of the enlisting shilling per man, he raised two full companies of one hundred each for the regiment then enrolling under the command of the Earl of Halifax, and marched them in person to Northampton, attended by four picked men on his four coach horses, where he was received on his entrance into the town with shouts and acclamations expressive of applause so fairly merited. The Earl of Halifax, then high in character and graceful in his person, received this tribute of my father's loyalty as might naturally be expected, and as a mark of his consideration insisted upon bestowing one of these companies upon me, for which I had the commission, though I was then too young to take command. An officer was named with the approbation of my father, to act in my place, and the regiment set out on their route for Carlisle, then in the hands of the Highlanders. There many of them lost their lives in the siege, and the smallpox made such cruel havoc amongst our young peasantry, that, although they had in the first instance been cheaply raised, the distresses of their families brought a very considerable and lasting charge upon the bounty of my father.

I remained at Westminster School, as well as I can recollect, half a year in the Shell, and one year in the sixth form, and I cannot reflect upon this period of my education without acknowledging the reason I have to be contented with the time so passed. I did not indeed drink long and deeply at the Helicon of that distinguished seminary, but I had a taste of the spring and felt the influence of the waters. In point of composition I particularly profited, for which I conceive there is in that school a kind of taste and character, peculiar to itself, and handed down perhaps from times long past, which seems to mark it out for a distinction, that it may indisputably claim, that of having been above all others the most favored cradle of the Muses. If any are disposed to question this assertion, let them turn to the lives and histories of the poets and satisfy their doubts. I know there is a tide, that flows from the very fountain-head of power, that has long run strongly in another channel, but the vicinity of Windsor Castle is of no benefit to the discipline and good order of Eton School.[1] A wise father will no more estimate his son's improvement by the measure of his boarding-house bills and pocket money amount, than a good soldier will fix his preference on a corps, because it happens to figure in the most splendid uniform, and indulge in the most voluptuous and extravagant mess.

When I returned to school I was taken as a boarder into the family of Edmund Ashby, Esq., elder brother of Waring, who had been married to my father's sister. This gentleman had a wife and three daughters, and occupied a spacious house in Peter Street, two doors from the turning out of College Street. Having been set aside by the will of his father, he was in narrow circumstances, and his style of living was that of economy upon the strictest scale. No visitor ever entered his doors, nor did he ever go out of them in search of amusement or society. Temperate in the extreme, placid and unruffled, he simply vegetated without occupation, did nothing, and had nothing to do, never seemed to trouble himself with much thinking, or interrupt the thoughts of others with much talking, and I don't recollect ever to have found him engaged with a newspaper, or a book, so that had it not been for the favors I received from a few Canary birds which the ladies kept, I might as well have boarded in the convent of La Trappe. I confess my spirit felt the gloomy influence of the sphere I lived in, and my nights were particularly long and heavy, annoyed as they were by the

[1] George III. was very partial to Eton School. Dr. Quincey thus relates the incident of his suddenly meeting the king in one of the walks at Frogmore, while, together with his young friend, Lord W——, he was 'practically commenting on the art of throwing stones.' 'The king,' says he, 'having first spoken with great kindness to my companion, inquiring circumstantially about his mother and grandmother, as persons particularly well known to himself, then turned his eye upon me. What passed was pretty nearly as follows: My name, it seems, from what followed, had been communicated to him as we were advancing; he did not, therefore, inquire about that. Was I of Eton? was his first question. I replied that I was not, but I hoped I should be. Had I a father living? I had not; my father had been dead about eight years. 'But you have a mother?' I had. 'And she thinks of sending you to Eton?' I answered that she had expressed such an intention in my hearing; but I was not sure whether *that* might not be in order to waive an argument with the person to whom she spoke, who happened to have been an Etonian. 'Oh, but all people think highly of Eton; everybody praises Eton; your mother does right to inquire; there can be no harm in that; but the more she inquires the more she will be satisfied; that I can answer for.'—*Life and Manners.*

yells and howlings of the crews of the depredators, which infest that infamous quarter, and sometimes even roused and alarmed us by their pilfering attacks. In some respects, however, I was benefited by my removal from Ludfords, as I was no longer under the strict confinement of a boarding-house, but was once or twice allowed to go, under proper convoy, to the play, where for the first time in my life I was treated with the sight of Garrick in the character of Lothario; Quin played Horatio, Ryan Altamont, Mrs. Cibber Calista, and Mrs. Pritchard condescended to the humble part of Lavinia. I enjoyed a good view of the stage from the front row of the gallery, and my attention was riveted to the scene. I have the spectacle even now as it were before my eyes. Quin presented himself upon the rising of the curtain in a green velvet coat embroidered down the seams, an enormous full-bottomed periwig, rolled stockings, and high-heeled square-toed shoes; with very little variation of cadence, and in a deep full tone, accompanied by a sawing kind of action, which had more of the senate than of the stage in it, he rolled out his heroics with an air of dignified indifference, that seemed to disdain the plaudits that were bestowed upon him. Mrs. Cibber, in a key high-pitched, but sweet withal, sung or rather recited Rowe's harmonious strain, something in the manner of the Improvisatores; it was so extremely wanting in contrast, that, though it did not wound the ear, it wearied it; when she had once recited two or three speeches, I could anticipate the manner of every succeeding one; it was like a long old legendary ballad of innumerable stanzas, every one of which is sung to the same tune, eternally chiming in the ear without variation or relief. Mrs. Pritchard was an actress of a different cast, had more nature, and of course more change of tone, and variety both of action and expression: in my opinion the comparison was decidedly in her favor; but when, after long and eager expectation, I first beheld little Garrick, then young and light and alive in every muscle and in every feature, come bounding on the stage, and pointing at the wittol Altamont and heavy-paced Horatio—heavens, what a transition!—it seemed as if a whole century had been stepped over in the transition of a single scene; old things were done away, and a new order at once brought forward, bright and luminous, and clearly destined to dispel the barbarisms and bigotry of a tasteless age, too long attached to the prejudices of custom, and superstitiously devoted to the illusions of imposing declamation. This heaven-born actor was then struggling to emancipate his audience from the slavery they were resigned to, and though at times he succeeded in throwing in some gleams of new-born light upon them, yet in general they seemed to love darkness better than light, and in the dialogue of altercation between Horatio and Lothario, bestowed far the greater show of hands upon the master of the old school than upon the founder of the new. I thank my stars, my feelings in those moments led me right; they were those of nature, and therefore could not err.[1]

At the house of Mr. Ashby I had a room to myself, a solitude within it, and silence without; I had no plea for neglecting my studies, for I had no avocations to draw me off, and no amusements to resort to. I pursued my private studies without intermission, and having taken up the Georgics for recreation's sake, I began to entertain myself with a translation in blank verse of Virgil's beautiful description of the plague amongst the cattle, beginning at verse 478 of the third book, and continued to the end of the same, viz:—

> Hic quondam morbo cœli miseranda coorta est
> Tempestas, &c. &c.

As this is one of the very few samples of my 'Juvenilia,' which I have thought well enough of to preserve, I shall now insert it *verbatim* from my first copy, and, without repeating former

[1] Garrick's appearance on the boards of a theatre in Goodman's Fields, the 19th of October, 1741, marked a change in the style of dramatic representations in England. He abandoned the artificial declamation of the prevailing school, and adhered to nature and truth. The effect was wonderful. 'All the town,' wrote Walpole to Sir Horace Mann, May 26, 1742, 'is now after Garrick, a wine merchant, who is turned player at Goodman's Fields. He plays all parts, and is a very good mimic. His acting I have seen, and may say to you, who will not tell it again here, I see nothing wonderful in it; but it is heresy to say so. The Duke of Argyle says he is superior to Betterton.' 'Garrick,' said Sir Joshua Reynolds, and surely he is a more reliable judge than Walpole, 'produces more amusement than anybody.' 'No wonder, sir, that he is vain,' said Johnson, 'a man who is perpetually flattered in every mode that can be conceived. So many bellows have blown the fire that one wonders he is not by this time become a cinder.' Boswell.—'And such bellows, too. Lord Mansfield, with his cheeks like to burst; Lord Chatham, like an Æolus. I have read such notes from them to him, as were enough to turn his head.' Johnson.—'True. When he whom everybody else flatters, flatters me, I then am truly happy.' . . . . .

> 'If there's delight in love, 'tis when I see
> That heart which others bleed for, bleed for me.'
>
> *Boswell's Johnson*, vol. ii. pp. 233, 241.

'Garrick,' said Johnson, on another occasion, 'was a very good man, the cheerfullest man of his age; a decent liver in a profession which is supposed to give indulgence to licentiousness; and a man who gives away freely, money acquired by himself. He began the world with a great hunger for money; the son of a half-pay officer, bred in a family whose study was to make fourpence do as much as others made fourpence-halfpenny do. But, when he had got money, he was very liberal.'—*Ibid.*, vol. iii. p. 417.

apologies, submit it unaltered in a single instance to the candor of the reader:—

'Here once from foul and sickly vapors sprung
A piteous plague, through all th' autumnal heats
Fatally raging: not a beast throughout,
Savage or tame, escap'd the general bane.
The foodful pasture and frequented pool
Lay charg'd with mischief; death itself assum'd
Strange forms of horror, for when fiery drought
Persuasive, coursing through the circling blood,
The feeble limbs had wasted, straight again
The oozy poison work'd its cursed way,
Sapping the solid bones: they by degrees
Sunk to corruption. Oft the victim beast,
As at the altar's sacred foot it stood,
With all its wreathy honors on its head,
Dropt breathless, and escap'd the tardy blow.
Or if its lingering spirit might chance t' await,
The priest's death-dealing hand, no flames arise
From the disposed entrails; there they lie
In thick and unpresaging smoke obscur'd.
The question'd augur holds his peace, and sees
His divination foil'd; the slaughtering blade
Scarce quits its paly hue, and the light sand
Scarce blushes with thin and meagre blood.
'Hence o'er the pasture rich and plenteous stalls
The tender herd in fragrant sighs expire;
Fell madness seizes the domestic dog;
The pursy swine heave with repeated groans.
A rattling cough inflames their swelling throats:
No toils secure, no palm the victor-horse
Availeth, now no more the wholesome spring
Delights, no longer now the once-lov'd mead;
The fatal ill prevails; with anguish stung
Raging he stamps, his ears hang down relax'd;
Sometimes an intermitting sweat breaks forth,
Cold ever at th' approach of death; again
The dry and staring hide grows stiff and hard,
Scorch'd and impasted with the feverish heat.
Such the first signs of ruin, but at length
When the accomplish'd and mature disease
With its collected and full vigor works,
The red'ning eyeballs glow with baneful fire,
The deep and hollow breath with frequent groans,
Piteous variety—! is sorely mix'd,
And long-drawn sighs distend the laboring sides:
Then forth the porches of the nose descends,
As from a conduit, blood defil'd and black,
And 'twixt the glew'd and unresolved jaws
The rough and clammy tongue sticks fast—at first
With generous wine they drench'd the closing throat—
Sole antidote, worse bane at last—for then
Dire madness—such as the just gods to none
Save to the bad consign!—at the last pang
Arose, whereat their teeth with fatal gripe,
Like pale and ghastly executioners,
Their fair and sightly limbs all mangled o'er.

'The lab'ring ox, while o'er the furrow'd land
He trails the tardy plough, down drops at once,
Forth issues bloody foam, till the last groan
Gives a long close to his labors: The sad hind
Unyokes his widow'd and complainful mate,
Leaving the blasted and imperfect work
Where the fix'd ploughshare points the luckless spot.
The shady covert, where the lofty trees
Form cold retreat, the lawns, whose springing herb
Yields food ambrosial, the transparent stream,
Which o'er the jutting stones to th' neighboring mead
Takes its fantastic course, these now no more
Delight as they were wont, rather afflict,
With him they cheer'd, with him their joys expir'd,
Joys only in participation dear;
Famine instead stares in his hollow sides,
His leaden eyeballs, motionless and fix'd,
Sleep in their sockets, his unnerved neck
Hangs drooping down, death lays his load upon him,
And bows him to the ground—what now avail
His useful toils, his life of service past?
What though full oft he turn'd the stubborn glebe,
It boots not now—yet have these never felt
The ills of riot and intemperate draughts,
Where the full goblet crowns the luscious feast:
Their only feast to graze the springing herb
O'er the fresh lawn, or from the pendant bough
To crop the savory leaf, from the clear spring,
Or active stream refined in its course,
They slake their sober thirst, their sweet repose
Nor cares forbid, nor soothing arts invite,
But pure digestion breeds and light repast.
'Twas then great Juno's altar ceas'd to smoke
With blood of bullocks, and the votive car
With huge misshapen buffaloes was drawn
To the high temples. Each one till'd his field,
Each sow'd his acres with their owner's hand,
Or, bending to the yoke with straining neck,
Up the high steep dragg'd the slow load along.
No more the wolf with crafty siege infests
The nightly fold; more pressing cares than these
Engage the sly contriver and subdue.
The fearful deer league with the hostile hound,
And ply about the charitable door
Familiar, unannoy'd. The mighty deep
At every mouth disgorg'd the scaly tribe,
And on the naked shore expos'd to view
The various wreck: the furthest rivers felt
The vast discharge and swarm'd with monstrous shapes.
In vain the viper builds his mazy cell;
Death follows him through all his wiles; in vain
The snake involves him deep beneath the flood,
Wond'ring he starts, erects his scales and dies.
The birds themselves confess the tainted air,
Drop while on wing, and as they soar expire.
Nought now avails the pasture fresh and new;
Each art applied turns opposite; e'en they,
Sage Chiron, sage Melampus, they despair,

Whilst pale Tisiphone, come fresh from hell,
Driving before her Pestilence and Fear,
Her ministers of vengeance to fulfil
Her dread commission, rages all abroad,
And lifts herself on ruin day by day
More and more high. The hollow banks resound,
The winding streams and hanging hills repeat
Loud groans from ev'ry herd, from ev'ry fold
Complaintive murmurs; heaps on heaps they fall,
There where they fall they lie, corrupt and rot
Within the loathsome stalls, fill'd and dam'd up
With impure carcasses, till they perform
The necessary office and confine
Deep under ground the foul offensive stench;
For neither might you dress the putrid hide,
Nor could the purifying stream remove,
The vigorous all-subduing flame expel
The close incorporate poison; none essayed
To shear the tainted fleece, or bind the wool,
For who e'er dar'd to clothe his desp'rate limbs
With that Nessean garment, a foul sweat,
A vile and lep'rous tetter bark'd about
All his smooth body, nor long he endur'd,
But in the sacred fire consum'd and died.'

A great and heavy affliction now befell my parents and myself. A short time before my holidays in autumn, my father and mother came to town, and brought my eldest sister Joanna with them, a very lovely girl, then in her seventeenth year. She caught the smallpox, and died in the house of the Reverend Doctor Cutts Barton, Rector of Saint Andrew's, Holborn, who kindly permitted my father to remove thither, when she sickened with that cruel disease. She was truly most engaging in her person, and, though much admired, her manners were extremely modest, and her temper mild and gentle. When I first visted her, after the symptoms of the disease were upon her, she told me she was persuaded she had caught the smallpox, and that it would be fatal to her. Her augury was too true; it was confluent, and assistance was in vain; the regimen then followed was exactly contrary to the present improved method of treating that disease, which, when it had kept her in torments for eleven days, having effectually destroyed her beauty, finally put an end to her life. My father, who tenderly loved her, submitted to the afflicting dispensation in silent sadness, never venting a complaint; my mother's sorrows were not under such control, and as to me, devoted to her as I had been from my cradle, the shock appeared to threaten me with such consequences, that my father resolved upon taking me out of town immediately, and we went down to our abode at Stanwick, a sad and melancholy party, while Mr. Ashby, my father's nephew, stayed in town and attended the body of his lamented cousin to the grave. My surviving sisters, Elizabeth and Mary, the elder of whom was six years younger than myself, had been left in the country; the attentions, which these young creatures had a claim to, the consolatory visits of our friends, and the healing hand of time by degrees assuaged the keenness of affliction, and patient resignation did the rest.

The alarm, which my father had been under on account of my health upon my sister's death, and the abhorrence he had conceived of London since that unfortunate event, determined him against my return to Westminster, and though another year, which my early age might well have dispensed with, was recommended by Dr. Nichols, and would most probably have been so employed with advantage to my education, yet the measure was taken, and, though only in my fourteenth year, I was admitted of Trinity College in Cambridge. There were yet some months of the vacation unexpired, and that I might pass this time at home with the more advantage, my father prevailed upon a neighboring clergyman, the Reverend Mr. Thomas Strong, to reside with us and assist me in my studies. A better man I never knew; a brighter scholar might easily have been found; yet we read together some few hours in every day, and those readings were almost entirely confined to the Greek Testament: there I had a teacher in Mr. Strong well worthy of my best attention, for none could better recommend by practice what he illustrated by precept, than this exemplary young man. He some time after married very happily, and resided on his living of Hargrave in our neighborhood universally respected, and I trust it is not amongst my sins of omission ever after to have forgotten his services, or failed in my attention to him.

When the time came for me to commence my residence in College, my father accompanied me and put me under the care of the Reverend Doctor Morgan, an old friend of our family, and a senior fellow of that society. My rooms were closely adjoining to his, belonging to that staircase which leads to the chapel bell; he was kind to me when we met, but as tutor I had few communications with him, for the gout afforded him not many intervals of ease, and with the exception of a few trifling readings in Tully's Offices, by which I was little edified, and to which I paid little or no attention, he left me and one other pupil, my friend and intimate, Mr. William Rudd, of Durham, to choose and peruse our studies as we saw fit. This dereliction of us was inexcusable, for Rudd was a youth of fine talents and a well-grounded scholar. In the course of no long time, however, Doctor Morgan left college, and went to reside upon his living of Gainford, in the bishopric of Durham, and I was turned over to the Reverend Doctor Philip Young, professor of oratory in the University, and afterwards Bishop of Norwich; what Morgan made a very light concern, Young made an absolute sinecure, for from him I never received a single lecture, and I hope his lordship's conscience was not much disturbed on my account, for, though he gave me free leave to be idle, I did not make idleness my choice.

CHAPTER II.

His studies—His habits—His style of reading—A present of books—Doctor Richard Walker—Disputation—Ill-health—Advantages of the system of instruction at Cambridge—*Collectanea*—Plan of reading—Mason's Elfrida—Politics—Change of life—Excursion to York—Elegiac verses—Candidate for a fellowship—Appointed Lord Halifax's private secretary—Sketch of Halifax—Dr. Crane—Cumberland goes to London—John Pownall—Visit to the Duke of Newcastle—Bishop of Peterborough—Charles Mason—Cumberland's examination for a fellowship—His success—His competitors—His course of life in London—Not fitted for public life—Demagogues—Charles Townshend—Lord and Lady Halifax—Ambrose Isted—Mr. Eskins—Jeffrey—Richard Reynolds—Poem on India—Death of Lady Halifax—Her character—Cumberland's father removes to Fulham—His popularity—Bishop Sherlock—Mrs. Sherlock—Richard Glover—Bubb Dodington—Cumberland's visit to—Character of—Henry Fox—Alderman Beckford—Lay-fellowship at Trinity College—The banishment of Cicero—Praised by Warburton—Recommended to Garrick by Lord Halifax—Garrick's refusal to put it on the stage—Cumberland's marriage.

In the last year of my being under graduate, when I commenced Soph, in the very first act that was given out to be kept in the mathematical schools, I was appointed to an opponency, when at that time I had not read a single proposition in Euclid; I had now been just turned over to Mr. Backhouse, the Westminster tutor, who gave regular lectures, and fulfilled the duties of his charge ably and conscientiously. Totally unprepared to answer the call now made upon me, and acquit myself in the schools, I resorted to him in my distress, and through his interference my name was withdrawn from the act; in the mean time I was sent for by the master, Doctor Smith, the learned author of the well-known Treatises upon Optics and Harmonics, and the worthy successor to my grandfather Bentley, who strongly reprobated the neglect of my former tutors, and recommended me to lose no more time in preparing myself for my degree, but to apply closely to my academical studies for the remainder of the year, which I assured him I would do.

As I did not belong to Mr. Backhouse till I had commenced Soph, but nominally to those who left me to myself, I had hitherto pursued those studies that were familiar to me, and indulged my passion for the classics, with an ardor that rarely knew any intermission or relief. I certainly did not wantonly misuse my time, or yield to any even of the slightest excesses, that youth is prone to: I never frequented any tavern, neither gave nor received entertainments, nor partook in any parties of pleasure, except now and then in a ride to the hills, so that I thank God I have not to reproach myself with any instances of misconduct towards a generous father, who at this tender age committed me to my own discretion and confided in me. I look back therefore upon this period of my life with a tranquil conscience; I even dwell upon it with peculiar delight, for within those maternal walls I passed years given up to study and those intellectual pure enjoyments, which leave no self-reproach, whilst with the works of my ancestors in my hands, and the impression of their examples on my heart, I flattered myself in the belief that I was pressing forward ardently and successfully to follow them in their profession, and peradventure not fall far behind them in their fame. This was the great aim and object of my ambition; for this I labored, to this point I looked, and all my world was centred in my college. Every scene brought to my mind the pleasing recollection of times past, and filled it with the animating hope of times to come: as my college duties and attendances were occupations that I took pleasure in, punctuality and obedience did not put me to the trouble of an effort, for when to be employed is our amusement, there is no self-denial in not being idle. If I had then had a tutor, who would have systematized and arranged my studies, it would have been happy for me; but I had no such director, and with my books before me (poets, historians and philosophers), sate down as it were to a *cœna dubia*, with an eager, rather than a discriminating, appetite; I am now speaking of my course of reading from my admission to my commencing Soph, when I was called off to my academical studies. In that period my stock of books was but slender, till Doctor Richard Bentley had the goodness to give me a valuable parcel of my grandfather's books and papers, containing his correspondence with many of the foreign literati upon points of criticism, some letters from Sir Isaac Newton, a pretty large body of notes for an edition of Lucan's Pharsalia, which I gave to my uncle Bentley, and were published under his inspection by Dodsley, at Mr. Walpole's press, with sundry other manuscripts, and a considerable number of Greek and Latin books, mostly collated by him, and their margins filled with alterations and corrections in his own hand, neatly and legibly written in a very small character. The possession of these books was most gratifying and acceptable to me; some few of them were extremely rare, and in the history I have given in 'The Observers' of the Greek writers, more particularly of the Comic Poets now lost, I have availed myself of them, and I am vain enough to believe no such collection of the scattered extracts, anecdotes and remains of those dramatists is anywhere else to be found. The donor of these books was the nephew of my grandfather, and inherited by will the whole of his library, which at his death was sold by auction in Leicestershire, where he resided in his latter years on his rectory of Nailstone: he was himself no inconsiderable collector, and it is much to be regretted that his executors took this method of disposing of his books, by which they became dispersed in small lots amongst many country purchasers, who probably did not know their value. He was an accurate collator, and for his judgment in editions much resorted to by Doctor Mead, with whom he lived in great intimacy. During the time that he resided in college, for he was one of the senior fellows of Trinity, he gave me every possible proof, not only in this instance of his donation, but in many others, of his favor and protection.

At the same time Doctor Richard Walker, the friend of my grandfather, and vice-master of the college, never failed to distinguish me by every kindness in his power. He frequently invited me to his rooms, which I had so often visited as a child, and which had the further merit with me as having been the residence of Sir Isaac Newton, every relic of whose studies and experiments were respectfully preserved to the minutest particular, and pointed out to me by the good old vice-master with the most circumstantial precision. He had many little anecdotes of my grandfather, which to me at least were interesting, and an old servant Deborah, whom he made a kind of companion, and who was much in request for the many entertaining circumstances she could narrate of Sir Isaac Newton, when she waited upon him as his bedmaker, and also of Doctor Bentley, with whom she lived for several years after Sir Isaac left college, and at the death of my grandfather was passed over to Doctor Walker, in whose service she died.

My mind in these happy days was so tranquil, and my time passed in so uniform a tenor of study and retirement, that though it is a period pleasing to me to reflect upon, yet it furnishes little that is worthy to be recorded. I believe I hardly ever employed myself upon English composition, except on the event of the Prince of Wales's death, when amongst others I sent in my contribution of elegiac verses to the university volume, and very indifferent ones they were. To my Latin declamations I paid my best attention, for these were recited publicly in the chapel after evening prayers on Saturdays, when it was open to all who chose to resort thither, and we were generally flattered by pretty full audiences.

The year of trial now commenced, for which, through the neglect of my tutors, I was, as an academical student, totally unprepared. Determined to use every effort in my power for redeeming my lost time, I began a course of study so apportioned as to allow myself but six hours sleep, to which I strictly adhered, living almost entirely upon milk, and using the cold bath very frequently. As I was then only seventeen years old, and of a frame by no means robust, many of my friends remonstrated against the severity of this regimen, and recommended more moderation, but the encouragement I met in the rapidity of my progress through all the dry and elementary parts of my studies, determined me to persist with ardor, and made me deaf to their advice. In the several branches of the mechanics, hydrostatics, optics and astronomy, I consulted the best treatises, and made myself master of them; I worked all propositions, formed all my minutes, and even my thoughts, in Latin, whereby I acquired a facility of expounding, solving and arguing in that language, in which I may presume to say I had advantages, which some of the best of my contemporaries in our public disputations were but too sensible of, for so long as my knowledge of a question could supply matter for argument, I never felt any want of terms for explanation.

When I found myself prepared to take my part in the public schools, I thirsted for the opportunity, which I no longer dreaded, and with this my ambition was soon gratified, being appointed to keep an act, and three respectable opponents singled out against me, the first of which was looked up to as the best of the year. When his name was given out for disputation, the schools never failed to be crowded, and as I had drawn my questions from Newton's Principia, I gave him fair scope for the display of his superiority, and was by all considered (for his fame was universal) as a mere child in his hands, justly to be punished for my temerity, and self-devoted to complete confutation. I was not only a mere novice in the schools, but also a perfect stranger to the gentleman opposed to me; when, therefore, mounted on a bass in the rostrum, which even then I could scarcely overtop, I contemplated, in the person of my antagonist, a North-country black-bearded philosopher, who at an advanced age had admitted at Saint John's to qualify for holy orders (even at that time a finished mathematician and a private lecturer in those studies), I did not wonder that the contrast of a beardless boy, pale and emaciated as I was then become, seemed to attract everybody's curiosity; for after I had

5

concluded my thesis, which precedes the disputation, when he ascended his seat under the rostrum of the Moderator——

> With grave
> Aspect he rose, and in his rising seem'd
> A pillar of strength; deep in his front engraven
> Deliberation sate—sage he stood
> With Atlantean shoulders fit to bear
> The weight of mightiest argument.

Formidable as he appeared, I did not feel my spirits sink, for I had taken a very careful survey of the ground I was upon, and thought myself prepared against any attack he could devise against me. I also saw that all advantages, resulting from the unequal terms on which we engaged, were on my side; I might obtain glory from him, and he could but little profit by his triumph over me. My heart was in my cause, and proudly measuring its importance by the crowd it had collected, armed, as I believed myself to be, in the full understanding of my questions, and a perfect readiness in the language in which our disputations were to be carried on, I waited his attack amidst the hum and murmur of the assembly. His argument was purely mathematical, and so enveloped in the terms of his art, as made it somewhat difficult for me to discover where his syllogism pointed without those aids and delineations, which our process did not allow of; I availed myself of my privilege to call for a repetition of it, when at once I caught the fallacy, and pursued it with advantage, keeping the clue firm in hand till I completely traced him through all the windings of his labyrinth. The same success attended me through the remaining seven arguments, which fell off in strength and subtlety, and his defence became sullen and morose, his latinity very harsh, inelegant and embarrassed, till I saw him descend with no very pleasant countenance, whilst it appeared evident to me that my whole audience were not displeased with the unexpected turn which our controversy had taken. He ought in course to have been succeeded by a second and third opponent, but our disputation had already been prolonged beyond the time commonly allotted, and the schools were broken up by the Moderator with a compliment addressed to me in terms much out of the usual course on such occasions.

If it is allowable for me to speak of such trifling events circumstantially, and with the importance which at that time I attached to them, when I knew nothing of this great world beyond the walls of my college, I hope this passage will be read with candor, and that I shall be pardoned for a long tale told in my old age of the first triumph of my youth, earned by extreme hard labor, and gained at the risk and hazard of my health by a perseverance in so severe a course of study, as brought me ultimately to the very brink of the grave.

Four times I went through these scholastic exercises in the course of the year, keeping two acts and as many first opponencies. In one of the latter, where I was pitched against an ingenious student of my own college, I contrived to form certain arguments, which by a scale of deductions so artfully drawn, and involving consequences which, by mathematical gradations (the premises being once granted), led to such unforeseen confutation, that even my tutor, Mr. Backhouse, to whom I previously imparted them, was effectually trapped, and could as little parry them as the gentleman who kept the act, or the Moderator who filled the chair.

The last time I was called upon to keep an act in the schools, I sent in three questions to the Moderator, which he withstood as being all mathematical, and required me to conform to the usage of proposing one metaphysical question in the place of that which I should think fit to withdraw. This was ground I never liked to take, and I appealed against his requisition; the act was accordingly put by till the matter of right should be ascertained by the statutes of the university, and in the result of that inquiry it was given for me, and my questions stood. This litigation between the Moderator and an under-graduate, whose interest in the distribution of honors at the ensuing degree lay so much at the mercy of his report, made a considerable stir, and gave rise to much conversation; so that when this long-suspended act took place, not only the floor of the schools was filled with the juniors, but many of high standing in the university assembled in the gallery. The Moderator had nominated the same gentleman as my first opponent, who no doubt felt every motive to renew the contest, and bring me to a proper sense of my presumption. The term was now drawing near to its close, and I began to feel very sensibly the effects of my too intense application, my whole frame being debilitated in a manner that warned me I had not long to continue my course of labor without the interruption of some serious attack; I had in fact the seeds of a rheumatic fever lurking in my constitution, and was led between two of my friends and fellow collegians to the schools in a very feeble state. I was, however, intellectually alive to all the purposes of the business we were upon, and when I observed that the Moderator exhibited symptoms of indisposition by resting his head upon the cushion on the desk, I cut short my thesis to make way for my opponent, who had hardly brought his argument to bear, when the Moderator, on the plea of sudden indisposition, dismissed me with a speech, which, though tinctured with some petulance, had more of praise in it than I expected to receive.

I yielded now to advice, and paid attention to my health, till we were cited to the senate house to be examined for our Bachelor's degree. It was hardly ever my lot during that examination to enjoy any respite. I seemed an object singled out as every man's mark, and was kept perpetually at the table under the process of question and answer. My constitution just held me up to the expiration of the scrutiny, and I immediately hastened to my own home to alarm my parents with my ghastly looks, and soon fell ill of a rheumatic fever, which for the space of six months kept me hovering between life and death. The skill of my physician, the afore-mentioned Dr. Wallis, of Stamford, and the tender attention of the dear friends about me, rescued me at length, and I recovered under their care. Whilst I was in this state, I had the pleasure of hearing from Cambridge of the high station which had been adjudged to me amongst 'The Wranglers' of my year, and I further understood how much I was indebted to the generous support of that very Moderator, whom I had thwarted in the matter of my questions, for this adjudication so much in my favor and perhaps above my merits, for my knowledge had been hastily attained; a conduct so candid on the part of the Reverend Mr. Ray (fellow of Corpus Christi, and the Moderator, of whom I have been speaking) was ever remembered by me with gratitude and respect: Mr. Ray was afterwards domestic chaplain to the Archbishop of Canterbury, and, when I was resident in town, I waited upon him at Lambeth palace to express my sensibility of the very liberal manner in which he had protected me.

I now found myself in a station of ease and credit in my native college, to which I was attached by every tie that could endear it to me. I had changed my under-graduate's gown, and obtained my degree of Bachelor of Arts with honors hardly earned by pains the more severe because so long postponed: and now, if I have been seemingly too elaborate in tracing my own particular progress through these exercises, to which the candidate for a degree at Cambridge must of necessity conform, it is not merely because I can quote my privilege for my excuse, but because I would most earnestly impress upon the attention of my reader the extreme usefulness of these academical exercises and the studies appertaining to them, by which I consider all the purposes of an university education are completed; and so convinced am I of this, that I can hardly allow myself to call that an education, of which they do not make a part; if therefore I am to speak for the discipline of the schools, ought I not first to show that I am speaking from experience, without which opinions pass for nothing? Having therefore first demonstrated what my experience of that discipline has been, I have the authority of that, as far as it goes, for an opinion in its favor, which every observation of my life has since contributed to establish and confirm. What more can any system of education hold out to those, who are the objects of it, than public honors to distinguish merit, public exercises to awaken emulation, and public examinations, which cannot be passed without extorting some exertion even from the indolent, nor can be avoided without a marked disgrace to the compounder? Now if I have any knowledge of the world, any insight into the minds and characters of those whom I have had opportunities of knowing (and few have lived more and longer amongst mankind), all my observations tend to convince me that there is no profession, no art, no station nor condition in life, to which the studies I have been speaking of will not apply and come in aid with profit and advantage. That mode of investigation step by step, which crowns the process of the student by the demonstration and discovery of positive and mathematical truth, must of necessity so exercise and train him in the habits of following up his subject, be it what it may, and working out his proofs, as cannot fail to find their uses, whether he who has them dictates from the pulpit, argues at the bar, or declaims in the senate; nay, there is no lot, no station (I repeat it with confidence), be it either social or sequestered, conspicuous or obscure, professional or idly independent, in which the man, once exercised in these studies, though he shall afterwards neglect them, will not to his comfort experience some mental powers and resources, in which their influence shall be felt, though the channels that conducted it may from disuse have become obscure, and no longer to be traced.

Hear the crude opinions, that are let loose upon society in our table conversations: mark the wild and wandering arguments that are launched at random without ever hitting the mark they should be levelled at; what does all this noise and nonsense prove, but that the talker has indeed acquired the fluency of words, but never known the exercise of thought, or attended to the development of a single proposition? Tell him that he ought to hear what may be said on the other side of the question—he agrees to it, and either begs leave to wind up with a few words more, which he winds and wire-draws without end; or, having paused to hear, hears with impatience a very little, foreknows everything you had further to say, cuts short your argument and bolts in upon you—with an answer to that argument—? No; with a continuation of his own gabble, and, having stifled you with the torrent of his trash, places your contempt to the credit of his own capacity, and foolishly conceives he talks with reason because he has not patience to attend to any reasoning but his own.

What are all the quirks and quibbles, that skirmishers in controversy catch hold of to escape the point of any argument, when pressed upon them? If a laugh, a jeer, a hit of mimicry, or buffoonery cannot parry the attack, they find themselves disarmed of the only weapons they can wield, and then, though truth should stare them in the face, they will affect not to see it: instead of receiving conviction as the acquirement of something, which they had not themselves, and have gained from you, they regard it as an insult to their understandings, and grow sullen and resentful; they will then tell you they shall leave you to your own opinions, they shall say no more, and with an air of importance wrap themselves up in a kind of contemptuous indifference, when their reason for saying nothing is only because they have nothing more to say. How many of this cast of character are to be met with in the world every man of the world can witness.

There are also others, whose vivacity of imagination having never felt the trammels of a syllogism is for ever flying off into digression and display—

Quo teneam nodo mutantem Protea formas?—

To attempt at hedging in these cuckoos is but lost labor. These gentlemen are very entertaining as long as novelties with no meaning can entertain you; they have a great variety of opinions, which, if you oppose, they do not defend, and if you agree with, they desert. Their talk is like the wild notes of birds, amongst which you shall distinguish some of pleasant tone, but out of which you compose no tune or harmony of song. These men would have set down Archimedes for a fool when he danced for joy at the solution of a proposition, and mistaken Newton for a madman, when in the surplice, which he put on for chapel over night, he was found the next morning in the same place and posture fixed in profound meditation on his theory of the prismatic colors. So great is their distaste for demonstration, they think no truth is worth the waiting for; the mountain must come to them, they are not by half so complaisant as Mahomet. They are not easily reconciled to truisms, but have no particular objection to impossibilities. For argument they have no ear; it does not touch them; it fetters fancy, and dulls the edge of repartee; if by chance they find themselves in an untenable position, and wit is not at hand to help them out of it, they will take up with a pun, and ride home upon a horse laugh: if they can't keep their ground, they won't wait to be attacked and driven out of it. Whilst a reasoning man will be picking his way out of a dilemma, they, who never reason at all, jump over it, and land themselves at once upon new ground, where they take an imposing attitude, and escape pursuit. Whatever these men do, whether they talk, or write, or act, it is without deliberation, without consistency, without plan. Having no expanse of mind, they can comprehend only in part; they will promise an epic poem, and produce an epigram: In short, they glitter, pass away, and are forgotten; their outset makes a show of mighty things; they stray out of their course into by-ways and obliquities, and when out of sight of their contemporaries, are forever lost to posterity.

When characters of this sort come under our observation, it is easy to discover that their levities and frivolities have their source in the errors and defects of education, for it is evident they have not been trained in any principles of right reasoning. Therefore it is that I hold in such esteem the academical studies pursued at Cambridge, and regard their exercises in the mathematical schools, and their examinations in the theatre, as forming the best system, which this country offers, for the education of its youth. Persuaded as I am of this, I must confess I have ever considered the election of scholars from the college of Eton to that of King's in Cambridge, as a bar greatly in their disfavor, forasmuch as by the constitution of that college they are not subjected to the same process for attaining their degrees, and of course the study of the mathematics makes no part of their system, but is merely optional. I leave this remark to those who may think it worthy of their consideration. Under-graduates of Trinity College, whether elected from Westminster or not, have no such exemptions.

Having now, at an age more than commonly early, obtained my Bachelor's degree, with the return of health I resumed my studies, and without neglecting those I had so lately been engaged in, again took up those authors who had lain by untouched for a whole twelvemonth. I supposed my line in life was decided for the church, the profession of my ancestors, and in the course of three years I had good reason to expect a fellowship with the degree of Master of Arts. These views, so suited to my natural disposition, were now before me, and I dwelt upon them with entire content.

Having now been in the habit of reading upon system, I resolved to put my thoughts together upon paper, and began to form a kind of *Collectanea* of my studies. With this view I got together all the tracts relative to the controversy between Boyle and Bentley, omitting none even of the authorities and passages they referred to, and having done this, I compressed the reasonings on both sides into a kind of statement and report upon the question in dispute, and if in the result my judgment went with him, to whom my inclination leant, no learned critic of the present age will condemn me for the decision.

When I had accomplished this, I meditated on a plan little short of what might be projected for an Universal History, or at least for that of the Great Empires in particular. For this purpose I began with studying the Sanchoniatho of Bishop Cumberland, contrasting the Phœnician and Egyptian Cosmogonies with that of Moses, by which I found myself at length involved in references to so many authors, which I had no means of consulting, and so hampered by Oriental languages, which I did not understand, that after filling a large folio foul-book, which I still keep in possession, I gave up the task, or, more properly speaking, reduced it to a more contracted scale, in which, however, I contrived to review all the several systems of the heathen philosophers, and discuss at large the tenets and opinions maintained and professed by their respective schools and academies. This was a work of labor and considerable research, and having had lately occasion to resort to it for certain purposes, which I have in hand, I must do myself the justice to say I found it very accurate, and derived all the aid and information from it that I expected or required. That I was at that age disposed and able to apply my mind to a work so operose and argumentative I ascribe entirely to the nature of the studies, and the habitudes of thinking I had so recently been engaged in.

Thus, after wandering at large for a considerable time, without any one to guide me, I was at last compelled to chalk out for myself a settled plan of reading, which, if I had not been disciplined, as above described, I certainly should have long postponed, or perhaps never have struck out. Why will not those whose duty it is to superintend the education of their pupils in our universities, when they discover talents and a thirst for learning, point out to the student the best and nearest road to its attainment? It is surely within their province to do it; and the benefit would be incalculable.

I well remember, when I was newly come to college, with what avidity I read the Greek tragedians, and with what reverence I swallowed the absurdities of their chorus, and was bigoted to their cold character and rigid unities; and when Mason,[1] of Pembroke-Hall, published his 'Elfrida' after their model, though I did not quite agree with him as to his choice of plot, or the perfect legitimacy of his chorus, yet I was warm in my praises of that generally admired production, and in imitation of it planned and composed an entire drama, of which Caractacus was the hero, with bards and Druids attached to it as a chorus, for whom I wrote odes in the manner of 'Elfrida.' I have this manuscript now in my possession, and it is flattering to my choice of subject that Mason, with whom I had no communication or correspondence, should afterwards strike upon the same character for the hero of his drama; but though in this particular I have the good chance to agree with him, in point of plot I strayed equally from him and from the history, for, not writing with any thought of publication, I wove into my drama some characters and several incidents perfectly fictitious. There is a good deal of fancy, and some strong writing in it; but, as a whole, it must be read with allowances, and I shall, therefore, pass it over, not wishing to make too many demands upon the candor of the reader.

Whilst I was thus living with my family at Stanwick, in the enjoyment of everything that could constitute my felicity, a strong contest took place upon the approach of the general election; and the county of Northampton was hotly canvassed by the rival parties of Knightly and Hanbury, or, in other words, by the Tories and the Whigs. My father, whose politics accorded with the latter, was drawn out upon this occasion, and gave a very active and effectual support to his party, and though the cause he embarked in was unsuccessful, yet his particular exertions had been such that he might truly have said—

Si Pergama dextrâ
Defendi possent, etiam hâc defensi fuissent.

---

[1] Mason was the son of a clergyman in Yorkshire, where he was born in 1725. He adopted his father's profession, and after the publication of 'Elfrida,' was appointed one of the royal chaplains. At the era of the American Revolution, Mason was an advocate for freedom, and, in consequence, lost his chaplaincy. The excesses of the French Revolution, however, brought about a change in his sentiments, or an abatement of his zeal; and, in the latter part of his life, his politics were conservative. Johnson, who disliked Mason, was in the habit of disparaging him as a poet. 'Surely, sir,' said Boswell, on one occasion, 'Mr. Mason's 'Elfrida' is a fine poem; at least you will allow there are some good passages in it.' Johnson.—'There are now and then some good imitations of Milton's bad manner.' Johnson had an equally low estimate of Gray. 'Mr. Mason's 'Elfrida,' says Boswell, 'is exquisite, both in political description and moral sentiment; and his 'Caractacus' is a noble drama. Nor can I omit paying my tribute of praise to some of his smaller poems, which I have read with pleasure, and which no criticism shall persuade me not to like. If I wondered at Johnson's not tasting the works of Mason and Gray, still more have I wondered at their not tasting his works.'—*Boswell's Johnson*, vol. ii. 348.

This second striking instance of his popularity and influence was by no means overlooked by the Earl of Halifax, then high in office, and Lord Lieutenant of the county. Offers, which he did not court, were pressed upon him; but though he was resolute in declining all favors personal to himself, yet he was persuaded to lend an ear to flattering situations pointed out for me, and my destiny was now preparing to reverse those tranquil and delectable scenes which I had hitherto enjoyed, and to transplant me from the cloisters of my college, and free range of my studies, to the desk of a private secretary, and the irksome, painful restraints of dependence.

Let me not, by my statement of this event, appear to lay anything to the charge of my ever dear and honored father; if I were unnaturally disposed to find a fault in his proceeding upon this occasion, I must search for it amongst his virtues. He was open, warm, and unsuspecting, apt to credit others for what was natural to himself, ever inclined to look only on the best side of men and things, and certainly not one of the children of this world. If I have cause to regret this departure from the line in which by education I had been trained, I am the author of my own misfortune; I was perfectly a free agent, and have nobody but myself to accuse. My youth, however, and the still unsettled state of my health, spared me for a time; and my father proposed an excursion to the city of York, for the double purpose of my relaxation and my sister's accomplishments in music and dancing. We had a near relation living there, a widow lady, niece to Doctor Bentley, who accommodated us with her house; and we passed half a year in the society and amusements of the place. This lady, Forster by name, and first cousin to my mother, was a woman of superior understanding. Her opinions were pronounced authoritatively, and without respect of person; they were considered in York as little less than oracular. The style of living in this place was so new to me and out of character, when contrasted by the habits of study and retirement which I had been accustomed to, that it seemed to enfeeble and depress that portion of genius which nature had endowed me with. I hunted in the mornings, danced in the evenings, and devoted but a small portion of my time to anything that deserved the name of study. I had no books of my own, and unfortunately got engaged with Spenser's 'Fairy Queen,' in imitation of which I began to string nonsensical stanzas to the same rhyming kind of measure. Though I trust I should not have surrendered myself for any length of time to this jingling strain of obsolete versification, yet I am indebted to my mother for the seasonable contempt she threw upon my imitations, felt the force of her reproof, and laid the 'Fairy Queen' upon its shelf.

The Earl of Galloway, father of the present Lord, was then residing at York with his family; a beautiful copy of elegiac verses, the composition of his daughter, Lady Susan, was communicated to me, of which the hint seemed to be taken from Hamlet's meditations on the skull of Yorick. I do not feel myself at liberty to publish the elegant poem of that lady, who lived to grace the high station which by her birth, virtues, and endowments she was entitled to, and when I now venture to insert my own, I am fully conscious how ill it would endure a comparison with that which gave occasion to it—

'True! We must all be chang'd by death,
 Such is the form the dead must wear,
And so, when Beauty yields its breath,
 So shall the fairest face appear.

But let thy soul survey the grace,
 That yet adorns its frail abode,
And through the wondrous fabric trace,
 The hand of an unerring God.

Why does the blood in stated round
 Its vital warmth throughout dispense?
Who tun'd the ear to every sound,
 And lent the hand its ready sense?

Whence had the eyes that subtle force,
 That languor, they by turns display?
Who hung the lips with prompt discourse,
 And tun'd the soft melodious lay?

What but thy Maker's image there
 In each external part is seen?
But 'tis thy better part to wear
 His image pictur'd best within.

Else what avail'd the raptur'd strain,
 Did not the mind her aid impart,
The melting eye would speak in vain,
 Flow'd not its language from the heart.

The blood with stated pace had crept
 Along the dull and sluggish veins,
The ear insensibly had slept,
 Though angels sung in choicest strains.

It is that spark of quick'ning fire,
 To every child of nature giv'n,
That either kindles wild desire,
 Or lights us on the road to heav'n.

That spark, if Virtue keeps it bright,
 And Genius fans it into flame,
Aspiring mounts, and in its flight,
 Soars far above this earthly frame.

Strong and expansive in its view,
It tow'rs amidst the boundless sky,
Sees planets other orbs pursue,
Whose systems other suns supply.

Such Newton was, diffusing far
His radiant beams; such Cotes had been,
This a bright comet; that a star,
Which glitter'd and no more was seen.

Blush then if thou hast sense of shame,
Inglorious, ign'rant, impious slave!
Who think'st this heav'n-created frame
Shall basely perish in the grave.

False as thou art, dar'st thou suggest
That thy Creator is unjust?
Wilt thou the truth with Him contest,
Whose wisdom form'd thee of the dust?

Say, dotard, hath he idly wrought,
Or are his works to be believ'd?
Speak, is the whole creation nought?
Mortal, is God or thou deceiv'd?

Thy harden'd spirit, convict at last,
Its damning error shall perceive,
Speechless shall hear its sentence past,
Condemn'd to tremble and believe.

But thou in reason's sober light
Death clad with terror can'st survey,
And from the foul and ghastly sight
Derive the pure and moral lay.

Go on, sweet Nymph, and when thy Muse
Visits the dark and dreary tomb,
Bright-rob'd Religion shall diffuse
Her radiance, and dispel the gloom.

And when the necessary day
Shall call thee to thy saving God,
Secure thou'lt choose that better way,
Which Conscience points and Saints have trod.

So shall thy soul at length forsake
The fairest form e'er soul receiv'd
Of those rich blessings to partake,
Which eye ne'er saw, nor heart conceiv'd.

There, 'midst the full angelic throng,
Praise Him, who those rich blessings gave,
There shall resume the grateful song,
A joyful victor o'er the grave.'

This excursion to York was indeed a relaxation, but not altogether of a sort that either suited my ease or accorded with my taste. Certain it is I had, for a time, impaired my health by too much application and the over-abstemious habits I imposed upon myself during my last year at college, but tranquillity, not dissipation, or what is called amusement, was the restorative I most needed. The allurements of public assemblies and the society of those who resort to them, form so great a contrast to the occupations of a student, that instead of being enlivened by the change, I felt a lassitude of mind, that put me out of humor with myself, and damped that ardent spirit of acquirement, which in my nature seemed to have been its ruling passion. Extremes of any sort are dangerous to youthful minds, and should be studiously avoided. The termination of our visit to York, and the prospect of returning to college were welcomed by me most cordially. I had brought no books with me to York, and of course had nothing to call off my mind from the listless idle style in which I dangled away my time, amusing myself only now and then with my pen, because my fancy would not be totally unemployed; sometimes, as I have before related, imitating Spenser's style, and at other times composing short elegies after the manner of Hammond; for this, when I was reprimanded by the same judicious monitress, who rallied me out of my imitations of the stanzas of 'The Fairy Queen,' I promised her I would write no more love elegies, and took leave of Hammond with the following lines, written almost extempore—

'When wise men love, they love to folly;
When blockheads love, they're melancholy;
When coxcombs love, they love for fashion,
And quaintly call it the belle passion.

Old bachelors, who wear the willow,
May dream of love and hug the pillow,
Whilst love, in poet's fancy rhyming,
Sets all the bells of folly chiming.

But women, charming women, prove
The sweet varieties of love;
They can love all, but none too dearly,
Their husbands, too, but not sincerely.

They'll love a thing, whose outward shape
Marks him twin brother to an ape;
They'll take a miser for his riches,
And wed a beggar without breeches.

Marry, as if in love with ruin,
A gamester to their sure undoing;
A drunkard, raving, swearing, storming,
For the dear pleasure of reforming.

They'll wed a lord, whose breath shall falter
Whilst he is crawling from the altar:
What is there women will not do,
When they love man and money too?'

These and numerous trifles of the like sort, not worth recording, amused my vacant hours at York, but when I returned home, I made a very short stay and hastened to college, where I was soon invited to the master's lodge by Doctor Smith, who was pleased to honor me with his approbation of my past exertions, and imparted to me a new arrangement, that he and the seniors had determined upon for annulling so much of the existing statutes as restricted all Bachelor of Arts, except those of the third year's standing, from offering themselves candidates for fellowships: when he had signified this to me, he kindly added, that as I should be in the second year of my degree at the next election, he recommended it to me by all means to present myself for examination, and to take my chance. This was a communication so flattering, that I knew not how to shape the answer, which he seemed to expect from me; I clearly saw that his meaning was to bring me into the society a year before any one had been elected since the statutes were in existence; I knew that by my election there must be an exclusion of some candidate of the year above me, who had only a single chance, whereas I had a double one; in the mean time, my circumstances were such as not to want the emoluments of a fellowship, and my age such as might well admit of a postponement. These were my reflections at that time, and I felt the force of them, but the regulation was gone forth, and there were others of my own year, who had announced their resolution of coming forward as candidates at the time of the election. There was no part therefore for me to take but to prepare myself for the examination and expect the result. To this I looked forward with much more terror and alarm than to all I had experienced in the schools and theatre, for I not only stood in awe of the master of Trinity, as being the deepest mathematician of his time, but as I had reason to believe he had been led to lay open the election in some degree on my account, I apprehended he would never suffer his partiality to single me out to the exclusion of any other without strict scrutiny into my pretensions, and as I had obtained a high honor when I took my degree, I greatly feared he might expect too much, and meet with disappointment.

Under these impressions, whilst I was preparing to resume my studies with increased attention, and repair the time not profitably passed of late, I received a summons, which opened to me a new scene of life. I was called for by Lord Halifax to assume the situation of his private confidential secretary; it was considered by my family and the friends and advisers of my family, as an offer, upon which there could be no hesitation. They took the question as it struck them in their view of it;

they could not look into futurity, neither could they take a perfect estimate either of my fitness for the situation held out to me, or of the eventual value of the situation, from which I was about to be displaced. What the prosecution of my studies might have led me to in that line of life, to which I had directed my attention, and fixed my attachment, is a matter of speculation and conjecture; what I might have avoided is now become matter of experience, and I can only say that had certain passages of my past life been then stated to me as probabilities to occur, I would have stuck to my college, and endeavored to have trodden in the steps of my ancestors.

I was not fitted for dependence; my nature was repugnant to it; I was most fortunately formed with feelings that could ill endure the assumed importance of some, or submit to take advantage of the weakness of others. I had ambition enough, and it may be more than enough; but it was the ambition of working out my own way by the labors of my mind, and raising to myself a character upon a foundation of my own laying. I certainly do not offend against truth when I say I had an ardent wish to earn a name in literature: I had studied books; I had not studied men, and perhaps I was too much disposed to measure my respect for their characters by the standard of their talents. I had no acquaintance with the noble lord, who now invited me to share his confidence, and receive my destiny from his hands. My good father did what was perfectly natural for a father to do in the like circumstances, he availed himself of the opportunity for placing me under the patronage of one of the most figuring and rising men of his time. There was something extremely brilliant and more than commonly engaging in the person, manners, and address of the Earl of Halifax. He had been educated at Eton, and came with the reputation of a good scholar to Trinity College, where he established himself in the good opinion of the whole society, not only by his orderly and regular conduct, but in a very distinguished manner by the attention which he paid to his studies, and the proofs he gave in his public exercises of his classical acquirements. He was certainly, when compared with men of his condition, to be distinguished as a scholar much above the common mark: he quoted well and copiously from the best authors, chiefly Horace; he was very fond of English poetry, and recited it very emphatically after the manner of Quin, who had been his master in that art: he had a partiality for Prior, which he seemed to inherit from the celebrated Lord Halifax, and would rehearse long passages from his Solomon, and Henry and Emma, with the whole of his verses, beginning with 'Sincere, oh tell me'—and these he would set off with great display of action, and in a style of declamation more than sufficiently theatrical. He was married to a virtuous aud exemplary lady, who brought him a considerable fortune, and from whom he took the name of Dunk, and was made a freeman of London to entitle him to marry in conformity to the condition of her father's will. His family, when I came to him, consisted of this lady, with whom he lived in great domestic harmony, and three daughters; there was an elderly clergyman of the name of Crane, an inmate also, who had been his tutor, and to whom he was most entirely attached. A better guide, and a more faithful counsellor he could not have, for amongst all the men it has been my chance to know, I do not think I have known a calmer, wiser, more right-headed man; in the ways of the world, the politics of the time, and the characters of those who were in the public management and responsibility of affairs, Doctor Crane was incomparably the best steersman that his pupil could take his course from, and so long as he submitted to his temperate guidance he could hardly go astray. The opinions of Doctor Crane were upon all points decisive, because in the first place they were always withheld till extorted from him by appeal, and secondly, because they never failed to carry home conviction of the prudence and sound judgment they were founded upon.

This was the state of the family to which I was now introduced. In the lord of the house I contemplated a man regular in his duties, temperate in his habits, and a strict observer of decorum: in the lady, a woman in which no fault or even foible could be discovered—mild, prudent, unpretending: in the tutor, a character not easy to develop, or rightly and correctly to appreciate, for whilst his qualities commanded respect, the dryness of his external repulsed familiarity: in short, I set him down as a man of a clear head and a cold heart: the daughters were children of the nursery.

I went to town attended by a steady and intelligent servant of my father's; this person, Anthony Fletcher by name, who then wore a livery, has since, by a series of good conduct and good fortune, established himself in an affluent and creditable situation at Bath, where he still lives in a very advanced age in the Crescent, well known and universally respected. Lord Halifax's house was in Grosvenor Square, but I found lodgings taken for me by his order in Downing Street, for the purpose, as I understood, of my being near Mr. John Pownall, then acting secretary to the Board of Trade, at which it was Lord Halifax's office to preside. This gentleman was to give me the necessary instructions for my obtaining some insight into the nature of the business likely to devolve upon me. My location was certainly very well pitched for those communications, for Mr. Pownall lodged and boarded at a house in the same street, and with him I was to mess when not invited out.

The morning after my arrival I waited on this gentleman at his office in Whitehall, and was received by him with all possible politeness, but in a style of such ceremony and form as I was little used to, and not much delighted with. How many young men at my time of life would have embraced this situation with rapture! The whole town indeed was before me, but it had not for me either friend or relation, to whom I could resort for comfort or for counsel. With a head filled with Greek and Latin, and a heart left behind me in my college, I was completely out of my element. I saw myself unlike the people about me, and was embarrassed in circles, which according to the manners of those days were not to be approached without a set of ceremonies and manœuvres, not very pleasant to perform, and, when awkwardly performed, not very edifying to behold. In these graces Lord Halifax was a model; his address was noble and impressive; he could never be mistaken for less than he was, whilst his official secretary Pownall, who egregiously overacted his imitations of him, could as little be mistaken for more than he was. In the world, which I now belonged to, I heard very little, except now and then a quotation from Lord Halifax, that in any degree interested me; there were talkers, however, who would take possession of a subject as a highwayman does of a purse, without knowing what it contained, or caring whom it belonged to: many of these gentlemen had doubtless found that ignorance had been no obstacle to their advancement, and now they seemed resolved it should be no bar to their assurance. I found there was a polite as well as a political glossary, which involved mysteries little less obscure than those which are couched under the hieroglyphics of Egypt, and I perceived that whosoever had the ready use and apt application of those pass-words, was by right looked up to as the best bred and best informed man in the company: when a single word can comprise the matter of a whole volume, those worthy gentlemen have a very sufficient plea for not wasting their time upon reading. I have lived long enough to witness such amazing feats performed by impudence, that I much wonder why modest men will allow themselves to be found in societies, where they are condemned to be annoyed by talkers, who turn all things upside down, whilst they are not permitted to utter that which would set them right.

When it was my chance to dine at our boarding-house table

with the afore-mentioned sub-secretary, I contemplated with surprise the importance of his air, and the dignity that seemed attached to his official situation. The good woman of the house, who was at once our provider and our president, regularly addressed him by the name of statesman, and in her distribution of the joint showed something more than an impartial attention to his plate. If he knew any state secrets, I will do him the justice to say that he never disclosed them; and if he talked *with* ministers and great nobles as he talked *of* them, I will venture to say he was extremely familiar with them; and I cannot doubt but that this was the case; for if he was thus high with his equals, it surely behoved him to be much higher with those who but for such self-swelling altitudes might stand a chance to pass for his superiors. He had a brother in the guards, a very amiable man, and with him I formed a friendship. Having been told to inform myself about the colonies, and shown some folio books of formidable contents, I began *more meo* with the discoverers of America, and proceeded to travel through a mass of voyages, which furnished here and there some plots for tragedies, dumb shows and dances, as they have since done, but in point of information applicable to the then existing state of the colonies, were most discouragingly meagre, and most oppressively tedious in communicating nothing. I got a summary but sufficient insight into the constitutions of the respective provinces, for what was worth knowing was soon learnt, and when I found that my whole employment in Grosvenor Square consisted in copying a few private letters to governors and civil officers abroad, I applied my thoughts to other objects, and particularly to the approaching election at my college; still, London lodgings and London hours were not quite so well adapted to study as I could have wished, though I changed my situation for the better when I removed to an apartment which was taken for me in Mount Street, within a very short walk of Lord Halifax's house, where I attended for his commands every morning, and dined twice or thrice in the week. One day he took me with him to Newcastle House, in Lincoln's Inn Fields, for the purpose of presenting me to the duke, then prime minister; his lordship was admitted without delay; I waited two hours for my audience, and was then dismissed in two minutes, whilst his grace, stripped to his shirt, with his sleeves rolled up to his elbows, was washing his hands.[1]

[1] Sir Robert Walpole used to say of the Duke of Newcastle—'He has a foolish head and a perfidious heart. His name is perfidy.' 'For nearly thirty years,' says Lord Mahon, 'was he Secretary of State; for nearly ten years First Lord of the Treasury. His character during that period has been, of course,

The recess took place at the usual time, when Lord Halifax left town and went to Horton in Northamptonshire; I accompanied him thither, and from thence went to Cambridge; he seemed interested in my undertaking, and offered me letters of recommendation, which with due acknowledgments I declined. On my arrival, I found Doctor Richard Bentley had come from his living of Nailstone, in Leicestershire, purposely to support my cause; the vice-master also welcomed me with his accustomed cordiality, and I found the candidates of both years had turned out strong for the contest. There were six vacancies, and six candidates of the year above me; of these Spencer Madan, now Bishop of Peterborough, was, as senior Westminster, secure of his election, and such was his merit, independent of any other claim, that it would have been impossible to pass him over. He was a young man of elegant accomplishments, and with the recommendation of a very interesting person and address, had derived from the Cowpers, of which family his mother was, no

observed and described by writers of every rank and every party; and it may well astonish us to find how much they agree in their accounts. His peculiarities were so glaring and ridiculous that the most careless glance could not mistake, nor the most bitter enmity exaggerate them. There could be no caricature where the original was always more laughable than the likeness. Ever in a hurry, yet seldom punctual, he seems, said Lord Wilmington, as if he had lost half an hour in the morning which he is hurrying after the rest of the day without being able to overtake it! He never walked, but constantly ran; 'insomuch,' writes Chesterfield, 'that I have sometimes told him that by his fleetness one should rather take him for the courier than the author of the letters.' His conversation was a sort of quick stammer—a strange mixture of slowness and rapidity; and his ideas sometimes were in scarcely less confusion. 'Annapolis! Annapolis! Oh yes, Annapolis must be defended; to be sure Annapolis should be defended! Pray, where is Annapolis?' Extremely timorous, and moved to tears on even the slightest occasions, he abounded in childish caresses, and in empty protestations. At his levees he accosted, hugged, clasped, and promised everybody with a seeming cordiality, so universal that it failed to please any in particular. Fretful and peevish with his dependents, always distrusting his friends, and always ready to betray them, he lived in a continual turmoil of harassing affairs, vexatious opposition, and burning jealousies. In business, Lord Hervey thus contrasts him to Sir Robert Walpole: 'We have one minister that does everything with the same seeming ease and tranquillity as if he was doing nothing; we have another that does nothing in the same hurry and agitation as if he did everything.' Yet in some points Newcastle might bear a more favorable parallel with Walpole. He built no palace at Haughton. He formed no splendid collection of paintings. He won no fortune in the South Sea speculations. In noticing his decease, Lord Chesterfield gives him this high testimony: 'My old kinsman and contemporary is at last dead, and, for the first time, quiet. . . . After all the great offices which he had held for fifty years, he died £300,000 poorer than he was when he came into them. A very unministerial proceeding!' Nor was disinterestedness the only merit of Newcastle. In private life, though a bundle of weaknesses, his character was excellent.'—*History of England*, vol. ii. p. 154.

The only thing dearer to Newcastle than his place, says Macaulay, was his neck.

small proportion of hereditary taste and talent; he was a good classical scholar, composed excellent declamation in the Ciceronian style, which he set off with all the grace of recitation and voice that can well be conceived: he had a great passion for music, sung well, and read in chapel to the admiration of every one. I have passed many happy hours with him in the morning of our lives, and I hope he will enjoy the evening of his days in comfort and tranquillity, having chosen that better lot, which has brought him into harbor, whilst I, who lost it, am left out at sea.

The senior Westminster of my year, and joint candidate with me at this time, was John Higgs, now Rector of Grandisburgh in Suffolk, and a senior fellow of Trinity College; a man who, when I last visited him, enjoyed all the vigor of mind and body in a green old age, the result of good humor, and the reward of temperance. We have spun out mutually a long measure of uninterrupted friendship, he in peace throughout, and I at times in perplexity; and if I survive to complete these memoirs, and he to read this page, I desire he will receive it as a testimony of my unaltered regard for him through life, and the bequest of my last good wishes at the close of it.

It would hardly be excusable in me to detail a process that takes place every year, but that in this instance the novelty of our case made it matter of very general attention. When the day of examination came, we went our rounds to the electing seniors; in some instances by one at a time, in others by parties of three or four; it was no trifling scrutiny we had to undergo, and here and there pretty severely exacted, particularly, as I well remember, by Doctor Charles Mason, a man of curious knowledge in the philosophy of mechanics and a deep mathematician; he was a true modern Diogenes, in manners, and apparel, coarse and slovenly to excess in both; the witty made a butt of him, but the scientific caressed him; he could ornament a subject at the same time that he disgusted and disgraced society. I remember when he came one day to dinner in the college hall, dirty as a blacksmith from his forge, upon his being questioned on his appearance, he replied—that he had been *turning*—then I wish, said the other, when you was about it, friend Charles, you had *turned* your shirt. This philosopher, as I was prepared to believe, decidedly opposed my election. He gave us a good dose of dry mathematics, and then put an Aristophanes before us, which he opened at a venture, and bade us give the sense of it. A very worthy candidate of my year declined having any thing to do with it, yet Mason gave his vote for that gentleman, and against me, who took his leavings.[1] Doctor Samuel Hooper gave us a liberal and well chosen examination in the more familiar classics; that indeed was a man in whom nothing could be found but what was gentle and engaging, whom suavity of temper and the charms of manners made dear to all that knew him; he died and was buried in the chapel of his college, where a marble tablet, erected to his memory, cannot fail to awaken the sensibility of all who, like me, were acquainted with his virtues.

The last, whom in order of our visits we resorted to, was the master; he called us to him one by one according to our standings, and of course it fell to me as junior candidate to wait till each had been examined in his turn. When in obedience to his summons I attended upon him, he was sitting, not in the room where my grandfather had his library, but in a chamber up stairs, encompassed with large folding screens, and over a great fire, though the weather was then uncommonly warm: he began by requiring of me an account of the whole course and progress of my studies in the several branches of philosophy, so called in the general, and as I proceeded in my detail of what I had read, he sifted me with questions of such a sort as convinced me he was determined to take nothing upon trust; when he had held me a considerable time under this examination, I expected he would have dismissed me, but on the contrary he proceeded in the like general terms to demand of me an account of what I had been reading before I had applied myself to academical studies, and when I had acquitted myself of this question as briefly as I could, and I hope as modestly as became me in presence of a man so learned, he bade me give him a summary account of the several great empires of the ancient world, the periods when they flourished, their extent when at the summit of their power, the causes of their declension and dates of their extinction. When summoned to give answer to so wide a question, I can only say it was well for me I had worked so hard upon my scheme of General History, which I have before made mention of, and which, though not complete in all the points of his inquiry, supplied me with materials for such a detail as seemed to give him more than tolerable satisfaction. This process being over, he gave me a sheet of paper written through in Greek with his own hand, which he ordered me to turn either into Latin or English, and I was

[1] We apprehend this is the same Charles Mason who, with Mr. Dixon, was sent out in 1763, to determine the limits of the provinces of Maryland and Pennsylvania.

shown into a room containing nothing but a table furnished with materials for writing, and one chair, and I was required to use dispatch. The passage was maliciously enough selected in point of construction, and also of character, for he had scrawled it out in a puzzling kind of hand with abbreviations of his own devising; it related to the arrangement of an army for battle, and I believe might be taken from Polybius, an author I had then never read. When I had given in my translation in Latin, I was remanded to the empty chamber with a subject for Latin prose and another for Latin verse, and again required to dispatch them in the manner of an impromptu. The chamber, into which I was shut for the performance of these hasty productions, was the very room, dismantled of the bed, in which I was born. The train of ideas it revived in my mind were not inappositely woven into the verses I gave in, and with this task my examination concluded.

Doctor Smith, who so worthily succeeded to the mastership of Trinity on my grandfather's decease, was unquestionably one of the most learned men of his time, as his works, especially his 'System of Optics,' effectually demonstrate. He led the life of a student, abstemious and recluse, his family consisting of a sister, advanced in years, and unmarried like himself, together with a niece, who in the course of her residence there, was married to a fellow of the college. He was a man, of whom it might be said—Philosophy *had marked him for her own;* of a thin spare habit, a nose prominently aquiline, and an eye penetrating as that of the bird, the semblance of whose beak marked the character of his face: the tone of his voice was shrill and nasal, and his manner of speaking such as denoted forethought and deliberation. How deep a theorist he was in harmony his treatise will evince; of mere melody he was indignantly neglectful, and could not reconcile his ear to the harpsichord, till by a construction of his own he had divided the half tones into their proper flats and sharps. Those who figured to themselves a Diogenes in Mason, might have fancied they beheld an Aristotle in Smith, who, had he lived in the age and fallen within the eye of the great designer of The School of Athens, might have left his image there without discrediting the group.

The next day the election was announced, and I was chosen, together with Mr. John Orde, now one of the masters in Chancery, who was of the same year with myself, and next to me upon the list of *wranglers.* This gentleman had also gained the prize adjudged to him for his Latin declamation; for his private worthiness he was universally esteemed, and for his public merits deservedly rewarded. By our election, two candidates of the year above us forever lost their chance; the one of these a Mr. Briggs, the other Mr. Penneck, a name well known, and a character much esteemed: he filled a situation in the British Museum with great respectability, was a very amiable worthy man, highly valued by his friends when living, and much lamented after death. His disappointment on this occasion was very generally regretted, and I think I can answer for the feelings of Mr. Orde as confidently as for my own.

When I waited upon the electing seniors to return my thanks, of course I did not omit to pay my compliments to Doctor Mason. 'You owe me no compliment,' he replied, 'for I tell you plainly I opposed your election, not because I have any personal objection to you, but because I am no friend to innovations, and think it hard upon the excluded candidates to be subjected on a sudden to a regulation which, according to my calculation, gives you two chances to their one, and takes away, as it has proved, even that one; but you are in, so there's an end of it, and I give you joy.'

Having stayed as long in college as in gratitude and propriety I conceived it right to stay, I went home to Stanwick, and from thence paid my duty in a short visit to Lord Halifax. This was certainly a moment of which I could have availed myself for returning into the line of life which I had stepped out of; and as neither now, nor in any day of my long attendance upon Lord Halifax, there ever was an hour when my father would not have lent a ready ear to my appeal, the reasons that prevailed with me for persisting were not dictated by him. In the mean time, the life I led in town during the first years of my attendance was almost as much sequestered from the world as if I had been resident in college. In my lodgings in Mount Street, I had stocked myself with my own books, some of my father's, and those which Doctor Richard Bentley had bestowed upon me. I sought no company, nor pushed for any new connections amongst those whom I occasionally met in Grosvenor Square. One or two of my fellow collegiates now and then looked in upon me; and about this time I made my first small offering to the press, following the steps of Gray with another churchyard elegy, written on Saint Mark's Eve, when, according to rural tradition, the ghosts of those who are to die within the year ensuing are seen to walk at midnight across the churchyard. I believe the public were very little interested by my plaintive ditty, and Mr. Dodsley, who was publisher, as little profited. I had written it at Stanwick in one of my college vacations, some time before I belonged to Lord Halifax, and had affixed to my title-page the following motto, with which I sent it into the world—

> '—— Διὸς δὲ τοι ἄγγελος εἶμι,
> Ὃς σευ, ἄνευθεν ἐὼν, μέγα κήδεται ηδ' ελεαιρει·
> —— Αλλὰ τὺ σῇσιν ἔχε φρεσὶ, μηδε σε ληθη
> Αἱρείτω εὖτ' ἄν σε μελιθρων ὕφνος ἀνήη.'

I had made my stay at Horton as short as I could with propriety, being impatient to avail myself of every day that I could pass in the society of my family. With them, I was happy; in their company, I enjoyed those tranquil and delicious hours, which were endeared to me still more by the contrast of what I suffered when in absence from them.

With all these sensations within me, these filial feelings and family attachment, I hardly need confess that, however time and experience may have changed my taste or capacity for public life, certain it is that I was not then fitted for it, nor had any of those worldly qualities and accommodations in my nature which are sure to push their possessors into notice, and form what may be called the very *nidus* of good fortune. A man who is gifted with these lucky talents is armed with hands, as a ship with grappling-irons, ready to catch hold of, and make himself fast to everything he comes in contact with, and such a man, with all these properties of adhesion, has also the property, like the polypus, of a most miraculous and convenient indivisibility; cut off his hold—nay, cut him how you will, he is still a polypus, whole and entire. Men of this sort shall work their way out of their obscurity like cockroaches out of the hold of a ship, and crawl into notice, nay, even into kings' palaces, as the frogs did into Pharaoh's; the happy faculty of noting times and seasons, and a lucky promptitude to avail themselves of moments with address and boldness, are alone such all-sufficient requisites, such marketable stores of worldly knowledge, that, although the minds of those who own them shall be, as to all the liberal sciences, a *rasa tabula*, yet knowing these things needful to be known, let their difficulties and distresses be what they may, though the storm of adversity threatens to overwhelm them, they are in a life-boat, buoyed up by corks, and cannot sink. These are the stray children turned loose upon the world, whom fortune, in her charity, takes charge of, and for whose guidance in the by-ways and cross-roads of their pilgrimage she sets up fairy finger-posts, discoverable by them whose eyes are near the ground, but unperceived by such whose looks are raised above it.

In a nation like this, where all ranks and degrees are laid open to enterprise, merit, or good fortune, it is fit, right, and natural that sudden elevations should occur and be encouraged; it is a spur to industry, and incites to emulation and laudable ambition. Whilst it leads to these good consequences, it must also tend to others of a different sort. In all communities so constituted, there will be a secret market for cunning, as well as a fair emporium for honesty; and a vast body of men, who can't support themselves without labor of some sort, and won't live by the labor of their hands, must contrive to live by their wits—

> Honest men
> Are the soft easy cushions, on which knaves
> Repose and fatten.

But there are more than these—vain men will have their flatterers, rich men their followers, and powerful men their dependents. A great man in office is like a great whale in the ocean; there will be a sword-fish and a thresher, a Junius and a John Wilkes, ever in his wake and arming to attack him: These are the vexed spirits of the deep, who trouble the waters, turning them up from the very bottom, that they may emerge from their mud, and float upon the surface of the billows in foam of their making.

The abstract history of some of these gentry is curious—when they have made a wreck of their own reputation, they assault and tear in pieces the reputations of others; they defame man and blaspheme God; they are punished for their enormities; this makes them martyrs; martyrdom makes them popular; they are crowned with praises, honors and emoluments, and they leave the world in admiration of their talents, before they have tasted the contempt which they deserve.[1]

But whilst these men may be said to fight their way into consequence, and so long as they can but live in notice are content to live in trouble, there is a vast majority of easy, unambitious, courteous humble servants, whose unoffending vanity aspires no higher than, like Samson's bees, to make honey in the bowels of a lion, and fatten on the offal of a rich man's superfluities. They ask no more of fortune than to float, like the horse dung with the apples, and enjoy the credit of good company as they travel down the smooth and easy stream of life. For these there is a vast demand, and their talents are as various as the uses they are put to. Every great, rich and consequential man, who has not the wisdom to hold his tongue, must enjoy his privilege

[1] This is a faithful description of the class of men referred to. They abound in every country, and under every form of government. In despotic countries they are conspirators; in Republics, demagogues.

of talking, and there must be dull fellows to listen to him; again, if, by talking about what he does not understand, he gets into embarrassments, there must be clever fellows to help him out of them. When he would be merry, there must be witty rogues to make him laugh; when he would be sorrowful, there must be sad rogues to sigh and groan and make long faces: as a great man must be never in the wrong, there must be hardy rascals, who will swear he is always in the right; as he must never show fear, of course he must never see danger; and as his courage must at no time sink, there must be friends at all times ready to prevent its being tried.

A great man is entitled to his relaxations; he who labors for the public, must recreate his spirit with his private friends: then it is that the happy moments, the *mollia tempora*, are to be found, which the adept in the art of rising knows so well how to make his use of. Of opportunities like these I have had my share; I never turned them to my own advantage; if at any time I undertook a small solicitation, or obtruded a request, it was for some humble client, who told a melancholy tale, and could advance no nearer to the principal than by making suit to me; in the mean time, I saw many a favor wrested by importunity out of that course which I had reason to expect they would have taken: I never remonstrated, and a very slight apology sufficed for me. These negative merits I may fairly claim without offence against the modesty of truth; I was assiduous in discharging all the duties of my small employ, and faithfully attached to my employer: if he had no call upon me for more or greater services than any man of the commonest capacity could have performed, it was because occasions did not occur; I had not the fault of neglecting what I had to do, nor the presumption of dictating in any single instance what should be done.

Lord Halifax wrote all his own dispatches, and with reason, for he wrote well; but I am tempted to record one opportunity, that was thrown in my way by the candor of Mr. Charles Townshend, whilst he was passing a few days at Horton; amongst a variety of subjects, which his active imagination was forever starting, something had recurred to his recollection of an enigmatical sort, that he wished to have the solution of, and could not strike upon it; it was only to be done by a geometrical process, which I was fortunate enough to hit upon; I worked it as a problem and gave him my solution in writing; I believe it pleased him, but I am very sure that his good nature was glad of the opportunity to say flattering things to a diffident young man, who said very little for himself, and further to do me grace he was pleased to put into my hands a very long and elaborate report of his own drawing up, for he was then one of the lords of trade, and this he condescended to desire I would carefully revise and give him my remarks without reserve. How highly I was gratified by this condescension in a man of his extraordinary and superior genius, I need not say, nor how well, or how ill, I executed my commission; I did it to the best of my abilities; there was much to admire, and something here and there in his paper to warrant a remark; if his compliments were sincere, I succeeded, and shortly after I had proofs, that put his kind opinion of me out of doubt.[1]

One morning, in conversation tete-à-tete, he said he recollected

[1] There seems but little diversity of opinion as to the merits and qualities of this extraordinary man. Burke's splendid tribute of affection and admiration to his memory, however, dwells too much on the lights, without contrasting the shades, of his character. That he was among the most versatile and accomplished men of his time is conceded. As an orator, he was eclipsed only by Pitt. As a wit, he yielded only to Selwyn. But vain, fickle, ambitious; himself, not country; glory, not truth, were the guiding lights of his career.

His speech on the famous Marriage Bill, when but twenty-eight years of age, first placed him in the rank of Parliamentary Orators. 'A second adversary appeared against the bill,' says Walpole, in describing the discussion. 'This was Charles Townshend, second son of my Lord Townshend, a young man of unbounded ambition, of exceeding application, and, as it now appeared, of abilities capable of satisfying that ambition, and of not wanting that application; yet to such parts and such industry he was fond of associating all the little arts and falsehoods that always depreciate, though so often thought necessary by, a genius. He had been an early favorite of Lord Halifax, and had already distinguished himself in affairs of trade, and in drawing plans and papers for that province; but, not rising in proportion to his ambition, he comforted himself with employing as many stratagems as had ever been imparted to the most successful statesmen. His figure was tall and advantageous, his action vehement, his voice loud, his laugh louder. He had art enough to disguise anything but his vanity.'—*Memoirs of the Reign of George II.*, vol. i. p. 340.

Such is Walpole's description of Townshend, when just setting out on his high career. Burke thus portrays him as an orator, when his light had 'passed and set for ever.' 'In truth, sir, he was the delight and ornament of this house, and the charm of every private society which he honored with his presence. Perhaps there never arose in this country, nor in any country, a man of a more pointed and finished wit; and (where his passions were not concerned) of a more refined, exquisite, and penetrating judgment. If he had not so great a stock, as some have had who flourished formerly, of knowledge long treasured up; he knew better by far, than any man I ever was acquainted with, how to bring together, within a short time, all that was necessary to establish, to illustrate, and to decorate that side of the question he supported. He stated his matter skilfully and powerfully. He particularly excelled in a most luminous explanation and display of his subject. His style of argument was neither trite and vulgar, nor subtle and abstruse. He hit the house just between wind and water. And not being troubled with too anxious a zeal for any matter in question, he was never more tedious, or more earnest than the preconceived opinions and present temper of his hearers required, to whom he was always in perfect unison. He conformed exactly to the temper of the House; and he seemed to guide, because he was always sure to follow it.'—*Speech on American Taxation.*

a quotation he had chanced upon in an anonymous author, who maintained opinions of a very impious sort.—The passage he repeated is as follows:—

Post mortem nihil est, ipsaq; mors nihil—

And he asked me if I knew where those words were to be found. I recollected them to be in one of the tragedies of Seneca; I believed it was that of the Troades, which I had lately chanced upon amongst my grandfather's books. As soon as I had access to these, I turned to the passage, and, according to his desire, copied and inclosed it to him. 'Tis found in the second act of the Troades; and, as it is a curious extract, and short withal, I have inserted it, together with the stanzas written at the time, and transmitted with it, which, though not very closely translated, I have transcribed verbatim as I find them.

Verum est, an timidos fabula decipit
Umbras corporibus vivere conditis?
Cum conjux oculis imposuit manum,
Supremusq; dies solibus obstitit,
Et tristes cineres urna courcuit,
Non prodest animam tradere funeri,
Sed restat miseris vivere longius,
An toti morimur, nullaq; pars manet
Nostri, cum profugo spiritus halitu
Immistus nebulis cessit in aera,
Et nudum tetigit subdita fax latus—?
Quidquid sol oriens, quidquid et occidens
Novit, cæruleis oceanus fretis
Quidquid vel veniens vel fugiens lavat,
Ætas pegaseo corripiet gradu.
Quo biscena volant sidera turbine,
Quo cursu properat secula volvere
Astrorum dominus, quo properat modo
Obliquis Hecate currere flexubus,
Hoc omnes petimus fata; nec amplius
Juratos Superis qui tetigit lacus
Usquam est: ut calidis fumus ab ignibus
Vanescit, spatium per breve sordidus,
Ut nubes gravidas, quas modo vidimus,
Arctoi Boreæ disjicit impetus,
Sic hic, quo regimur, spiritus effluet.
Post mortem nihil est, ipsaq; mors nihil;
Velocis spatii meta novissima.
Spem ponant avidi, sollicit metum!
Quæris quo jaceas post obitum loco—?
Quo non nata jacent.
Tempus nos avidum devorat, et chaos:
Mors individua est; noxia corpori,
Nec parcens animæ. Tænara, et aspero
Regnum sub domino, limen et obsidens
Custos non facili Cerberus ostio,
Rumores vacui, verbaq; inania,
Et par sollicito fabula somnio.

Chorus of Trojan Women.

'Is it a truth, or fiction all,
  Which only cowards trust,
Shall the soul live beyond the grave,
  Or mingle with our dust?

When the last gleam of parting day
  Our struggling sight hath blest,
And in the pale array of death
  Our clay-cold limbs are drest,

Did the kind friend who clos'd our eyes,
  Speak peace to us in vain?
Is there no peace, and have we died
  To live and weep again?

Or sigh'd we then our souls away,
  And was that sigh our last,
Or e'er upon the flaming pile
  Our bare remains were cast?

All the sun sees, the ocean laves,
  Kingdoms and kings shall fall,
Nature and nature's work shall cease,
  And time be lord of all.

Swift as the monarch of the skies
  Impels the rolling year,
Swift as the gliding orb of night
  Pursues her prone career,

So swift so sure we all descend
  Down life's continual tide,
Till in the void of fate profound
  We sink with worlds beside.

As in the flame's resistless glare
  'Th' envelop'd smoke is lost,
Or as before the driving North
  The scatter'd clouds are tost,

So this proud vapor shall expire,
  This all-directing soul,
Nothing is after death; you've run
  Your race and reach'd the goal.

Dare not to wish, nor dread to meet
  A life beyond the grave;
You'll meet no other life than now
  The unborn ages have.

Time whelms us in the vast Inane,
  A gulf without a shore;
Death gives the exterminating blow,
  We fall to rise no more.

Hell, and its triple-headed guard,
  And Lethe's fabled stream,
Are tales that lying gossips tell,
  And moon-struck Sibyls dream.'

It was the good old custom of the Earl of Halifax to pass the Christmas at his family seat of Horton in great hospitality, and upon these occasions he never failed to be accompanied by parties of his friends and intimates from town; the chief of these were the Lords Dupplin and Barrington, Mr. Charles Townshend, Mr. Francis Fane, Mr. James Oswald, Mr. Hans Stanley, Mr. Narbonne Berkeley, Lord Hillsborough, Mr. Dodington, Colonel James Johnstone, the husband of his sister, Lady Charlotte, and Mr. Ambrose Isted, of Ecton, near Northampton, his neighbor and constant visitor at those seasons; these, with the addition of Doctor Crane and the Reverend Mr. Spencer, an elderly clergyman, long attached to the family, formed a society highly respectable. I ever entertained a perfect and sincere regard for Lady Halifax; her mild, complacent character was to me far more engaging than the livelier spirits and more figuring talents of many who engrossed that attention which she did not aspire to. She was uniform in her kindness to me, and whilst she lived, I flatter myself I had a friend who esteemed and understood me; when she died, I had more reason to regret her loss than for myself alone.

My father was still fixed in his residence at Stanwick; and there I ever found unvaried felicity, unabated affection. He had some excellent friends, and many pleasant neighbors, with whom he lived upon the most agreeable terms; for in his house everybody seemed to be happy. His table was admirably managed by my mother, his cellar, servants, equipage in the best order, and without parade unbecoming of his profession, or unsuitable to his fortune—no family could be better conducted; and here I must indulge myself in dilating on the character of one of his best friends and best of men, Ambrose Isted, Esq., of Ecton, afore-mentioned. Through every scene of my life, from my childhood to the lamented event of his death, which happened whilst I was in Spain, he was invariably kind, indulgent, and affectionate to me. I conceive there is not upon record one, who more perfectly fulfilled the true character of a country gentleman, in all its most respectable duties and departments, than did this exemplary person; nor will his name be forgotten in Northamptonshire so long as the memory or tradition of good deeds shall circulate, or gratitude be considered as a tribute due to the benevolent. He was the pattern and very model of hospitality most worthy to be copied; for his family and affairs were administered and conducted with such measured liberality, such correct and wise economy, that the friend, who found nothing wanting, which could constitute his comforts, found nothing wastefully superfluous to occasion his regret.

Though Mr. Isted's estate was not large, yet by the process of inclosure, and above all by his prudent and well-ordered management, it was augmented without extortion, and left in excellent condition to his son and heir. The benefits he conferred upon his poorer neighbors were of a nature far superior to the common acts of alms-giving (though these were not omitted), for in all their difficulties and embarrassments, he was their counsellor and adviser, not merely in his capacity of acting justice of the peace, but also from his legal knowledge and experience, which were very considerable, and fully competent to all their uses; by which numbers, who might else have fallen under the talons of country attorneys, were saved from pillage and beggary. With this gentleman my father acted as justice, and was united in friendship and in party, and to him he resorted upon all occasions, where the opinion and advice of a judicious friend were wanted. Our families corresponded in the utmost harmony, and our interchange of visits was frequent and delightful. The house of Ecton was to me a second home, and the hospitable master of it a second father; his gayety of heart, his suavity of temper, the interest he took in giving pleasure to his guests, and the fund of information he possessed in the stores of a well-furnished memory and a lively animated genius, are ever fresh in my recollection, and I look back upon the days I have passed with him as some of the happiest in my life. For many years before his death, I saw this excellent man by intervals excruciated with a tormenting and incurable disease, which lay too deep and undiscoverable in his vitals to admit of any other relief than laudanum in large doses could at times administer: nothing but a soul serene and piously resigned as his was, could have borne itself up against a visitation at once so agonizing and so hopeless; a spirit, however, fortified by faith, and a conscience clear of reproach, can effect great things, and my heroic friend, through all his trials, smiled in the midst of sufferings, and submitted unrepining to his fate. One of the last letters he lived to write I received in Spain: I saw it was the effort of an exhausted frame, a generous zeal to send one parting testimony of his affection to me, and being at that time myself extremely ill, I was hardly in a capacity to dictate a reply.

I was also at this time in habits of the most intimate friendship with two young men of my own age, sons of a worthy clergyman in our neighborhood, the Reverend Mr. Ekins. Jeffery, the elder, now deceased, was Dean of Carlisle, and Rector of Morpeth; John, the younger, is yet living, and Dean of Salisbury. Few men have been more fortunate in life than these brothers; fewer still have probably so well deserved their good success. With the elder of these my intimacy was the greatest. The same passion for poetry possessed us both, the same attachment to the drama; our respective families indulged us in our propensities, and were mutually amused with our domestic exhibitions. My friend Jeffery was in my family as I was in his, an inmate ever welcome; his genius was quick and brilliant, his temper sweet, and his nature mild and gentle in the extreme. I loved him as a brother; we never had the slightest jar, nor can I recollect the moment in our lives that ever gave occasion of offence to either. Our destinations separated us in the more advanced period of our time; his duties drew him to a distance from the scenes I was engaged in. His lot was prosperous and placid, and well for him it was; for he was not made to combat with the storms of life. In early youth, long before he took orders, he composed a drama of an allegorical cast, which he entitled 'Florio; or, the Pursuit of Happiness.' There was a great deal of fancy in it; and I wrote a comment upon it almost as long as the drama itself, which I sent to him as a mark of my admiration of his genius, and my affection for his person. He also wrote a poem upon Dreams, which had great merit; but as I wished my friend to employ his talents upon subjects of a more elevated nature, I addressed some lines to him in the style of remonstrance, of which I shall transcribe no more than the concluding stanza—

> '—— But thou, whose powers can wield a weightier theme,
> Why waste one thought upon an empty dream?
> Why all this genius, all this art display'd
> To paint a vapor and arrest a shade?
> Can fear-drawn shapes and visions of the night
> Assail thy fancy, or deceive thy sight?
> Wilt thou to air-built palaces resort,
> Where the sylphs flutter and the fairies sport?
> No, let them soothe the love-enfeebled brain,
> Thy Muse shall seize her harp and strike a loftier strain.'

During the time I lived in this pleasing intercourse with the family of these worthy brothers, there was an ingenious friend and school-fellow of theirs, pretty constantly resident with them, of the name of Arden, a young man very much to be loved for the amenity of his temper and the vivacity of his parts. He was the life and soul of our dramatic amusements, and had an energy of character, as well as a fund of humor, that enabled him to give its true force and expression to every part he assumed in our private exhibitions; and here let me not omit to mention a near relation, and once my most dear friend, Richard, son of the Reverend Doctor George Reynolds, and grandson of

Bishop Reynolds, who married the daughter of Bishop Cumberland. This mild and amiable young man had, in early life, so far attached himself to the Earl of Sandwich as to accompany him to the Congress at Aix-la-Chapelle; but, being perfectly independent in his fortune, and of an unambitious, placid nature, he declined pursuing any further the unquiet track of public life, and sat down, with his family, at their house of Paxton, in Huntingdonshire, to the possession of which he succeeded, and where he still resides. I am here speaking of the days of my intimacy with this gentleman, and I look back to them with none but grateful recollection; in the course of these memoirs, I shall have to speak of other days, that will recall sensations of another sort.

If ever this once-valued friend shall be my reader, let me appeal to his candor for a fair interpretation of my feelings when I cannot pass this period over without recalling to his memory and my own the name of his departed sister, who merited and possessed my best affections in their purest sense. The hospitable welcome I always received from the parents of this amiable lady, and their encouraging politeness to me, might have tempted one less respectful of her comforts, and less sensible of her superior pretensions, to have presumed upon their favor, and made tender of his addresses; but my precarious dependency and unsettled state of life forbade such hopes, and I was silent. I now return to my narrative, in which I am prepared to speak both of others and myself no more than I know, or verily believe to be true.

It was about this time I employed myself in collecting materials from the history of India for the plan of a poem in heroic verse, many fragments of which I find amongst my old papers, which prove I had bestowed considerable labor on the work, and made some progress. Whether I found the plan could not be made to accord to my idea of the epic, or whether any other project called me off, I cannot now recollect; but at that time I had not attempted anything professedly for the stage. I must, however, lament that it has lain by, unlooked at, for so great a length of time, as there have been intermediate periods of leisure when it would have been well worth my pains to have taken it up; it is now too late, and the only use I can apply it to is humbly to lay before the public a specimen, faithfully transcribed from that part of the poem where the discoveries of the Portuguese are introduced. I might perhaps have selected passages less faulty; but I give it correctly as I find it, trusting that the candid reader will make allowances for that too florid style which juvenile versifiers are so apt to indulge themselves in, whilst the fancy is too prurient, and the judgment not mature.

Fragment.

'—— Long time had Afric's interposing mound,
Stretching athwart the navigator's way,
Fenc'd the rich East, and sent th' advent'rous bark
Despairing home, or whelm'd her in the waves.
Gama the first on bold discovery bent,
With prow still pointing to the further pole,
Skirted Caffraria till the welcome cape,
Thence call'd of *Hope*—but not to Asia's sons—
Spoke the long coast exhausted; still 'twas hope,
Not victory; nature in one effort foil'd,
Still kept the contest doubtful, and enrag'd,
Rous'd all the elements to war. Meanwhile,
As once the Titans with Saturnian Jove,
So he in happier hour and his bold crew
Undaunted conflict held; old Ocean storm'd,
Loud thunder rent the air, the leagued winds
Roar'd in his front, as if all Afric's gods
With necromantic spells had charm'd the storm
To shake him from his course—in vain; for Fate,
That grasp'd his helm with unrelenting hand,
Had register'd his triumph: through the breach
All Lusitania pour'd; Arabia mourn'd,
And saw her spicy caravans return
Shorn of their wealth; the Adriatic bride
Like a neglected beauty pin'd away;
Europe which by her hand of late receiv'd
India's rich fruits, from the deserted mart
Now turn'd aside and pluck'd them as they grew.
  A new-found world from out the waves arose.
Now Soffala, and all the swarming coast
Of fruitful Zanguebar, till where it meets
The sultry Line, pour'd forth their odorous stores.
The thirsty West drank deep the luscious draught,
And reel'd with luxury: Emmanuel's throne
Blaz'd with barbaric gems; aloft he sate
Encanopied with gold, and circled round
With warriors and with chiefs in Eastern pomp
Resplendent with their spoils. Close in the rear
Of conquest march'd the motley papal host,
Monks of all colors, brotherhoods and names:
Frowning they rear'd the cross; th' affrighted tribes
Look'd up aghast, and whilst the cannon's mouth
Thunder'd obedience, dropt the unwilling knee
In trembling adoration of a God,
Whom, as by nature tutor'd, in his works
They saw, and only in his mercy knew.
But creeds, impos'd by terror, can ensure
No fix'd allegiance, but are strait dismiss'd
From the vext conscience, when the sword is sheath'd.
  Now when the barrier, that so long had stood
'Twixt the departed nations, was no more,
Like fire once kindled, spreading in its course,
Onward the mighty conflagration roll'd.

As if the Atlantic and the Southern seas,
Driv'n by opposing winds and urg'd amain
By fierce tornadoes, with their cumbrous weight
Should on a sudden at the narrowing pass
Of Darién burst the continental chain
And whelm together, so the nations rush'd
Impetuous through the breach, where Gama forc'd
His desperate passage; terrible the shock,
From Ormus echoing to the Eastern isles
Of Java and Sumatra; India now
From th' hither Tropic to the Southern Cape
Show'd to the setting sun a shore of blood:
In vain her monarchs from a hundred thrones
Sounded the arbitrary word for war;
In vain whole cataracts of dusky slaves
Pour'd on the coast: earth trembled with the weight;
But what can slaves? What can the nerveless arm,
Shrunk by that soft emasculating clime,
What the weak dart against the mailed breast
Of Europe's martial sons? On sea, on shore
Great Almeed triumph'd, and the rival sword
Of Albuquerque, invincible in arms,
Wasted the nations, humbling to the yoke
Kings, whom submissive myriads in the dust
Prostrate ador'd, and from the solar blaze
Of majesty retreating veil'd their eyes.
As when a roaming vulture on the wing
From Mauritania or the cheerless waste
Of sandy Thibet, by keen hunger press'd,
With eye quick glancing from his airy height
Haply at utmost need descries a fawn,
Or kid, disporting in some fruitful vale,
Down, down at once the greedy felon drops
With wings close cow'ring in his hollow sides
Full on the helpless victim; thence again
Tow'ring in air he bears his luscious prize,
And in his native wild enjoys the feast:
So those forth issuing from the rocky shore
Of distant Tagus on the quest for gain
In realms unknown, which feverish fancy paints
Glittering with gems and gold, range the wide seas,
Till India's isthmus, rising with the sun
To their keen sight, her fertile bosom spreads,
Period and palm of all their labors past;
Whereat with avarice and ambition fir'd,
Eager alike for plunder and for fame,
Onward they press to spring upon their prey;
There every spoil obtain'd, with greedy haste
By force or fraud could ravage from the hands
Of Nature's peaceful sons, again they mount
Their richly freighted bark; she, while the cries
Of widows and of orphans rend the strand,
Striding the billows, to the venal winds
Spreads her broad vans, and flies before the gale.
Here as by sad necessity I tell
Of human woes to rend the hearer's heart,
Truth be my Muse, and thou, my bosom's star,
The planetary mistress of my birth,

Parent of all my bliss, of all my pain,
Inspire me gentle Pity and attune
Thy numbers, heavenly cherub, to my strain
Thou, too, for whom my heart breathes every wish,
That filial love can form, fairest of isles,
Albion, attend and deign to hear a son,
Who for afflicted millions, prostrate slaves
Beneath oppression's scourge, and waning fast
By ghastly famine and destructive war,
No venal suit prefers; so may thy fleets,
Mistress of commerce, link the Western world
To thy maternal bosom, chase the sun
Up to his source, and in the bright display
Of empire, and the liberal search of fame
Belt the wide globe—but mount, ye guardian waves,
Stand as a wall before the spoiler's path!
Ye stars, your bright intelligence withdraw,
And darkness cover all, whom lust of gold,
Fell rapine, and extortion's guilty hope
Rouse from their native dust to rend the thrones
Of peaceful princes, and usurp that soil,
Where late as humble traffickers they sought
And found a shelter: thus what they obtain'd
By supplication they extend by force,
Till in the wantonness of power they grasp
Whole provinces, where millions are their slaves.
Ah whither shall I turn to meet the face
Of love and human kindness in this world,
On which I now am ent'ring? Gracious heaven,
If, as I trust, thou hast bestow'd a sense
Of thy best gift, benevolence, on me,
Oh visit me in mercy, and preserve
That spark of thy divinity alive,
Till time shall end me! So when all the blasts
Of malice and unkindness, which my fate
May have in store, shall vent their rage upon me,
Feeling, but still forgiving, the assault,
I may persist with patience to devote
My life, my love, my labors to mankind.'

The severest misfortune that could menace my unhappy patron, was now hanging over him. The state of Lady Halifax's health became daily more and more alarming; she seemed to be sinking under a consumptive and exhausted constitution. It was then the custom for the chief families in Northamptonshire to attend the country races in great form, and the Lord Lieutenant on that occasion made it a point to assemble his friends and party in their best equipage and array to grace the meeting: this was ever a formidable task for poor Lady Halifax, whose tender spirits and declining health were ill suited to such undertakings; but upon the last year of her accompanying her lord to this meeting, I found her more than usually apprehensive, and she too truly predicted that it would accelerate her death. I attended upon her at that meeting, and when I expressed my hopes that she had escaped her fatigues without any material injury, as I was handing her to her coach on the morning of her departure, she shook her head and again repeated her entire conviction that she should not long survive. My heart sank as I took leave of her under this melancholy impression: we met no more: she languished for a time, and to the irreparable loss of her afflicted husband died.

Lady Halifax was by birth of humble rank, and not endowed by nature with shining talents or superior charms of person. She did not aim at that display which conciliates popularity, nor affect those arts which invite admiration; without any of those brilliant qualities which, whilst they gratify a husband's vanity, too often endanger his honor and his peace, the virtues of her heart and the serenity of her temper were so happily adapted to allay and tranquillize the more impassioned character of her lord, that every man, who knew his nature, could not fail to foresee the dangers he would be exposed to when she was no longer at his side. He had still a true and faithful friend in Doctor Crane, and to him Lady Halifax had been most entirely attached. He merited all her confidence, and sincerely lamented her loss, foreseeing, as I had good reason to know, the unhappy consequences it might lead to, for by this time I was favored with some tokens of his regard, that could not be mistaken, and though his feelings never forced him into warm expressions, yet his heart was kind, and his friendship sincere. Many days passed before I was summoned to pay my respects to the afflicted widower, who was represented to me as being almost frantic with his grief. I divided this time between my own home and the house of Ecton: at length I was invited to Horton, and the meeting was a very painful moment to us both.

We soon removed to town for the winter season, and there, whilst politics and public office began to occupy his thoughts and by degrees to wean him from his sorrows, I resumed my solitary lodgings in Mount Street, where, with my old Swiss servant for my caterer and cook, I lived in all the temperance and nearly all the retirement of a hermit. Then it was that I derived all my resources in the books I possessed, and the talents God had given me. I read and wrote incessantly, and should have been in absolute solitude but for the kind visits of my friend Higgs, who, not forgetting our late intimacy at college and at school, nor disdaining my poor fare and dull society, cheered and relieved my spirits with the liveliness and hilarity natural to him: these are favors I can never forget; for they supported me at a time when I felt all the gloominess of my situation, and yet wanted energy to extricate myself from it, and renounce those expectations, to which I had devoted so much time in profitless dependence. I lived indeed upon the narrowest system I could adopt, but nevertheless I could not make the income of my fellowship bear me through without the generous assistance of my father, and that reflection was the only painful concomitant of a disappointment, that I should not in my own particular else have wasted a regret upon.

In the mean time, the long and irksome residence in town which my attendance upon Lord Halifax entailed upon me, and the painful separation from my family, became almost insupportable, and whilst I was meditating a retreat, my good father, who participated with me and his whole family in these sensations, projected and concluded an exchange for his living of Stanwick with the Reverend Mr. Samuel Knight, and with permission of the Bishop of London, took the vicarage of Fulham as an equivalent, and thereby opened to me the happy prospect of an easier access to those friends so justly valued and so justly dear.

In point of income the two livings were as nearly equal as could well be, therefore no pecuniary compensation passed between the contracting parties; but the comforts of tranquillity in point of duty, or of conveniences in respect of locality, were all in favor of Mr. Knight, and nothing could have prevailed with my father for leaving those, whom he had so long loved and cherished as his flock, but the generous motive of giving me an asylum in the bosoms of my family. With this kind and benevolent object in his view, he submitted to the pain of tearing himself from his connections, and amidst the lamentations of his neighbors and parishioners came up to Fulham to take upon himself the charge of a great suburban parish, and quitted Stanwick, where he had resided for the space of thirty years in peace, beloved by all around him.

He found a tolerably good parsonage house at Fulman, in which, with my mother and my sisters, he established himself with as much content as could be looked for. Wherever he went the odor of his good name, and of course his popularity, was sure to follow him; but the task of preaching to a large congregation after being so long familiarized to the service of his little church at Stanwick, oppressed his modest mind, and though his person, matter and manner were such as always left favorable impressions on his hearers, yet it was evident to us who knew him and belonged to him, that he suffered by his exertions.

Bishop Sherlock was yet living and resided in the palace, but in the last stage of bodily decay. The ruins of that luminous and powerful mind were still venerable, though his speech was almost unintelligible, and his features cruelly disarranged and distorted by the palsy: still his genius was alive, and his judgment discriminative, for it was in this lamentable state that he performed the task of selecting sermons for the last volume he committed to the press, and his high reputation was in no respect lowered by the selection. I had occasionally the honor of being admitted to visit that great man in company with my father, to whom he was uniformly kind and gracious, and in token of his favor bestowed on him a small prebend in the church of St. Paul, the only one that became vacant within his time.

Mrs. Sherlock was a truly respectable woman, and my mother enjoyed much of her society till the bishop's death brought a successor in his place.

In the adjoining parish of Hammersmith lived Mr. Dodington, at a splendid villa, which by the rule of contraries he was pleased to call La Trappe, and his inmates and familiars the monks of the convent; these were Mr. Windham, his relation, whom he made his heir, Sir William Breton, privy purse to the king, and Doctor Thompson, a physician out of practice; these gentlemen formed a very curious society of very opposite characters; in short it was a trio consisting of a misanthrope, a courtier, and a quack. Mr. Glover, the author of Leonidas, was occasionally a visitor, but not an inmate as those above mentioned.[1] How a man of Dodington's sort came to single out men of their sort (with the exception of Mr. Glover) is hard to say, but though his instruments were never in unison, he managed to make music out of them all. He could make and find amusement in contrasting the sullenness of a Grumbetonian with the egregious vanity and self-conceit of an antiquated coxcomb, and as for the Doctor, he was a juck-pudding ready to his hand at any time. He was understood to be Dodington's body physician, but I believe he cared very little about his patient's health, and his patient cared still less about his prescriptions; and when in his capacity of superintendent of his patron's dietetics, he cried out one morning at breakfast to have the *muffins* taken

[1] Richard Glover, the author of 'Leonidas,' 'Progress of Commerce,' and the celebrated ballad of 'Hosier's Ghost,' was the son of a London merchant, and born in 1712. He was, at one time, a member of Parliament, and esteemed by the mercantile interest for his activity and abilities. The letters of Junius, upon very slight and insubstantial grounds, have been attributed to him. In 1742, he was selected by the London merchants to conduct an application to Parliament, complaining of the neglect of trade. His speech on the occasion was much applauded. Walpole, however, who always depreciates him, thus refers to this passage of his life: 'We have at last finished the merchant's petition, under the conduct of the Lord Mayor and Mr. Leonidas; the greatest coxcomb and the greatest oaf that ever met in blank verse or prose.'—*Letters*, vol. i. p. 110. Mr. Glover died in 1785, at the age of seventy-three.

away, Dodington aptly enough cried out at the same time to the servant to take away the *ragamuffin*, and truth to say, a more dirty animal than poor Thompson was never seen on the outside of a pigsty; yet he had the plea of poverty and no passion for cold water.

It is about a short and pleasant mile from this villa to the parsonage house of Fulham, and Mr. Dodington having visited us with great politeness, I became a frequent guest at La Trappe, and passed a good deal of my time with him there, in London also, and occasionally in Dorsetshire. He was certainly one of the most extraordinary men of his time, and as I had opportunities of contemplating his character in all its various points of view, I trust my readers will not regret that I have devoted some pages to the further delineation of it.

I have before observed that the nature of my business as private secretary to Lord Halifax was by no means such as to employ any great portion of my time, and of course I could devote many hours to my own private pursuits without neglecting those attendances, which were due to my principal. Lord Halifax had also removed his abode to Downing Street, having quitted his house in Grosvenor Square upon the decease of his lady, so that I rarely found it necessary to sleep in town, and could divide the rest of my time between Fulham and La Trappe. It was likewise entirely correspondent with Lord Halifax's wishes that I should cultivate my acquaintance with Mr. Dodington, with whom he not only lived upon intimate terms as a friend, but was now in train to form, as it seemed, some opposition connections; for at this time it happened that upon a breach with the Duke of Newcastle, he threw up his office of First Lord of Trade and Plantations, and detached himself from administration. This took place towards the latter end of the late king's reign, and the ground of the measure was a breach of promise on the part of the Duke to give him the Seals and a seat in the Cabinet as Secretary of State for the Colonies.

In the summer of this year, being now an ex-secretary of an ex-statesman, I went to Eastbury, the seat of Mr. Dodington, in Dorsetshire, and passed the whole time of his stay in that place. Lord Halifax, with his brother-in-law, Colonel Johnstone, of the Blues, paid a visit there, and the Countess Dowager of Stafford, and old Lady Hervey, were resident with us the whole time. Our splendid host was excelled by no man in doing the honors of his house and table; to the ladies he had all the courtly and profound devotion of a Spaniard, with the ease and gayety of a Frenchman towards the men. His mansion was magnificent, massy, and stretching out to a great extent of front, with an enormous portico of Doric columns, ascended by a stately flight of steps; there were turrets and wings that went I know not whither, though now they are levelled with the ground, and gone to more ignoble uses. Vanbrugh, who constructed this superb edifice, seemed to have had the plan of Blenheim in his thoughts, and the interior was as proud and splendid as the exterior was bold and imposing. All this was exactly in unison with the taste of its magnificent owner, who had gilt and furnished the apartments with a profusion of finery, that kept no terms with simplicity, and not always with elegance or harmony of style. Whatever Mr. Dodington's revenue then was, he had the happy art of managing it with that regularity and economy, that I believe he made more display at less cost than any man in the kingdom but himself could have done. His town house in Pall-Mall, his villa at Hammersmith, and the mansion above described, were such establishments as few nobles in the nation were possessed of. In either of these he was not to be approached but through a suite of apartments, and rarely seated but under painted ceilings and gilt entablatures. In his villa you were conducted through two rows of antique marble statues ranged in a gallery floored with the rarest marbles, and enriched with columns of granite and lapis lazuli; his saloon was hung with the finest Gobelin tapestry, and he slept in a bed encanopied with peacock's feathers in the style of Mrs. Montague. When he passed from Pall-Mall to La Trappe, it was always in a coach, which I could suspect had been his ambassadorial equipage at Madrid, drawn by six fat unwieldy black horses, short docked, and of colossal dignity: neither was he less characteristic in apparel than in equipage; he had a wardrobe loaded with rich and flaring suits, each in itself a load to the wearer, and of these I have no doubt but many were coeval with his embassy above mentioned, and every birth-day had added to the stock. In doing this he so contrived as never to put his old dresses out of countenance by any variations in the fashion of the new; in the mean time, his bulk and corpulency gave full display to a vast expanse and profusion of brocade and embroidery, and this, when set off with an enormous tye-periwig and deep laced ruffles, gave the picture of an ancient courtier in his gala habit, or Quin in his stage dress; nevertheless, it must be confessed this style, though out of date, was not out of character, but harmonized so well with the person of the wearer, that I remember when he made his first speech in the House of Peers, as Lord Melcombe, all the flashes of his wit, all the studied phrases and well-turned periods of his rhetoric, lost their effect, simply because the orator had laid aside his magisterial tye, and put on a modern bag wig, which was as much out of costume upon the broad expanse of his shoulders, as a cue would have been upon the robes of the Lord Chief Justice.

Having thus dilated more than perhaps I should have done upon this distinguished person's passion for magnificence and display, when I proceed to inquire into those principles of good taste which should naturally have been the accompaniments and directors of that magnificence, I fear I must be compelled by truth to admit that in these he was deficient. Of pictures, he seemed to take his estimate only by their cost—in fact, he was not possessed of any; but I recollect his saying to me one day, in his great saloon at Eastbury, that if he had half a score pictures, of a thousand pounds apiece, he would gladly decorate his walls with them, in place of which, I am sorry to say, he had stuck up immense patches of gilt leather, shaped into bugle-horns, upon hangings of rich crimson velvet, and round his state-bed he displayed a carpeting of gold and silver embroidery, which too glaringly betrayed its derivation from coat, waistcoat, and breeches by the testimony of pockets, buttonholes, and loops, with other equally incontrovertible witnesses, subpœnaed from the tailor's shopboard. When he paid his court at St. James's to the present queen upon her nuptials, he approached to kiss her hand decked in an embroidered suit of silk, with lilac waistcoat and breeches, the latter of which, in the act of kneeling down, forgot their duty, and broke loose from their moorings in a very indecorous and uncourtly manner.

In the higher provinces of taste, we may contemplate his character with more pleasure; for he had an ornamented fancy and a brilliant wit. He was an elegant Latin classic, and well versed in history, ancient and modern. His favorite prose writer was Tacitus; and I scarce ever surprised him in his hours of reading without finding that author upon his table before him. He understood him well, and descanted upon him very agreeably, and with much critical acumen. Mr. Dodington was in nothing more remarkable than in ready perspicuity and clear discernment of a subject thrown before him on a sudden. Take his first thoughts, then, and he would charm you; give him time to ponder and refine, you would perceive the spirit of his sentiments and the vigor of his genius evaporate by the process, for though his first view of the question would be a wide one, and clear withal, when he came to exercise the subtlety of his disquisitorial powers upon it, he would so ingeniously dissect and break it into fractions, that as an object, when looked upon too intently for a length of time, grows misty and confused, so would the question under his discussion when the humor took him to be hypercritical. Hence it was that his impromptus in Parliament were generally more admired than his studied speeches, and his first suggestions in the councils of his party better attended to than his prepared opinions.

Being a man of humble birth, he seemed to have an innate respect for titles, and none bowed with more devotion to the robes and fasces of high rank and office; he was decidedly aris tocratic. He paid his court to Walpole in panegyric poems, apologizing for his presumption by reminding him that it was better to be pelted with roses than with rotten eggs. To Chesterfield, to Winnington, Pulteney, Fox, and the luminaries of his early time, he offered up the oblations of his genius, and incensed them with all the odors of his wit; in his latter days, and within the period of my acquaintance with him, the Earl of Bute, in the plenitude of his power, was the god of his idolatry. That noble lord was himself too much a man of letters and a patron of the sciences to overlook a witty head that bowed so low; he accordingly put a coronet upon it, which, like the *barren sceptre* in the hand of Macbeth, merely served as a ticket for the coronation procession, and, having nothing else to leave to posterity in memory of its owner, left its mark upon the lid of his coffin.[1]

During my stay at Eastbury, we were visited by the late Mr. Henry Fox[2] and Mr. Alderman Beckford; the solid good sense

[1] 'In an age of low and dirty prostitution—in the age of Dodington and Sandys—it was something to have a man,' thus does Macaulay refer to Dodington in connection with the Elder Pitt, 'who might, perhaps, under some strong excitement, have been tempted to ruin his country, but who never would have stooped to pilfer from her; a man whose errors arose, not from a sordid desire of gain, but from a fierce thirst for power, for glory, and for vengeance.'—*Essays*, vol. ii. p. 246. Dodington was son of an apothecary; but got his name and estate from a maternal uncle. 'He had,' says Walpole, 'a great deal of wit, great knowledge of business, and was an able speaker in Parliament, though an affected one, and though most of his speeches were premeditated. He was, as his diary shows, vain, fickle, ambitious, servile, and corrupt.'—*Memoirs of the Reign of George II.*, vol. i. p. 437.

[2] The father of Charles James Fox. He was younger son of Sir Stephen Fox, and born in 1705. His youth, like the youth of his renowned son, was characterized for wild and reckless dissipation. His morals were profligate; his politics venal; but his abilities of the highest order. Distrusted as a statesman, he was beloved as a man. When he had nearly reached the age of forty, he made a runaway match with the eldest daughter of Charles, Duke of Richmond, grandson of King Charles II. 'Mr. Fox fell in love with Lady Caroline Lennox;' thus wrote Walpole on the occasion, 'asked her, was refused, and stole her. His father was a footman; her great grandfather a king: *hinc illæ lacrymæ;* all the blood royal have been up in arms.'—*Letters*, vol. i. p. 284. 'Fox,' says Lord Chesterfield, 'had not the least notion of or regard for the public good or the constitution, but despised those cares as the objects of narrow minds.'—*Lord Chesterfield's Characters.* On the other hand, he had many attractive virtues.

of the former, and the dashing loquacity of the latter[1] formed a striking contrast between the characters of these gentlemen. To Mr. Fox, our host paid all that courtly homage which he so well knew how to time, and where to apply; to Beckford, he did not observe the same attentions, but in the happiest flow of his raillery and wit combated this intrepid talker with admirable effect. It was an interlude truly comic and amusing. Beckford, loud, voluble, self-sufficient, and galled by hits which he could not parry, and probably did not expect, laid himself more and more open in the vehemence of his argument. Dodington, lolling in his chair in perfect apathy and self-command, dozing, and even snoring at intervals in his lethargic way, broke out every now and then into such gleams and flashes of wit and irony as, by the contrast of his phlegm with the other's impetuosity, made his humor irresistible, and set the table in a roar;[2]

'In natural disposition, as well as in talents,' says Macaulay, 'he bore a great resemblance to his more celebrated son. He had the same sweetness of temper, boldness, and impetuosity, the same cordiality towards friends, the same placability towards enemies. No man was more warmly or justly beloved by his family or by his associates.'—*Essays*, vol. ii. p. 266. As a speaker, he was inferior only to Pitt; as a debater, he surpassed him. 'Fox,' says Walpole, 'with a great hesitation in his elocution, and a barrenness of expression, had conquered these impediments, and the prejudices they had raised against his speaking, by a vehemence of reasoning, and closeness of argument, that beat all the orators of the time. His spirit, his steadiness, and humanity, procured him strong attachments, which the more jealous he grew of Pitt the more he cultivated. Fox always spoke to the question; Pitt to the passions. Fox, to carry the question; Pitt to raise himself. Fox pointed out, Pitt lashed the errors of his antagonists. Pitt's talents were likely to make him soonest; Fox's to keep him First Minister longest.'—*Memoirs of the Reign of George II.*, vol. i. p. 93.

[1] Beckford, whom Walpole styles a 'noisy, good-humored flattering bombast, as became the priest of such an idol' (referring to Pitt), 'and vulgar and absurd as was requisite to captivate any idol's devotees, the mob,' was Pitt's personal friend and efficient supporter. 'He was pompous in his expense, or rather in his expressions, but he knew his interest, and was attentive to it.'—*Walpole's Memoirs of the Reign of George II.*, vol. iii. p. 177. His fortune was large, and lay chiefly in Jamaica. He 'was a man of neglected education,' says Mahon, 'noted in the House of Commons for his loud tones and his faulty Latin, but upright and fearless, and ever prompt and ready; of much commercial weight and especial popularity in the city of London, which he represented in Parliament.'—*History of England*, vol. v. p. 174. Beckford was on intimate terms with Horne Tooke, and, on several occasions, availed himself of the talents of his friend. His celebrated address to the king (George III.), which is inscribed on the base of the statue erected to his honor, by the grateful citizens of London, is said to have been composed by Tooke. He died in 1770, leaving his enormous fortune to his only son, known as the author of 'Vathek,' 'the fastidious man of taste—the fantastic decorator of Ramalhao and Fonthill.'

[2] This it was that gave such zest to the wit of Lord North and Selwyn. It came unexpectedly, bursting forth as it were from their sleep. Their 'prime distinction' was—

'Social wit; which, never kindling strife,
Blazed in the small, sweet courtesies of life;
Those little sapphires round the diamond shone,
Lending soft radiance to the richer stone.'

he was here upon his very strongest ground, for no man was better calculated to exemplify how true the observation is—

> Ridiculum acri
> Fortius ac melius.

At the same time, he had his serious hours and graver topics, which he would handle with all due solemnity of thought and language; and these were to me some of the most pleasing hours I have passed with him, for he could keep close to his point if he would, and could not be less argumentative than he was eloquent when the question was of magnitude enough to interest him. It is with singular satisfaction I can truly say that I never knew him flippant upon sacred subjects; he was, however, generally courted and admired as a gay companion rather than as a grave one.

I have said that the dowager Ladies Stafford and Hervey made part of our domestic society, and as the trivial amusement of cards was never resorted to in Mr. Dodington's house, it was his custom in the evenings to entertain his company with reading, and in this art he excelled; his selections, however, were curious, for he treated these ladies with the whole of Fielding's 'Jonathan Wild,' in which he certainly consulted his own turn for irony rather than theirs for elegance, but he set it off with much humor after his manner, and they were polite enough to be pleased, or at least to appear as if they were.

His readings from Shakspeare were altogether as whimsical, for he chose his passages only where buffoonery was the character of the scene; one of these I remember was that of the clown, who brings the asp to Cleopatra. He had, however, a manuscript copy of Glover's 'Medea,' which he gave us *con amore*, for he was extremely warm in his praises of that classical drama, which Mrs. Yates afterwards brought upon the stage, and played in it with her accustomed excellence; he did me also the honor to devote an evening to the reading of some lines, which I had hastily written to the amount of about four hundred, partly complimentary to him as my host, and in part consolatory to Lord Halifax upon the event of his retiring from public office; they flattered the politics then in favor with Mr. Dodington, and coincided with his wishes for detaching Lord Halifax from the administration of the Duke of Newcastle. I was not present, as may well be conceived, at this reading, but I confess I sat listening in the next room, and was not a little gratified by what I overheard. Of this manuscript I have long since destroyed the only copy that I had, and if I had it now in my hands it would be only to consign it to the flames, for it was of that occasional class of poems for the day, which have no claim upon posterity, and in such I have not been ambitious to concern myself: it served the purpose, however, and amused the moment; it was also the tribute of my mite to the lares of that mansion, where the Muse of Young had dictated his tragedy of The Revenge, and which the genius of Voltaire had honored with a visit: here Glover had courted inspiration, and Thompson caught it: Dodington also himself had a lyre, but he had hung it up, and it was never very high sounding; yet he was something more than a mere admirer of the Muse. He wrote small poems with great pains, and elaborate letters with much terseness of style, and some quaintness of expression: I have seen him refer to a volume of his own verses in manuscript, but he was very shy, and I never had the perusal of it. I was rather better acquainted with his *diary*, which since his death has been published, and I well remember the temporary disgust he seemed to take, when upon his asking what I would do with it, should he bequeath it to my discretion, I instantly replied that I would destroy it. There was a third, which I more coveted a sight of than either of the above, as it contained a miscellaneous collection of anecdotes, repartees, good sayings and humorous incidents, of which he was part author and part compiler, and out of which he was in the habit of refreshing his memory, when he prepared himself to expect certain men of wit and pleasantry either at his own house or elsewhere.[1] Upon this practice, which he did not affect to conceal, he observed to me one day, that it was a compliment he paid to society, when he submitted to steal weapons out of his own armory for their entertainment, and ingenuously added, that although his memory was not in general so correct as it had been, yet he trusted it would save him from the disgrace of repeating the same story to the same hearers, or foisting it into conversation in the wrong place or out of time. No man had fewer oversights of that sort to answer for, and fewer still were the men, whose social talents could be compared with those of Mr. Dodington.

[1] It was in like manner a trick of Sheridan to use the *bon-mots* of his acquaintance; but with such address and embellishment as almost to entitle him to the credit of original creation. 'Like all men of genius,' says his biographer, 'he had, in addition to the resources of his own wit, a quick apprehension of what suited his purpose in the wit of others, and a power of enriching whatever he adopted from them with such new grace as gave him a sort of claim of paternity over it, and made it all his own.' 'It is certain, that even his *bon-mots* in society were not always to be set down to the credit of the occasion; but that frequently, like skilful priests, he prepared the miracle of the moment beforehand.' —*Moore's Life of Sheridan.*

Upon my return out of Dorsetshire, I was invited by my friends at Trinity College to come and offer myself as a candidate for the Lay-fellowship then vacant by the death of Mr. Titley, the Danish envoy. There are but two fellowships of this description, and there were several solicitors for an exemption so desirable, but the unabated kindness of the master and seniors patronized my suit, and honored me with that last and most distinguished mark of their favor and protection. I did not hold it long, for Providence had a blessing in store for me, which was an effectual disqualification from holding any honors on the terms of celibacy.

About this time I wrote my first legitimate drama in five acts, and entitled it 'The Banishment of Cicero.' I was led to this by the perusal of Middleton's account of his life, which afforded me much entertainment. As the hero of a drama I was not happy in my choice of Cicero, and banishment is a tame incident to depend upon for the interest and catastrophe of a tragic plot. I knew that his philosophy had deserted him on this occasion, and that I could find no feature of Coriolanus in the character of my exile, but as I began it without any view of offering it to the stage, as long as I found amusement I continued to write. As a classical composition, which tells its story in fair language, and has stood the test of the press both in England and Ireland, with the approbation of some who were most competent to decide upon it, I may venture to say it was creditable to its author as a first attempt. It has been long out of print, and when, after a period of more than forty intermediate years, I read it (as I have now been doing) with all the impartiality in my power, I certainly can discover inaccuracies in the diction here and there, and in the plot an absolute inaptitude to scenic exhibition, yet I think I may presume to say, that as a dramatic poem for the closet it will bear examination, though I cannot expect that any of its readers at this time would pass so favorable a judgment upon it as I was honored with by Primate Stone and Bishop Warburton, from the latter of whom I received a letter, which I have preserved, and which I cannot withstand the temptation of inserting, though I am thoroughly conscious it bestows praises far above the merits of my humble work—

To Richard Cumberland, Esq.

Grosvenor Square, May 15, 1767.

Dear Sir: Let me thank you for the sight of a very fine dramatic poem. It is (like Mr. Mason's) much too good for a prostitute stage. Yesterday I received a letter from the Primate. He was on the point of leaving Bath for Ireland; so that my letter got to him just in time. 'It gives me great satisfaction,' says he, 'that my opinion of Bishop Cumberland's grandson agrees with yours,' &c. &c.

I have the honor to be,
Dear sir, your very faithful
And assured humble servant,
W. GLOUCESTER.

It is a singular circumstance, though perhaps not a favorable one, that in the dramatis personæ of this play there is not one auxiliary character; they are all principals, and such in respect of consequence as few authors ever brought together, in one point of view, for they consist of the two Consuls L. Calphurnius Piso and Aulus Gabinius, the Tribune P. Clodius, Cicero and Pomponius Atticus, Caius Piso Frugi, Terentia and Tullia, wife and daughter of Cicero, and Clodia, sister of the Tribune, without one speaking attendant or interloper throughout the piece, except a very few words from one Apollodorus.

To give display to characters like these, the bounds of any single drama would hardly serve, and of course the arrangement was so far injudicious; yet the author, as if he had not enough on his hands, goes aside to speak of Cato in the scene betwixt Gabinius and Clodius—

GABINIUS.

'Cato is still severe, is still himself;
Rough and unshaken in his squalid garb,
He told us he had long in anguish mourn'd,
Not in a private but the public cause,
Not for the wrong of one, but wrong of all,
Of Liberty, of Virtue, and of Rome.

CLODIUS.

'No more: I sleep o'er Cato's drowsy theme.
He is the senate's drone, and dreams of liberty,
When Rome's vast empire is set up to sale,
And portioned out to each ambitious bidder
In marketable lots——'

In the further progress of the same scene, Pompey is mentioned, and Calphurnius Piso introduced in the following terms:—

GABINIUS.

'——Oh! who shall attempt to read
In Pompey's face the movements of his heart?
The same calm artificial look of state,
His half-clos'd eyes in self-attention wrap'd,
Serve him alike to mask unseemly joy,
Or hide the pangs of envy and revenge.

CLODIUS.

See, yonder your old colleague Piso comes!
But name hypocrisy and he appears.
How like his grandsire's monument he looks!

He wears the dress of holy Numa's days,
The brow and beard of Zeno; trace him home,
You'll find his house the school of vice and lust,
The foulest sink of Epicurus' sty,
And him the rankest swine of all the herd.'

I find the two first acts are wound up with some couplets in rhyme after the manner of the middle age. It will, I hope, be pardonable if I here insert the lines, with which Clodius concludes the first act—

'When flaming comets vex our frighted sphere,
Though now the nations melt with awful fear,
From the dread omen fatal ill presage,
Dire plague and famine and war's wasting rage;
In time some brighter genius may arise,
And banish signs and omens from the skies,
Expound the comet's nature and its cause,
Assign its periods and prescribe its laws,
Whilst man grown wise, with his discoveries fraught,
Shall wonder how he needed to be taught.'

I shall only add that the dialogue between Cicero and Atticus in the third act seems in point of poetry one of the happiest efforts of its author: in short, although this drama has not all the finishing of a veteran artist, yet in parts it has a warmth of coloring and a strength of expression, which might induce a candid reader to augur not unfavorably of the novice who composed it.

It is here I begin more particularly to feel the weight of those difficulties, which at my outset I too rashly announced myself prepared to meet. When I review what I have been saying about this my first drama, and recollect what numbers are behind, I am almost tempted to shrink back from the task, to which I am committed. If indeed the candor and liberality of my readers will allow me to step out of myself (if I may so term it), whilst I am speaking of myself, I have little to fear; but if I must be tied down to my individuality, and not allowed my fair opinion without incurring the charge of self-conceit, I am in a most unenviable situation, and must either abandon my undertaking, or abide by the conditions of it with what fortitude I can muster. If, when I am professedly the recorder of my own writings, I am to record nothing in them or about them but their simple titles and the order in which they were written, I give the reader nothing more than a catalogue, which any magazine might furnish, or the prompter's register as well supply; if, on the contrary, I proceed to fulfill the real purposes of biographer and critic, ought I not to act as honestly and conscientiously in my own case, as I would in the instance of another person? I think I ought: It is what the title of my book professes; how I am to execute it I do not know, and how my best endeavors may be received I can form no guess. In the mean time, I will strive to arm myself with an humble but honest mind, resolving, as far as in me lies, not to speak partially of my works because they are my own, nor slightingly against my conscience from apprehension that readers may be found to differ from me, where my thoughts may seem more favorable than theirs. The latter of these consequences may perhaps frequently occur, and when it does, my memoirs must encounter it, and acquit themselves of it as they can; for myself, it cannot be long before I am alike insensible to censure or applause.

This play, of which I have been speaking, lay by me for a considerable time; till Lord Halifax one day, when we were at Bushey Park, desired me to show it to him; he read it, and immediately proposed to carry it to Garrick, and recommend it to him for representation. Garrick was then at Hampton, and I went with Lord Halifax across the Park to his house. This was the first time I found myself in company with that extraordinary man. He received his noble visitor with profound obeisance, and in truth there were some claims upon his civility for favors and indulgences granted to him by Lord Halifax as Ranger of Bushey Park. I was silently attentive to every minute particular of this interview, and soon discovered the embarrassment, which the introduction of my manuscript occasioned; I saw my cause was desperate, though my advocate was sanguine, and in truth the first effort of a raw author did not promise much to the purpose of the manager. He took it, however, with all possible respect, and promised an attentive perusal, but those tell-tale features, so miraculously gifted in the art of assumed emotions, could not mask their real ones, and I predicted to Lord Halifax, as we returned to the lodge, that I had no expectation of my play being accepted. A day or two of what might scarce be called suspense, confirmed this prediction, when Mr. Garrick having stated his despair of accommodating a play on such a plan to the purposes of the stage, returned the manuscript to Lord Halifax with many apologies to his lordship, and some few qualifying words to its author, which certainly was as much as in reason could be expected from him, though it did not satisfy the patron of the play, who warmly resented his non-compliance with his wishes, and for a length of time forbore to live in habits of his former good neighborhood with him.

When I published this play, which I soon after did, I was conscious that I published Mr. Garrick's justification for refusing it, and I made no mention of the circumstances above stated.

George Ridge, Esq., of Kilmiston, in the county of Hants, had two sons and one daughter by Miss Brooke, niece to my grandfather Bentley; with this family we had lived as friends and relations in habits of the greatest intimacy. It was upon an excursion, as I have before related, to this gentleman's house that I founded my school-boy poem written at Bury, and our families had kept up an interchange of annual visits for a course of time. From these meetings I had been for several years excluded by my avocations at college or London, till upon Mr. Ridge's coming to town accompanied by his wife and daughter, and taking lodgings in the near neighborhood of Mount Street, where I held my melancholy abode, I was kindly entertained by them, and found so many real charms in the modest manners and blooming beauty of the amiable daughter, that I passed every hour I could command in her society, and devoted all my thoughts to the attainment of that happiness, which it was in her power to bestow upon my future days. As soon, therefore, as I obtained, through the patronage of Lord Halifax, a small establishment as Crown Agent for the province of Nova Scotia, I began to hope the object I aspired to was within my reach, when upon a visit she made with her parents to mine at Fulham, I tendered my addresses, and had the unspeakable felicity to find them accepted, and sanctioned by the consent of all parties concerned; thus I became possessed of one, whom the virtues of her heart and the charms of her person had effectually endeared to me, and on the 19th day of February, 1759 (being my birth-day), I was married by my father in the church of Kilmiston, to Elizabeth, only daughter of George and Elizabeth Ridge.

CHAPTER III.

Lord Halifax, first lord of trade and plantations—Earl of Bute at the head of affairs—Dodington—Lord Halifax, lord-lieutenant of Ireland—His arrangements—William Gerard Hamilton—Cumberland, Ulster secretary—'The Banishment of Cicero'—Lord Melcombe—Bentley—'The Wishes'—Opening speech of the Lord Lieutenant—Edmund Burke—Mr. Roseingrave—Cumberland's disinterestedness—Offered a baronetcy—Hamilton as an orator—Quarrel with Burke—Cumberland's father raised to the bishopric—Society in Dublin—Primate Stone—Dr. Robinson—Colonel Ford—George Faulkner—Mrs. Dancer—Cumberland returns to England—Health of his family—Bishop Cumberland—Cumberland's disappointment—Situation at the Board of Trade—Cumberland's estimate of Halifax—The Summer's tale—Bickerstaff—Smith the actor—Cumberland visits his father—'The brothers'—Garrick—Fitzherbert—The West Indian—Mr. Talbot—Lord Eyre—Anecdote of a Catholic priest—The O'Roukes—Sir Thomas Cuffee—Mr. Geoghegan—Doctor of laws.

Lord Halifax, upon some slight concessions from the Duke of Newcastle, had reassumed his office of First Lord of Trade and Plantations, and I returned with my wife to Fulham, taking a house for a short time in Luke Street, Westminster, and afterwards in Abington Buildings.

In the following year, upon the death of the king, administration it is well known took a new shape, and all eyes were turned towards the Earl of Bute, as dispenser of favors and awarder of promotions.[1] Mr. Dodington, whom I had visited a second

[1] 'Lord Bute,' said Dr. Johnson, 'though a very honorable man—a man who meant well—a man who had his blood full of prerogative—was a theoretical statesman—a book minister—and thought this country could be governed by the influence of the crown alone.'—*Boswell's Johnson*, vol. ii. p. 355. How mistaken he was, his short, unpopular, and inglorious administration will attest.

'The Earl of Bute,' says Walpole, 'was a Scotchman, who, having no estate, had passed his youth in studying mathematics and mechanics in his own little island, then simples in the hedges about Twickenham, and at five-and-thirty had fallen in love with his own figure, which he produced at masquerades in becoming dresses, and in plays, which he acted in private companies, with a set of his own relations.'—*Memoirs of the Reign of George II.*, vol. i. p. 46.

Bute married the only daughter of the celebrated Mary Wortley Montague. After the death of her father, and brother, the eccentric Edward Wortley Montague, she came into possession of a large landed property. After living several years in profound retirement, on his patrimonial estate, in the Isle of Bute, he emerged from his retreat, and took a house on the banks of the Thames. Accident made him acquainted with Frederic, Prince of Wales, and

time at Eastbury with my wife and her father, Mr. Ridge, obtained an English peerage, and Lord Halifax was honored with the high office of Lord Lieutenant of Ireland, and was preparing to open his majesty's first Parliament in that kingdom; I had reason to believe myself at this time very much in his confidence, and in the conduct of a certain private transaction, which I am not called upon to explain, I had done him

father of George III. He became a great favorite with the Prince and Princess; took a part in the private theatricals exhibited for their amusement, and gradually laid the foundations of his subsequent elevation. After the death of the Prince, his intimacy with the Princess gave rise to rumors which compromised her character and injuriously affected him. The Earl's handsome person was supposed to be an irresistible attraction to the plastic and pleasure-loving Princess. To his external accomplishments, says Wraxall, 'he added a cultivated mind, illuminated by a taste for many branches of the fine arts and letters. For the study of botany he nourished a decided passion, which he gratified to the utmost; and, in the indulgence of which predilection, he manifested on some occasions a princely liberality. Of a disposition naturally retired and severe, he was not formed for an extensive commerce with mankind, or endowed by nature with talents for managing popular assemblies. Even in his family he was austere, harsh, difficult of access, and sometimes totally inaccessible to his own children. In the House of Lords he neither displayed eloquence nor graciousness of manners. But he proved himself likewise deficient in a quality still more essential for a first minister, firmness of character. Yet, with these political defects of mind, and of personal deportment, he undertook to displace, and he aspired to succeed Mr. Pitt, at a moment when that minister had carried the glory of the British arms to an unexampled height by sea and land. We cannot sufficiently regret that George the Third should not have contented himself with heaping honors and dignities on him, carefully excluding him from any political employment. Few princes, however, of whom history preserves any record, have manifested, at twenty-three, a judgment so superior to the natural partialities of youth. Even Elizabeth, though she placed Cecil at the head of her councils, yet committed her armies successively to Leicester and to Essex. After an administration of about two years, passed either in the post of Secretary of State or as First Lord of the Treasury, during which time he brought the war with France and Spain to a conclusion, Lord Bute, abandoning his royal master, quitted his situation, and again withdrew to privacy; no testimonies of national regret, or of national esteem, accompanied him at his departure from office. His magnificent residence in Berkeley Square exposed him to very malignant comments, respecting the means by which he had reared so expensive a pile. His enemies asserted that he could not possibly have possessed the ability, either from his patrimonial fortune, or in consequence of his marriage, to erect such a structure. As little could he be supposed to have amassed wherewithal, during his very short administration, to suffice for its construction. The only satisfactory solution of the difficulty, therefore, lay in imagining that he had either received presents from France, or had made large purchases in the public funds previous to the signature of the preliminaries.'—*Historical Memoirs*, p. 175, vide *Mahon's Character of Bute, History of England*, vol. iv. p. 23; and *Chesterfield's Characters*. The violence of his opponents and the lukewarmness of his friends drove Bute into retirement. The popular displeasure followed him even there, and his influence was supposed still to control public measures. He was disliked by his contemporaries, and his character seems to have inspired no other feeling in their posterity.

faithful service; happy for him it would have been, and the prevention of innumerable troubles and vexations, if my zealous efforts had been permitted to take effect, but a fatal propensity had again seized possession of him, and probably the more strongly for the interruption it had received—but of this enough.

His family was now to be formed upon an establishment suitable to his high office. In these arrangements there was much to do, and I was fully occupied. Some few persons of obscure characters were pressed upon him for subordinate situations from a quarter where I had no communication or connection; but I had the satisfaction to see his old and faithful friend, Doctor Crane, prepare himself to head the list of his chaplains, and Doctor Oswald, afterwards Bishop of Raphoe, with my good father, completed that department. I obtained a situation for a gentleman, who had married my eldest sister, but what gave me peculiar satisfaction was to have it in my power to gratify the wishes of one of the best and bravest young officers of his time, Captain William Ridge, brother to my wife. He had served the whole war in America with distinguished reputation; had been shot and carried off the field in the fatal affair of Ticonderoga, and was now returned with honorable wounds and the praises and esteem of his general and brother officers. This amiable, this excellent friend, whose heart was as it were my own, and whose memory will be ever dear to me, I caused to be put upon the staff of aids-de-camp, and had the happiness of making him one of my family during the whole time of my residence in Dublin Castle, as Ulster Secretary.

William Gerard Hamilton, a name well known, had negotiated himself into the office of Chief Secretary.[1] I need say no more than that he did not owe this to the choice of Lord Halifax; of course it was not easy for that gentleman to find himself in the confidence of his principal, to whom he was little known, and in the first instance not altogether acceptable. I do not think he

[1] William Gerard Hamilton was born in 1729, at Lincoln's Inn, where his father was a barrister. 'His father,' says Walpole, 'had been the first Scot who ever pleaded at the English bar, and, as it was said of him, should have been the last; the son had much more parts.'—*Memoirs of the Reign of George II.*, vol. ii. p. 44. Hamilton was educated at Winchester School, and Oriel College, Oxford. He studied his father's profession; but was never called to the bar. In 1754, he was elected a member of Parliament, and made the memorable speech, which gave him the name of Single Speech Hamilton. 'He spoke for the first time,' wrote Walpole to Conway, 'and was at once perfection; his speech was set and full of antitheses, but these antitheses were full of argument; indeed, his speech was the most argumentative of the whole day, and he broke through the regularity of his own composition, answered other people, and fell

took much pains to conquer first impressions, and recommend himself to the confidence of Lord Halifax; it is certain he did not possess it, and the consequence was, that I, who held the secondary post of Ulster Secretary, became involved in business of a nature, that should not in the course of office have belonged to me. Affairs of this sort, which I did not court, and had no right to be concerned in, made my situation very delicate and not a little dangerous, whilst at the same time the entire superintendence of Lord Halifax's private finances, then very far from being in a flourishing condition, was a task which no prudent man would covet, yet such an one as for his sake I made no scruple to undertake. It was his lot to succeed the Duke of Bedford, and his high spirit would not suffer him to sink upon the comparison; I found him therefore resolute to start on his career with great magnificence, and leave behind him all attentions to expense. All that was in my power I did with unwearied diligence and attention to his interest, inspecting his accounts and paying his bills every week, to the minutest article. I put his Green Cloth upon a liberal, but regulated, establishment; I placed a faithful and well experienced servant of my father's at the head of his stables and equipages, and gave charge of the household articles to his principal domestic, of whose honesty he had many years' experience.

I had published my tragedy of 'The Banishment of Cicero,' by Mr. J. Walter, at Charing Cross, upon quarto paper in a handsome type; I found it pirated and published in a sixpenny edition at Dublin, from the press of George Faulkner of immortal memory; if he had subjoined a true and faithful list of errata, I doubt if he could have afforded it at the price. I also, upon the king's accession, composed and published a poem addressed to the young sovereign, in which I attempted to delineate the character of the people he was to govern, and the principles of that conduct, which, if pursued, would insure their

into his own track again with the greatest ease.' Nov. 15, 1755. 'His voice, manner, and language,' says the same ear-witness, in recording this display on the historic page, 'were most advantageous; his arguments sound, though pointed; and his command of himself easy and undaunted.'—*Memoirs of the Reign of George II.*, vol. ii. p. 51. Hamilton was subsequently made one of the lords of trade; and, as stated by Cumberland, went to Ireland as the Secretary of Lord Halifax. In the Irish Parliament, he stood high as an orator; though he did not realize the promise of excellence, which his famous speech had made, *vide* post, p. 120. He held for many years the office of Chancellor of the Exchequer in Ireland; and when he retired from that employment, in 1784, he gave the remainder of his life to literary pursuits. He died in 1796. On a subsequent page the reader will find Cumberland's estimate of his character and talents. (*Post*, p. 120.)

attachment, and establish his own happiness and glory. This I wrote in blank verse; it was published by Mr. Dodsley, and I did not give my name to it. Of the extent of its circulation I cannot speak, neither did I make any search into the reviews of that time for the character, good or ill, which they thought fit to give it.

I had taken leave of Lord Melcombe the day preceding the coronation, and found him before a looking-glass in his new robes practising attitudes and debating within himself upon the most graceful mode of carrying his coronet in the procession. He was in high glee with his fresh and blooming honors, and I left him in the act of dictating a billet to Lady Hervey, apprising her that a *young lord* was coming to throw himself at her feet.[1] He conjured me to keep my Lord Lieutenant firmly attached to Lord Bute, and we parted.

Here, however, I must take leave to pause upon a period in the life of my uncle, Mr. Bentley, when fortune smiled upon him, and his genius was drawn forth into exertion by the patronage of Lord Bute. Through my intimacy with Mr. Dodington, I had been the lucky instrument of opening that channel which, for a time at least, brought him affluence, comfort, and consideration. There was not a man of literary talents then in the kingdom who stood so high, and so deservedly in fame and favor with the Premier as Mr. Bentley; and though when that great personage went out of office, my uncle lost every place of profit that could be taken from him, he continued to enjoy a pension of five hundred pounds per annum, in which his widow had her life, and received it many years after his decease.

Lord Bute had all the disposition of a Mecænas, and fondly hoped he would be the auspicious instrument of opening an Augustan reign. He sent out his runners upon the search for men of talents; and Dodington was perfectly reconciled to the honor of being his provider in that laudable pursuit, for which no man was better qualified. He was not wanting in intuition to discern what the powers of Bentley's genius were; and none could better point out the purposes to which they might be usefully directed. Opposition was then beginning to look up, and soon felt the sharp point of Bentley's pen in one of the

[1] 'To my Lord Melcombe; address as many lords and lordships as you please, and you cannot err; he is as fond of his title as his child could be, if he had one.'—*Walpole to Sir Horace Man*, May 14, 1761, vide *Walpole's Letters*. Dodington did not live long to enjoy his coveted honors. He died July 28, 1762, of a dropsy in his stomach, 'just when,' says Walpole, 'the views of his life were nearest being realized.'

keenest and wittiest satires extant in our language; Lord Temple, Wilkes, and others of the party were attacked with unsparing asperity and much classical acumen. Churchill, the Dryden of his age, and indisputably a man of first-rate genius, was too candid not to acknowledge the merit of the poem; and when he declined taking up the gauntlet so pointedly thrown down to him, it was not because he held his challenger in contempt. It was this poem that brought an accumulation of favors on its author; but I don't know that he ever had an interview with the bestower of them, and I am rather inclined to think they never met. About the same time, my uncle composed his witty, but eccentric drama of 'The Wishes,' in which he introduces the speaking harlequin, after the manner of the Italians. This curious production, after being circulated in manuscript, admired and applauded by all who had seen it, and those the very party which led the taste of the time under the auspices of Lord Bute, was privately rehearsed at Lord Melcombe's villa of La Trappe. It was on a beautiful summer's evening when it was recited upon the terrace on the banks of the Thames by Obrien, Miss Elliot, Mrs. Haughton, and some few others, under the management of Foote and Murphy, who attended on the occasion.[1] At this rehearsal, there was present *a youth unknown to fame*, who was understood to be protected by Lord Bute, and came thither in a

[1] Walpole, in a letter to George Montague, thus *gossips* about his quondam friend Bentley's play: 'If you will stay with me a fortnight or three weeks, perhaps I may be able to carry you to a play of Mr. Bentley's—you stare, but I am in earnest; nay, and *de par le roy*. In short, here is the history of it. You know the passion he always had for the Italian comedy; about two years ago, he wrote one, intending to get it offered to Rich, but without his name. He would have died to be supposed an author and writing for gain. I kept this an inviolable secret. Judge, then, of my surprise, when about a fortnight or three weeks ago, I found my Lord Melcombe reading this very Bentleian in a circle at my Lady Hervey's. Cumberland had carried it to him with a recommendatory copy of verses, containing more incense to the King and my Lord Bute, than the Magi brought in their portmanteaus to Jerusalem. The idols were propitious, and, to do them justice, there is a great deal of wit in the piece, which is called 'The Wishes, or Harlequin's Mouth Opened.' A bank note of two hundred pounds was sent from the treasury to the author, and the play ordered to be performed by the summer company. Foote was summoned to Lord Melcombe's, where Parnassus was composed by the Peer himself, who, like Apollo, as I am going to tell you, was dozing, the two Chief Justices and Lord B. Bubo read the play himself, 'with handkerchief and orange by his side.' But the curious part is a prologue, which I never saw. It represents the God of Verse fast asleep by the side of Helicon; the race of modern bards try to wake him, but the more they repeat their works the louder he snores. At last 'ruin, seize thee, ruthless king!' is heard, and the god starts from his trance. This is a good thought, but will offend the bards so much that I think Dr. Bentley's son will be abused at least as much as his father was. The prologue concludes with young Augustus, and how much he excels the ancient one by the choice

hackney-coach with Mrs. Haughton. This gentleman was of the party at the supper with which the evening's entertainment concluded; he modestly resigned the conversation to those who were more disposed to carry it on, whilst it was only in the contemplation of an intelligent countenance that we could form any conjecture as to that extraordinary gift of genius which in course of time advanced him to the Great Seal of the kingdom, and the Earldom of Rosslyn.[1]

of his friend. Foote refused to act this prologue, and said it was too strong. 'Indeed,' said Augustus's friend, 'I think it is.' They have softened it a little, and I suppose it will be performed.'—*Letters*, vol. iii. p. 129, June 18, 1761.

[1] This was Alexander Wedderburn, the son of a Scotch advocate at Edinburgh, where the future Chancellor was born, in 1733. He adopted the profession of his father, and was called to the Scottish bar. But quarrelling with the Dean of Faculty, and doubtless ambitious of a success which he could not attain in his own country, he suddenly bade adieu to Scotland, and sought his fortune in London. At the time referred to by Cumberland, he had been four years at the English bar; his rise was slow. He was brought into Parliament by Lord Bute, and at a time when the popular prejudice was setting strongly against the inhabitants of the Northern Island. Thus is he described by Churchill—

'A pert prim prater of the Northern race,
Guilt in his heart, and famine in his face!
Mute at the bar, and in the Senate loud,' &c.

Unscrupulous, dexterous, able, with his eye fixed steadily on office, Wedderburn, through the mazes of treachery, attained the objects of his ambition. 'It is the imperative duty of the historian,' says Lord Brougham, 'to dwell upon the fate, while he discloses with impartial fulness, and marks with just reprobation, the acts of such men; to the end that their great success, as it is called, may not mislead others, and conceal behind the glitter of worldly prosperity, the baser material with which the structure of their fortune is built up. This wholesome lesson, and indeed needful warning, is above all required when we are called upon to contemplate a professional and political life so eminently prosperous as the one which we have been contemplating, which rolled on in an uninterrupted tide of worldly gains and worldly honors, but was advanced only by shining and superficial talents, supported by no fixed principles, illustrated by no sacrifices to public virtue, embellished by no feats of patriotism, nor made memorable by any monuments of national utility, and which, being at length closed in the disappointment of many unworthy desires, ended amidst universal neglect, and left behind it no claim to the respect or gratitude of mankind, though it may have excited the admiration or envy of the contemporary vulgar.'

Wedderburn, though an accomplished debater, full of resources of argument and illustration, and occasionally rising into the regions of oratory, seems to have failed in conversation. 'He did not seek, like Thurlow,' says Lord Campbell, 'to gain distinction by a display of his colloquial powers; and, thinking of the superior *eclat* to be obtained by a brilliant speech in *Parliament*, he was contented with being rather obscure in the *salon*. According to some accounts, he submitted to this necessity after having found by experience that his genius did not fit him for talk. Boswell, having told us that Johnson, in allusion to Lord Mansfield, had said, 'It is wonderful, sir, with how little real superiority of mind men can make an eminent figure in public life,' thus proceeds: 'He expressed himself to the same purpose concerning another law

Foote, Murphy, and Obrien were then joint conductors of the summer theatre, and performed their plays upon the stage of Drury Lane, and here they brought out 'The Wishes,' which had now been so much the topic of conversation, that it drew all the wit and fashion then in town to its first representation. The brilliancy of its dialogue, and the reiterated strokes of point and repartee kept the audience in good humor with the leading acts, and seemed to augur favorably for the conclusion, till when the last of the Three Wishes produced the ridiculous catastrophe of the hanging of Harlequin in full view of the audience, my uncle, the author, then sitting by me, whispered in my ear—'If they don't damn this, they deserve to be damn'd themselves,' and whilst he was yet speaking the roar began, and 'The Wishes' were irrevocably condemned.[1] Mr. Harris

lord,* who, it seems, once took a fancy to associate with the wits of London; but with so little success that Foote said: 'What can he mean by coming among us? He is not only dull himself, but the cause of dulness in others.' Trying him by the test of his colloquial powers, Johnson had found him very defective. He once said to Sir Joshua Reynolds, 'This man has been ten years now about town, and has made nothing of it;' meaning as a companion. He said to me: 'I never heard anything from him in company that was at all striking; and depend upon it, sir, it is when you come close to a man in conversation that you discover what his real abilities are; to make a speech in a public assembly is a knack.''—*Boswell's Johnson.—Campbell's Lives of the Chancellors.*

[1] 'I came to town yesterday,' writes Walpole to George Montague, 'through clouds of dust, to see the 'Wishes,' and went, actually feeling for Mr. Bentley, and full of the emotions he must be suffering. What do you think, in a house crowded, was the first thing I saw? Mr. and Madame Bentley, perched up in the front boxes, and acting audience at his own play! No, all the impudence of false patriotism never came up to it. Did one ever hear of an author that had courage to see his own first night in public? I don't believe Fielding or Foote himself ever did; and this was the modest, bashful Mr. Bentley, that died at the thought of being known for an author, even by his own acquaintance! In the stage-box was Lady Bute, Lord Halifax, and Lord Melcombe. I must say the two last entertained the house as much as the play; your king was prompter, and called out to the actor every minute to speak louder. . . . The audience were extremely fair; the first act they bore with patience, though it promised very ill; the second is admirable, and was much applauded; so was the third; the fourth woful; the beginning of the fifth it seemed expiring, but was revived by a delightful burlesque of the ancient chorus, which was followed by two dismal scenes, at which people yawned, but were awakened on a sudden by Harlequin's being drawn up to a gibbet, nobody knew why or wherefore. This raised a prodigious and continued hiss, Harlequin all the while suspended in the air. At last they were suffered to finish the play, but nobody attended to the conclusion. Modesty and his lady all the while sat with the utmost indifference. . . . To add to the judgment of his conduct, Cumberland two days ago published a pamphlet to abuse him.'—July 28, 1761.

---

* Evidently Wedderburn, though not named.

some years after gave it a second chance upon his stage: the judgment of the public could not take away the merit of the poet, but it decided against his success. Upon the hint of this play, and the entertainment at La Trappe, where Foote had been a guest, that wicked wit took measure of his host, and founded his satirical drama of 'The Patron'—in short, he feasted, flattered and lampooned.

Mr. Bentley also wrote a very elegant poem, and addressed it as an epistle to Lord Melcombe: it was in my opinion a most exquisite composition, in no respect inferior to his satire, but for reasons I could never understand, nor even guess, it was coolly received by Melcombe, and stopped with him. If that poem is in the hands of any of Mr. Bentley's family, it is much to be regretted that they withhold it from the public, though all that was then temporary is now long past and forgotten.

What may be the nature or amount of the manuscripts which my uncle may have left behind him, I do not know: I can speak only of two dramas; one of these, entitled Philodamus, has been given to the public by Mr. Harris, and Henderson performed the character, that gives its name to the play. The ingenious author always wrote for the reader, he did not study how to humor the spectator: Philodamus has much of the old cast in its style, with a considerable portion of originality and a bold vein of humor running through it, occasionally intermixed even with the pathos of the scene, which in a modern composition, professing itself to be a tragedy, is a perilous experiment. Such it proved to Philodamus: its very best passages in perusal were its weakest points in representation, and it may be truly said it was ruined by its virtues: but in the galleries of our theatres the Graces have no seats, and he that writes to the populace must not borrow the pen of the author of Philodamus. Poet Gray wrote a long and elaborate critique upon this drama, which I saw, and though his flattery was outrageously pedantic, yet the incense of praise from author to author is always sweet, and perhaps not the less acceptable on account of its being so seldom offered up. The other drama, on the Genoese Conspiracy, I saw in its unfinished state, and can only say that I was struck by certain passages, but cannot speak of it as a whole.

When the ceremony of the coronation was over, the Lord Lieutenant set out for Ireland with a numerous cavalcade. I was now the father of two infant children, a daughter and a son; these I left with their grandmother Mrs. Ridge, and was accompanied by my wife, though in a state ill calculated to endure the rough roads by land, and the more rough passage by sea: my father, mother and sisters were with us in the yacht; they took a house in Dublin, and I was by office an inhabitant of the castle, and lodged in very excellent and commodious apartments.

The speech of the Lord Lieutenant upon the opening of the session is upon record. It was generally esteemed a very brilliant composition. His graceful person and impressive manner of delivery set it off to its best advantage, and all things seemed to augur well for his success. When I was called in jointly with Secretary Hamilton to take the project and rough copy of this speech into consideration, I could not help remarking the extraordinary efforts, which that gentleman made, to engraft his own very peculiar style upon the sketch before him; in this I sometimes agreed with him, but more commonly opposed him, till Lord Halifax, whose patience began to be exhausted, no longer submitted his copy to be dissected, but took it to himself with such alterations as he saw fit to adopt, and those but few. I must candidly acknowledge that at times when I have heard people searching for internal evidence in the style of Junius as to the author of those famous letters, I have called to recollection this circumstance, which I have now related, and occasionally said that the style of Junius bore a strong resemblance to what I had observed of the style of Secretary Hamilton; beyond this I never had the least grounds for conjecture, nor any clue to lead me to the discovery of that anonymous writer beyond what I have alluded to.

I remember a conversation he held with me some time before we left England on the subject of Mr. Edmund Burke, whom he had then attached to himself, and for whom he wished me to assist in projecting some establishment. I had then never seen that eminent person, nor did I meet him till after my arrival in Dublin, when I had merely the opportunity of introducing myself to him in passing through the apartment, where he was in attendance upon Mr. Hamilton. He had indeed his fortune to make, but he was not disposed to make it by any means but such as perfectly accorded with his feelings and his honor; for when Mr. Hamilton contrived to accommodate him by some private manœuvre, which I am not correctly possessed of, he saw occasion in a short time after his acceptance of it to throw it up, and break from all connection with that gentleman and his politics. With the Lord Lieutenant he had little, if any, correspondence or acquaintance, for though Lord Halifax's intuition could not have failed to discover the merits of Mr. Burke, and rightly to have appreciated them, had they ever come cordially into contact, it was not from the quarter, in which he was then placed, that favor and promotion were to be looked for.[1]

Without entering upon the superannuated politics of that time, it is enough to say that the king's business was carried through the session with success, and when the vote was passed for augmenting the revenue of the Lord Lieutenant, and settling it at the standard to which it is now fixed, he accepted and passed it in favor of his successors, but peremptorily rejected it for himself. At this very time I had issued to the amount of twenty thousand pounds expended in office, whilst he had been receiving about twelve, and I know not where that man could have been found, to whom those exceedings were more severely embarrassing than to this disinterested personage; but in this case he acted entirely from the dictates of his own high spirit, scarce deigning to lend an ear to the remonstrances even of Doctor Crane, and taking his measures with such rapidity, as to preclude all hesitation or debate.

His popularity, however, was so established by this high-minded proceeding, that, upon his departure from Ireland, all parties seemed to unite in applauding his conduct and invoking his return; the shore was thronged with crowds of people, that followed him to the water's edge, and the sea was in a manner covered with boats and vessels, that accompanied the yacht through the bay, studious to pay to their popular chief governor every valedictory honor, that their zeal and attention could devise.

The patronage of the Lord Lieutenant was at that time so extremely circumscribed, that except in the church and army few expectants could have been put in possession of their wishes, had not my under-secretary, Mr. Roseingrave, discovered a number of lapsed patents that had laid dormant in my office for a length of time, neither allowances nor perquisites being annexed to them. When a pretty considerable number of these patents were collected, and a list of them made out, I laid them before

[1] When Burke went to Ireland as Hamilton's secretary, his talents had given him a name in literature; but, unaccompanied with those more substantial rewards, in the absence of which, merit is supposed to rise slowly. '*Nitor in adversum*, is the motto for a man like me,' he afterwards remarked. At the time of receiving this post of secretary from Hamilton, he had attained the age of thirty-three. After a service of little more than a twelve-month he obtained a pension of £300 a year; but this he did not long enjoy. The friendship that had subsisted between Hamilton and himself was broken. The circumstances of the quarrel are not clearly known; but enough has appeared to justify the imputation on Hamilton of tyranny and meanness. 'To get rid of him completely,' says Burke, 'and not to carry a memorial of such a person about me, I offered to transmit my pension to his attorney in trust for him. This offer he thought proper to accept.'

the Lord Lieutenant for his disposal in such manner as he saw fit. He at once discerned the great accommodation they would afford him, and very gladly availed himself of them, obtaining grants of Parliament for each respectively, which, though virtually pensions, were not so glaringly obnoxious, nor were any of them in fact such absolute sinecures, some duty being attached to every one of them. They were certainly a very seasonable accession to his patronage, and I make no doubt a very acceptable one to the circumstances of those on whom he bestowed them. I sought no share in the spoil, but rather wished to stand correctly clear of any interested part in the transaction; some small thing, however, I asked and obtained for my worthy second Mr. Roseingrave, who had all the merit of the manœuvre, and many other merits of a much superior sort, for which I sincerely esteemed him, and, till his death put an end to our correspondence, preserved a constant interchange of friendly sentiments, and at times of visits, when either he came to England, or I passed over to Ireland.

And here, in justice to myself, I must take credit for a disinterestedness which never could be betrayed into the acceptance of anything, however covered or contrived (and many were the devices then ingeniously practised upon me) which delicacy could possibly interpret as a gratuity, whether tendered as an acknowledgment for favors past, or as an inducement for services to come. As I went to Ireland so I returned from it, perfectly clean-handed, not having profited my small fortune in the value of a single shilling, except from the fair income of my office arising from the established fees upon wool licenses, which netted, as well as I can recollect, about 300*l.* per annum, and did not clear my extraordinary expenses.

Towards the close of the session the Lord Lieutenant took occasion one morning, when I waited upon him with his private accounts, to express his satisfaction in my services, adding that he wished to mark his particular approbation of me by obtaining for me the rank of baronet: a title, he observed, very fit in his opinion for me to hold, as my father would in all probability be a bishop, and had a competent estate, which would descend to me. I confess it was not the sort of favor I expected, and struck me as a gaudy insubstantial offer, which as a mere addition to my name without any to my circumstances, was (as my friend Isted afterwards described it) a mouthful of moonshine. I received the tender notwithstanding with all due respect, and only desired time to turn it in my thoughts. I was now the father of three children, for I had a daughter born in the castle, and when I found my father and my whole family adverse to the proposal, I signified to Lord Halifax my wish to decline the honor he had been pleased to offer to me: I certainly did not make my court to him by this refusal, and vanity, if I had listened to it, would in this instance have taught me better policy, but to err on the side of moderation and humility is an error that ought not to be repented of; though I have reason to think, from ensuing circumstances, that it contributed to weaken an interest, which so many engines were at work to extinguish. In fact, I plainly saw it was not for me to expect any lasting tenure in the share I then possessed of favor, unless I kept it up by sacrifices I was determined not to make; in short, I had not that worldly wisdom, which could prevail with me to pay my homage in that quarter, from which my patron derived his ruin, and purchase by disgraceful attentions a continuance of that claim to his protection and regard, which I had earned by long and faithful services for ten years past (the third part of my life) without intermission, and for the longer half of that time without consideration or reward.

As sure as ever my history brings me to the mention of that fatal step, which took me out of the path I was in, and turned me from the prosecution of those peaceful studies, to which I was so cordially devoted, and which were leading me to a profession, wherein some that went before me had distinguished themselves with such credit, so sure am I to feel at my heart a pang, that wounds me with regret and self-reproach for having yielded to a delusion at the inexperienced age of nineteen, since which I have seen more than half a century go by, every day of which has only served to strengthen more and more the full conviction of my error.

Hamilton, who in the English Parliament got the nick-name of Single-speech, spoke well, but not often, in the Irish House of Commons. He had a promptitude of thought, and a rapid flow of well-conceived matter, with many other requisites, that only seemed waiting for opportunities to establish his reputation as an orator. He had a striking countenance, a graceful carriage, great self-possession and personal courage: he was not easily put out of his way by any of those unaccommodating repugnances, that men of weaker nerves or more tender consciences might have stumbled at, or been checked by; he could mask the passions, that were natural to him, and assume those that did not belong to him; he was indefatigable, meditative, mysterious; his opinions were the result of long labor and much reflection, but he had the art of setting them forth as if they were the starts of ready genius and a quick perception: he had as much seeming steadiness as a partisan could stand in need of, and all the real flexibility that could suit his purpose or advance his interest. He would fain have retained his connection with Edmund Burke, and associated him to his politics, for he well knew the value of his talents, but in that object he was soon disappointed: the genius of Burke was of too high a cast to endure debasement.

The bishopric of Elphin became vacant, and was offered to Doctor Crane, who, though moderately beneficed in England, withstood the temptation of that valuable mitre, and disinterestedly declined it. This was a decisive instance of the purity as well as moderation of his mind, for had he not disdained all ideas of negotiation in church preferments, he might have accepted the see of Elphin, and traded with it in England, as others have done both before and since his time. He was not a man of this sort; he returned to his prebendal house at Westminster in the little cloisters, and some years before his death resided in his parsonage house at Sutton, a living given him by Sir Roger Burgoyne, near to which I had a house, from which I paid him frequent visits, and with unspeakable concern saw that excellent man resign himself with patience truly Christian to the dreadful and tormenting visitation of a cancer in his face. I was at my house at Tetworth near Sutton in Bedfordshire, when he rode over to me one morning, and complained of a soreness on his lip, which he said he had hurt in shaving himself; it was hardly discernible, but alas! it contained the seeds of that dire disease, and from that moment kept spreading over his face with excruciating agony, which allowed him no repose, till it laid him in his grave.

By his refusal of Elphin, Doctor Oswald was promoted to an inferior bishopric, and my father thereby stood next upon the roll for a mitre: in the mean time, he formed his friendships in Ireland with some of the most respectable characters, and made a visit, accompanied by my mother, to Doctor Pocock, Bishop of Ossory, at his episcopal house at Kilkenny. That celebrated oriental traveller and author was a man of mild manners and primitive simplicity: having given the world a full detail of his researches in Egypt, he seemed to hold himself excused from saying anything more about them, and observed in general an obdurate taciturnity. In his carriage and deportment he appeared to have contracted something of the Arab character, yet there was no austerity in his silence, and though his air was solemn, his temper was serene. When we were on our road to Ireland, I saw from the windows of the inn at Daventry a cavalcade of horsemen approaching on a gentle trot, headed by an elderly chief in clerical attire, who was followed by five servants, at distances geometrically measured and most precisely maintained, and who, upon entering the inn, proved to be this distinguished prelate, conducting his horde with the phlegmatic patience of a scheik.

I found the state of society in Dublin very different from what I had observed in London: the professions more intermixed, and ranks more blended; in the great houses I met a promiscuous assembly of politicians, lawyers, soldiers and divines; the profusion of their tables struck me with surprise; nothing that I had seen in England could rival the Polish magnificence of Primate Stone, or the Parisian luxury of Mr. Clements. The style of Dodington was stately, but there was a watchful and well-regulated economy over all, that here seemed out of sight and out of mind. The professional gravity of character maintained by our English dignitaries was here laid aside, and in several prelatical houses the mitre was so mingled with the cockade, and the glass circulated so freely, that I perceived the spirit of conviviality was by no means excluded from the pale of the church of Ireland.

Primate Stone was at that time in the zenith of his power; he had a great following; his intellect was as strong as ever, but his constitution was in its wane. I had frequent occasions to resort to him, and much reason to speak highly of his candor and condescension. No man faced difficulties with greater courage, none overcame them with more address; he was formed to hold command over turbulent spirits in tempestuous seasons; for if he could not absolutely rule the passions of men, he could artfully rule men by the medium of their passions; he had great suavity of manners when points were to be carried by insinuation and finesse; but if authority was necessarily to be enforced, none could hold it with a higher hand: he was an elegant scholar, a consummate politician, a very fine gentleman, and in every character seen to more advantage than in that which, according to his sacred function, should have been his chief and only object to sustain.

Dr. Robinson was by Lord Halifax translated from the see of Ferns to that of Kildare. I had even then a presentiment that we were forwarding his advancement towards the primacy, and persuaded myself that the successor of Stone would be found in the person of the Bishop of Kildare. Of him I shall probably have occasion to speak more at large hereafter, for the acquaintance, which I had the honor to form with him at this time, was in the further course of it ripened into friendship and an intimacy which he never suffered to abate, and I prized too highly to neglect.

I made but one short excursion from Dublin, and this was to the house of that gallant officer Colonel Ford, who perished in his passage to India, and who was married to a relation of my wife. Having established his fame in the battle of Plassey and several other actions, he seated himself at Johnstown, in the centre of an inveterate bog, but the soil, such as it was, had the recommendation to him of being his native soil, and all its deformities vanished from his sight.

I had more than once the amusement of dining at the house of that most singular being, George Faulkner, where I found myself in a company so miscellaneously and whimsically classed, that it looked more like a fortuitous concourse of oddities, jumbled together from all ranks, orders, and descriptions, than the effect of invitation and design. Description must fall short in the attempt to convey any sketch of that eccentric being to those who have not read him in the notes of Jephson, or seen him in the mimicry of Foote, who, in his portraits of Faulkner, found the only sitter whom his extravagant pencil could not caricature; for he had a solemn intrepidity of egotism, and a daring contempt of absurdity, that fairly out-faced imitation, and like Garrick's ode on Shakspeare, which Johnson said 'defied criticism,' so did George, in the original spirit of his own perfect buffoonery, defy caricature. He never deigned to join in the laugh he had raised, nor seemed to have a feeling of the ridicule he had provoked: at the same time, that he was pre-eminently, and by preference, the butt and buffoon of the company, he could find openings and opportunities for hits of retaliation, which were such left-handed thrusts as few could parry: nobody could foresee where they would fall, nobody of course was fore-armed, and as there was in his calculation but one super-eminent character in the kingdom of Ireland, and he the printer of the 'Dublin Journal,' rank was no shield against George's arrows, which flew where he listed, and fixed or missed as chance directed, he cared not about consequences. He gave good meat and excellent claret in abundance; I sat at his table once from dinner till two in the morning, whilst George swallowed immense potations with one solitary sodden strawberry at the bottom of the glass, which he said was recommended to him by his doctor for its cooling properties. He never lost his recollection or equilibrium the whole time, and was in excellent foolery; it was a singular coincidence, that there was a person in company, who had received his reprieve at the gallows, and the very judge who had passed sentence of death upon him. This did not in the least disturb the harmony of the society, nor embarrass any human creature present. All went off perfectly smooth, and George, adverting to an original portrait of Dean Swift, which hung in his room, told us abundance of excellent and interesting anecdotes of the Dean and himself with minute precision and an importance irresistibly ludicrous. There was also a portrait of his late lady, Mrs. Faulkner, which either made the painter or George a liar, for it was frightfully ugly, whilst he swore she was the most divine object in creation. In the mean time, he took credit to himself for a few deviations in point of gallantry, and asserted that he broke his leg in flying from the fury of an enraged husband, whilst Foote constantly maintained that he fell down an area with a tray of meat upon his shoulder, when he was journeyman to a butcher: I believe neither of them spoke the truth. George prosecuted Foote for lampooning him on the stage of Dublin; his counsel, the prime-sergeant, compared him to Socrates, and his libeller to Aristophanes; this I believe was all that George got by his course of law; but he was told he had the best of the bargain in the comparison, and sat down contented under the shadow of his laurels. In process of time he became an alderman; I paid my court to him in that character, but I thought he was rather marred than mended by his dignity. George grew grave and sentimental, and sentiment and gravity sat as ill upon George, as a gown and a square cap would upon a monkey.

Mrs. Dancer,[1] then in her prime, and very beautiful, was acting with Barry at the Crow Street theatre, and Miss Elliot,[2] who had played in Mr. Bentley's 'Wishes,' came over with the recommendation of Mr. Arthur Murphy, who interested himself much in her success. This young uneducated girl had great

[1] This lady, says Taylor, was an excellent actress, both in tragedy and comedy. 'Her Rosalind was,' he adds, 'in my opinion, one of the most perfect performances I ever attended.'—*Records of my Life*, p. 64.

[2] Miss Elliott was of humble origin, and possessing the 'fatal gift' of beauty; she was betrayed into that unfortunate mode of life to which charms like hers too frequently lead. She was brought upon the stage by Murphy. 'He lived with her in a cottage near Richmond,' says Taylor, 'and she resided there while he went upon the circuit. Returning unexpectedly, on one of these occasions, he found a fine haunch of venison roasting at the fire. Upon inquiry, he found that the Earl of Bristol was a constant visitor to the lady, and expected to dine there that day. This circumstance put an end at once to the connection, and to his rural retirement. The lady at length lived under the protection of a member of the royal family, now deceased. Mr. Murphy never withdrew his countenance from her, and she was glad to retain so valuable a friend. At her desire, her royal admirer permitted Mr. Murphy to visit her when he was at home, and was much pleased with his conversation. Miss Elliott died in this situation, and such was her regard for Mr. Murphy, that she would have left the bulk of her property to him, but he declined it, and took care to secure it for her relations; of whom one, as far as I can recollect, was her sister. By all accounts she was one of the most original and spirited actresses that ever appeared on the stage.'—*Records of my Life*, p. 120.

natural talents, and played the part of Maria in her patron's farce of 'The Citizen,' with admirable spirit and effect. The whimsical mock-opera of Midas was first brought upon the Dublin stage in this season, and had all the protection which the castle patronage could bestow, and that could not be more than its pleasantry and originality deserved.

When the time for our departure was in near approach, the Lord Lieutenant expressed his wish that I would take the conduct of his daughters and the ladies of his family on their journey home, whilst he went forward, and would expect us at Bushey Park. Circumstanced as I was, I could not undertake the charge of his family without abandoning that of my own, which I did with the utmost regret, though my brother-in-law, Captain Ridge, kindly offered himself to conduct his sister and her infant to the place of their destination, and accordingly embarked with them in a packet for Holyhead some days before my departure. Painful as this parting was, I had yet the consolation of surrendering those objects of my affection to the care of him whom I would have chosen out of all men living for the trust. They were to repose for a few days at a house called Tyringham, within a short distance of Newport Pagnell, which I had taken of the heir of the Bakewell family. It was a large and venerable old mansion, situated on the banks of the Ouse, and had caught my eye as I was on my road to Ireland; understanding it was furnished, and to be let, I crossed the river, and in a few minutes' conversation with the steward agreed to take it, and in this I was in some degree biassed by the consideration of its near neighborhood to Lord Halifax, at Horton. It was a hasty bargain, but one of the cheapest ever made, and I had no occasion at any time after to repent of it.

When we arrived at Bushey Park, and I had surrendered my charge to Lord Halifax, I lost no further time, but hastened to my wife, who was then in Hampshire at her father's, where the children we left behind us had been kindly harbored; them indeed I found in perfect health, but that and every other joy attendant on my return was at once extinguished in the afflicting persuasion, that I had only arrived in time to take a last leave of my dying wife, who was then in the crisis of a most violent fever, exhausted, senseless, and scarce alive. Many florid writers would seize the opportunity of describing scenes of this sort; I shall decline it. It was my happy lot to see her excellent constitution surmount the shock, and to witness her recovery in her native air by the blessing of Providence and the unwearied attentions of her hospitable parents. As soon as she was re-established in her health, we removed with our children to

Tyringham, where my wife had left her infant fellow traveller in the care of an excellent young woman, who, from the day of our marriage to the day of her death, lived with me and my family, faithfully attached and strictly fulfilling every part of her duty.

A short time before Lord Halifax quitted the government of Ireland, in which he was succeeded by the Duke of Northumberland, a vacancy happened in the bench of bishops, and my father was promoted to the see of Clonfert. This vacancy fell so close upon the expiration of Lord Halifax's government, that great efforts were made and considerable interest exerted to wrest the nomination out of his Lordship's patronage, and throw it into the disposal of his successor; it was proposed to recompense my father by preferment of some other description; but this was firmly resisted by Lord Halifax, and the mitre was bestowed upon one, who wore it to the last hour of his life with unblemished reputation, honored, beloved, and I may say (almost without a figure) adored by the people of Ireland for his benevolence, his equity, his integrity, and every virtue that could make him dear to his fellow-creatures, and acceptable to his Creator.

The expectant, who, if I was rightly informed, would have obtained the bishopric of Clonfert in the event of my father's being deprived of it, has had reason to felicitate himself on his disappointment, if, as I just now observed, I am not mistaken in believing Dr. Markham was the person whose happy destiny sent my father to Ireland, and reserved him for better fortune at home, and higher dignities most worthily bestowed and most honorably enjoyed.

My father, in the mean time, had returned to his vicarage of Fulham, and sat down without repining at the issue of his expedition, which now seemed to close upon him without any prospect of success, when I hastened to impart to him the intelligence I had just received from Secretary Hamilton, whom I had accidentally crossed upon in Parliament Street. He received it in his calm manner, modestly remarking, that his talents were not turned to public life, nor did he foresee any material advantages likely to accrue to such as belonged to him from his promotion to an Irish bishopric; it was not consistent, he said, with his principles to avail himself of the patronage in that country to the exclusion of the clergy of his diocese, and of course he must deny himself the gratification of serving his friends and relations in England, if any such should solicit him. This did happen in more instances than one, and I can witness with what pain he withstood requests, which he would have been so happy to have complied with; but his conscience was a rule to him, and he never deviated from it in a single instance. He further observed, in the course of this conversation with me, what I have before noticed in my remarks upon Bishop Cumberland's appropriation of his episcopal revenue, and, alluding to that rule as laid down by his grandfather, expressed his approbation of it, and said, that though he could not aspire to the most distant comparison with him in greater matters, yet he trusted he should not be found degenerate in principle; and certainly he did not trust in himself without reason. In conclusion, he said, that having visited Ireland, and formed many pleasing and respectable connections there, he would quietly wait the event without embarrassing Lord Halifax with any solicitation, and when he thought he perceived me in a disposition to be not quite so tranquil and sedentary in the business, he positively forbade me to make any stir, or give Lord Halifax any trouble on his account—'You have shown your moderation,' added he, 'in declining the title that was offered to you; let me at least betray no eagerness in courting that, which may or may not devolve upon me. Had it not been for you, it would never have come under my contemplation; I should still have remained parson of Stanwick, but the same circumstances that have drawn you from your studies, have taken me from my solitude, and if you are thus zealous to transport me and your mother into another kingdom, I hope you will be not less solicitous to visit and console us with the sight of you, when we are there.'

I bless God I have not to reproach myself with neglecting this tender and paternal injunction. Not a year passed during my father's residence in Ireland that I did not happily devote some months of it to the fulfilment of this duty, always accompanied by my wife, and, with the exception of one time only, by some part of my young family.

In a few days after this conversation, I was authorized to announce to my father his nomination to the bishopric of Clonfert. He lost no time in arranging his affairs, and preparing for his departure with my mother and my younger sister, then unmarried. Lord Halifax, in the mean time, had received the Seals of Secretary of State; he had to name one Under Secretary, and his choice fell upon a gentleman of the name of Sedgewicke, who had attended upon him to Ireland in the capacity of Master of the Horse, and on this promotion vacated an employ, which he held in the office of Trade and Plantations under the denomination of Clerk of the Reports. He was a civil, mannerly, and, as far as suited him, an obsequious little gentleman; fond of business, and very busy in it, be it what it might; his training had been in office, and his education stamped his character with marks that could not be mistaken; he well knew how to follow up preferment to its source, and though the waters of that spring were not very pure, he drank devoutly at the fountain head, and was rewarded for his perseverance.

I could not be said to suffer any disappointment on the occasion of this gentleman's promotion; I had due warning of the alternative that presented itself to my choice. I had a holding on Lord Halifax, founded on my father's merits, and a long and faithful attachment on my own part; but, as I had hitherto kept the straight and fair track in following his fortunes, I would not consent to deviate into indirect roads, and disgrace myself in the eyes of his and my own connections, who would have marked my conduct with deserved contempt. In attending upon him to Ireland, I had the example of Dr. Crane to refer to; and I had his advice and approbation on this occasion for tendering my services when he received the seals as a point of duty, though not with any expectation of my tender being accepted. The answer was exactly what I looked to receive, cool in its terms, repulsive in its purport; *I was not fit for every situation.* Nothing could be more true; neither did I oppose a single word to the conviction it carried with it. In that, I acquiesced respectfully and silently; but I said a few words in thankful acknowledgment of the favor he had conferred upon my father, and for that which I had received in my own person, namely, the Crown-Agency of Nova Scotia. Perhaps he did not quite expect to have disposed of me with so little trouble to himself; for my manner seemed to waken some sensations, which led him to dilate a little on his motives for declining to employ me, inasmuch as I did not speak French. This also was not less true than his first remark, for as certainly as I was not fit for all situations, so surely was I unfit for this if speaking French fluently (though I understood it as a language) was a qualification not to be dispensed with; in short, I admitted this objection in its full force, well persuaded that if I had possessed the elegance and perfection of Voltaire himself in that language, I should not have been a step nearer to the office in question. When we know ourselves to be put aside for reasons that do not touch the character, but will not truly be revealed, we do well to acquiesce in the very first civil, though evasive apology that is passed upon us in the way of explanation.

Finding myself thus cast out of employ, and Mr. Sedgewicke in possession of his office, I began to think it might be worth my while to endeavor at succeeding him in his situation at the Board of Trade, and submit to follow him as he had once followed, and now passed me in this road to preferment. After above eleven years attendance, my profit was the sole attainment of a place of two hundred pounds per annum; my loss was that of the expense I had put my father to for my support and maintenance in a style of life very different from that in which I was found. This expense I had the consolation of being enabled to replace to my father upon the receipt of my wife's fortune; but by this act of justice and duty, so gratifying to my conscience, the balance upon £3,000, which was the portion allotted to Miss Ridge, was very inconsiderable when it reached me. I had already three children, and the prospect of an increasing family; my father's bishopric was not likely to benefit me, neither could it be considered as a compensation for my services, inasmuch as the past exertions of his influence and popularity in Northamptonshire might fairly give him a claim to a favor not less than that of appointing him second chaplain to Dr. Oswald, who was a perfect stranger to his lordship till introduced and recommended by his brother James. These considerations induced me to hope I could not be thought a very greedy or presumptuous expectant when I ventured to solicit him in competition with a gentleman who had only been in his immediate service as Master of the Horse for one session in Ireland; and at the same time they served as motives with me for endeavoring to succeed that gentleman, whose office, if I could obtain it, would be an addition to my income of two hundred per annum. The Earl of Hillsborough was the first Lord of Trade and Plantations, and, being an intimate friend of Lord Halifax, was, I presume, not indisposed towards me. I thereupon went to Bushey Park to wait upon Lord Halifax, and communicated to him the idea which had occurred to me of making suit for the office that Mr. Sedgewicke had vacated. He received this intimation in a manner that did not merely denote embarrassment; it made it doubtful to me whether he meant to take it up as matter of offence, or turn it off as matter of indifference. For some time, he seemed inclined to put an interpretation upon the measure proposed which certainly it could not bear, and to consider it as an abandonment on my part of a connection that had uninterruptedly subsisted for so many years. When a very few words on my part convinced him that this charge could not lie against me, he stated it in another view, as a degradation, which he was surprised I could think of submitting to after the situation I had stood in with respect to him; this was easily answered, and in terms that could not give offence. Thus, whilst I was guarding my expressions from any semblance of disgust, and his lordship was holding a language that could not come from his heart, we broke up the conference without any other decision than that of referring it to my own choice and discretion, as a measure he neither advised nor opposed.

As it was from this interview with the noble person to whom I had attached myself for so long a term of years, that my future line in life took a new direction, I could not pass it over in silence; but though my mind retains the memory of many particulars which, if my own credit only was at stake, I should be forward to relate, I shall forbear, convinced that when I lost the favor and protection of that noble person I had not forfeited his real good opinion. Of this truth, he survived to give, and I to receive proofs that could not be mistaken. I had known him too intimately not to know, in the very moment of which I have been speaking, that what he was by accident he was not by nature. I am persuaded he was formed to be a good man; he might also have been a great one. His mind was large, his spirit active, his ambition honorable; he had a carriage noble and imposing. His first approach attracted notice; his consequent address insured respect. If his talents were not quite so solid as some, nor altogether so deep as others, yet they were brilliant, popular, and made to glitter in the eyes of men; splendor was his passion. His good fortune threw opportunities in his way to have supported it; his ill fortune blasted all those energies which should have been reserved for the crisis of his public fame. The first offices of the state, the highest honors which his sovereign could bestow, were showered upon him, when the spring of his mind was broken; and his genius, like a vessel overloaded with treasure, but far gone in decay, was only precipitated to ruin by the very freight that in its better days would have crowned it with prosperity and riches.

I now addressed a letter to the Earl of Hillsborough, tendering my humble services in Mr. Sedgewicke's room, and was accepted without hesitation. Thus I entered upon an office, the duties of which consisted of taking minutes of the debates and proceedings at the Board, and preparing for their approbation and signature, such reports as they should direct to be drawn up for his Majesty, or the Council, and, on some occasions, for the Board of Treasury, or Secretaries of State. It was at most an office of no great labor, but as Mr. Pownall, now actual Secretary, was much in the habit of digesting these reports himself, my task was greatly lightened, and I had leisure to address myself to other studies, and indulge my propensities towards composition in whatever way they might incline me to employ them.

Bickerstaff[1] having at this time brought out his operas of 'Love in a Village' and 'The Maid of the Mill' with great suc-

[1] Bickerstaff was a native of Ireland, and was born about the year 1735. As a writer, he was very successful; but as a man, he had no claims to respect.

cess, some friends persuaded me to attempt a drama of that sort, and engaged Simpson, conductor of the band at Covent Garden and a performer on the hautboy, to compile the airs and adapt them to the stage. With very little knowledge of stage-effect, and as little forethought about plot, incident, or character, I sat down to write, and soon produced a thing in three acts, which I named the 'Summer's Tale,' though it was a tale about nothing and very indifferently told; however, being a vehicle for some songs, not despicably written, and some of these very well set, it was carried by my friends to Beard, then manager of the theatre, and accepted for representation. My friends, who were critics merely in music, took as little concern about revising the drama, as I took pains in writing it: they brought me the music of old songs, and I adapted words to it, and wove them into the piece, as I could. I saw, however, how very ill this plan was adapted for any credit that could be expected to accrue to me from my share in it, and to mark how little confidence I placed in the composition of the drama, I affixed as motto to the title page the following words: *Vox, et prœterea nihil.*—Abel furnished the overture, Bache, Doctor Arne and Arnold supplied some original compositions; Beard, Miss Brent (then in high reputation), Mr. and Mrs. Mattocks and Shuter filled the principal characters. It was performed nine or ten nights to moderate houses without opposition, and very deservedly without much applause, except what the execution of the vocal performers, and some brilliant compositions justly obtained; but even with these, it was rather overloaded, and was not sufficiently contrasted and relieved by familiar airs.

The fund for the support of decayed actors being then recently established by the company of Covent Garden Theatre, I appropriated the receipts of my ninth night to that benevolent institution, which the conductors were pleased to receive with much good will, and have honored me with their remembrance at their annual audits ever since.

The Summer's Tale was published by Mr. Dodsley, and as I received no complaint from him on account of the sale, I hope that liberal purchaser of the copy had no particular reason to be discontented with his bargain.

Bickerstaff, who had established himself in the public favor by the success of his operas above mentioned, seemed to consider me as an intruder upon his province, with whom he was to keep no terms, and he set all engines of abuse to work upon me and my poor drama, whilst it was yet in rehearsal, not repress-

He was compelled to flee his country, to escape punishment for crime, and died abroad, poor and despised.

ing his acrimony till it had been before the public; when to have discussed it in the spirit of fair criticism might have afforded him full matter of triumph, without convicting him of any previous malice or personality against an unoffending author. I was no sooner put in possession of the proofs against him, which were exceedingly gross, than I remonstrated by letter to him against his uncandid proceeding; I have no copy of that letter; I wish I had preserved it, as it would be in proof to show that my disposition to live in harmony with my contemporaries was, at my very outset as a writer for the stage, what it has uniformly been to the present hour, and that, although this attack was one of the most virulent and unfair ever made upon me, yet I no otherwise appealed against it, than by telling him 'that if his contempt of my performance was really what he professed it to be, he had no need to fear me as a rival, and might relax from his intemperance; on the contrary, if alarm for his own interest had any share in the motives for his animosity, I was perfectly ready to purchase his peace of mind and good-will by the sacrifice of those emoluments, which might eventually accrue from my nights, in any such way as might relieve his anxiety, and convince him of my entire disinterestedness in commencing author; adding, in conclusion, that he might assure himself he would never hear of me again as a writer of operas.' This I can perfectly recollect was the purport of my letter, which I dictated in the belief of what was reported to me as an apology for his conduct, and entirely ascribed his hostility to his alarm on the score of interest, and not to the evil temper of his mind. This was the interpretation I put upon what Mr. Bickerstaff had written of me, and my real motive for what I wrote to him: I understood he was wholly dependent on the stage, and that the necessity of his circumstances made him bitter against any one who stepped forward to divide the favor of the public with him. To insult his poverty, or presume on my advantage over him in respect of circumstances, was a thought that never found admission to my heart, nor did Bickerstaff himself so construe my letter, or suspect me of such baseness; for Mr. Garrick afterwards informed me that Bickerstaff showed this letter to him as an appeal to his feelings of such a nature, as ought to put him to silence; and when Mr. Garrick represented to him, that he also saw it in that light, he did not scruple to confess that his attack had been unfair, and that he should never repeat it against me or my productions. I led him into no further temptations, for whilst he continued to supply the stage with musical pieces, I turned my thoughts to dramas of another cast, and we interfered no longer with each other's labors.

One day as I was leaving the theatre after a rehearsal of the Summer's Tale, I was met by Mr. Smith, then engaged at Covent Garden, and whom I had known at the University, as an under-graduate of Saint John's College. We had of course some conversation, during which he had the kindness to remonstrate with me upon the business I was engaged in, politely saying, that I ought to turn my talents to compositions of a more independent and a higher character; predicting to me, that I should reap neither fame nor satisfaction in the operatic department, and demanding of me, in a tone of encouragement, why I would not rather aim at writing a good comedy, than dabbling in these sing-song pieces. The animating spirit of this friendly remonstrance, and the full persuasion that he predicted truly of the character and consequences of my undertaking then on foot, made a sensible impression on my mind, and in the warmth of the moment I formed my resolution to attempt the arduous project he had pointed out. If my old friend and contemporary ever reads this page, perhaps he can call to mind the conversation I allude to; though he has not the same reasons to keep in his remembrance this circumstance, as I have, who was the party favored and obliged, yet I hope he will at all events believe that I record it truly as to the fact, and gratefully for the effects of it. As his friend, I have lived with him, and shared his gentlemanly hospitality; as his author, I have witnessed his abilities, and profited by his support; and though I have lost sight of him ever since his retirement from the stage, yet I have ever retained at heart an interest in his welfare, and as he and I are too nearly of an age to flatter ourselves that we have any very long continuance to come upon the stage of this life, I beg leave to make this public profession of my sincere regard for him, and to pay the tribute of my plaudits now, before he makes his final exit, and the curtain drops.

Before I had ushered my melodious nonsense to the audience, I had clearly discovered the weakness of the tame and lifeless fable on which I had founded it; there were still some scenes between the characters of Henry and Amelia, which were tolerably conceived, and had preserved themselves a place in the good opinion of the audience by the simplicity of the style, and the address of Mrs. Mattocks and Mr. Dyer, to whom those parts were allotted. It was thereupon thought advisable to cut down the Summer's Tale to an after-piece of two acts, and exhibit it in the next season under the title of Amelia. In this state it stood its ground, and took its turn with very tolerable success 'behind the foremost and before the last.' Simpson published the music in a collection, and I believe he got home pretty well upon the sale of it. The good judges of that time thought it good music, but the better judges of this time would probably think it good for nothing.

In the summer of this year, as soon as the Board of Trade broke up for their usual recess, I went with my wife and part of my young family to pay my duty and fulfil my promise to my father and mother in Ireland. They waited for us in Dublin, where my father had taken the late Bishop of Meath's house in Kildare Street, next door to the Duke of Leinster's. When we had reposed ourselves for a few days, after the fatigues of a turbulent passage, we all set off for Clonfert in the county of Galway. Everybody who has travelled in Ireland, and witnessed the wretched accommodation of the inns, particularly in the west, knows that it requires some forecast and preparation to conduct a large family on their journey. It certainly is as different from travelling in England as possible, and not much unlike travelling in Spain; but with my father for our provider, whose appointments of servants and equipage were ever excellent, we could feel few wants, and arrived in good time at our journey's end, where, upon the banks of the great river Shannon, in a nook of land, on all sides, save one, surrounded by an impassable bog, we found the episcopal residence, by courtesy called palace, and the Church of Clonfert, by custom called cathedral. This humble residence was not devoid of comfort and convenience, for it contained some tolerable lodging rooms, and was capacious enough to receive me and mine without straitening the family. A garden of seven acres, well planted and disposed into pleasant walks, kept in the neatest order, was attached to the house, and at the extremity of a broad gravel walk in front stood the cathedral. Within this boundary the scene was cheerful; all without it was either impenetrable bog, or a dreary undressed country; but whilst all was harmony, hospitality and affection underneath the parental roof, 'the mind was its own place,' and every hour was happy. My father lived, as he had ever done, beloved by all around him; the same benevolent and generous spirit, which had endeared him to his neighbors and parishioners in England, now began to make the like impressions on the hearts of a people as far different in character, as they were distant in place, from those whom he had till now been concerned with. Without descending from the dignity he had to support, and condescending to any of the paltry modes of courting popularity, I instantly perceived how high he stood in their esteem; these observations I was perfectly in the way to make, for I had no forms to keep, and was withal uncommonly delighted with their wild eccentric humors, mixing with all ranks and descriptions of men, to my infinite amusement. If I have been successful in my dramatic sketches of the Irish character, it was here I studied it in its purest and most primitive state; from high to low it was now under my view. Though I strove to present it in its fairest and best light upon the stage, truth obliges me to confess there was another side of the picture, which could not have been contemplated without affright and horror! Atrocities and violences, which set all law and justice at defiance, were occasionally committed in this savage and licentious quarter, and suffered to pass over with impunity. In the neighboring town of Eyre Court, they had by long usage assumed to themselves certain local and self-constituted privileges and exemptions, which rendered it unapproachable by any officers or emissaries of the civil power, who were universally denounced as mad dogs, and subjected to be treated as such, and even put to death with as little ceremony or remorse. I speak of what actually occurred within my own immediate knowledge, whilst I resided with my father, in more instances than one, and those instances would be shocking to relate. To stem these daring outrages, and to stand in opposition to these barbarous customs, was an undertaking that demanded both philanthropy and courage, and my father of course was the very man to attempt it. Justice and generosity were the instruments he employed, and I saw the work of reformation so auspiciously begun, and so steadily pursued by him, as convinced me that minds the most degenerate may be to a degree reclaimed by actions, that come home to their feelings, and are evidently directed to the sole purposes of amending their manners, and improving their condition. To suppose they were a race of beings stupidly vicious, devoid of sensibility, and delivered over by their natural inertness to barbarism and ignorance, would be the very falsest character that could be conceived of them; it is, on the contrary, to the quickness of their apprehensive faculties, to the precipitancy and unrestrained vivacity of their talents and passions, that we must look for the causes, and in some degree for the excuse of their excesses; together with their ferocious propensities there are blended and compounded humors so truly comic, eccentricities so peculiar, and attachments and affections at times so inconceivably ardent that it is not possible to contemplate them in their natural characters without being diverted by extravagances which we cannot seriously approve, and captivated by professions which we cannot implicitly give credit to.

The bishop held a considerable parcel of land, arable and grazing, in his hands, or more properly speaking in the phrase of the country, a large demesne, with a numerous tribe of laborers, gardeners, turf-cutters, herdsmen and handicraft-men of various denominations. His first object, and that not an easy one to attain, was to induce them to pursue the same methods of husbandry as were practised in England, and to observe the same neat and cleanly course of cultivation. This was a great point gained; they began it with unwillingness, and watched it with suspicion: their idle neighbors, who were without employ, ridiculed the work, and predicted that their hay-stacks would take fire, and their corn be rendered unfit for use; but in the further course of time, when they experienced the advantages of this process, and witnessed the striking contrast of these productive lands, compared with the slovenly grounds around them, they began to acknowledge their own errors and to reform them. With these operations the improvements of their own habitations were contrived to keep pace; their cabins soon wore a more comfortable and decent appearance; they furnished them with chimneys, and emerged out of the smoke, in which. they had buried and suffocated their families and themselves. When these old habits were corrected within doors, on the outside of every one of them there was to be seen a stack of hay, made in the English fashion, thatched and secured from the weather, and a lot of potatoes carefully planted and kept clean, which, with a suitable proportion of turf, secured the year's provision both for man and beast. When these comforts were placed in their view, they were easily led to turn their attention to the better appearance of their persons, and this reform was not a little furthered by the premium of a Sunday's dinner to all, who should present themselves in clean linen and with well-combed hair, without the customary addition of a scare-crow wig, so that the swarthy Milesian no longer appeared with a yellow wig upon his coal-black hair, nor the yellow Dane with a coal-black wig upon his long red locks: the old barbarous custom also of working in a great coat loosely thrown over the shoulders, with the sleeves dangling by the sides, was now dismissed, and the bishop's laborers turned into the field, stripped to their shirts, proud to show themselves in whole linen, so that in them vanity operated as a virtue, and piqued them to excel in industry as much as they did in appearance. As for me, I was so delighted with contemplating a kind of new creation, of which my father was the author, that I devoted the greatest portion of my time to his works, and had full powers to prosecute his good intentions to whatever extent I might find opportunities for carrying them. This commission was to me most gratifying, nor have any hours in my past life been more truly satisfactory, than those in which I was thus occupied as the administrator of his unbounded benevolence to his dependent fellow creatures. My father being one of the governors of the Linen Board, availed himself also of the opportunity for introducing a branch of that valuable manufacture in his neighborhood, and a great number of spinning-wheels were distributed, and much good linen made in consequence of that measure. The superintendence of this improving manufacture furnished an interesting occupation to my mother's active mind, and it flourished under her care.

In the month of October my father removed his family to Dublin, and from thence I returned to resume my official duty at the Board of Trade. In the course of this winter I brought out my first comedy, entitled 'The Brothers,' at Covent Garden theatre, then under the direction of Mr. Harris and his associates, joint proprietors with him. I had written this play, after my desultory manner, at such short periods of time and leisure, as I could snatch from business or the society of my family, and sometimes even in the midst of both, for I could then form whole scenes in my memory, and afterwards write them down when opportunity afforded; neither was it any interruption, if my children were playing about me in the room. I believe I was indebted to Mr. Harris singly for the kind reception which this offer met; for if I rightly remember what passed on that occasion, my Brothers were not equally acceptable to his brethren as to him. He took it, however, with all its responsibility, supported it, and cast it with the best strength of his company. Woodward in the part of Ironsides, and Yates in that of Sir Benjamin Dove, were actors that could keep their scene alive, if any life was in it. Quick, then a young performer, took the part of Skiff, and my friend Smith, who had prompted me to the undertaking, was the young man of the piece; Mrs. Green performed Lady Dove, and Mrs. Yates was the heroine Sophia.

The play was successful, and I believe I may say that it brought some advantage to the theatre as well as some reputation to its author. It has been much played on the provincial stages, and occasionally revived on the royal ones. There are still such excellent successors in the lines of Yates and Woodward to be found in both theatres, that perhaps it would not even now be a loss of labor, if they took it up afresh. I recollect that I borrowed the hint of Sir Benjamin's assumed valor, upon being forced into a rencounter, from one of the old comedies, and if I conjecture rightly, it is 'The Little French Lawyer.' It may be said of this comedy, as it may of most, it has some merits and some faults; it has its scenes that tell, and its scenes that tire; a start of character, such as that of the tame Sir Benjamin, is always a striking incident in the construction of a drama, and when a revolution of that sort can be brought about without violence to nature, and for purposes essential to the plot, it is a point of art well worthy the attention and study of a writer for the stage. The comedy of 'Rule a Wife and have a Wife,' and particularly that of Massinger's 'City Madam,' are strong instances in point. It is to be wished that some man of experience in stage effect would adapt the latter of these comedies to representation.

Garrick was in the house at the first night of 'The Brothers,' and as I was planted in the back seat of an upper box, opposite to where he sat, I could not but remark his action of surprise when Mrs. Yates opened the epilogue with the following lines:—

'Who but hath seen the celebrated strife,
Where Reynolds calls the canvas into life,
And 'twixt the tragic and the comic muse,
Courted of both, and dubious where to choose,
Th' immortal actor stands—?'

My friend Fitzherbert, father of Lord St. Helen, was then with Garrick, and came from his box to me across the house, to tell me that the immortal actor had been taken by surprise, but was not displeased with the unexpected compliment from an author with whom he had supposed he did not stand upon the best terms; alluding no doubt to his transaction with Lord Halifax respecting 'The Banishment of Cicero.' From this time Mr. Garrick took pains to cultivate an acquaintance, which he had hitherto neglected, and after Mr. Fitzherbert had brought us together at his house, we interchanged visits, and it is nothing more than natural to confess I was charmed with his company and flattered by his attentions. I had a house in Queen Ann Street, and he then lived in Southampton Street, Covent Garden, where I frequently went to him and sometimes accompanied him to his pleasant villa at Hampton. In the mean time, whilst I was thus fortunate in conciliating to myself one eminent person by my epilogue, I soon discovered to my regret how many I had offended by my prologue. A host of newspaper writers fell upon me for the pertness and general satire of that incautious composition, and I found myself assailed from various quarters with unmitigated acrimony. I made no defence, and the only one I had to make would hardly have brought me off, for I could have opposed nothing to their charge against me, but the simple and sincere assertion that I alluded personally to no man, and being little versed in the mock modesty of modern addresses to the audience, took the old style of prologue for my model, and put a bold countenance upon a bold adventure. Numerous examples were before me of prologues arrogant in the extreme; Johnson abounds in such instances, but I did not advert sufficiently to the change, which time had wrought in the circumstances of the dramatic poet, and how much it behoved him to lower his tone in the hearing of his audience: neither did Smith, who was speaker of the prologue, and an experienced actor, warn me of any danger in the lines he undertook to deliver. In short, mine was the error of inexperience, and their efforts to rebuff me only gave a fresh spring to my exertions, for I can truly say, that, although I have been annoyed by detraction, it never had the property of depressing me. I was silly enough to send this comedy into the world with a dedication to the Duke of Grafton, a man with whom I had not the slightest acquaintance, nor did I seek to establish any upon the merit of this address; he was Chancellor of the University of Cambridge, and this was my sole motive for inscribing my first comedy to him. As for the play itself, whilst the prologue and the prologue's author run the gauntlet, that kept possession of the stage, and Woodward and Yates lost no credit by the support they gave it.

I will not trouble the reader with many apologies or appeals, yet just now, whilst I am beginning to introduce a long list of dramas, such as I presume no English author has yet equalled in point of number, I would fain intercede for a candid interpretation of my labors, and recommend my memory to posterity for protection after death from those unhandsome cavils, which I have patiently endured whilst living.

I am not to learn that dramatic authors are to arm themselves with fortitude before they take a post so open to attack; they, who are to act in the public eye, and speak in the public ear, have no right to expect a very smooth and peaceful career. I have had my full share of success, and I trust I have paid my tax for it always without mutiny, and very generally without murmuring. I have never irritated the town by making a sturdy stand against their opposition, when they have been pleased to point it against any one of my productions; I never failed to withdraw myself on the very first intimation that I was unwelcome, and the only offence I have been guilty of is, that I have not always thought the worse of a composition only because the public did not think well of it. I solemnly protest that I have never written, or caused to be written, a single line to puff and praise myself, or to decry a brother dramatist, since I had life; of all such anonymous and mean manœuvres I am clearly innocent and proudly disdainful; I have stood firm for the corps, into which I enrolled myself, and never disgraced my colors by abandoning the cause of the legitimate comedy, to whose service I am sworn, and in whose defence I have kept the field for nearly half a century, till at last I have survived all true national taste, and lived to see buffoonery, spectacle, and puerility so effectually triumphant, that now to be repulsed from the stage is to be recommended to the closet, and to be applauded by the theatre is little else than a passport to the puppet-show. I only say what everybody knows to be true; I do not write from personal motives, for I have no more cause for complaint than is common to many of my brethren of the corps. It is not my single misfortune to have been accused of vanity, which I did not feel, of satires, which I did not write, and of invectives, which I disdained even to meditate. It stands recorded of me in a review to this hour, that on the first night of 'The School for Scandal' I was overheard in the lobby endeavoring to decry and cavil at that excellent comedy. I gave my accuser proof positive, that I was at Bath during the time of its first run, never saw it during its first season, and exhibited my pocket-journal in confirmation of my alibi; the gentleman was convinced of my innocence, but as he had no opportunity of correcting his libel, everybody that read it remains convinced of my guilt.[1] Now, as none who ever heard my name, will fail to suppose I must have said what is imputed to me in bitterness of heart, not from defect in head, this false aspersion of my character was cruel and injurious in the extreme. I hold it right to explain that the reviewer I am speaking of has been long since dead.

[1] It was said, and reported to Sheridan, that while the whole house was convulsed with laughter, during the representation of the School for Scandal, Cumberland never smiled, nor relaxed a feature. Sheridan replied that there was some ingratitude in Cumberland's refusal to laugh at his comedy, since he had laughed at one of his tragedies from beginning to end. This tale appeared in print, and hence Cumberland's denial. It is supposed that Sheridan intended the character of Sir Fretful Plagiary, in 'The Critic,' for Cumberland, but the latter, unmindful of the supposition, invariably speaks in terms of respect of Sheridan's talents.

'Cumberland,' says Taylor, 'came one night to Mr. Sheridan's box in the theatre, somewhat late, and stumbled at the entrance. Mr. Sheridan sprang forward and assisted him. 'Ah! sir,' said Cumberland, 'you are the only man to assist a *falling* author.' Mr. Sheridan, in waggery or forgetfulness, said: '*Rising*, you mean,' the very words which Mr. Sheridan has assigned to Sir Fretful Plagiary, in 'The Critic,' a character commonly understood to be drawn for Mr. Cumberland.'—*Records of my Life*, p. 328.

In the ensuing year I again paid a visit to my father at Clonfert, and there, in a little closet at the back of the palace, as it was called, unfurnished and out of use, with no other prospect from my single window but that of a turf-stack, with which it was almost in contact, I seated myself by choice, and began to plan and compose 'The West-Indian.'

As the writer for the stage is a writer to the passions, I hold it matter of conscience and duty in the dramatic poet to reserve his brightest coloring for the best characters, to give no false attractions to vice and immorality, but to endeavor, as far as is consistent with that contrast, which is the very essence of his art, to turn the fairer side of human nature to the public, and, as much as in him lies, to contrive so as to put men into good humor with one another. Let him, therefore, in the first place, strive to make worthy characters amiable, but take great care not to make them insipid; if he does not put life and spirit into his man or woman of virtue, and render them entertaining as well as good, their morality is not a whit more attractive than the morality of a Greek chorus. He had better have let them alone altogether.

Congreve, Farquhar, and some others have made vice and villany so playful and amusing, that either they could not find in their hearts to punish them, or not caring how wicked they were, so long as they were witty, paid no attention to what became of them: Shadwell's comedy is little better than a brothel. Poetical justice, which has armed the tragic poet with the weapons of death, and commissioned him to wash out the offence in the blood of the offender, has not left the comic writer without his instruments of vengeance; for surely, if he knows how to employ the authority that is in him, the scourge of ridicule alone is sharp enough for the chastisement of any crimes, which can fall within his province to exhibit. A true poet knows that, unless he can produce works whose fame will outlive him, he will outlive both his works and his fame; therefore, every comic author who takes the mere clack of the day for his subject, and abandons all his claims upon posterity, is no true poet; if he dabbles in personalities, he does considerably worse. When I began, therefore, as at this time, to write for the stage, my ambition was to aim at writing something that might be lasting and outlive me; when temporary subjects were suggested to me, I declined them: I formed to myself in idea what I conceived to be the character of a legitimate comedy, and that alone was my object, and though I did not quite aspire to attain, I was not altogether in despair of approaching it. I perceived that I had fallen upon a time when great eccentricity of character was pretty nearly gone by, but still I fancied there was an opening for some originality, and an opportunity for showing at least my good-will to mankind, if I introduced the characters of persons who had been usually exhibited on the stage, as the butts for ridicule and abuse, and endeavored to present them in such lights as might tend to reconcile the world to them, and them to the world. I thereupon looked into society for the purpose of discovering such as were the victims of its national, professional, or religious prejudices; in short, for those suffering characters which stood in need of an advocate, and out of these I meditated to select and form heroes for my future dramas, of which I would study to make such favorable and reconciliatory delineations, as might incline the spectators to look upon them with pity, and receive them into their good opinion and esteem.

With this project in my mind, and nothing but the turf-stack to call off my attention, I took the characters of an Irishman and a West Indian for the heroes of my plot, and began to work it out into the shape of a comedy. To the West Indian I devoted a generous spirit, and a vivacious giddy dissipation; I resolved he should love pleasure much, but honor more; but as I could not keep consistency of character without a mixture of failings, when I gave him charity, I gave him that which can cover a multitude, and thus protected, thus recommended, I thought I might send him out into the world to shift for himself.

For my Irishman I had a scheme rather more complicated; I put him into the Austrian service, and exhibited him in the livery of a foreign master, to impress upon the audience the melancholy and impolitic alternative, to which his religious disqualification had reduced a gallant and a loyal subject of his natural king: I gave him courage, for it belongs to his nation; I endowed him with honor, for it belongs to his profession, and I made him proud, jealous, susceptible, for such the exiled veteran will be, who lives by the earnings of his sword, and is not allowed to draw it in the service of that country which gave him birth, and which of course he was born to defend: for his phraseology I had the glossary ready at my hand; for his mistakes and trips, vulgarly called bulls, I did not know the Irishman of the stage then existing, whom I would wish to make my model: their gross absurdities, and unnatural contrarieties have not a shade of character in them. When his imagination is warmed, and his ideas rush upon him in a cluster, 'tis then the Irishman will sometimes blunder; his fancy having supplied more words than his tongue can well dispose of, it will occasionally trip. But the imitation must be delicately conducted; his meaning is clear, he conceives rightly, though in delivery he is confused; and the art, as I conceive it, of finding language for the Irish character on the stage consists not in making him foolish, vulgar, or absurd, but, on the contrary, whilst you furnish him with expressions that excite laughter, you must graft them upon sentiments that deserve applause.

In all my hours of study, it has been through life my object so to locate myself as to have little or nothing to distract my attention, and therefore brilliant rooms or pleasant prospects I have ever avoided. A dead wall, or, as in the present case, an Irish turf-stack, are not attractions, that can call off the fancy from its pursuits; and whilst in those pursuits it can find interest and occupation, it wants no outward aids to cheer it. My mother, who had a fellow-feeling with me in these sensations, used occasionally to visit me in this hiding hole, and animated me with her remarks upon the progress of my work: my father was rather inclined to apologize for the meanness of my accommodation, and I believe rather wondered at my choice: in the mean time, I had none of those incessant avocations which forever crossed me in the writing of 'The Brothers.' I was master of my time, my mind was free, and I was happy in the society of the dearest friends I had on earth. In parents, sister, wife and children, greater blessings no man could enjoy. The calls of office, the cavillings of angry rivals, and the jibings of newspaper critics could not reach me on the banks of the Shannon, where all within doors was love and affection, all without was gratitude and kindness devolved on me through the merits of my father. In no other period of my life have the same happy circumstances combined to cheer me in any of my literary labors.

During an excursion of a few days upon a visit to Mr. Talbot, of Mount Talbot, a very respectable and worthy gentleman in those parts, I found a kind of hermitage in his pleasure grounds, where I wrote some few scenes, and my amiable host was afterwards pleased to honor the author of the West Indian with an inscription, affixed to that building, commemorating the use that had been made of it; a piece of elegant flattery very elegantly expressed.

On this visit to Mr. Talbot I was accompanied by Lord Eyre, of Eyre Court, a near neighbor and friend of my father. This noble lord, though pretty far advanced in years, was so correctly indigenous as never to have been out of Ireland in his life, and not often so far from Eyre Court as in this tour to Mr. Talbot's. Proprietor of a vast extent of soil, not very productive, and inhabiting a spacious mansion, not in the best repair, he lived according to the style of the country with more hospitality than elegance: whilst his table groaned with abundance, the order and good taste of its arrangement were little thought of: the slaughtered ox was hung up whole, and the hungry servitor supplied himself with his dole of flesh, sliced from off the carcass. His lordship's day was so apportioned as to give the afternoon by much the larger share of it, during which, from an early dinner to the hour of rest, he never left his chair, nor did the claret ever quit the table. This did not produce inebriety, for it was sipping rather than drinking that filled up the time, and this mechanical process of gradually moistening the human clay was carried on with very little aid from conversation, for his lordship's companions were not very communicative, and fortunately he was not very curious. He lived in an enviable independence as to reading, and of course he had no books. Not one of the windows of his castle was made to open, but luckily he had no liking for fresh air, and the consequence may be better conceived than described.

He had a large and handsome pleasure-boat on the Shannon, and men to row it. I was of two or three parties with him on that noble water as far as to Pertumna, the then deserted castle of the Lord Clanrickarde; upon one of these excursions, we were hailed by a person from the bank, who somewhat rudely called us to take him over to the other side. The company in the boat making no reply, I inadvertently called out: 'Ay, ay, sir! Stay there till we come.' Immediately, I heard a murmur in the company, and Lord Eyre said to me: 'You'll hear from that gentleman again, or I am mistaken. You don't know perhaps that you have been answering one of the most irritable men alive, and the likeliest to interpret what you have said as an affront.' He predicted truly, for the very next morning the gentleman rode over to Lord Eyre, and demanded of him to give up my name; this his lordship did, but informed him withal that I was a stranger in the country, the son of Bishop Cumberland, at Clonfert, where I might be found if he had any commands for me. He instantly replied, that he should have received it as an affront from any other man; but Bishop Cumberland's was a character he respected, and no son of his could be guilty of an intention to insult him. Thus, this valiant gentleman permitted me to live, and only helped me to another feature in my sketch of Major O'Flaherty.

A short time after this, Lord Eyre, who had a great passion for cock-fighting, and whose cocks were the crack of all Ireland, engaged me in a main at Eyre Court. I was a perfect novice in that elegant sport; but the gentlemen from all parts sent me in their contributions, and, having a good feeder, I won every battle in the main but one. At this meeting, I fell in with my hero from the Shannon bank. Both parties dined together; but when I found that mine, which was the more numerous, and infinitely the most obstreperous and disposed to quarrel, could no longer be left in peace with our antagonists, I quitted my seat by Lord Eyre, and went to the gentleman above alluded to, who was presiding at the second table, and, seating myself familiarly on the arm of his chair, proposed to him to adjourn our party, and assemble them in another house, for the sake of harmony and good fellowship. With the best grace in life, he instantly assented; and when I added that I should put them under his care, and expect from him, as a man of honor and my friend, that every mother's son of them should be found forthcoming and alive the next morning, 'Then, by the soul of me,' he replied, 'and they shall, provided only that no man in company shall dare to give *the glorious and immortal memory* for his toast, which no gentleman who feels as I do will put up with.' To this, I pledged myself, and we removed to a whiskey-house, attended by half a score pipers, playing different tunes; here we went on very joyously and lovingly for a time, till a well-dressed gentleman entered the room, and, civilly accosting me, requested to partake of our festivity, and join the company, if nobody had an objection. 'Ah, now, don't be too sure of that!' a voice was instantly heard to reply; 'I believe you will find plenty of objection in this company to your being one amongst us.' What had he done, the gentleman demanded. 'What have you done?' rejoined the first speaker. 'Don't I know you for the miscreant that ravished the poor wench against her will in presence of her mother? And didn't your Pagans that held her down ravish the mother afterwards in presence of her daughter? And do you think we will admit you into our company? Make yourself sure that we shall not; therefore, *get out of this* as speedily as you can, and away wid you!' Upon this, the whole company rose; and in their rising the civil gentleman made his exit, and was off. I relate this incident exactly as it happened, suppressing the name of the gentleman, who was a man of property and some consequence. When my surprise had subsided, and the punch began to circulate with a rapidity the greater for this gentleman's having troubled the waters, I took my departure, having first cautioned a friend who sat by me (and the only Protestant in the company) to keep his head cool, and beware of the *glorious memory*. This gallant young officer, son to a man who held lands of my father, promised faithfully to be sober and discreet, as well knowing the company he was in; but my friend, having forgot the first part of his promise, and getting very tipsy, let the second part slip out of his memory, and became very mad, for stepping aside for his pistols, he re-entered the room, and, laying them on the table, took the cockade from his hat and dashed it into the punch-bowl, demanding of the company to drink *the glorious and immortal memory of King William* in a bumper, or abide the consequences. I was not there; and if I had been present I could neither have stayed the tumult nor described it. I only know he turned out the next morning merely for honor's sake; but as it was one against a host, the magnanimity of his opponents let him off with a shot or two that did no execution. I returned to the peaceful family at Clonfert, and fought no more cocks.

The fairies were extremely prevalent at Clonfert. Visions of burials, attended by long processions of mourners, were seen to circle the churchyard by night; and there was no lack of oaths and attestations to enforce the truth of it. My mother suffered a loss by them of a large brood of fine turkeys, who were every one burnt to ashes, bones and feathers, and their dust scattered in the air by their provident nurse and feeder to appease those mischievous little beings, and prevent worse consequences. The good dame credited herself very highly for this act of atonement; but my mother did not see it quite in so meritorious a light.

A few days after, as my father and I were riding in the grounds, we crossed upon the Catholic priest of the parish. My father began a conversation with him, and expressed a wish that he would caution his flock against this idle superstition of the fairies; the good man assured the bishop that in the first place he could not do it if he would, and in the next place confessed that he himself was far from being an unbeliever in their existence. My father thereupon turned the subject, and observed to him with concern that his steed was a very sorry one, and in very wretched condition. 'Truly, my good lord,' he replied, 'the beast himself is but an ugly garron, and, whereby I have no provender to spare him, mightily out of heart, as I may truly say; but your lordship must think a poor priest like me has a mighty deal of work, and very little pay.' 'Why, then, brother,' said my good father, whilst benevolence beamed in his countenance, ''tis fit that I, who have the advantage of you in both respects, should mount you on a better horse, and furnish you with provender to maintain him.' This parley with the priest passed in the very hayfield where the bishop's people were at work. Orders were instantly given for a stack of hay to be made at the priest's cabin; and in a few days after a steady horse was purchased and presented to him. Surely, they could not be true born Irish fairies that would spite my father, or even his turkeys after this.

Amongst the laborers in my father's garden there were three brothers of the name of O'Rourke, regularly descended from the kings of Connaught, if they were exactly to be credited for the correctness of their genealogy. There was also an elder brother of these, Thomas O'Rourke, who filled the superior station of hind, or headman; it was his wife that burnt the bewitched turkeys, whilst Tom burnt his wig for joy of my victory at the cock-match, and threw a proper parcel of oatmeal into the air as a votive offering for my glorious success. One of the younger brothers was upon crutches in consequence of a contusion on his hip, which he literally acquired as follows: When my father came down to Clonfert from Dublin, it was announced to him that the bishop was arrived: the poor fellow was then in the act of lopping a tree in the garden; transported at the tidings, he exclaimed: 'Is my lord come? Then I'll throw myself out of this same tree for joy.' He exactly fulfilled his word, and laid himself up for some months.

When I accompanied my mother from Clonfert to Dublin, my father having gone before, we passed the night at Killbeggan, where Sir Thomas Cuffee (knighted in a frolic by Lord Townshend) kept the inn. A certain Mr. Geoghegan was extremely drunk, noisy and brutally troublesome to Lady Cuffee the hostess: Thomas O'Rourke was with us, and being much scandalized with the behavior of Geoghegan, took me aside, and in a whisper said: 'Squire, will I quiet this same Mr. Geoghegan?' When I replied by all means, but how was it to be done?—Tom produced a knife of formidable length and demanded—'Haven't I got this? And won't this do the job, and hasn't he wounded the woman of the inn with a chopping knife, and what is this but a knife, and wouldn't it be a good deed to put him to death like a mad dog? Therefore, Squire, do you see, if it will pleasure you and my lady there above stairs, who is ill enough, God he knows, I'll put this knife into that same Mr. Geoghegan's ribs, and be off the next moment on the gray mare; and isn't she in the stable? Therefore only say the word, and I'll do it.' This was the true and exact proposal of Thomas O'Rourke, and, as nearly as I can remember, I have stated it in his very words.

We arrived safe in Dublin, leaving Mr. Geoghegan to get sober at his leisure, and dismissing O'Rourke to his quarters at Clonfert. When we had passed a few days in Kildare Street, I well remember the surprise it occasioned us one afternoon, when, without any notice, we saw a great gigantic dirty fellow walk into the room and march straight up to my father, for what purpose we could not devise. My mother uttered a scream, whilst my father with perfect composure addressed him by the name of Stephen, demanding what he wanted with him, and what brought him to Dublin—'Nay, my good lord,' replied the man, 'I have no other business in Dublin itself but to take a bit of a walk up from Clonfert to see your sweet face, long life to it, and to beg a blessing upon me from your lordship; that is all.' So saying, he flounced down on his knees, and, in a most piteous kind of howl, closing his hands at the same time, cried out—'Pray, my lord, pray to God to bless Stephen Costello.' The scene was sufficiently ludicrous to have spoiled the solemnity, yet my father kept his countenance, and gravely gave his blessing, saying, as he laid his hands on his head—'God bless you, Stephen Costello, and make you a good boy!' The giant sung out a loud amen, and arose, declaring he should immediately set out and return to his home. He would accept no refreshment, but with many thanks and a thousand blessings in recompense for the one he had received, walked out of the house, and I can well believe, resumed his pilgrimage to the westward without stop or stay. I should not have considered this and the preceding anecdotes as worth recording, but that they are in some degree characteristic of a very curious and peculiar people, who are not often understood by those who profess to mimic them, and who are too apt to set them forth as objects for ridicule only, when oftentimes even their oddities, if candidly examined, would entitle them to our respect.

I will here mention a very extraordinary honor, which the city of Dublin was pleased to confer upon my father in presenting him with his freedom in a gold box; a form of such high respect as they had never before observed towards any person below the rank of their chief governor: I state this last-mentioned circumstance from authorities that ought not to be mistaken; if the fact is otherwise, I have been misinformed, and the honor conferred upon the Bishop of Clonfert was not without a precedent. The motives assigned in the deed which accompanied the box, are in general for the great respectability of his character, and in particular for his disinterested protection of the Irish clergy. Under this head it was supposed they alluded to the benefice, which he had bestowed upon a most deserving clergyman, his own particular friend and chaplain, the Reverend Dixie Blondel, who happened also to be at that time chaplain to the Lord Mayor of Dublin. I have the box at this time in my possession.

To the same merits, which influenced the city to bestow this distinguished honor on my father, I must ascribe that which I received from the University of Dublin, by the honorary grant of the degree of Doctor of Laws. Upon this I have only to observe that to be within the sphere of my father's good name, was to me at once a security against danger and a recommendation to favor and reward.

CHAPTER IV.

The West Indian—Garrick—Vindication of Dr. Bentley—Pride—Duke of Alva—The Rev. Mr. Reynolds—Neis Nill Society—Garrick—Reynolds—Johnson—Jenyns—Anecdote of Garrick—Foote—Anecdote of Thomas Mills—The Fashionable Lover—Anonymous defamation—Oliver Goldsmith—Dr. Johnson—Goldsmith's comedies—Retaliation, Goldsmith's poems—Bishop Cumberland, transferred to Kilmore—Death of—The choleric man—Mrs. Abington—Henderson—Death of the Earl of Halifax—Lord George Germain—Cumberland's promotion.

When I returned to England I entered into an engagement with Mr. Garrick to bring out 'The West Indian' at his theatre. I had received fair and honorable treatment from Mr. Harris, and had not the slightest cause of complaint against him, his brother patentees or his actors. I had, however, no engagement with him, nor had he signified to me his wish or expectation of any such in future. If, notwithstanding, the obligation was honorably such, as I was not free to depart from, in which light I am pretty sure he regarded it, my conduct was no otherwise defensible than as it was not intentionally unfair. My acquaintance with Mr. Garrick had become intimacy between the acting of the 'Brothers' and the acceptance of the 'West Indian.' I resorted to him again and again with the manuscript of my comedy; I availed myself of his advice, of his remarks, and I was neither conscious of doing what was wrong in me to do, nor did any remonstrance ever reach me to apprise me of my error.

I was not indeed quite a novice to the theatre, but I was clearly innocent of knowing or believing myself bound by any rules or usage, that prevented me from offering my production to the one or the other at my own free option. I went to Mr. Garrick; I found in him what my inexperience stood in need of, an admirable judge of stage effect; at his suggestion I added the preparatory scene in the house of Stockwell, before the arrival of Belcour, where his baggage is brought in, and the domestics of the merchant are setting things in readiness for his coming. This insertion I made by his advice, and I punctually remember the very instant when he said to me in his chariot on our way to Hampton—'I want something more to be announced of your West Indian before you bring him on the stage to give eclat to his entrance, and rouse the curiosity of the audience; that they may say—Ay, here he comes, with all his colors flying.' When I asked how this was to be done, and who was to do it, he considered awhile and then replied—'Why, that is your look out, my friend, not mine; but if neither your merchant nor his clerk can do it, why, why send in the servants, and let them talk about him. Never let me see a hero step upon the stage without his trumpeters of some sort or other.' Upon this conversation it was that I engrafted the scene above mentioned, and this was in truth the only alteration of any consequence that the manuscript underwent in its passage to the stage.

After we came to Hampton, where that inimitable man was to be seen in his highest state of animation, we began to debate upon the cast of the play. Barry was extremely desirous to play the part of the Irish Major, and Garrick was very doubtful how to decide, for Moody was then an actor little known and at a low salary. I took no part in the question, for I was entitled to no opinion, but I remember Garrick, after long deliberation, gave his decree for Moody with considerable repugnance, qualifying his preference of the latter with reasons that in no respect reflected on the merits of Mr. Barry—but he did not quite see him in the whole part of O'Flaherty; there were certain points of humor, where he thought it likely he might fail, and in that case his failure, like his name, would be more conspicuous than Moody's. In short, Moody would take pains; it might make him, it might mar the other; so Moody had it, and succeeded to our utmost wishes. Mr. King, ever justly a favorite of the public, took the part of Belcour, and Mrs. Abington, with some few salvos on the score of condescension, played Charlotte Rusport, and though she would not allow it to be anything but a sketch, yet she made a character of it by her inimitable acting.

The production of a new play was in those days an event of much greater attraction than from its frequency it is now become, so that the house was taken to the back rows of the front boxes for several nights in succession before that of its representation; yet in this interval I offered to give its produce to Garrick for a picture that hung over his chimney piece in Southampton Street, and was only a copy from a Holy Family of Andrea del Sarto; he would have closed with me upon the bargain, but that the picture had been a present to him from Lord Baltimore. My expectations did not run very high when I made this offer.

A rumor had gone about that the character which gave its

title to the comedy, was satirical; of course the gentlemen who came under that description, went down to the theatre in great strength, very naturally disposed to chastise the author for his malignity, and their phalanx was not a little formidable. Mrs. Cumberland and I sat with Mr. and Mrs. Garrick in their private box. When the prologue-speaker had gone the length of the first four lines, the tumult was excessive, and the interruption held so long, that it seemed doubtful if the prologue would be suffered to proceed. Garrick was much agitated; he observed to me that the appearance of the house, particularly in the pit, was more hostile than he had ever seen it. It so happened that I did not at that moment feel the danger, which he seemed to apprehend, and remarked to him that the very first word, which discovered Belcour's character to be friendly, would turn the clamor for us, and so far I regarded the impetuosity of the audience as a symptom in our favor. Whilst this was passing between us, order was loudly issued for the prologue to begin again, and in the delivery of a few lines more than they had already heard they seemed reconciled to wait the development of a character from which they were told to expect—

'Some emanations of a noble mind.'

Their acquiescence, however, was not set off with much applause; it was a suspicious truce, a sullen kind of civility, that did not promise more favor than we could earn; but when the prologue came to touch upon the Major, and told his countrymen in the galleries, that—

'His heart can never trip,'

they, honest souls, who had hitherto been treated with little else but stage kicks and cuffs for their entertainment, sent up such a hearty crack, as plainly told us we had not indeed little cherubs, but lusty champions, who sat up aloft.

Of the subsequent success of this lucky comedy there is no occasion for me to speak; eight and twenty successive nights it went without the buttress of an afterpiece, which was not then the practice of attaching to a new play.[1] Such was the good fortune of an author, who happened to strike upon a popular and taking plan, for certainly the moral of the West Indian is not quite unexceptionable, neither is the dialogue above the level of others of the same author, which have been much less favored. The snarlers snapped at it, but they never

[1] This is a mistake, which Cumberland has corrected in the supplement. (Vide *post.*)

set their teeth into the right place; I don't think I am very vain when I say that I could have taught them better. Garrick was extremely kind, and threw his shield before me more than once, as the St. James's evening paper could have witnessed. My property in the piece was reserved for me with the greatest exactness; the charge of the house upon the author's nights was then only sixty pounds, and when Mr. Evans the Treasurer came to my house in Queen Ann Street in a hackney coach with a huge bag of money, he spread it all in gold upon my table, and seemed to contemplate it with a kind of ecstasy, that was extremely droll; and when I tendered him his customary fee, he peremptorily refused it, saying he had never paid an author so much before, I had fairly earned it, and he would not lessen it a single shilling, not even his coach-hire, and in that humor he departed. He had no sooner left the room than one entered it, who was not quite so scrupulous, but quite as welcome; my beloved wife took twenty guineas from the heap, and instantly bestowed them on the faithful servant who had attended on our children; a tribute justly due her unwearied diligence and exemplary conduct.

I sold the copyright to Griffin in Catharine Street for 150*l.*, and if he told the truth when he boasted of having vended 12,000 copies, he did not make a bad bargain; and if he made a good one, which it is pretty clear he did, it is not quite so clear that he deserved it: he was a sorry fellow.

I paid respectful attention to all the floating criticisms that came within my reach, but I found no opportunities of profiting by their remarks, and very little cause to complain of their personalities; in short, I had more praise than I merited, and less cavilling than I expected.[1] One morning when I called upon Mr. Garrick, I found him with the St. James's evening paper in his hand, which he began to read with a voice and action of surprise, most admirably counterfeited, as if he had discovered a mine under my feet, and a train to blow me up to destruction. 'Here, here,' he cried, 'if your skin is less thick than a rhinoceros's hide, egad, here is that will cut you to the bone. This is a terrible fellow; I wonder who it can be.' He began to sing out his libel in a high declamatory tone, with a most comic countenance, and pausing at the end of the first sentence, which seemed to favor his contrivance for a little ingenious tormenting, when he found he had hooked me, he laid down the paper, and began to comment upon the cruelty of newspapers,

[1] No man was more sensitive to criticism than Cumberland. Garrick once described him as 'The man without a skin.'

and moan over me with a great deal of malicious fun and good humor—'Confound these fellows, they spare nobody. I dare say this is Bickerstaff, again; but you don't mind him; no, no, I see you don't mind him; a little galled, but not much hurt: you may stop his mouth with a golden gag, but we'll see how he goes on.' He then resumed his reading, cheering me all the way as it began to soften, till winding up in the most professed panegyric, of which he was himself the writer, I found my friend had had his joke, and I had enjoyed his praise, seasoned and set off in his inimitable manner, which to be comprehended must have been seen.

It was the remark of Lord Lyttleton upon this comedy, when speaking of it to me one evening at Mrs. Montague's, that had it not been for the incident of O'Flaherty's hiding himself behind the screen, when he overhears the lawyer's soliloquy, he should have pronounced it a faultless composition. This flattery his lordship surely added against the conviction of his better judgment merely as a sweetener to qualify his criticism, and by so doing convinced me that he suspected me of being less amenable to fair correction than I really am and ever have been. But be this as it may, a criticism from Lord Lyttleton must always be worth recording, and this especially, as it not only applies to my comedy in particular, but is general to all.

'I consider listening,' said he, 'as a resource never to be allowed in any pure drama, nor ought any good author to make use of it.' This position being laid down by authority so high, and audibly delivered, drew the attention of the company assembled for conversation, and all were silent. 'It is in fact,' he added, 'a violation of those rules, which original authorities have established for the constitution of the comic drama.' After all due acknowledgments for the favor of his remark, I replied that if I had trespassed against any rule laid down by classical authority in the case alluded to, I had done it inadvertently, for I really did not know where any such rule was to be found.

'What did Aristotle say?—Were there no rules laid down by him for comedy?' None that I knew; Aristotle referred to the Margites and Ilias Minor as models, but that was no rule, and the models being lost, we had neither precept nor example to instruct us. 'Were there any precedents in the Greek or Roman drama, which could justify the measure?' To this I replied that no precedent could justify the measure in my opinion, which his lordship's better judgment had condemned; being possessed of that, I should offend no more; but as my error was committed when I had no such advice to guide me, I did recollect that Aristophanes did not scruple to resort to listening, and drawing conclusions from what was overheard, when a man rambled and talked broken sentences in his bed asleep and dreaming; and as for the Roman stage, if anything could apologize for the Major's screen, I conceived there were screens in plenty upon that, which formed separate streets and entrances, which concealed the actors from each other, and gave occasion to a great deal of listening and overhearing in their comedy.

'But this occurs,' said Lord Lyttleton, 'from the construction of the scene, not from the contrivance and intent of the character, as in your case; and when such an expedient is resorted to by an officer like your Major, it is discreditable and unbecoming of him as a man of honor.' This was decisive, and I made no longer any struggle. What my predecessors in the drama, who had been dealers in screens, closets and keyholes for a century past, would have said to this doctrine of the noble critic, I don't pretend to guess; it would have made sad havoc with many of them, and cut deep into their property; as for me, I had so weak a cause and so strong a majority against me (for every lady in the room denounced listeners) that all I could do was to insert without loss of time a few words of palliation into the Major's part, by making him say, upon resorting to his hiding place—'I'll step behind this screen and listen; a good soldier must sometimes fight in ambush as well as in the open field.'

I now leave this criticism to the consideration of those ingenious men who may in future cultivate the stage; I could name one now living, who has made such happy use of his screen in a comedy of the very first merit, that if Aristotle himself had written a whole chapter professedly against *screens*, and Jerry Collier had edited it with notes and illustrations, I would not have placed Lady Teazle out of ear-shot to have saved their ears from the pillory; but if either of these worthies could have pointed out an expedient to have got Joseph Surface off the stage, pending that scene, with any reasonable conformity to nature, they would have done more good to the drama than either of them have done harm; and that is saying a great deal.

There never have been any statute laws for comedy; there never can be any; it is only referable to the unwritten law of the heart, and that is nature; now, though the natural child is illegitimate, the natural comedy is, according to my conception of it, what in other words we denominate the legitimate comedy. If it represents men and women as they are, it pictures nature; if it makes monsters, it goes out of nature. It has a right to command the aid of spectacle, as far as spectacle is properly incidental to it, but if it makes its serving-maid its mistress, it becomes a puppet-show, and its actors ought to speak through a comb behind the scenes, and never show their foolish faces on the stage. If the author conceives himself at liberty to send his characters on and off the stage exactly as he pleases, and thrust them into gentlemen's houses and private chambers, as if they could walk into them as easily as they can walk through the side scenes, he does not know his business; if he gives you the interior of a man of fashion's family, and does not speak the language, or reflect the manners, of a well-bred person, he undertakes to describe company he has never been admitted to, and is an impostor; if he cannot exhibit a distressed gentleman on the scene, without a bailiff at his heels to arrest him, nor reform a dissipated lady without a sponging-house to read his lectures in, I am sorry for his dearth of fancy, and lament his want of taste; if he cannot get his Pegasus past Newgate without his restively stopping like a post horse at the end of his stage, it is a pity he has taught him such unhandsome customs; if he permits the actor, whom he deputes to personate the rake of the day, to copy the dress, air, attitude, straddle, and outrageous indecorum of those caricatures in our print-shops, which keep no terms with nature, he courts the galleries at the expense of decency, and degrades himself, his actor, and the stage, to catch those plaudits that convey no fame, and do not elevate him one inch above the keeper of the beasts of the Tower, who puts his pole between the bars to make the lion roar. In short it is much better, more justifiable, and infinitely more charitable, to write nonsense and set it to good music, than to write ribaldry, and impose it upon good actors. But of this more fully and explicitly hereafter, when committing myself and my works to the judgment of posterity, I shall take leave of my contemporaries, and with every parting wish for their prosperity shall bequeath to them honestly and without reserve all that my observation and long experience can suggest for their edification and advantage.

However, before I quite bid farewell to the West Indian, I must mention a criticism, which I picked up in Rotten-Row from Nugent Lord Clare, not *ex cathedrâ*, but from the saddle on an easy trot. His lordship was contented with the play in general, but he could not relish the five wives of O'Flaherty; they were four too many for an honest man, and the over-abundance of them hurt his lordship's feelings; I thought I could not have a better criterion for the feelings of other people, and desired Moody to manage the matter as well as he could; he put in the qualifier of *en militaire*, and his five wives brought him into no further trouble; all but one were left-handed, and he had German practice for his plea. Upon the whole I must take the world's word for the merit of 'The West Indian,' and thankfully suppose that what they best liked was in fact best to be liked.

A little straw will serve to light a great fire, and after the acting of the West Indian, I would say, if the comparison was not too presumptuous, I was almost the 'Master Betty' of the time; but as I dare say that young gentleman is even now too old and too wise to be spoiled by popularity, so was I then not quite boy enough to be tickled by it, and not quite fool enough to confide in it. In short, I took the same course then which he is taking now; as he keeps on acting part after part, so did I persist in writing play after play; and this, if I am not mistaken, is the surest course we either of us could take of running through our period of popularity, and of finding our true level at the conclusion of it.

I recollect the fate of a young artist in Northamptonshire, who was famous for his adroitness in pointing and repairing the spires of church steeples; he formed his scaffolds with consummate ingenuity, and mounted his ladders with incredible success. The spire of the church of Raunds was of prodigious height; it over-peered all its neighbors, as Shakspeare does all his rivals; the young adventurer was employed to fix the weather-cock; he mounted to the topmost stone, in which the spindle was bedded; universal plaudits hailed him in his ascent; he found himself at the very acme of his fame, but glorious ambition tempted him to quit his ladder, and occupy the place of the weather-cock, standing upon one leg, while he sung a song to amaze the rustic multitude below: what the song was, and how many stanzas he lived to get through, I do not know; he sung it in too large a theatre, and was somewhat out of hearing; but it is in my memory to know that he came to his cadence before his song did, and falling from his height, left the world to draw its moral from his melancholy fate.

I now for the first time entered the lists of controversy, and took up the gauntlet of a renowned champion to vindicate the insulted character of my grandfather, Doctor Bentley.[1] The

[1] 'Tenacious alike of his own literary fame and that of his family connections,' say the authors of the 'Cabinet Cyclopedia,' 'Cumberland took up the pen in great indignation against Bishop Lowth, who, in an attack upon Warburton, had censured his maternal grandfather, Dr. Richard Bentley. The long and angry pamphlet which he published upon this occasion met with no reply, Lowth not choosing to enter into a controversy upon the subject. Cumberland, in yielding to resentful feelings upon so slight a cause, since every

offensive passage met me in a pamphlet written by Bishop Lowth professedly against Warburton, acrimonious enough of all conscience, and unepiscopally intemperate in the highest degree, even if his lordship had not gone out of his course to hurl this dirt upon the coffin of my ancestor. The bishop is now dead, and I will not use his name irreverently; my grandfather was dead, yet he stepped aside to hook him in as a mere verbal critic, who in matters of taste and elegant literature he asserts was contemptibly deficient, and then he resorts to his Catullus for the most disgraceful names he can give him as a scholar or a gentleman, and says he was *aut caprimulgus aut fossor*, terms that, in English, would have been downright blackguardism.

All the world knows that Warburton and Lowth had mouthed and mumbled each other till their very bands blushed and their lawn-sleeves were bloody. I should have thought that the prelate, who had Warburton for his antagonist, would hardly have found leisure from his own self-defence to have turned aside and fixed his teeth in a by-stander. Yet so it was, and it struck me that the unmanly unprovoked attack not only warranted, but demanded, a remonstrance from the descendants of Doctor Bentley. I stood only in the second degree from my uncle Richard, and as much below him in controversial ability as I was in lineal descent. I appealed, therefore, in the first place to him, as nearest in blood, and strongest in capacity. His blood, however, was not in the temper to ferment as mine did, and with a philosophical contempt for this sparring of pens he positively declined having anything to do with the affair. I well remember, but I won't describe the scene; he was very pleasant with me, and reminded me with great kindness how utterly unequal I ought to think myself for undertaking to hold an argument against Bishop Lowth. He was perfectly right; it was exactly so that a sensible Roman would have talked to Curtius before he took his foolish leap, or a charitable European to a Bramin widow before she devoted herself to the flames; but my obstinacy was incorrigible. At length, having warned me that I was about to draw a complete discomfiture on my cause, he prudently conditioned with me so to mark myself out, either by name

person who gives his writings to the public is fairly obnoxious to criticism, shows how easily he could be irritated by the strictures which his own voluminous works, of very different degrees of merit, were calculated to provoke. His assurance, that he bore the observations of hostile writers with perfect equanimity, must be insufficient to produce conviction, when opposed to the extreme sensitiveness betrayed upon trifling occasions, a sensitiveness which seems to justify the imputations of his associates, who represent him as writhing under the slightest infliction of the critic's lash.'—Vol. iii. p. 353.

or description, in the title of my pamphlet, as that he should stand excused, and out of chance of being mistaken for its author. Nothing could be more reasonable, and I promised to comply with his injunctions, and be duly careful of his safety. This I fulfilled by describing myself under such a signature, as all but told my name, and could not possibly, as I conceived, be fathered upon him. With this he was content, and with great politeness, in which no man exceeded him, gave me his hand at parting and wished me a good deliverance.

I lost no time in addressing myself to this task; it soon grew into the size of a pamphlet; my heart was warm in the subject, and as soon as my appeal appeared, I was publicly known to be the author of it. I may venture to say, that weak as my bow was presumed to be, the arrow did not miss its aim, and justice universally decided for me. Warburton had candidly apologized to Lowth for having unknowingly hurt his feelings by some glances he had made at the person of a deceased relation of the Bishop of Oxford, and I now claimed from Lowth the same candor, which he had experienced in the apology of Warburton. This was unanswerable, and though Bishop Lowth would not condescend to offer the atonement to me which he had exacted and received from another, still he had the grace to keep silence, and not attempt a justification of himself, and that which he did not do *per se*, he would not permit to be done *per alium;* for I have reason to know he refused the voluntary reply tendered to him by a certain clergyman of his diocese, acknowledging that I had just reason for retaliation, and he thought it better that the affair should pass over in silence on his part.

In the mean time, my pamphlet went through two full editions, and I had every reason to believe the judgment of the public was in my favor. I entitled it 'A Letter to the Right Reverend the Lord Bishop of O——d, containing some animadversions upon a character given of the late Doctor Bentley in a letter from a late Professor in the University of Oxford, to the Right Reverend Author of the Divine Legation of Moses demonstrated.' To this I subjoined, by way of motto,

Jam parce sepulto.

The following paragraph occurs in the 9th page of this pamphlet, and is fairly pressed upon the party complained of—'Recollect, my Lord, the warmth, the piety, with which you remonstrated against Bishop W——'s treatment of your father in a passage of his Julian:—It is not (you therein say) in behalf of myself that I expostulate, but of one for whom I am much more concerned, that is—my father. These are your lordship's words—amiable, affecting expression! instructive lesson of filial devotion! alas, my lord, that you, who were thus sensible to the least speck, which fell upon the reputation of your father, should be so inveterate against the fame of one, at least as eminent and perhaps not less dear to his family.'

I had traced his *caprimulgas aut fossor* up to its source in one of the most uncleanly samples in Catullus,[1] and in that same satire I was led to the character of Suffenus, who seemed made for the very purposes of retort. My Uncle Bentley stood clear from all suspicion of being guilty of the pamphlet, with the exception of one old gentleman only, Mr. Commissary Greaves, of Fulborne in Cambridgeshire, a man of fortune and consequence in his county, who had ever professed a great esteem for the memory of my grandfather, with whom he had lived in great intimacy, and to whom, I believe, he acknowledged some important obligations. This worthy old gentleman had made a small mistake as to the merit of the pamphlet, and a great one as to the author; for he complimented the writing, and sent a handsome present to the supposed writer. When this mistake was no longer a secret from Mr. Greaves, and I received not a syllable on the subject from him, I sent him the following letter, of which I chanced upon the copy, for the better understanding of which I must premise that he had sent me notice, through my relation, Dr. Bentley, of Nailstone, of a present of books, which he had designed for me when I was a student at college, amounting in value to twenty pounds, but which promise he excused himself from performing, because there had been a wet season, and some of his fen lands had been under water.

My letter was as follows:—

'Dear Sir: When in the warmth of your affection for the memory of my grandfather, you could praise a pamphlet written by me, and address your praises to my uncle, as supposing him to be the author of it, I am more flattered by your mistake, than I will attempt to express to you. You have ever been so good to me, that had your commendations been directed rightly, I must have ascribed the greater share of them to your charitable interpretation of my zeal, and the rest I should have placed to the account of your politeness.

When I was an under-graduate at Trinity College, you was so obliging as to let me be informed of your intention to encourage and assist me in my studies, and though circumstances at that time intervened to postpone your kind design, you have so abundantly overpaid me, that I have no greater ambition now at heart than that I may continue so to write as to be mistaken for my uncle, and you so to approve of what you read, as to see fresh cause of applauding him, who is so truly deserving of every favor you can bestow.

I have the honor to be, &c.

To William Greaves, Esquire, *Fulbourne*.'

---

[1] This Cumberland admits is a palpable error. (*Vide* the supplement.)

Before I quite dismiss this subject, I beg leave to address a very few words to my friend Mr. Hayley, who in his desultory remarks, prefixed to his third volume of Cowper's Letters, has in his mild and civil manner made merciless and uncivil sport with Dr. Bentley's character. I give him notice that I meditate to wreak an exemplary vengeance upon him, for I will publish in these memoirs a copy of his verses (very elegant in themselves, and extremely flattering to me), which I have carefully preserved, and from which I shall derive two very considerable advantages —the one will be the credit of having such a sample of good poetry in my book; the other the malicious gratification of convincing my readers that Mr. Hayley, with all his genius, does not know where to apply it, praising the grandson, who is not worthy of his praise, and censuring the grandfather, whom, as a scholar of the highest class, he of all men living ought not to have treated with flippancy and derision.

And now methinks since I have vowed this vengeance, I will not let it rankle in my heart, neither will I longer withhold from my readers the verses I have promised them, which, though entitled an impromptu by their elegant author, I have not suffered to vanish out of my possession with the rapidity that they have probably slipped out of his recollection. If he shall be angry with me for publishing them, I desire he will believe, there is not a man living, who would not do as I have done, when flattered by the muse of Hayley: if the following hasty and unstudied stanzas are not so good as others of his finished compositions, they are still better than any one else would write, or could write, upon so barren a subject:—

'*Impromptu on a Letter of Mr. Cumberland's, most liberally commending a Poem of the Author's.*

'Kind nature with delight regards,
And glories to impart,
To her bold race of genuine bards
Simplicity of heart.

But gloomy spleen, who still arraigns
Whate'er we lovely call,
Hath said that all poetic veins
Are tinged with envious gall.

Each bard, she said, would strike to earth
His rival's wreath of fame,
Nor ever to inferior worth
Allow its humbler claim.

But nature with a noble pride
Maintain'd her injur'd cause—
'O Spleen, peruse these lines,' she cried,
'Of Cumberland's applause!

Enough by me hast thou been told
Of his poetic art;
Now in his generous praise behold
The genius of his heart!'

The sullen sprite with shame confess'd
Her sordid maxim vain,
And own'd the true poetic breast
Unconscious of the stain.'

Whilst I have been relating the circumstances that induced me to appeal to the world against so great a man as Bishop Lowth, and considering within myself how far I was justified in that apparently presumptuous measure, some thoughts have struck me, as I went on with my detail, which all arose out of the subject I was upon, though they do not personally apply to the parties I have been speaking of. And, after all, where is the difference between man and man, so ascendant on one side, and so depressive on the other, as should give to this an authority to insult, and take from that the privilege of remonstrance? It is a truth not sufficiently enforced, and when enforced, not always admitted, though one of the most useful and important for the government of our conduct, and this it is—that every man, however great in station or in fortune, is mutually dependent upon those who are dependent upon him. In a social state, no man can be truly said to be safe who is not under the protection of his fellow-creatures; no man can be called happy, who is not possessed of their good-will and good opinion; for God never yet endowed a human creature with sensibility to feel an insult, but that he gave him also powers to express his feelings, and propensity to revenge it.

The meanest and most feeble insect, that is provided with a sting, may pierce the eye of the elephant, on whose very ordure it subsists and feeds.

Every human being has a sting; why then does an overgrown piece of mortal clay arrogantly attempt to bestride the narrow world, and launch his artificial thunder from a bridge of brass upon us poor underlings in creation? And when we venture to lift up our heads in the crowd, and cry out to the folks about us—'This is mere mock thunder; this is no true Jupiter; we'll not truckle to his tyranny,'—why will some good-natured friend be ever ready to pluck us by the sleeve, and whisper in our ear—'What are you about? Recollect yourself! he is a giant, a man-mountain; you are a grub, a worm, a beetle; he'll crush you under his foot; he'll tread you into atoms—' not considering, or rather not caring—

'That the poor beetle, which he trode upon,
In mental suff'rance felt a pang as great,
As what a monarch feels.'

Let no man who belongs to a community presume to say that he is independent; there is no such condition in society. Thank God, our virtues are our best defence; conciliation, mildness, charity, benevolence. *Hæ tibi erunt artes.*

Are there not spirits continually starting out from the mass of mankind like red-hot flakes from the hammer of the blacksmith? And are not these to be feared, who are capable of setting a whole city, ay, even a whole kingdom, in flames, let them only fall upon the train that is prepared for them? Who, then, will underwrite a strutting fellow in a lofty station, puffed up with brief authority, who won't answer a gentleman's letter, or allow his visit when he asks admission? If he had the integrity of Aristides, the wisdom of Solon, and the eloquence of Demosthenes, there would be the congregation of an incalculable multitude to sing 'Te Deum' at his downfall. He will find himself in the plight of the poor Arab, who made his cream-tarts without pepper; for want of a little wholesome seasoning, he will have marred his whole batch of pastry, and be condemned for a bad baker to the pillory.

A man shall sin against the whole decalogue, and in this world escape with more impunity than the proud fellow who offends against no commandment, yet provokes you to detest him. I know not how to liken him to anything alive except it be to the melancholy mute recluse of the convent of La Trappe, who has no employment in life but to dig his own grave, no other society but to keep company with his own coffin. If I look for his resemblance amongst the irrationals, I should compare him to a poor, disconsolate ass, whom nobody owns, and nobody befriends. The man who has a cudgel bestows it on his back, and when he brays out his piteous lamentations the dissonance of his tones provoke no compassion; they jar the ear, but never move the heart.

A certain Duke of Alva, about a century ago, was the most popular man in Spain; the people perfectly adored him. He had a revolution in his power every day that he stepped without his doors. The prime minister truckled to him; the king trembled at him. How he acquired this extraordinary degree of influence was a mystery that seemed to puzzle all conjecture. Not by his eloquence, or those powers of declamation which captivate a mob; the illustrious personage could not string three sentences together into common sense or uncommon nonsense. Wit, he had none, and virtue he by no means abounded in; few men in Spain were supposed to be more unprincipled. If you conceived it was by his munificence and generosity, he could have told you no man bought his popularity so cheap; for when the secret came out, he confessed that the whole mystery consisted in his wearing out a few more hats in the year than others sacrificed who did not take off theirs so often.

I knew a gentleman who was the very immediate contrast to this Spanish duke; he was a man of strict morality, who fulfilled the duties, and observed the decorum of his profession in the most exemplary manner. In his meditative walk one summer morning, he was greeted by a country fellow with the customary salutation: 'Good-morning to you, sir! A fine day; a pleasant walk to you!' 'I don't know you,' he replied. 'Why do you interrupt me with your familiarity? I did not speak to you. Put your hat upon your head, and pass on.' 'So I will,' cried the fellow, 'and never take it off again to such a proud puppy whilst I have a head upon my shoulders.' There never was a hat stirred to that man from that day, and had he fallen into a ditch, I question if there would have been a hand stirred to have helped him out of it.

I return to my narrative. I had a house in Queen Ann Street West, at the corner of Wimpole Street; I lived there many years. My friend, Mr. Fitzherbert, lived in the same street, and Mr. Burke nearly opposite to me. I was surprised one morning, at an early hour, by a visit from an old clergyman, the Reverend Decimus Reynolds. I knew there was such a person in existence, and that he was the son of Bishop Reynolds by my father's aunt, and, of course, his first cousin; but I had never seen him to my knowledge in my life, and he came now at an hour when I was so particularly engaged that I should have denied myself to him but that he had called once or twice before, and been disappointed of seeing me. I had my office papers before me; and my wife was making my tea that I might get down to Whitehall in time for my business, and the coach was waiting at the door. He was shown into the room; a more uncouth person, habit, and address was hardly to be met with. He advanced, stopped, and stood staring, with his eyes fixed upon me, for some time, when, putting his hand into a pocket in the lining of the breast of his coat, he drew out an old packet of paper, rolled up and tied with whip-cord, and very ceremoniously desired me to peruse it. I begged to know what it was; for it was a work of time to unravel the knots. He replied: 'My will.' 'And what am I to do with your will, sir?' 'My heir.' 'Well, sir, and who is your heir?' I really did not understand him. 'Richard Cumberland—look at the date—left it to you twenty years ago—my whole estate, real and personal—come to town on purpose—brought up my little deeds—put them into your hands—sign a deed of gift, and make them over to you hard and fast.'

All this while I had not looked at his will; I did not know he had any property, or, if he had, I had no guess where it lay, nor did I so much as know whereabouts he lived. In the mean time, he delivered himself in so strange a style, by starts and snatches, with long pauses and strong sentences, that I suspected him to be deranged, and I saw by the expression of my wife's countenance, that she was under the same suspicion also. I now cast my eye upon the will; I found my name there as his heir under a date of twenty years past; it was therefore no sudden caprice, and I conjured him to tell me if he had any cause of quarrel or displeasure with his nearer relations. Upon this he sat down, took some time to compose himself, for he had been greatly agitated, and having recovered his spirits, answered me deliberately and calmly, that he had no immediate matter of offence with his relations, but he had no obligations to them of any sort, and had been entirely the founder of his own fortune, which by marriage he had acquired and by economy improved. I stated to him that my friend and cousin, Mr. Richard Reynolds, of Paxton, in Huntingdonshire, was his natural heir, and a man of most unexceptionable worth and good character; he did not deny it, but he was wealthy and childless, and he had bequeathed it to me, as his will would testify, twenty years ago, as being the representative of the maternal branch of his family; in fine, he required of me to accompany him to my conveyancer, and direct a positive deed of gift to be drawn up, for which purpose he had brought his title-deeds with him, and should leave them in my hands. He added, in further vindication of his motives, that my father had been ever his most valued friend, that he had constantly watched my conduct and scrutinized my character, although he had not seen occasion to establish any personal acquaintance with me. Upon this explanation, and the evidence of his having inherited no atom of his fortune from his paternal line, I accepted his bounty so far as to appoint the next morning for calling on Mr. Heron, who then had chambers in Gray's Inn, when I would state the case to him, and refer myself to his judgment and good counsel. The result of my conference with the lately deceased Sir Richard Heron was the insertion of a clause of resumption, empowering the donor to revoke his deed at any future time when he should see fit, and this clause I particularly pointed out to my benefactor when he signed the deed.

It was with difficulty I prevailed upon him to admit it, and can witness to the uneasiness it gave him, whilst he prophetically said I had left him exposed to the solicitations and remonstrances of his nephews, and that the time might come, when in the debility of age and irresolution of mind, he might be pressed into a revocation of what he had decided upon as the most deliberate act of his life.

My kind old friend stood a long siege before he suffered his prediction to take place; for it was not till after nearly ten years of uninterrupted cordiality, that, weak and wearied out by importunity, he capitulated with his besiegers, and sending his nephew into my house in Queen Ann Street unexpectedly one morning, surprised me with a demand that I would render back the whole of his title deeds. I delivered them up exactly as I had received them; his messenger put them into his hackney coach and departed.

In consequence of this proceeding, I addressed the following letter to the Reverend Mr. Decimus Reynolds, at Clophill, in Bedfordshire.

'*Queen Ann Street,* Monday, 13th Jan., 1779.

Dear Sir: I received your letter by the conveyance of Major George Reynolds, and in obedience to your commands have resigned into his hands all your title deeds, intrusted to my custody. I would have had a schedule taken of them by Mr. Kipling for your better satisfaction and security, but as your directions were peremptory, and Major Reynolds, who was ill, might have been prejudiced by any delay, I thought it best to put them into his hands without further form, which be assured I have done without the omission of one, for they have lain under seal at my banker's ever since they have been committed to my care.

Whatever motives may govern you, dear sir, for recalling either your confidence, or your bounty, from me and my family, be assured you will still possess and retain my gratitude and esteem. I have only a second time lost a father, and I am now too much in the habit of disappointment and misfortune not to acquiesce with patience under the dispensation.

You well can recollect, that your first bounty was unexpected and unsolicited: it would have been absolute, if I had not thought it for my reputation to make it conditional, and subject to your revocation: perhaps I did not believe you would revoke it, but since you have been induced to wish it, believe me, I rejoice in the reflection, that everything has been done by me for your accommodation, and I had rather my children should inherit an honorable poverty, than an ample patrimony, which caused the giver of it one moment of regret.

I believe I have some few papers still at Tetworth, which I received from you in the country. I shall shortly go down thither, and will wait upon you with them. At the same time, if you wish to have the original conveyance of your lands, as drawn up by Sir Richard Heron, I shall obey you by returning it: the uses being cancelled, the form can be of little value, and I can bear in memory your former goodness without such a remembrancer.

Mrs. Cumberland and my daughters join me in love and respects to you and Mrs. Reynolds, whom by this occasion I beg to thank for all her kindness to me and mine. I spoke yesterday to Sir Richard Heron' [Sir Richard Heron was Chief Secretary in Ireland] 'and pressed with more than common earnestness upon him to fulfil your wishes in favor of Mr. Decimus Reynolds in

Ireland. It would be much satisfaction to me to hear the deeds came safe to hand, and I hope you will favor me with a line to say so.

I am, &c. &c. R. C.'

I have been the more particular in the detail of this transaction, because I had been unfairly represented by a relation, whom in the former part of these memoirs I have recorded as the friend of my youth; a man, whom I dearly loved, and towards whom I had conducted myself through the whole progress of this affair with the strictest honor and good faith, voluntarily subjecting myself, the father of six children, to be deprived of a valuable gift, which the bestower of it wished to have been absolute and irrevocable.

That relation is yet living, and by some few years an older man than I am. Though I may have ceased to live in his remembrance, he has not lost his place in my affection and regard. I wish him health and happiness for the remainder of his days, and, in the perfect consciousness of having merited more kindness than I have received, bid him heartily farewell.

There was more celebrity attached to the success of a new play in the days of which I am speaking, than in the present time, when—

> Portents and prodigies are grown so frequent,
> That they have lost their name.

The happy hit of The West Indian drew a considerable resort of the friends and followers of the Muses to my house. I was superlatively blest in a wife who conducted my family with due attention to my circumstances, yet with every elegance and comfort that could render it a welcome and agreeable rendezvous to my guests. I had six children, whose birth-days were comprised within the period of six years, and they were by no means trained and educated with that laxity of discipline which renders so many houses terrible to the visitor, and almost justifies Foote in his professed veneration for the character of Herod. My young ones stood like little soldiers to be reviewed by those who wished to have them drawn up for inspection, and were dismissed like soldiers at a word. Few parents had more excuse for being vain than my wife and I had, for I may be allowed to say my daughters even then gave promise of that grace and beauty, for which they afterwards became so generally and conspicuously noticed; and my four boys were not behind them in form or feature, though hot climates and hard duty by sea and land, in the service of their king and country, have laid two of them in distant graves, and rendered the survivors war-worn veterans before their time. Even poor Fitzherbert, my unhappy and lamented friend, with all his fond benignity of soul, could not with his caresses introduce a relaxation of discipline in the ranks of our small infantry; and though Garrick could charm a circle of them about him whilst he acted the turkey-cocks, and peacocks, and water-wagtails to their infinite and indescribable amusement, yet at the word or even look of the mother *hi motus animorum* were instantly composed, and order re-established, whenever it became time to release their generous entertainer from the trouble of his exertions.

Ah! I would wish the world to believe, that they take but a very short and impartial estimate of that departed character, who only appreciate him as the best actor in the world; he was more and better than that excellence alone could make him by a thousand estimable qualities, and much as I enjoyed his company, I have been more gratified by the emanations of his heart than by the sallies of his fancy and imagination. Nature had done so much for him, that he could not help being an actor; she gave him a frame of so manageable a proportion, and from its flexibility so perfectly under command, that by its aptitude and elasticity he could draw it out to fit any sizes of character, that tragedy could offer to him, and contract it to any scale of ridiculous diminution, that his Abel Drugger, Scrub, or Fribble, could require of him to sink it to. His eye, in the mean time, was so penetrating, so speaking; his brow so movable, and all his features so plastic, and so accommodating, that wherever his mind impelled them they would go, and before his tongue could give the text, his countenance would express the spirit and the passion of the part he was encharged with.

I always studied the assortment of the characters, who honored me with their company, so as never to bring uncongenial humors into contact with each other. How often have I seen all the objects of society frustrated by inattention to the proper grouping of the guests! The sensibility of some men of genius is so quick and captious, that you must first consider whom they can be happy with, before you can promise yourself any happiness with them. A rivalry in wit and humor will oftentimes render both parties silent, and put them on their guard: if a chance hit, or lucky sally, on the part of a competitor, engrosses the applause of the table, ten to one if the stricken cock ever crows upon the pit again: a matter of fact man will make a pleasant fellow sullen, and a sullen fellow, if provoked by raillery, will disturb the comforts of the whole society.

It is tiresome listening to the nonsense of those who can talk nothing else, but nonsense talked by men of wit and understanding, in the hour of relaxation, is of the very finest essence of conviviality, and a treat delicious to those who have the sense to comprehend it. I have known, and could name many, who understood this art in its perfection, but as it implies a trust in the company, not always to be risked, their practice of it was not very frequent.

Raillery is of all weapons the most dangerous and two-edged; of course it ought never to be handled but by a gentleman, and never should be played with but upon a gentleman; the familiarity of a low-born vulgar man is dreadful; his raillery, his jocularity, like the shaking of a water-spaniel, can never fail to soil you with some sprinkling of the dunghill, out of which he sprung.

A disagreement about a name or a date will mar the best story that was ever put together. Sir Joshua Reynolds luckily could not hear an interrupter of this sort; Johnson would not hear, or if he heard him, would not heed him; Soame Jenyns heard him, heeded him, set him right, and took up his tale, where he had left it, without any diminution of its humor, adding only a few more twists to his snuff-box, a few more taps upon the lid of it, with a preparatory grunt or two, the invariable forerunners of the amenity that was at the heels of them. He was the man, who bore his part in all societies with the most even temper and undisturbed hilarity of all the good companions whom I ever knew. He came into your house at the very moment you had put upon your card; he dressed himself to do your party honor in all the colors of the jay; his lace indeed had long since lost its lustre, but his coat had faithfully retained its cut since the days when gentlemen wore embroidered figured velvets with short sleeves, boot cuffs, and buckram skirts; as nature had cast him in the exact mould of an ill-made pair of stiff stays, he followed her so close in the fashion of his coat, that it was doubted if he did not wear them: because he had a protuberant wen just under his pole, he wore a wig, that did not cover above half his head. His eyes were protruded like the eyes of the lobster, who wears them at the end of his feelers, and yet there was room between one of these and his nose for another wen that added nothing to his beauty; yet I heard this good man very innocently remark, when Gibbon published his history, that he wondered anybody so ugly could write a book.

Such was the exterior of a man, who was the charm of the circle, and gave a zest to every company he came into; his pleasantry was of a sort peculiar to himself; it harmonized with everything; it was like the bread to our dinner; you did not perhaps make it the whole, or principal part, of your meal, but it was an admirable and wholesome auxiliary to your other viands. Soame Jenyns told you no long stories, engrossed not much of your attention, and was not angry with those that did; his thoughts were original, and were apt to have a very whimsical affinity to the paradox in them: he wrote verses upon dancing, and prose upon the origin of evil, yet he was a very indifferent metaphysician and a worse dancer; ill nature and personality, with the single exception of his lines upon Johnson, I never heard fall from his lips; those lines I have forgotten, though I believe I was the first person to whom he recited them; they were very bad, but he had been told that Johnson ridiculed his metaphysics, and some of us had just then been making extemporary epitaphs upon each other: though his wit was harmless, yet the general cast of it was ironical; there was a terseness in his repartees that had a play of words as well as of thought, as when speaking of the difference between laying out money upon land, or purchasing into the funds, he said, 'One was principal without interest, and the other interest without principal.'[1] Certain it is he had a brevity of expression that never hung upon the ear, and you felt the point in the very moment that he made the push. It was rather to be lamented that his lady, Mrs. Jenyns, had so great a respect for his good sayings, and so imperfect a recollection of them, for though she always prefaced her recitals of them with—*as Mr. Jenyns says*—it was not always what Mr. Jenyns said, and never, I am apt to think, *as* Mr. Jenyns said; but she was an excellent old lady, and twirled her fan with as much mechanical address as her ingenious husband twirled his snuff-box.[2]

The brilliant vivacity of Garrick was subject to be clouded; little flying stories had too much of his attention, and more of his credit than they should have had; and certainly there were too many babblers who had access to his ear. There was some

[1] A similar remark is attributed to Lord Mansfield. 'The funds,' said he, 'give interest without principal, and land principal without interest; but mortgages both principal and interest.'

[2] Soame Jenyns, distinguished as a wit, author, and companion, was born in the year 1704, and died 1787. He 'was possessed,' says Boswell, 'of lively talents, and a style eminently pure and easy, and could very happily play with a light subject, either in prose or verse; but when he speculated on that most difficult and excruciating question, the Origin of Evil, he ventured far beyond his depth, and, accordingly, was exposed by Johnson, both with acute argument and brilliant wit.'—*Life of Johnson*, vol. i. p. 294.

Jenyns submitted in silence, while Johnson lived; but after his death he published an attack on him in the form of an epitaph, which was copied into the leading newspapers and magazines of the time. This provoked retort on the part of Johnson's friends and admirers, and Jenyns, himself nearly sinking into the grave, was treated with great severity.

precaution necessary as to the company you associated with him at your table; Fitzherbert understood that in general admirably well, yet he told me of a certain day, when Garrick, who had perhaps been put a little out of his way, and was missing from the company, was found in the back yard acting a turkey-cock to a black boy, who was capering for joy and continually crying out—'Massa Garrick, do so make me laugh: I shall die with laughing.' The story I have no doubt is true; but I rather think it indicates the very contrary from a ruffled temper, and marks good humor in its strongest light. To give amusement to children, and to take pleasure in the act, is such a symptom of suavity, as can never be mistaken.

I made a visit with him by his own proposal to Foote at Parson's Green; I have heard it said he was reserved and uneasy in his company; I never saw him more at ease and in a happier flow of spirits than on that occasion.

Where a loud-tongued talker was in company, Edmund Burke declined all claims upon attention,[1] and Samuel Johnson, whose ears were not quick, seldom lent them to his conversation, though he loved the man, and admired his talents; I have seen a dull damping matter-of-fact man quell the effervescence even of Foote's unrivalled humor.[2]

[1] Talking of conversation, on one occasion, Johnson said, 'There must, in the first place, be knowledge, there must be materials; in the second place, there must be command of words; in the third place, there must be imagination, to place things in such views as they are not commonly seen in; and in the fourth place, there must be presence of mind, and a resolution that is not to be overcome by failures; this last is an essential requisite; for want of it many people do not excel in conversation.'—*Boswell's Johnson*, vol. iv. p. 181. He thus described Burke's conversation: 'Burke's talk is the ebullition of his mind; he does not talk from a desire of distinction, but because his mind is full.'—*Ibid.*, p. 182. 'If a man,' he said, on another occasion, 'were to go by chance at the same time with Burke under a shed, to shun a shower, he would say 'this is an extraordinary man.' If Burke should go into a stable to see his horse drest, the ostler would say, 'we have had an extraordinary man here.' . . . . When Burke does not descend to be merry, his conversation is very superior indeed. There is no proportion between the powers which he shows in serious talk, and in jocularity.'—*Ibid.* Boswell differed from his great friend as to Burke's pleasantry; and in this was supported by Mr. Windham, who thought Burke was often very happy in his merriment.

[2] 'For loud, obstreperous, broad-faced mirth, I know not his equal,' said Johnson of Foote. 'I have been surprised,' says Taylor, 'that my old friend, Arthur Murphy, should have entertained so high an opinion of Foote as a wit, since there are very few proofs of such original jocularity as might be expected, considering he had acquired so high a reputation for *bons mots* and repartees. I have often wished there had been some record of that facetious fecundity which rendered Foote's conversational powers so entertaining to people of all ranks, for those sallies of his inexhaustible humor which have reached public notice, by no means afford such samples of original wit as to give adequate

But I remember full well, when Garrick and I made him the visit above mentioned, poor Foote had something worse than a dull man to struggle with, and matter of fact brought home to him in a way, that for a time entirely overthrew his spirits, and most completely frighted him from his propriety. We had taken him by surprise, and of course were with him some hours before dinner, to make sure of our own if we had missed of his. He seemed overjoyed to see us, engaged us to stay, walked with us in his garden, and read to us some scenes roughly sketched for his 'Maid of Bath.' His dinner was quite good enough, and his wine superlative; Sir Robert Fletcher, who had served in the East Indies, dropped in before dinner and made the fourth of our party. When we had passed about two hours in perfect harmony and hilarity, Garrick called for his tea, and Sir Robert rose to depart; there was an unlucky screen in the room, that hid the door, and behind which Sir Robert hid himself for some purpose, whether natural or artificial I know not; but Foote, supposing him gone, instantly began to play off his ridicule at the expense of his departed guest. I must confess it was (in the cant phrase) a way that he had, and just now a very unlucky way, for Sir Robert, bolting from behind the screen, cried out: 'I am not gone, Foote; spare me till I am out of hearing; and now, with your leave, I will stay till these gentlemen depart, and then you shall amuse me at their cost, as you have amused them at mine.'

A remonstrance of this sort was an electric shock, that could not be parried. No wit could furnish an evasion, no explanation could suffice for an excuse. The offended gentleman was to the full as angry as a brave man ought to be with an unfor-

support to his high reputation, and I conceive that his dramatic works may be considered as the chief foundation of his intellectual character.' —*Records of my Life*, p. 433. Foote being mentioned on one occasion, Johnson said: 'He is not a good mimic.' One of the company added, 'A merry-Andrew, a buffoon.' Johnson.—'But he has wit, too, and is not deficient in ideas, or in fertility and variety of imagery, and not empty of reading; he has knowledge enough to fill up his part. One species of wit he has in an eminent degree, that of escape. You drive him into a corner with both hands, but he's gone, sir, when you think you have got him—like an animal that jumps over your head. Then he has a great range for wit; he never lets truth stand between him and a jest, and he is sometimes mighty coarse. Garrick is under many restraints from which Foote is free.' Wilkes.—'Garrick's wit is more like Lord Chesterfield's.' Johnson.—'The first time I was in company with Foote, was at Fitzherbert's. Having no good opinion of the fellow, I was resolved not to be pleased; and it is very difficult to please a man against his will. I went on eating my dinner pretty sullenly, affecting not to mind him. But the dog was so very comical, that I was obliged to lay down my knife and fork, throw myself back upon my chair, and fairly laugh it out. No, sir, he was irresistible.'—*Boswell's Johnson*, vol. iii. pp. 70, 71.

tunate wit, who possessed very little of that quality, which he abounded in. This event, which deprived Foote of all presence of mind, gave occasion to Garrick to display his genius and good nature in their brightest lustre; I never saw him in a more amiable light; the infinite address and ingenuity that he exhibited, in softening the enraged guest, and reconciling him to pass over an affront, as gross as could well be put upon a man, were at once the most comic and the most complete I ever witnessed. Why was not James Boswell present to have recorded the dialogue and the action of the scene? My stupid head only carried away the effect of it. It was as if Diomed (who being the son of Tydeus, was I conclude a great hero in a small compass) had been shielding Thersites from the wrath of Ajax; and so wrathful was our Ajax that if I did not recollect there was a certain actor at Delhi, who in the height of the massacre charmed away the furious passions of Nadir Shaw, and saved a remnant of the city, I should say this was a victory without a parallel. I hope Foote was very grateful, but when a man has been completely humbled, he is not very fond of recollecting it.

There was a gentleman of very general notoriety at this time, who had the address to collect about him a considerable resort of men of wit and learning at no other expense on his part than of the meat and drink, which they consumed; for as he had no predilection for reading their works, he did not put himself to the charge of buying them. The gentleman himself was of the Scottish nation; in that nobody could be mistaken; all beyond that was matter of conjecture, save only that it was universally understood that Mr. Thomas Mills was under the protection of the great Lord Mansfield. Having been Town Major of Quebec, he took the title of a field officer, and having been squire to a knight of the Bath on the ceremony of an installation, he became Sir Thomas, and a knight himself. It was chiefly through my acquaintance with this gentleman that I became a member of a very pleasant society (for we never had the establishment of a club) who used to dine together upon stated days at the British Coffee House, then kept by Mrs. Anderson, a person of great respectability. Many of the members of this society were men of the first eminence for their talents, and as there was no exclusion in our system of any member's friend or friends, our parties were continually enlivened by the introduction of new guests, who of course furnished new sources for conversation from which politics and party seemed by general consent decidedly proscribed. Foote, Reynolds, Fitzherbert, Goldsmith, Garrick, Macpherson, Doctors Carlisle, Robinson, Beattie, Caleb Whitefoord, with many others, resorted there as they saw fit.

In one of these meetings it was suggested and recommended to me to take up the character of a North Briton, as I had those of an Irishman and West Indian. I observed, in answer to this, that I had not the same chance for success as I had in my sketch of O'Flaherty, for I had never resided in Scotland, and should be perfectly to seek for the dialect of my hero. 'How could that be,' Fitzherbert observed, 'when I was in the very place to find it (alluding to the British Coffee House and the company we were in); 'however,' he added, 'give your Scotchman character, and take your chance for dialect. If you bring a Roman on the stage, you don't make him speak Latin.' 'No, no,' cried Foote, 'and if you don't make him wear breeches, Garrick will be much obliged to you. When I was at Stranraer I went to the Kirk, where the Mess-John was declaiming most furiously against luxury, and, as heaven shall judge me, there was not a pair of shoes in the whole congregation.'

This turned the conversation from my comedy to matters more amusing, but the suggestion had taken hold of my fancy, and I began to frame the character of Colin Macleod upon the model of a Highland servant, who with scrupulous integrity, and a great deal of nationality about him, managed all the domestic affairs of Sir Thomas Mills's household, and being a great favorite of everybody who resorted there, became in time, as it were, one of the company. With no other guide for the dialect of my Macleod than what the Scotch characters of the stage supplied me with, I endowed him with a good heart, and sent him to seek his fortune.

I was aware I had some little fame at stake, and bestowed my utmost care and attention upon the writing of this comedy: I availed myself of Mr. Garrick's judgment at all proper intervals as I advanced towards the completion of it. This I have acknowledged in the advertisement, and though I did not form sanguine hopes of its obtaining equal success with 'The West-Indian' in representation, I confess I flattered myself that I had outgone that drama in point of composition. When I found that Garrick thought of it as I did, I ventured to avow my preference in the prologue. I have been reading it over with attention, and so many years have passed since I wrote it, that I have very little of the feeling of the author when I speak of it. I rather think I was right in giving it the preference to the 'West Indian,' though I am far from sure I was unprejudiced in my judgment at that time. An author, who is conscious that his new work will not be equally popular with his preceding one, will be very apt to imitate the dealer, who, having a pair of horses to sell, will bestow all his praise upon the worst, and leave the best to recommend himself. I verily believe if 'The Fashionable Lover' was not my composition, and I were called upon to give my opinion of it (speaking only of its merits, and reserving to myself my opinion of its faults), I should be inclined to say it was a drama of a moral, grave, and tender cast, inasmuch as I discover in it sentiments laudably directed against national prejudice, breach of trust, seduction, gaming, and the general dissipation of the time then present. I could not deny it a preference to the 'West Indian' in a moral light, and, perhaps, if I were in very good humor with its author, I might be tempted to say that, in point of diction, it approached very nearly to what I conceived to be the true style of comedy—*Joca non infra soccum, seria non usque cothurnum.*

At the time when this play came out, the demands of the stage for novelty were much limited, and of course the excluded many had full leisure to wreak their malice on the selected few. I was silly enough to be in earnest, and make serious appeals against cavillers and slanderers below notice: this induced my friend Garrick to call me the man without a skin, and sure enough I should have been without a skin, if the newspaper beadles could have had their will of me, for I constantly stood out against them, and would never ask quarter. I have been long since convinced of my folly, but I am not at all ashamed of my principle, for I always made common cause with my contemporaries, and never separated my own particular interests from those of literature in general, as will in part appear by the following paragraph, extracted from the advertisement, which I prefixed to this comedy on its publication: 'Whether the reception of this comedy,' I therein say, 'may be such as shall encourage me to future efforts, is of small consequence to the public, but if it should chance to obtain some little credit with the candid part of mankind, and its author once escape without those personal and unworthy aspersions, which writers, who hide their own names, fling on them, who publish theirs, my success, it may be hoped, will draw forth others to the undertaking with far superior requisites; and that there are numbers under this description, whose sensibility keeps them silent, I am well persuaded, when I consider how general it is for men of the finest parts to be subject to the finest feelings; and I would submit whether this unhandsome practice of abuse is not calculated to create in the minds of men of genius not only a disinclination to engage in dramatic compositions, but a languid and unanimated manner of executing them, &c. &c.'

The remark is just, but I remember Lord Mansfield on a certain occasion said to me, that if a single syllable from his pen could at once confute an anonymous defamer, he would not gratify him with the word.[1] This might be a very becoming rule for him to follow, and yet it might by no means apply to a man of my humble sort, and in truth there was a filthy nest of vipers at that time in league against every name, to which any degree of celebrity was attached, and they kept their hold upon the papers till certain of their leaders were compelled to fly their country, some to save their ears and some to save their necks. They were well known, and I am sorry to say some men, whose minds should have been superior to any terrors they could hold out, made suit to them for favor, nay, even combined with them on some occasions, and were mean enough to enroll themselves under their despicable banners. It is to the honor of the present time, and infinitely to the repose of the present writers for the stage, that all these dirty doings are completely done away, and an era of candor and human kindness has succeeded to one that was scandalously its opposite.

At this time I did not know Oliver Goldsmith even by person; I think our first meeting chanced to be at the British Coffee-House; when we came together, we very speedily co-

[1] If Lord Mansfield did not invoke the aid of the press in his own particular case, to attack opponents or shield himself from libels, it is well known that he was perfectly aware of the immense power of this popular engine. He once said to the Duke of Northumberland, that the newspapers, if they went on as they had done, would finally write the duke out of his titles and estates, and the king out of his kingdom. His celebrated address to the public, on the occasion of reversing the outlawry of Wilkes, exhibited a noble defiance of lawless threats and calumnious assaults.

'I pass over,' said he, 'many anonymous letters I have received. Those in print are public; and some of them have been brought judicially before the court. Whoever the writers are, they take the wrong way. I will do my duty unawed. What am I to fear? That *mendax infamia* from the press, which daily coins false facts and motives? The lies of calumny carry no terror to me. I trust that my temper of mind, and the color and conduct of my life have given me a suit of armor against these arrows. If, during this king's reign, I have ever supported his government, and assisted his measures, I have done it without any other reward than the consciousness of doing what I thought right. If I have ever opposed, I have done it upon the points themselves; without mixing in party or faction, and without any collateral views. I honor the king, and respect the people; but many things acquired by the favor of either, are, in my account, objects not worth ambition. I wish popularity; but it is the popularity which follows, not that which is run after; it is that popularity which, sooner or later, never fails to do justice to the pursuit of noble ends by noble means. I will not do that which my conscience tells me is wrong upon this occasion, to gain the huzzas of thousands, or the daily praise of all the papers which come from the press. I will not avoid doing what I think is right, though it should draw on me the whole artillery of libels; all that falsehood and malice can invent, or the credulity of a deluded populace can swallow. I can say, with a great magistrate, upon an occasion, and under circumstances not unlike, 'Ego hoc animo semper fui, ut invidiam virtute partam, gloriam, non invidiam putarem.''

alesced, and I believe he forgave me for all the little fame I had got by the success of my West Indian, which had put him to some trouble, for it was not his nature to be unkind, and I had soon an opportunity of convincing him how incapable I was of harboring resentment, and how zealously I took my share in what concerned his interest and reputation. That he was fantastically and whimsically vain all the world knows, but there was no settled and inherent malice in his heart. He was tenacious to a ridiculous extreme of certain pretensions, that did not, and by nature could not, belong to him, and at the same time inexcusably careless of the fame which he had powers to command. His table-talk was, as Garrick aptly compared it, like that of a parrot, whilst he wrote like Apollo; he had gleams of eloquence, and at times a majesty of thought, but in general his tongue and his pen had two very different styles of talking. What foibles he had he took no pains to conceal, the good qualities of his heart were too frequently obscured by the carelessness of his conduct, and the frivolity of his manners.[1]

[1] There is no name, perhaps, in English literature, which so naturally attracts our affections as Oliver Goldsmith. Even his infirmities appeal to the heart; and, exciting our sympathies and regrets, attach to him our kindliest feelings. 'The epithet so often heard,' says one of his biographers, 'and in such kindly tones, of 'poor Goldsmith,' speaks volumes. Few, who consider the rich compound of admirable and whimsical qualities which form his character, would wish to prune away its eccentricities, trim its grotesque luxuriance, and clip it down to the decent formalities of rigid virtue.' 'Let not his frailties be remembered,' said Johnson; 'he was a very great man.' But for our parts, we rather say, 'Let them be remembered;' for we question whether he himself would not feel gratified in hearing his readers, after dwelling with admiration on the proofs of his greatness, close the volume with the kind-hearted phrase, so fondly and familiarly ejaculated, of 'Poor Goldsmith!'

Much must be allowed, in our estimate of Goldsmith, for the native characteristics, and unfortunate circumstances of his life. Though it certainly is no justification of fault or error, to say that it arose from an original bias or obliquity of moral principle; yet it may soften our judgments when we know that while the temptation was strong, the power of resistance, though sufficient, was nevertheless weak. Boswell's sketch of Goldsmith, if not altogether charitable, is on the whole not unjust. 'No man,' he says, 'had the art of displaying with more advantage as a writer, whatever literary acquisitions he made. 'Nihil quod tetigit non ornavit.' His mind resembled a fertile but thin soil. There was a quick, but not a strong vegetation, of whatever chanced to be thrown upon it. No deep root could be struck. The oak of the forest did not grow there; but the elegant shrubbery, and the fragrant parterre, appeared in gay succession. It has been generally circulated and believed that he was a mere fool in conversation; but, in truth, this has been greatly exaggerated. He had, no doubt, a more than common share of that hurry of ideas which we often find in his countrymen, and which sometimes produces a laughable confusion in expressing them. He was very much what the French call *un etourdi*, and from vanity and an eager desire of being conspicuous wherever he was, he frequently talked carelessly, without knowledge of the subject, or even without thought. His person was short, his countenance coarse and vulgar, his deportment that of a scholar awkwardly affecting

Sir Joshua Reynolds was very good to him, and would have drilled him into better trim and order for society, if he would have been amenable, for Reynolds was a perfect gentleman, had good sense, great propriety with all the social attributes, and all the graces of hospitality, equal to any man. He well knew how to appreciate men of talents, and how near a kin the Muse of poetry was to that art, of which he was so eminent a master. From Goldsmith he caught the subject of his famous Ugolino; what aids he got from others, if he got any, were worthily bestowed and happily applied.

There is something in Goldsmith's prose, that to my ear is uncommonly sweet and harmonious; it is clear, simple, easy to be understood; we never want to read his period twice over, except for the pleasure it bestows; obscurity never calls us back to a repetition of it. That he was a poet there is no doubt, but the paucity of his verses does not allow us to rank him in that high station, where his genius might have carried him. There must be bulk, variety and grandeur of design to constitute a first-rate poet. The Deserted Village, Traveller, and Hermit are all specimens beautiful as such, but they are only birds' eggs on a string, and eggs of small birds too. One great magnificent *whole* must be accomplished before we can pronounce upon the *maker* to be the ὁ ποιητής.[1] Pope himself never earned this title by a work of any magnitude but his Homer, and that being a translation only constitutes him an accomplished

the easy gentleman. Those who were in any way distinguished, excited envy in him to so ridiculous an excess, that the instances of it are hardly credible. When accompanying two beautiful young ladies with their mother, on a tour in France, he was seriously angry that more attention was paid to them than to him; and once, at the exhibition of the *Fantoccini* in London, when those who sat next him observed with what dexterity a puppet was made to toss a pike, he could not bear that it should have such praise, and exclaimed with some warmth: 'Pshaw! I can do it better myself.'' [It is said that he made the attempt, and broke his shin in consequence.]

'He, I am afraid, had no settled system of any sort, so that his conduct must not be strictly scrutinized; but his affections were social and generous, and when he had money he gave it away liberally. His desire of imaginary consequence predominated over his attention to truth. When he began to rise into notice, he said he had a brother who was Dean of Durham' [Dr. Isaac Goldsmith, his relative, was Dean of Cloyne, in 1747, and he might have referred to him; and hence the tale], 'a fiction so easily detected that it is wonderful how he should have been so inconsiderate as to hazard it. He boasted to me at this time of the power of his pen in commanding money, which I believe was true in a certain degree, though in the instance he gave he was by no means correct.'—*Boswell's Johnson*, vol. i. pp. 395, 397.

[1] *Poetic power* may be evinced in few as well as in many lines. And it is precisely the exhibition of this power that constitutes a poet; whether he writes more or less. It is the *excellence* of the power, and not the extent to which it has been exercised, that constitutes a first-rate poet.

versifier. Distress drove Goldsmith upon undertakings, neither congenial with his studies, nor worthy of his talents. I remember him, when in his chamber in the Temple, he showed me the beginning of his 'Animated Nature;' it was with a sigh, such as genius draws, when hard necessity diverts it from its bent to drudge for bread, and talk of birds, and beasts, and creeping things, which Pidcock's show-man would have done as well. Poor fellow, he hardly knew an ass from a mule, nor a turkey from a goose, but when he saw it on the table. But publishers hate poetry, and Paternoster Row is not Parnassus. Even the mighty Doctor Hill, who was not a very delicate feeder, could not make a dinner out of the press till by a happy transformation into Hannah Glass, he turned himself into a cook, and sold receipts for made dishes to all the savory readers in the kingdom. Then indeed the press acknowledged him second in fame only to John Bunyan; his feasts kept pace in sale with Nelson's fasts, and when his own name was fairly written out of credit, he wrote himself into immortality under an alias. Now though necessity, or I should rather say the desire of finding money for a masquerade, drove Oliver Goldsmith upon abridging histories and turning Buffon into English, yet I much doubt if without that spur he would ever have put his Pegasus into action; no, if he had been rich, the world would have been poorer than it is by the loss of all the treasures of his genius and the contributions of his pen.[1]

Who will say that Johnson himself would have been such a champion in literature, such a front-rank soldier in the fields of fame, if he had not been pressed into the service, and driven on to glory with the bayonet of sharp necessity pointed at his back? If fortune had turned him into a field of clover, he

[1] Speaking of a dinner at General Oglethorpe's (April 10, 1772), where he met Goldsmith, Boswell, after detailing the conversation of the host and his guests, thus proceeds: 'Goldsmith told us that he was now busy in writing a natural history; and that he might have full leisure for it, he had taken lodgings at a farmer's house, near to the six milestone, on the Edgeware road, and had carried down his books in two returned postchaises. He said, he believed the farmer's family thought him an odd character, similar to that in which the Spectator appeared to his landlady and her children: he was *the gentleman*. Mr. Mickle, the translator of 'The Lusiad,' and I, went to visit him at this place, a few days afterwards. He was not at home; but having a curiosity to see his apartments, we went in, and found curious scraps of descriptions of animals, scrawled upon the wall with a black lead pencil.'—*Life of Johnson*, vol. ii. p. 186. 'Goldsmith,' said Johnson, 'was a man, who, whatever he wrote, did it better than any other man could do.' The same authority emphatically said, that he would make his 'Animated Nature,' 'as entertaining as a Persian tale.' The result justified his judgment; for notwithstanding the defects of knowledge, observable in the work, the charm of its style has preserved its popularity.

would have laid down and rolled in it. The mere manual labor of writing would not have allowed his lassitude and love of ease to have taken the pen out of the inkhorn, unless the cravings of hunger had reminded him that he must fill the sheet before he saw the table cloth. He might indeed have knocked down Osbourne for a blockhead, but he would not have knocked him down with a folio of his own writing. He would perhaps have been the dictator of a club, and wherever he sat down to conversation, there must have been that splash of strong bold thought about him, that we might still have had a collectanea after his death; but of prose I guess not much, of works of labor none, of fancy perhaps something more, especially of poetry, which under favor I conceive was not his tower of strength. I think we should have had his Rasselas at all events, for he was likely enough to have written at Voltaire, and brought the question to the test, if infidelity is any aid to wit. An orator he must have been; not improbably a parliamentarian, and, if such, certainly an oppositionist, for he preferred to talk against the tide. He would indubitably have been no member of the Whig Club, no partisan of Wilkes, no friend of Hume, no believer in Macpherson; he would have put up prayers for early rising, and laid in bed all day, and with the most active resolutions possible, been the most indolent mortal living. He was a good man by nature, a great man by genius; we are now to inquire what he was by compulsion.

Johnson's first style was naturally energetic, his middle style was turgid to a fault, his latter style was softened down and harmonized into periods, more tuneful and more intelligible. His execution was rapid, yet his mind was not easily provoked into exertion; the variety we find in his writings was not the variety of choice arising from the impulse of his proper genius, but tasks imposed upon him by the dealers in ink, and contracts on his part submitted to in satisfaction of the pressing calls of hungry want; for, painful as it is to relate, I have heard that illustrious scholar assert (and he never varied from the truth of fact) that he subsisted himself for a considerable space of time upon the scanty pittance of four-pence half-penny per day. How melancholy to reflect that his vast trunk and stimulating appetite were to be supported by what will barely feed the weaned infant! Less, much less, than Master Betty has earned in one night, would have cheered the mighty mind, and maintained the athletic body of Samuel Johnson in comfort and abundance for a twelvemonth. Alas! I am not fit to paint his character; nor is there need of it; Etiam mortuus loquitur: every man who can buy a book, has bought a *Boswell*; Johnson is known to all the reading world. I also knew him well, respected him highly, loved him sincerely: it was never my chance to see him in those moments of moroseness and ill humor, which are imputed to him, perhaps with truth, for who would slander him? But I am not warranted by any experience of those humors to speak of him otherwise than of a friend, who always met me with kindness, and from whom I never separated without regret. When I sought his company, he had no capricious excuses for withholding it, but lent himself to every invitation with cordiality, and brought good humor with him, that gave life to the circle he was in. He presented himself always in his fashion of apparel; a brown coat with metal buttons, black waistcoat and worsted stockings, with a flowing bob wig, was the style of his wardrobe, but they were in perfectly good trim, and with the ladies, which he generally met, he had nothing of the slovenly philosopher about him; he fed heartily, but not voraciously, and was extremely courteous in his commendations of any dish that pleased his palate; he suffered his next neighbor to squeeze the China oranges into his wineglass after dinner, which else perchance had gone aside, and trickled into his shoes, for the good man had neither straight sight nor steady nerves.

At the tea-table he had considerable demands upon his favorite beverage, and I remember when Sir Joshua Reynolds at my house reminded him that he had drank eleven cups, he replied: 'Sir, I did not count your glasses of wine, why should you number up my cups of tea?' And then laughing in perfect good humor he added: 'Sir, I should have released the lady from any further trouble, if it had not been for your remark; but you have reminded me that I want one of the dozen, and I must request Mrs. Cumberland to round up my number.' When he saw the readiness and complacency with which my wife obeyed his call, he turned a kind and cheerful look upon her, and said: 'Madam, I must tell you for your comfort, you have escaped much better than a certain lady did awhile ago, upon whose patience I intruded greatly more than I have done on yours; but the lady asked me for no other purpose but to make a Zany of me, and set me gabbling to a parcel of people I knew nothing of; so, madam, I had my revenge of her; for I swallowed five and twenty cups of her tea, and did not treat her with as many words.' I can only say my wife would have made tea for him as long as the New River could have supplied her with water.

It was on such occasions he was to be seen in his happiest moments, when animated by the cheering attention of friends whom he liked, he would give full scope to those talents for narration, in which I verily think he was unrivalled both in the brilliancy of his wit, the flow of his humor, and the energy of his language. Anecdotes of times past, scenes of his own life, and characters of humorists, enthusiasts, crack-brained projectors and a variety of strange beings, that he had chanced upon, when detailed by him at length, and garnished with those episodical remarks, sometimes comic, sometimes grave, which he would throw in with infinite fertility of fancy, were a treat, which, though not always to be purchased by five and twenty cups of tea, I have often had the happiness to enjoy for less than half the number. He was easily led into topics; it was not easy to turn him from them; but who would wish it? If a man wanted to show himself off by getting up and riding upon him, he was sure to run restive and kick him off: you might as safely have backed Bucephalus, before Alexander had lunged him. Neither did he always like to be over-fondled; when a certain gentleman out-acted his part in this way, he is said to have demanded of him: 'What provokes your risibility, sir? Have I said anything that you understand?—Then I ask pardon of the rest of the company.' But this is Henderson's anecdote of him, and I won't swear he did not make it himself. The following apology, however, I myself drew from him, when speaking of his tour I observed to him upon some passages as rather too sharp upon a country and people who had entertained him so handsomely: 'Do you think so, Cumbey?' he replied. 'Then I give you leave to say, and you may quote me for it, that there are more gentlemen in Scotland than there are shoes.'

But I don't relish these sayings, and I am to blame for retailing them; we can no more judge of men by these droppings from their lips, than we can guess at the contents of the river Nile by a pitcher of its water. If we were to estimate the wise men of Greece by Laertius's scraps of their sayings, what a parcel of old women should we account them to have been!

The expanse of matter which Johnson had found room for in his intellectual storehouse, the correctness with which he had assorted it, and the readiness with which he could turn to any article that he wanted to make present use of, were the properties in him, which I contemplated with the most admiration. Some have called him a savage; they were only so far right in the resemblance, as that, like the savage, he never came into suspicious company without his spear in his hand and his bow and quiver at his back. In quickness of intellect few ever equalled him, in profundity of erudition many have surpassed him. I do not think he had a pure and classical taste, nor was apt to be best pleased with the best authors, but as a general scholar he ranks very high. When I would have consulted him upon certain points of literature, whilst I was making my collections from the Greek dramatists for my essays in 'The Observer,' he candidly acknowledged that his studies had not lain amongst them, and certain it is there is very little show of literature in his 'Ramblers,' and in the passage where he quotes Aristotle, he has not correctly given the meaning of the original. But this was merely the result of haste and inattention, neither is he so to be measured, for he had so many parts and properties of scholarship about him, that you can only fairly review him as a man of general knowledge. As a poet, his translations of Juvenal gave him a name in the world, and gained him the applause of Pope. He was a writer of tragedy, but his 'Irene' gives him no conspicuous rank in that department. As an essayist he merits more consideration; his 'Ramblers' are in everybody's hands; about them opinions vary, and I rather believe the style of these essays is not now considered as a good model; this he corrected in his more advanced age, as may be seen in his 'Lives of the Poets,' where his diction, though occasionally elaborate and highly metaphorical, is not nearly so inflated and ponderous as in the 'Ramblers.' He was an acute and able critic; the enthusiastic admirers of Milton and the friends of Gray will have something to complain of, but criticism is a task which no man executes to all men's satisfaction. His selection of a certain passage in the 'Mourning Bride of Congreve,' which he extols so rapturously, is certainly a most unfortunate sample; but unless the oversights of a critic are less pardonable than those of other men, we may pass this over in a work of merit, which abounds in beauties far more prominent than its defects, and much more pleasing to contemplate. In works professedly of fancy he is not very copious; yet in his 'Rasselas' we have much to admire, and enough to make us wish for more. It is the work of an illuminated mind, and offers many wise and deep reflections, clothed in beautiful and harmonious diction. We are not, indeed, familiar with such personages as Johnson has imagined for the characters of his fable, but if we are not exceedingly interested in their story, we are infinitely gratified with their conversation and remarks. In conclusion, Johnson's era was not wanting in men to be distinguished for their talents, yet, if one was to be selected out as the first great literary character of the time, I believe all voices would concur in naming him. Let me here insert the following lines, descriptive of his character, though not long since written by me and to be found in a public print :—

'*On Samuel Johnson.*

Herculean strength and a Stentorian voice,
Of wit a fund, of words a countless choice:
In learning rather various than profound,
In truth intrepid, in religion sound:
A trembling form and a distorted sight,
But firm in judgment and in genius bright:
In controversy seldom known to spare,
But humble as the Publican in prayer;
To more, than merited his kindness, kind,
And, though in manners harsh, of friendly mind;
Deep ting'd with melancholy's blackest shade,
And, though prepar'd to die, of death afraid—
Such Johnson was; of him with justice vain,
When will this nation see his like again?'[1]

---

[1] Those who were brought into intimate relations with Johnson, and under his rugged exterior, striking, and occasionally repulsive peculiarities of manner, discovered his large heart, strong will, penetrating judgment, and giant intellectual powers, came to regard him with a feeling little short of idolatry. On the other hand, courtiers, and men of the world, those who had long indulged in the frivolities of life, until, at last, all earnestness and zeal were obliterated from their hearts, until they were literally without God in the world, had no sympathy with that strong, earnest being; but regarded him as little better than a rude boor. Of this class was Walpole. 'With a lumber of learning and some strong parts,' thus does he describe the author of 'Rasselas,' 'Johnson was an odious and mean character. By principle a Jacobite, arrogant, self-sufficient, and overbearing by nature, ungrateful through pride, and of *feminine* bigotry, he had prostituted his pen to party, even in a dictionary, and had afterwards, for a pension, contradicted his own definitions. His manners were sordid, supercilious, and brutal; his style ridiculously bombastic and vicious; and, in one word, with all the pedantry he had all the gigantic littleness of a country schoolmaster.'—*Memoirs of the Reign of George III.*, vol. ii. p. 323.

To this uncharitable and unjust characterization of Johnson, I am happy to oppose the authority of a mild but truthful and discriminating delineator of men and manners, whose pen has not often nor intentionally been led astray by misconception and prejudice. I refer to Lord Mahon. Referring to the prevalence of scepticism, in the days of Chesterfield, of Hume and Gibbon, he thus proceeds:—

'If, then, it be asked, who first, in England, at this period, breasted the waves, and stemmed the tide of infidelity—who, enlisting wit and eloquence together with argument and learning on the side of revealed religion, first turned the literary current in its favor, and mainly prepared the reaction which succeeded: that praise seems most justly to belong to Dr. Samuel Johnson. Religion was to him no mere lip-service, nor cold formality; he was mindful of it in his social hours as much as in his graver lucubrations; and he brought to it, not merely erudition such as few indeed possessed, but the weight of the highest character, and the respect which even his enemies could not deny him. It may be said of him that, though not in orders, he did the Church of England better service than most of those who at that listless era ate her bread. . . . . . Besides the gratitude due to Dr. Johnson, as the steadfast and able champion of the Christian Church, there is another point of view in which his character most justly claims respect. No man at any

Oliver Goldsmith began at this time to write for the stage, and it is to be lamented that he did not begin at an earlier period of life to turn his genius to dramatic compositions, and much more to be lamented, that, after he had begun, the succeeding period of his life was so soon cut off. There is no doubt but his genius, when more familiarized to the business, would have inspired him to accomplish great things. His first comedy of 'The Good-natured Man' was read and applauded in its manuscript by Edmund Burke, and the circle in which he then lived and moved: under such patronage it came with those testimonials to the director of Covent Garden theatre, as could not fail to open all the avenues to the stage, and bespeak all the favor and attention from the performers and the public, that the applauding voice of him, whose applause was fame itself, could give it. This comedy has enough to justify the good opinion of its literary patron, and secure its author against any loss of reputation, for it has the stamp of a man of talents upon it, though its popularity with the audience did not quite keep pace with the expectations that were grounded on the fiat it had antecedently been honored with. It was a first effort, however, and did not discourage its ingenious author

period has more worthily upheld the dignity of literature. When first he began to write, he had to struggle with all the bitterness of poverty. There were nights when he had no resting-place to lay his head. There were days when he had no money to buy food. Several of his early notes to Mr. Cave, the bookseller, have appended to his name the mournful word *impransus.* Once when Mr. Harte, the biographer of Gustavus Adolphus, was the guest of Mr. Cave, he observed that a plateful of the dinner was sent behind a screen; this, it seems, was for Johnson, who had been ashamed to join the company in his threadbare clothes. Yet through all these difficulties the 'retired and uncourtly scholar'—for thus he describes himself—never swerved from the path of principle, nor was once betrayed into any mean or dishonorable action. Still did he hold fast his opposition politics. Still did he assert his manly independence. His worst enemies might accuse him of churlishness and rudeness, but certainly never of flattery or fawning. His letter to Lord Chesterfield, in 1755, proves how sternly, upon the smallest provocation, real or imagined, he would thrust aside the hand of patronage. When, at last, by no hand besides his own, he had secured both bread and fame—when he found his society courted, and his ascendency acknowledged—when the bounty of the crown, unsought and unexpected, had raised him into affluence—he showed the remembrance of his past condition by the most generous relief of other men's distress. 'He loved the poor,' says his friend, Mrs. Thrale, 'as I never yet saw any one else love them, with an earnest desire to make them happy. In pursuance of these principles,' continues the same lady, 'he nursed whole nests of people in his house, where the lame, the blind, the sick, and the sorrowful found a sure retreat.' And when in those days Johnson communed with the great, he did not indeed omit that civil deference of manner which he deemed their due, but he felt that now he met them at least on equal, if not on superior terms; and made them respect in him both the inborn pride of genius, and the well-earned dignity of learning.'—*History of England*, vol. vi. pp. 313, 314.

from invoking his Muse a second time.[1] It was now, whilst his labors were in projection, that I first met him at the British Coffee-House, as I have already related somewhat out of place. He dined with us as a visitor, introduced, as I think, by Sir Joshua Reynolds, and we held a consultation upon the naming of his comedy, which some of the company had read, and which he detailed to the rest after his manner with a great deal of good humor. Somebody suggested 'She Stoops to Conquer,' and that title was agreed upon. When I perceived an embarrassment in his manner towards me, which I could readily account for, I lost no time to put him at his ease, and I flatter myself I was successful. As my heart was ever warm towards my contemporaries, I did not counterfeit, but really felt a cordial interest in his behalf, and I had soon the pleasure to perceive that he credited me for my sincerity. 'You and I,' said he, 'have very different motives for resorting to the stage. I write for money, and care little about fame.' I was touched by this melancholy confession, and from that moment busied myself assiduously amongst all my connections in his cause. The whole company pledged themselves to the support of the ingenuous poet, and faithfully kept their promise to him. In fact, he needed all that could be done for him, as Mr. Colman, then manager of Covent Garden theatre, protested against the comedy, when, as yet, he had not struck upon a name for it. Johnson at length stood forth in all his terrors as champion for the piece, and backed by us, his clients and retainers, demanded a fair trial. Colman again protested, but, with that salvo for his own reputation, liberally lent his stage to one of the most eccentric productions that ever found its way to it, and 'She Stoops to Conquer' was put into rehearsal.

We were not over-sanguine of success, but perfectly deter-

[1] 'This comedy,' says one of Goldsmith's biographers, 'was offered to Garrick, to be brought out at his theatre of Drury Lane; but after much fluctuation between doubt and encouragement, with his customary hesitation and uncertainty, he at length declined it. The conduct of Garrick in this instance was the more surprising, as the piece had been read and applauded in manuscript by most of the author's literary friends, and had not only the sanction of Burke's critical judgment, but Johnson himself had engaged to write the prologue. Colman, the manager of Covent Garden theatre, was, however, not so scrupulous, especially when he found it presented under such patronage. It was, therefore, agreed that it should be produced at his theatre; and it was represented there for the first time, on the 29th of January, 1768. Contrary to the expectations of the author and his friends, it did not meet with unqualified applause; and though it kept possession of the stage nine nights, it was finally withdrawn. The peculiar genius of its author was apparent in the ease and elegance of the dialogue, and throughout the whole there were many keen remarks on men and manners; but the piece was deficient in stage effect.'—*Works of Goldsmith,* edited by Washington Irving.

mined to struggle hard for our author: we accordingly assembled our strength at the Shakspeare Tavern in a considerable body for an early dinner, where Samuel Johnson took the chair at the head of a long table, and was the life and soul of the corps: the poet took post silently by his side, with the Burkes, Sir Joshua Reynolds, Fitzherbert, Caleb Whitefoord, and a phalanx of North British predetermined applauders, under the banner of Major Mills, all good men and true. Our illustrious president was in inimitable glee, and poor Goldsmith that day took all his raillery as patiently and complacently as my friend Boswell would have done any day, or every day of his life. In the mean time, we did not forget our duty, and though we had a better comedy going, in which Johnson was chief actor, we betook ourselves in good time to our separate and allotted posts, and waited the awful drawing up of the curtain. As our stations were preconcerted, so were our signals for plaudits arranged and determined upon in a manner that gave every one his cue where to look for them, and how to follow them up.

We had amongst us a very worthy and efficient member, long since lost to his friends and the world at large, Adam Drummond, of amiable memory, who was gifted by nature with the most sonorous, and at the same time the most contagious, laugh that ever echoed from the human lungs. The neighing of the horse of the son of Hystaspes was a whisper to it; the whole thunder of the theatre could not drown it. This kind and ingenuous friend fairly forewarned us that he knew no more when to give his fire than the cannon did that was planted on a battery. He desired, therefore, to have a flapper at his elbow, and I had the honor to be deputed to that office. I planted him in an upper box, pretty nearly over the stage, in full view of the pit and galleries, and perfectly well situated to give the echo all its play through the hollows and recesses of the theatre. The success of our manœuvres was complete. All eyes were upon Johnson, who sat in a front row of a side box, and when he laughed everybody thought themselves warranted to roar. In the mean time, my friend followed signals with a rattle so irresistibly comic, that, when he had repeated it several times, the attention of the spectators was so engrossed by his person and performances, that the progress of the play seemed likely to become a secondary object, and I found it prudent to insinuate to him that he might halt his music without any prejudice to the author; but alas, it was now too late to rein him in; he had laughed upon my signal where he found no joke, and now unluckily he fancied that he found a joke in almost everything that was said; so that nothing in nature could be more *mal-apropos* than some of his bursts every now and then were. These were dangerous moments, for the pit began to take umbrage; but we carried our play through, and triumphed not only over Colman's judgment, but our own.[1]

As the life of poor Oliver Goldsmith was now fast approaching to its period, I conclude my account of him with gratitude for the epitaph he bestowed on me in his poem called 'Retaliation.' It was upon a proposal started by Edmund Burke, that a party of friends who had dined together at Sir Joshua Reynolds' and my house, should meet at the St. James's Coffee-House, which accordingly took place, and was occasionally repeated with much festivity and good fellowship. Dr. Bernard, Dean of Derry, a very amiable and old friend of mine, Dr. Douglas, since Bishop of Salisbury, Johnson, David Garrick, Sir Joshua Reynolds, Oliver Goldsmith, Edmund and Richard Burke, Hickey, with two or three others, constituted our party. At one of these meetings an idea was suggested of extemporary epitaphs upon the parties present; pen and ink were called for, and Garrick off hand wrote an epitaph with a good deal of humor upon poor Goldsmith, who was the first in jest, as he proved to be in reality, that we committed to the grave. The dean also gave him an epitaph, and Sir Joshua illuminated the

[1] If the end of comedy is to make an audience merry, then, 'She Stoops to Conquer' deserves high commendation. The objection to it, however, is that, notwithstanding the purity and elegance of the language, the wit and humor with which it abounds, are too nearly allied to farce. 'The chief diversion,' says Johnson, in a letter to Boswell, 'arises from a stratagem, by which a lover is made to mistake his future father-in-law's house for an inn. This, you see, borders upon farce. The dialogue is quick and gay, and the incidents are so prepared as not to seem improbable.'

It is related of Goldsmith, that on the first night of performance he did not come to the house till towards the close of the representation, having rambled into St. James's Park, to ruminate on the probable fate of his piece; and such were his anxiety and apprehension that he was with much difficulty prevailed on to repair to the theatre, on the suggestion of a friend, who pointed out the necessity of his presence, in order to mark any objectionable passages, for the purpose of omission or alteration in the repetition of the performance. With expectation suspended between hope and fear, he had scarcely entered the passage that leads to the stage, when his ears were shocked with a hiss, which came from the audience as a token of their disapprobation of the farcical supposition of Mrs. Hardcastle being so deluded as to suppose herself at a distance of fifty miles from home, while she was actually not distant fifty yards. Such was our poor author's tremor and agitation on this unwelcome salute, that running up to the manager, he exclaimed: 'What's that? what's that?' 'Pshaw, doctor,' replied Colman, in a sarcastic tone, 'don't be terrified at *squibs*, when we have been setting these two hours upon a barrel of *gunpowder*.' The pride of Goldsmith was so mortified by this remark, that the friendship which had subsisted between him and the manager was from that moment dissolved.—*Life of Goldsmith.*

dean's verses with a sketch of his bust in pen and ink, inimitably caricatured. Neither Johnson nor Burke wrote anything, and when I perceived Oliver was rather sore, and seemed to watch me with that kind of attention which indicated his expectation of something in the same kind of burlesque with theirs, I thought it time to press the joke no further, and wrote a few couplets at a side-table, which, when I had finished and was called upon by the company to exhibit, Goldsmith with much agitation besought me to spare him, and I was about to tear them, when Johnson wrested them out of my hand, and in a loud voice read them at the table. I have now lost all recollection of them, and in fact they were little worth remembering, but as they were serious and complimentary, the effect they had upon Goldsmith was the more pleasing for being so entirely unexpected. The concluding line, which is the only one I can call to mind, was—

'All mourn the poet, I lament the man.'

This I recollect, because he repeated it several times, and seemed much gratified by it. At our next meeting he produced his epitaphs as they stand in the little posthumous poem above mentioned, and this was the last time he ever enjoyed the company of his friends.[1]

As he had served up the company under the similitude of various sorts of meat, I had in the mean time figured them under that of liquors, which little poem I rather think was printed, but of this I am not sure. Goldsmith sickened and died, and we had one concluding meeting at my house, when it was decided to publish his 'Retaliation,' and Johnson at the same time

[1] The following is the epitaph on Cumberland:—

'Here Cumberland lies, having acted his parts,
The Terence of England, the mender of hearts;
A flattering painter, who made it his care
To draw men as they ought to be, not as they are.
His gallants are all faultless, his women divine,
And Comedy wonders at being so fine;
Like a tragedy queen he has dizen'd her out,
Or rather like tragedy giving a rout.
His fools have their follies so lost in a crowd
Of virtues and feeling, that folly grows proud;
And coxcombs, alike in their failings alone,
Adopting his portraits, are pleased with their own;
Say, where has our poet this malady caught,
Or, wherefore his characters thus without fault?
Say, was it that vainly directing his view
To find out men's virtues, and finding them few,
Quite sick of pursuing each troublesome elf,
He grew lazy at last, and drew from himself?'

undertook to write an epitaph for our lamented friend, to whom we proposed to erect a monument by subscription in Westminster Abbey. This epitaph Johnson executed; but in the criticism, that was attempted against it, and in the Round-Robin signed at Mr. Beauclerc's house I had no part. I had no acquaintance with that gentleman, and was never in his house in my life.

Thus died Oliver Goldsmith, in his chambers in the Temple, at a period of life when his genius was yet in its vigor, and fortune seemed disposed to smile upon him. I have heard Dr. Johnson relate with infinite humor the circumstance of his rescuing him from a ridiculous dilemma by the purchase-money of his 'Vicar of Wakefield,' which he sold on his behalf to Dodsley, and, as I think, for the sum of ten pounds only. He had run up a debt with his landlady for board and lodging of some few pounds, and was at his wit's-end how to wipe off the score and keep a roof over his head, except by closing with a very staggering proposal on her part, and taking his creditor to wife, whose charms were very far from alluring, whilst her demands were extremely urgent. In this crisis of his fate he was found by Johnson in the act of meditating on the melancholy alternative before him. He showed Johnson his manuscript of 'The Vicar of Wakefield,' but seemed to be without any plan, or even hope, of raising money upon the disposal of it; when Johnson cast his eye upon it, he discovered something that gave him hope, and immediately took it to Dodsley, who paid down the price above mentioned in ready money, and added an eventual condition upon its future sale. Johnson described the precautions he took in concealing the amount of the sum he had in hand, which he prudently administered to him by a guinea at a time. In the event he paid off the landlady's score, and redeemed the person of his friend from her embraces. Goldsmith had the joy of finding his ingenious work succeed beyond his hopes, and from that time began to place a confidence in the resources of his talents, which thenceforward enabled him to keep his station in society, and cultivate the friendship of many eminent persons, who, whilst they smiled at his eccentricities, esteemed him for his genius and good qualities.[1]

[1] Goldsmith's situation on the occasion referred to in the text, has been variously and erroneously described. Cumberland is among the number of those who have either misstated it from defective recollection, or embellished it from design. Boswell gives an authentic detail of it as narrated by Johnson himself.

'I received one morning,' says the doctor, 'a message from poor Goldsmith that he was in great distress, and as it was not in his power to come to me, begging that I would come to him as soon as possible. I sent him a guinea, and promised to come to him directly. I accordingly went as soon as I was dressed, and found that his landlady had arrested him for his rent, at which

My father had been translated to the see of Kilmore, which placed him in a more civilized country, and lodged him in a more comfortable house. I continued my yearly visits, and again went over to Ireland with part of my family, and passed my whole summer recess at Kilmore. I had with unspeakable regret perceived some symptoms of an alarming nature about him, which seemed to indicate the breaking up of a most excellent constitution, which, nursed by temperance and regularity, had hitherto been blest with such an uninterrupted course of health, that he had never through his whole life been confined a single day to his bed, except when he had the smallpox in his childhood. In all his appetites and passions he was the most moderate of men: ever cheerful in his family and with his friends, but never yielding to the slightest excess. My mother, in the mean time, had been gradually sinking into a state of extreme debility and loss of health, and I plainly saw that my father's ceaseless agitation and anxiety on her account had deeply affected his constitution. He had flattered me with the hope that he would attempt a journey to England with her, and in that expectation, when my time was expired, I painfully took leave of him—and, alas! never saw him, or my mother, more.

In the winter of that same year, whilst I was at Bath by advice for my own health, I received the first afflicting intelligence of his death from Primate Robinson, who loved him truly and lamented him most sincerely. This sad event was speedily succeeded by the death of my mother, whose weak and exhausted frame sunk under the blow: those senses so acute, and that mind so richly endowed, were in an instant taken from her, and, after languishing in that melancholy state for a short but distressful period, she followed him to the grave.

Thus was I bereft of father and mother without the consolation of having paid them the last mournful duties of a son. One surviving sister, the best and most benevolent of human beings, attended them in their last moments, and performed those duties which my hard fortune would not suffer me to share.

In a small patch of ground, inclosed with stone walls, ad-

he was in a violent passion: I perceived that he had already changed my guinea, and had a bottle of Madeira and a glass before him. I put the cork into the bottle, desiring he would be calm, and began to talk to him of the means by which he might be extricated. He then told me that he had a novel ready for the press, which he produced to me. I looked into it, and saw its merit; told the landlady I should soon return; and hurrying to a bookseller, sold it for sixty pounds. I brought Goldsmith the money, and he discharged his rent, not without rating his landlady in a high tone for having used him so ill.'—*Boswell's Johnson*, vol. i. p. 398.

joining to the churchyard of Kilmore, but not within the pale of the consecrated ground, my father's corpse was interred beside the grave of the venerable and exemplary Bishop Bedel. This little spot, as containing the remains of that good and great man, my father had fenced and guarded with particular devotion, and he had more than once pointed it out to me as his destined grave, saying to me, as I well remember, in the words of the Old Prophet of Bethel, 'When I am dead, then bury me in this sepulchre, wherein the man of God is buried; lay my bones beside his bones.' This injunction was exactly fulfilled, and the Protestant Bishop of Kilmore, the mild friend of mankind, the impartial benefactor and unprejudiced protector of his Catholic poor, who almost adored him whilst living, was not permitted to deposit his remains within the precincts of his own churchyard, though they howled over his grave, and rent the air with their savage lamentations.

Thus, whilst their carcasses monopolize the consecrated ground, his bones, and the bones of Bedel, make sacred the unblest soil in which they moulder; but whilst I believe and am persuaded that his incorruptible is received into bliss eternal, what concerns it me where his corruptible is laid? The corpse of my lamented mother, the instructress of my youth, the friend and charm of my maturer years, is deposited by his side.

My father's patronage at Kilmore was very considerable, and this he strictly bestowed upon the clergy of his diocese, promoting the curates to the smaller livings, as vacancies occurred, and exacting from every man, whom he put into a living, where there was no parsonage-house, a solemn promise to build; but I am sorry to say that in no single instance was that promise fulfilled; which breach of faith gave him great concern, and in the cases of some particular friends, whom he had promoted in full persuasion of their keeping faith with him, afflicted him very sensibly, as I had occasion to know and lament. The opportunities he had of benefiting his fortune and family by fines, and the lapse of leases, which might have been considerable, he honorably declined to avail himself of, for when he had tendered his renewals upon the most moderate terms, and these had been delayed or rejected in his days of health, he peremptorily withstood their offers, when he found his life was hastening to its period, esteeming it, according to his high sense of honor, not perfectly fair to his successor to take what he called the packing-penny, and sweep clean before his departure. He left his see, therefore, much more valuable than he found it by this liberal and disinterested conduct, by which it was natural to hope he had secured to his executors the good offices and assistance of his successor in recovering the outstanding arrears due to his survivors—but in that hope we were shamefully disappointed; neither these arrears, nor even his legal demands for moneys expended on improvements, beneficial to the demesne, and regularly certified by his diocesan, could be recovered by me for my sister's use, till the Lord Primate took the cause in hand, and enforced the sluggish and unwilling satisfaction from the bishop who succeeded him.

Previous to these unhappy events I had written my fourth comedy of 'The Choleric Man,' and left it with Mr. Garrick for representation. Whilst I was at Bath the rehearsals were going on, and the play was brought upon the stage during my absence. It succeeded to the utmost of my wishes, but when I perceived that the malevolence of the public prints suffered no abatement, and saw myself charged with having vented contemptuous and illiberal speeches in the theatre, where I could not have been, against productions of my contemporaries, which I had neither heard nor seen, galled with such false and cruel aspersions, which, under the pressure of my recent losses and misfortunes, fell on me with accumulated asperity, I was induced to retort upon my defamers, and accordingly prefixed to the printed copy of my comedy 'A Dedication to Detraction,' in which I observe that 'ill health and other melancholy attentions, which I need not explain, kept me at a distance from the scene of its decision.' The chief object of this dedication was directed to a certain tract then in some degree of circulation, entitled 'An Essay on the Theatre,' in which the writer professes to draw 'a comparison between laughing and sentimental comedy,' and under the latter description particularly points his observations at 'The Fashionable Lover.' There is no occasion for me to speak further of this dedication, as it is attached to the comedy, which is yet in print, except to observe that I can still repeat with truth what I there assert to my imaginary patron, that 'I can take my conscience to witness I have paid him no sacrifice, devoted no time or study to his service, nor am a man in any respect qualified to repay his favors.'

Garrick wrote the epilogue to this comedy, as he also did that to the 'West Indian,' and Mrs. Abington spoke it.[1] That

[1] 'As an actress,' says Taylor, 'Mrs. Abington was distinguished for spirit and humor, rather than for high-breeding and elegance. She excelled in the delivery of sarcastic humor, to which the shrewdness of her mind, and the tartness of her tone gave the most effective piquancy. Her manners were not sufficiently graceful and well-bred for Congreve's 'Millimont,' altogether, but in those passages where she taunts Murwood, there was a stinging severity in her delivery that would have fully satisfied the author. Beatrice has more wit and pertness than good-breeding, and in that part she was excellent; and also

charming actress was now at the height of her fame, and performed the part of Lætitia in a style that gave great support to the representation. 'The Two Brothers,' formed upon the plan of 'Terrence's Adelphi,' were well cast between Mr. King and Mr. Aickin, and Western personated Jack Nightshade with inimitable humor. The chief effect in this play is produced by the strong contrast of character between Manlove and the Choleric Man, and again, with more comic force, between Charles, the courtly gentleman, and Jack, the rustic booby, who, at the first meeting with his brother, exclaims, 'Who would think you and I were whelps of the same breed? You are as sleek as my lady's lapdog, I am rough as a water-spaniel, bedaggled and bemired, as if I had come out of the fens with wild fowl; why, I have brought off as much soil upon my boots only, as would set up a Norfolk farmer!'

It was observed of this comedy that the spirit of the first two acts was not kept up through the concluding three, and the general sense of the public was said to confirm this remark, therefore I presume it is true. It was a successful play in its time, though it has not been so often before the public as any of the three which preceded it, and since Weston's decease it has been consigned to the shelf. If ever there shall be found an editor of my dramatic works as an entire collection, this comedy will stand forward as one of the most prominent amongst them. The plot, indeed, is not original, but the characters are humorously contrasted, and there is point and spirit in the dialogue. Such as it is, it was the fourth produced in four succeeding seasons, and if I acquired any small share of credit by those which preceded it, I did not forfeit it by the publication of this. To this comedy I appositely affixed the following motto from Plautus:—

> Jam istæc insipientia est
> Sic iram in promptu gerere.

In the autumn of this year I made a tour in company with my friend, the Earl of Warwick, to the lakes in Cumberland.

in Estifania, another character that demands vivacity and humor, not elegance. She was the first Lady Teazle, and that character was admirably suited to her talents. It was understood that she was well acquainted with the French authors, and could converse in Italian. She was received in many good families as an admired companion. When or why she married I know not. Her husband, I understood, was a musician. They had been separated many years, and it was reported that she allowed him an annuity not to molest her.'—*Records of my Life*, p. 230, *et seq.* Mrs. Abington's origin was obscure, and her morals profligate. Her maiden name was Barton; but little is known of her, and that little not at all to her credit, until she appeared on the boards of the Metropolitan theatres as a first-rate comic actress. She was born in 1735, and died in 1815.

He took with him Mr. Smith, well known to the public for his elegant designs after nature in Switzerland, Italy, and elsewhere: my noble friend himself is a master in the art of drawing and designing landscapes in a bold and striking character, of which our tour afforded a vast variety. Whilst we passed a few days at Keswick, I hastily composed an irregular ode, 'which was literally struck out on the spot, and is addressed to the sun; for as the season was advancing towards winter, we had frequent temptations to invoke that luminary, who was never very gracious to our suit, except whilst we were viewing the lake of Keswick and its accompaniments.'

With this invocation my ode commences:—

'Soul of the world, refulgent Sun,
Oh, take not from my ravish'd sight
Those golden beams of living light,
Nor, ere thy daily course be run,
Precipitate the night.
Lo, where the ruffian clouds arise,
Usurp the abdicated skies,
And seize th' ethereal throne:
Sullen sad the scene appears,
Huge Helvellyn streams with tears;
Hark! 'tis giant Skiddaw's groan;
I hear terrific Lawdoor roar;
The sabbath of thy reign is o'er,
The anarchy's begun.
Father of light, return; break forth refulgent Sun!'
&c. &c.

This ode, with one addressed to Doctor James, was published and sold by Mr. Robson, in New Bond Street, in the year 1776, and is, I believe, to be found in 'The Tour to the Lakes.' The ode to Doctor Robert James was suggested by the recovery of my second son from a dangerous fever, effected, under Providence, by his celebrated powders. I am tempted to insert the following short extract, descriptive of the person of Death:—

'On his pale steed erect the monarch stands,
His dirk and javelin glittering in his hands:
This from a distance deals th' ignoble blow,
And that despatches the resisting foe:
Whilst all beneath him, as he flies,
Dire are the tossings, deep the cries,
The landscape darkens and the season dies.'
&c. &c.

These odes I addressed to Mr. George Romney, then lately returned from pursuing his studies at Rome.[1]

[1] On Romney's return from Italy he met with extraordinary success—in one year painting portraits to the value of £3,635. He was born in Lancashire, in 1734, and died in 1802.

'There are not many things in biography more striking,' says Lord Mahon,

The next piece that I presented to the stage under the management of Mr. Garrick was 'Timon of Athens,' altered from Shakspeare, to which I prefixed the following advertisement, when it was published by Becket:—

'I wish I could have brought this play upon the stage with less violence to its author, and not so much responsibility on my own part. New characters of necessity require some display. Many original passages of the first merit are still retained, and in the contemplation of them, my errors, I hope, will be overlooked or forgiven. In examining the brilliancy of a diamond, few people throw away any remarks upon the dulness of the foil.' Barry played the part of Timon, and Mrs. Barry that of Evanthe, which was engrafted on the original for the purpose of writing up the character of Alcibiades, in which a young actor of the name of Crofts made his first appearance on the stage. As the entire part of Evanthe, and with very few exceptions the whole of Alcibiades are new, the author of this alteration has much to answer for, and much it behoved him to make his new matter harmonize with the old; with what degree of success this is done it scarce becomes me to say; the public approbation seemed to sanction the attempt at the first production of the play, the neglect with which the stage has passed it over since disposes us to draw conclusions less in favor of its merit.

As few, who read these memoirs, have ever met, or probably ever will meet with this altered play, which is now out of print,

'than the tale how, at the age of twenty-seven, he forsook his young wife at Kendal, and went forth to seek his fortune in London; how, after seven-and-thirty years of desertion, he returned to her, rich, indeed, and famous, but worn out in body and in mind; and how, with patient forgiveness, she nursed him during his remaining span of decay, and, at last, of imbecility. When in full possession of his powers he had been deemed a rival to Sir Joshua himself, and it is by no means to the credit of the president, that Romney never was elected even an associate of the Royal Academy. Indeed, whenever Reynolds had occasion to refer to him, he would call him only "the man in Cavendish Square." In those days Lord Thurlow had said: "There are two factions in art, and for my part I am of the Romney faction." But, as Mr. Southey observes, time has reversed the chancellor's decision.'—*History of England*, vol. vi. p. 325.

Cumberland, like Thurlow, was also of the Romney faction. Garrick, one day, speaking of Cumberland to the President, said: 'He hates you, Sir Joshua, because you do not admire the painter whom he considers as a second Corregio.' 'Who is that,' replied Reynolds. 'Why, his Corregio,' answered Garrick, 'is Romney.' Except the desertion of his wife, whom he visited but twice in thirty years, and which will remain forever a fatal blot on his character, there is but little in the life of Romney which can be condemned. He was amiable, kind, upright, and liberal. His heart and purse were ever open to the calls of distress.

I trust that such at least will forgive me if I extract a short specimen from my own new matter in the second act—

'ACT 2. SCENE 3.

LUCULLUS AND LUCIUS.

Lucul.—How now, my lord; in private?
Luc.—Yes, I thought so,
Till an unwelcome intermeddling lord
Stept in and ask'd the question.
Lucul.—What, in anger!
By heav'ns I'll gall him! for he stands before me,
In the broad sunshine of Lord Timon's bounty,
And throws my better merits into shade. [*Aside.*
Luc.—Now would I kill him if I durst. [*Aside.*
Lucul.—Methinks
You look but coldly. What has cross'd your suit?
Alas, poor Lucius! but I read your fate
In that unkind one's frown.
Luc.—No doubt, my lord,
You, that receive them ever, are well vers'd
In the unkind one's frowns: as the clear stream
Reflects your person, so may you espy
In the sure mirror of her scornful brow
The clouded picture of your own despair.
Lucul.—Come, you presume too far; talk not thus idly
To me, who know you.
Luc.—Know me?
Lucul.—Ay, who know you.
For one that courses up and down on errands,
A stale retainer at Lord Timon's table;
A man grown great by making legs and cringes,
By winding round a wanton spendthrift's heart,
And gulling him at pleasure. Now do I know you?
Luc.—Gods, must I bear this? bear it from Lucullus?
I who first brought thee to Lord Timon's stirrup,
Set thee in sight and breath'd into thine ear
The breath of hope? What hadst thou been, ingrateful,
But that I took up Jove's imperfect work,
Gave thee a shape and made thee into man?

Alcibiades to them.

Alcib.—What, wrangling, lords, like hungry curs for crusts?
Away with this unmanly war of words!
Pluck forth your shining rapiers from their shells,
And level boldly at each other's hearts.
Hearts did I say? Your hearts are gone from home,
And hid in Timon's coffers. Fie upon it!
Luc.—My Lord Lucullus, I shall find a time.
Alcib.—Ha! find a time! the brave make time and place.
Gods, gods, what things are men! You'll find a time?
A time for what? To murder him in 's sleep?
The man who wrongs me, at the altar's foot
I'll seize, yea, drag him from the sheltering ægis
Of stern Minerva.
Luc.—Ay; 'tis your profession.
Alcib.—Down on your knees and thank the gods for that,
Or woe for Athens, were it left to such

As you are to defend. Do ye not hate
Each other heartily? Yet neither dares
To bear his trembling falchion to the sun.
How tame they dangle on your coward thighs!
Lucul.—We are no soldiers, sir.
Alcib.—No, ye are lords:
A lazy, proud, unprofitable crew:
The vermin gender'd from the rank corruption
Of a luxurious state. No soldiers, say you?
And wherefore are ye none? Have ye not life,
Friends, honor, freedom, country to defend?
He, that hath these, by nature is a soldier,
And, when he wields his sword in their defence,
Instinctively fulfils the end he lives for.'
&c. &c.

When Moody, from the excellence of his acting in the part of Major O'Flaherty, became the established performer of Irish characters, I wrote in compliance with his wishes another Hibernian upon a smaller scale, and composed the entertainment of 'The Note of Hand, or, Trip to Newmarket,' which was the last piece of my writing, which Mr. Garrick produced upon his stage before he disposed of his property in Drury Lane Theatre, and withdrew from business.

During my residence at Bath I had been greatly pleased with the performance of the part of Shylock by Mr. Henderson, and, upon conversing with him, found that his wishes strongly pointed to an engagement, if that could be obtained, at Drury Lane, then under the direction of Mr. Garrick. When I had seen him in different characters, and became confirmed in my opinion of his merit, I warmly recommended him to Mr. Garrick, and was empowered to contract for his engagement upon terms that, to my judgment, and that of other intermediate friends, appeared to be extremely reasonable. At first I conceived the negotiation as good as concluded, but some reports, that rather clashed with mine, rendered Mr. Garrick cool in the business, and disposed to consult other opinions as to Mr. Henderson's abilities; and amongst these he seemed greatly to depend upon his brother George's judgment, whose report was by no means of the same sanguine complexion with mine. Poor George had come to Bath in a lamentable state of health, and must have seen Henderson with distempered eyes to err so egregiously as he did in his account of him. It proved, however, in the upshot, decisive against my advice, and after a languishing negotiation, which got at length into other hands than mine, Garrick made the transfer of his property in the theatre without the name of Henderson upon the roll of his performers. Truth obliges me to say that the negotiation in all its parts and passages was not creditable to Mr. Garrick, and left impressions on the mind of Henderson, that time did not speedily wear out.

He had wit, infinite pleasantry and inimitable powers of mimicry, which he felt himself privileged to employ, and employed only too successfully. The season of the winter theatres passed over, and when the Haymarket house opened, Henderson came from Bath with all the powers of his genius on the alert, and upon the summer stage fully justified everything that I and others had said of him through the winter, and established himself completely in the public favor.[1] A great resort of men of talents now flocked around him; the town considered him as a man injuriously rejected, and though, when they imputed it to envy, I am sure they were mistaken, yet when Garrick found that by lending his ear to foolish opinions, and quibbling about terms, he had missed the credit of engaging the best actor of the time, himself excepted, it is not to be wondered at if the praise bestowed on Henderson's performances was not the most agreeable topic that could be chosen for his entertainment. He could not indeed always avoid hearing these applauses, but he did not hold himself obliged to second them, and when curiosity drew him to the summer theatre to see Henderson in the part of Shylock, he said nothing in his dispraise, but he discovered great merit in 'Tubal,' which of course had been the cast of some second-rate performer.

Henderson, in the mean time, was transferred from the Haymarket Theatre to Drury Lane, under the direction of Mr.

[1] On a subsequent page, Cumberland has given his estimate of Henderson's character and talents more at length. That he was an actor of uncommon and versatile powers, is generally conceded. Comedy, however, was his forte. Unlike Garrick, he had many disadvantages to overcome, in order to obtain, as he did, the first honors of his profession. His person,' says the 'Biographia Dramatica,' 'was not striking, nor were his features interesting. He had nothing in his appearance to create, at first sight, that surprise and admiration which conciliate favor and prejudice judgment.' 'On the other hand,' says the same authority, 'his excellences were of the most solid kind; they depended on a mind gifted with wonderful powers of feeling, and with powers of expression equally wonderful. Of the great compass of his talents, the proof is easy: he was the lineal successor of almost all the first performers in the preceding age; of Quin, in Falstaff; Woodward, in Bobadil; Macklin, in Shylock; Mossop, in Zanga; Digges, in Wolsey; Barry, in Evander; and Garrick, in Richard, Lear, Benedick, Sir John Brute, and almost all his other characters; but the greatest triumph of the comic muse, perhaps, was Henderson's representation of the fat knight, Falstaff; it is probable, 'We ne'er shall look upon its like again!'' Vol. i. p. 42, Introduc.

In this high praise the critics are not unanimous. 'His defects are said to have been an occasional sawing of the air, and latterly a habit of impregnating every character with a tinge of Falstaff.'—*Life of Henderson, Modern British Biography*, vol. iv. p. 380. 'Henderson's face and person,' says Taylor, 'were not fitted for tragedy, but he was an excellent comedian; and though his Falstaff was the most facetious I ever saw, yet it always struck me that it was a mixture of the old woman with the old man.'—*Records of my Life*, p. 213.

As a man, Henderson is said to have been estimable. His failings were an inordinate love of money, and inordinate vanity.

Sheridan, where I brought out my tragedy of 'The Battle of Hastings,' in which he played the part of Edgar Atheling, not indeed with the happiest effect, for he did not possess the graces of person or deportment, and as that character demanded both, an actor might have been found, who, with inferior abilities, would have been a fitter representative of it. As for the play itself, it was published, and is to be found in more collections than one; its readers will probably be of opinion, that it is better written than planned; a judgment to which I shall most readily submit, not only in this instance but in several others.

About this time died the Earl of Halifax. He had filled the high stations of First Lord of Trade and Plantations, Lord Lieutenant of Ireland, Principal Secretary of State, First Lord of the Admiralty, Lord Lieutenant of the county of Northampton, and Knight of the Garter. He had no son, and his title is extinct. His fine mansion and estate of Stansted, left to him by Mr. Lumley, was sold after his decease. I saw him in his last illness, when his constitution was an absolute wreck; I was subpœnaed to give evidence on this point before the Lord Chief Justice Mansfield, and according to my conscience deposed what was my opinion of his hopeless state; his physician, Sir Noah Thomas, whose professional judgment had justly more authority and influence than mine, by his deposition superseded mine, and the death of his patient very shortly after contradicted his. I never knew that man, whose life, if circumstantially detailed, would furnish a more striking moral and a more tragical catastrophe. Nature endowed him liberally with her gifts, Fortune showered her favors profusely upon him, Providence repeatedly held forth the most extraordinary vouchsafements—what a mournful retrospection! I am not bound to dwell upon it. I turn from it with horror.[1]

A brighter scene now meets me, for whilst I was yet a subaltern in the Board of Trade, uncomfortably executing the office of clerk of the reports, by the accession of Lord George Germain to the seals for the colonial department I had a new principal to look up to. I had never been in a room with him in my life, except during his trial at the Horse Guards for the affair of Minden, which I attended through the whole of its progress, and regularly reported what occurred to Mr. Dodington, who was then out of town; some of his letters I preserved, but of my own, according to custom, I took no copies. When Lord George had taken the seals, I asked my friend Colonel James Cunningham to take me with him to Pall Mall, which he did,

[1] Halifax had abilities; but lacked cautious, prudent self-control. He fell a victim to intemperance.

and the ceremony of paying my respects was soon dismissed. I confess I thought my new chief was quite as cold in his manner as a minister need be, and rather more so than my intermediate friend had given me reason to expect. I was now living in great intimacy with the Duke of Dorset, and asked him to do me that grace with his uncle, which the honor of being acknowledged by him as his friend would naturally have obtained for me. This I am confident he would readily have done but for reasons which precluded all desire on my part to say another word upon the business. I was therefore left to make my own way with a perfect stranger, whilst I was in actual negotiation with Mr. Pownall for the secretaryship, and had understood Lord Clare to be friendly to our treaty, in the very moment when he ceased to be our first lord, and the power of accommodating us in our wishes was shifted from his hands into those of Lord George. I considered it, therefore, as an opportunity gone by, and entertained no further hopes of succeeding. A very short time sufficed to confirm the idea I had entertained of Lord George's character for decision and dispatch in business; there was at once an end to all our circumlocutory reports and inefficient forms, that had only impeded business, and substituted ambiguity for precision; there was (as William Gerard Hamilton, speaking of Lord George, truly observed to me), no trash in his mind; he studied no choice phrases, no superfluous words, nor ever suffered the clearness of his conceptions to be clouded by the obscurity of his expressions, for these were the simplest and most unequivocal that could be made use of for explaining his opinions, or dictating his instructions. In the mean while, he was so momentarily punctual to his time, so religiously observant of his engagements, that we, who served under him in office, felt the sweets of the exchange we had so lately made in the person of our chief.

I had now no other prospect but that of serving in my subordinate situation under an easy master with security and comfort, for as I was not flattered with the show of any notices from him but such as I might reasonably expect, I built no hopes upon his favor, nor allowed myself to think I was in any train of succeeding in my treaty with our secretary for his office; and as I had reason to believe he was equally happy with myself in serving under such a principal, I took for granted he would move no further in the business.

One day, as Lord George was leaving the office, he stopped me on the outside of the door, at the head of the stairs, and invited me to pass some days with him and his family at Stoneland, near Tunbridge Wells. It was on my part so unexpected, that I doubted if I had rightly understood him, as he had spoken in a low and submitted voice, as his manner was, and I consulted his confidential secretary, Mr. Doyley, whether he would advise me to the journey. He told me that he knew the house was filled from top to bottom with a large party, that he was sure there would be no room for me, and dissuaded me from the undertaking. I did not quite follow his advice by neglecting to present myself, but I resolved to secure my retreat to Tunbridge Wells, and kept my chaise in waiting to make good my quarters. When I arrived at Stoneland I was met at the door by Lord George, who soon discovered the precaution I had taken, and himself conducting me to my bedchamber, told me it had been reserved for me, and ever after would be set apart as mine, where he hoped I would consent to find myself at home. This was the man I had esteemed so cold, and thus was I at once introduced to the commencement of a friendship, which day by day improved, and which no one word or action of his life to come ever for an instant interrupted or diminished.

Shortly after this it came to his knowledge that there had been a treaty between Mr. Pownall and me for his resignation of the place of Secretary, and he asked me what had passed; I told him how it stood, and what the conditions were, that my superior in office expected for the accommodation. I had not yet mentioned this to him, and probably never should. He said he would take it into his own hands, and in a few days signified the king's pleasure that Mr. Pownall's resignation was accepted, and that I should succeed him as Secretary in clear and full enjoyment of the place, without any compensation whatsoever. Thus was I, beyond all hope and without a word said to me that could lead me to expect a favor of that sort, promoted by surprise to a very advantageous and desirable situation. I came to my office at the hour appointed, not dreaming of such an event, and took my seat at the adjoining table, when Mr. Pownall being called out of the room, Lord George turned round to me and bade me take his chair at the bottom of the table, announcing to the Board his majesty's commands as above recited, with a positive prohibition of all stipulations. When I had endeavored to express myself as properly on the occasion, as my agitated state of spirits would allow of, I remember Lord George made answer, 'That if I was as well pleased upon receiving his majesty's commands as he was in being the bearer of them, I was indeed very happy.' If I served him truly, honestly, and ardently ever after, till I followed him to the grave, where is my merit? How could I do otherwise?

CHAPTER V.

The American contest—Services to Lord George Sackville—His children—Opera of Calypso—'The Widow of Delphi'—Lady Frances Burgoyne—Robert Perreau—Dr. Dodd—Rodney—Anecdote of Germain—Anecdote of Rodney—Character of—His nautical manœuvre—Lines to Lord Mansfield.

THE conflict in America was now raging at its height; that was a business out of my office to be concerned in, and I willingly pass it over; but it was in my way to know the effects it had upon the anxious spirit of my friend, and very much it was both my wish and my endeavor by every means in my capacity to be helpful at those hours, which were necessary for his relaxation, and take to my share as many of those burdensome and vexatious concerns, as without intrusion upon other people's offices I could relieve him from. All that I could I did, and as I was daily with him, and never out of call, I reflect with comfort, that there were occasions when my zeal was not unprofitably exerted for his alleviation and repose. I might say more, for those were trying and unquiet times. It is not a very safe or enviable predicament to be marked out for a known attachment to an unpopular character, and be continually under arms to turn out and encounter the prejudices of mankind. There is a middle kind of way, which some men can hit off, between doing all and doing nothing, which saves appearances and satisfies easy consciences; but some consciences are not so easily satisfied.

I had now four sons at Westminster school boarding at one house, and my two daughters coming into the world, so that the accession to my circumstances, which my promotion in office gave me, put me greatly at my ease, and enabled me to press their education with advantage. My eldest son Richard went through Westminster with the reputation of an excellent school-scholar, and I admitted him of Trinity College, but in one of his vacations having prevailed with me to let him volunteer a cruise with Sir Charles Hardy, then commander of the home fleet, the rage of service seized him, and by his importunity I may say, in the words of Polonius, he 'wrung from me my slow leave' to let him enter himself an ensign in the first regiment of foot-guards. This at once gave fire to the train, and the three remaining heroes breathed nothing but war: my second boy, George, took to the sea, and sailed for America; my third, Charles, enrolled himself an ensign in the tenth, and my youngest, William, disposed of himself as my second had done, and also took his departure for America under the command of the late Sir Richard Hughes.

I had been dispossessed of my delightful residence at Tyringham, near to which Mr. Praed, the present possessor, has now built a splendid mansion, and I had taken a house at Tetworth in Bedfordshire to be near my kind and ever honored friend Lady Frances Burgoyne, sister to Lord Halifax. Here I passed the summer recesses, and in one of these I wrote the Opera of 'Calypso,' for the purpose of introducing to the public the compositions of Mr. Butler, then a young man, newly returned from Italy, where he had studied under Piccini, and given early proofs of his genius. He passed the summer with me at Tetworth, and there he wrote the music for 'Calypso' in the style of a serious opera. 'Calypso' was brought out at Covent Garden, but that theatre was not by any means possessed of such a strength of vocal performers, as have of late years belonged to it.[1] Mrs. Kennedy, in the part of Telemachus, and Leoni in that of Proteus, were neither of them very eminently qualified to grace the action of an opera, yet as that was a consideration subordinate to the music, it was to them that Mr. Butler addressed his chief attention, and looked up for his support. I believe I may venture to say that more beautiful and original compositions were never presented to the English stage by a native master, though I am not unmindful of the fame of Artaxerxes; but 'Calypso,' supported only by Leoni and Mrs. Kennedy, did not meet success proportioned to its merit, and I should humbly conceive upon the same stage, which has since been so power-

[1] 'Calypso' was performed only a few nights. Cumberland had adopted the readiest means to procure its condemnation, by imprudently attacking newspaper editors, in his prelude, as a set of unprincipled fellows. 'Mr. Cumberland,' wrote Walpole, 'has given the town a masque, called Calypso, which is a prodigy of dulness. Would you believe that such a sentimental writer would be so gross as to make cantharides one of the ingredients of a love-potion for enamoring Telemachus? If you think I exaggerate, here are the lines:—

'To these, the hot Hispanian fly,
Shall bid his languid pulse beat high.'

Proteus and Antiope are Minerva's missioners for securing the prince's virtue, and in recompènse they are married and crowned king and queen.'—*To the Rev. Mr. Cole*, March 28, 1779.

fully mounted by Braham, Incledon and Storace, it might have been revived with brilliant effect. Why Mr. Butler did not publish his music, or a selection at least of those airs which were most applauded, I cannot tell; but so it was, and the score now remains in the depot of Covent Garden, whilst a few only of the songs, and those in manuscript, are in the possession of my second daughter Sophia, whom he instructed in singing, and with the aid of great natural talents on her part, accomplished her very highly. 'Calypso' as a drama has been published, therefore of my share in it as an opera I need not say much; it is before the reader, but I confess I lament that music, which I conceive to be so exquisitely beautiful, should be buried in oblivion. Mr. Butler has been long since settled at Edinburgh as a teacher and writer of music, and is well known to the professors and admirers of that art.

That I may not again recur to my dramatic connections with this ingenious composer, I will here observe that in the following season I wrote a comic opera, which I entitled 'The Widow of Delphi, or The Descent of the Deities,' the songs of which he set to music. Mr. Butler published a selection of songs, &c. from this opera, but as I was going out of England I did not send my copy to the press, and having now had it many years in my hands, by the frequent revisions and corrections which I have had opportunities of giving to this manuscript, I am encouraged to believe that if I, or any after me, shall send it into the world, this drama will be considered as one of my most classical and creditable productions.

Having adverted to the happiness and honor which I enjoyed in the friendship of Lady Frances Burgoyne, it occurs to me to relate the part which, at her request, I undertook in the behalf of the unfortunate Robert Perreau, when under trial for his life. The defence, which he read at the bar, was to a word drawn up by me, under the revision of his counsel Mr. Dunning, who did not change a syllable. I dined with Garrick on the very day when Robert Perreau had delivered it in court; there was a large company, and he was expatiating upon the effect of it, for he had been present; he even detailed the heads of it with considerable accuracy, and was so rapturous in his praises of it, that he predicted confidently, though not truly, that the man who drew up that defence had saved the prisoner's life, and what would he not give to know who it was? I confess my vanity was strongly moved to tell him; but he shortly after found it out, and perhaps repented of his hyperboles, for it was not good policy in him to over-praise a writer for the stage. When poor Dodd fell under the like misfortune, he applied to me in the first instance for the like good offices, but as soon as I understood that application had been made to Doctor Johnson, and that he was about to be taken under his shield, I did what every other friend to the unhappy would have done, consigned him to the stronger advocate, convinced that if the powers of Johnson could not move mercy to reach his lamentable case, there was no further hope in man; his penitence alone could save him.

I had known Sir George Brydges Rodney in early life, and whilst he was residing in France, pending the uneasy state of his affairs at home, had spared no pains to serve his interest and pave the way for his return to his own country, where I was not without hopes, by the recommendation of Lord George Germain, to procure him an employment worthy of his talents and high station in the navy.[1] I drew up from his minutes a memorial of his services, and petitioned for employ: he came home at the risk of his liberty to refute some malicious imputations that had been glanced at his character: this he effectually and honorably accomplished, and I was furnished with testimonials very creditable to him as an officer; his situation in the mean while was very uncomfortable, and his exertions circumscribed, yet in this pressure of his affairs, to mark his readiness and zeal for service, he addressed a letter to the king, tendering himself to serve as volunteer under an admiral, then going out, who, if I do not mistake, was his junior on the list. In this forlorn, unfriended state, with nothing but exclusion and despair before his eyes, when not a ray of hope beamed upon him from the admiralty, and he dared not set a foot beyond the limits of his privilege, I had the happy fortune to put in train that statement of his claim for service and employ, which, through the immediate application of Lord George, taking all the responsibility on himself, obtained for that adventurous and gallant admiral the command of that squadron, which on its passage to the West

[1] In the elections for 1768, Rodney was returned to the House of Commons for Northampton; but so great was his expenditure, that he was subsequently obliged to retire to France, in order to avoid his creditors. Here, he was offered, through the Duke de Biron, high rank in the French Navy. He thus replied: 'It is true, Monsieur le Duc, that my distresses have driven me from my country, but no temptation can estrange me from her service; had this offer been voluntary on your part, I should have considered it an insult; but I am glad it proceeds from a source that can do no wrong.' It is said that this spirited and patriotic reply, on reaching the admiralty, obtained for Rodney the rank of Admiral.

Rodney had fine qualities of heart, and distinguished talents as a commander. For his great services, it has been thought, his country bestowed on him an inadequate reward. The greater portion of his life was embittered by pecuniary difficulties. He died in 1792, at the advanced age of seventy-four.

Indies made capture of the Spanish fleet fitted out for the Caraccas. The degree of gratification, which I then experienced, is not easily to be described. It was not only that of a triumph gained, but of a terror dismissed, for the West India merchants had been alarmed, and clamored against the appointment so generally and so decidedly as to occasion no small uneasiness to my friend and patron, and drew from him something that resembled a remonstrance for the risk I had exposed him to. But in the brilliancy of this exploit all was done away, and past alarms were only recollected to contrast the joy which this success diffused.

Here I hope to be forgiven if I record an answer of Lord George Germain's to an officious gentleman, who upon some reference to me in his concerns expressed himself with surprise at the degree of influence which I appeared to have—'You are very right,' replied my friend, 'that gentleman has a great deal to do with me and my affairs, and if you can find any other to take his place as disinterestedly attached to me and as capable of serving me, I am confident he will hold himself very highly obliged to you for relieving him from a burden that brings him neither profit nor advantage, and only subjects him to such remarks as you have now been making.'

It happened to me to be present, and sitting next to Admiral Rodney at table, when the thought seemed first to occur to him of breaking the French line by passing through it in the heat of action. It was at Lord George Germain's house at Stoneland after dinner, when having asked a number of questions about the manœuvring of columns, and the effect of charging with them on a line of infantry, he proceeded to arrange a parcel of cherry stones, which he had collected from the table, and forming them as two fleets drawn up in line and opposed to each other, he at once arrested our attention, which had not been very generally engaged by his preparatory inquiries, by declaring he was determined so to pierce the enemy's line of battle, (arranging his manœuvre at the same time on the table) if ever it was his fortune to bring them into action. I dare say this passed with some as mere rhapsody, and all seemed to regard it as a very perilous and doubtful experiment, but landsmen's doubts and difficulties made no impression on the admiral, who having seized the idea held it fast, and in his eager, animated way went on manœuvring his cherry stones, and throwing his enemy's representatives into such utter confusion, that, already possessed of that victory in imagination, which in reality he lived to gain, he concluded his process by swearing he would lay the French admiral's flag at his sovereign's feet; a promise which he actually pledged to his majesty in his closet, and faithfully and gloriously performed.[1]

He was a singular and extraordinary man; there were some prominent and striking eccentricities about him, which on a first acquaintance might dismiss a cursory observer with inadequate and false impressions of his real character; for he would very commonly indulge himself in a loose and heedless style of talking, which for a time might intercept and screen from observation the sound, good sense that he possessed, and the strength and dignity of mind that were natural to him. Neither ought it to be forgotten that the sea was his element, and it was there, and not on land, that the standard ought to be planted by which his merits should be measured. We are apt to set that man down as vain-glorious and unwise, who fights battles over the table, and in the ardor of his conversation, though amongst enviers and enemies, keeps no watch upon his words, confiding in their candor and believing them his friends. Such a man was Admiral Lord Rodney, whom history will record amongst the foremost of our naval heroes, and whoever doubts his courage might as well dispute against the light of the sun at noon-day.

That he carried this projected manœuvre into operation, and that the effect of it was successfully decisive all the world knows. My friend, Sir Charles Douglas, captain of the fleet, confessed to me that he himself had been adverse to the experiment, and in discussing it with the admiral had stated his objections; to these he got no other answer but that 'his counsel was not called for; he required obedience only, he did not want advice.' Sir Charles also told me that whilst the project was in operation (the battle then raging), his own attention being occupied by the gallant defence made by the French Glorieux against the ships that were pouring their fire into her, upon his crying out, 'Behold, Sir George, the Greeks and Trojans contending for the body of Patroclus!' The admiral, then pacing the quarter deck in great agitation pending the experiment of his manœuvre (which in the instance of one ship had unavoidably miscarried), peevishly exclaimed: 'Damn the Greeks and damn the Trojans; I have other things to think of.' When, in a few minutes after, his supporting ship having led through the French line in a gallant style,

[1] This plan of breaking through the centre of the enemy's line, was not, it seems, original with Rodney. (*Vide* the Supplement, Chap. XIII.) Its author is said to be John Clerk, who wrote a work on Naval Tactics. It is asserted, that Rodney once observed to Mr. Dundas: 'A countryman of yours, Clerk, has taught us how to fight; and if ever I meet the French fleet, I will try his way;' and during his last illness, in a conversation with Lord Haddington, relative to the action with the Count De Grasse, Rodney is reported to have waved his hand, and shouted, 'Clerk, of Elgin, forever!'

turning with a smile of joy to Sir Charles Douglas, he cried out: 'Now, my dear friend, I am at the service of your Greeks and Trojans, and the whole of Homer's Iliad, or as much of it as you please, for the enemy is in confusion, and our victory is secure.' This anecdote, correctly as I relate it, I had from the gallant officer, untimely lost to his country, whose candor scorned to rob his admiral of one leaf of his laurels, and who, disclaiming all share in the manœuvre, nay, confessing he had objected to it, did in the most pointed and decided terms again and again repeat his honorable attestations of the courage and conduct of his commanding officer on that memorable day.

In a short time after, when, upon a change of the administration, this victorious admiral was superseded and called home,[1] he confirmed by his practice that maxim, which he took every opportunity to inculcate (and a very wise one and well worthy of being recorded it is), viz: 'That our naval officers have nothing to do with parties and politics, being simply bound to carry their instructions into execution to the best of their abilities, without deliberating about men and measures, which forms no part of their duty, and for which they are in no degree responsible.' It was to this transaction I alluded in the following lines, which I wrote and inclosed to Lord Mansfield about this time. I had the honor and happiness of enjoying his society frequently, but the immediate reason for my addressing him in this style has no connection with the subject here referred to:—

TO THE EARL OF MANSFIELD.

'Shall merit find no shelter but the grave,
And envy still pursue the wise and brave?
Sticks the leech close to life, and only drops
When its food fails and the heart's current stops?
Though sculptur'd laurels grace the hero's bust,
And tears are mingled with the poet's dust,
Review their sad memorials, you will find
This fell by faction, that in misery pin'd.

---

[1] 'The party prejudice against him,' says Mahon, 'may be forgiven in a landsman like Burke; less readily in that experienced Admiral to whom the naval administration was intrusted. Lord Keppel, whom we have seen so keenly sensitive to any supposed slight or disparagement to himself, appears to have acted with the coldest disdain, with the most unjustifiable severity towards an officer, it may be said without offence, greatly his superior in professional renown. Not only did he decide on recalling Rodney from the post he so ably filled, but he did so without an expression of kindness or concern; he did so, not even in his own hand or name, but in a dry official letter from his secretary, Mr. Stephens. That letter of revocation bears date the 1st of May. But even before that date, Rodney, by the blessing of Providence, had secured to all ages his country's glory and his own, and turned the Rockingham minister, however unwillingly, from his contemptuous recall to his promotion and his praise.'—*History of England*, vol. vii. p. 172.

When France and Spain the subject ocean swept,
Whilst Briton's tame inglorious lion slept,
Or lashing up his courage now and then,
Turn'd out and growl'd, and then turn'd in again,
Rodney in that ill-omen'd hour arose,
Crush'd his own first and next his country's foes;
Though all that fate allow'd was nobly won,
Envy could squint at something still undone;
Injurious faction stript him of command,
And snatch'd the helm from his victorious hand,
Summon'd the nation's brave defender home,
Prejudg'd his cause and warn'd him to his doom;
Whilst hydra-headed malice open'd wide
Her thousand mouths, and bay'd him till he died.

The poet's cause comes next—and you my lord,
The muse's friend, will take a poet's word;
Trust me our province is replete with pain;
They say we're irritable, envious, vain:
They say—and Time has varnish'd o'er the lie
Till it assumes Truth's venerable dye—
That wits, like falcons soaring for their prey,
Pounce every wing that flutters in their way,
Plunder each rival songster's tuneful breast
To deck with others' plumes their own dear nest;
They say—but 'tis an office I disclaim
To brush their cobwebs from the roll of fame,
There let the spider hang and work his worst,
And spin his flimsy venom till he burst;
Reptiles beneath the holiest shrine may dwell,
And toads engender in the purest well.

Genius must pay its tax like other wares
According to the value which it bears;
On sterling worth detraction's stamp is laid,
As gold before 'tis current is assay'd.
Fame is a debt time present never pays,
But leaves it on the score to future days;
And why is restitution thus deferr'd
Of long arrears from year to year incurr'd?
Why to posterity this labor given
To search out frauds and set defaulters even?
If our sons hear our praise 'tis well, and yet
Praise in the father's ear had sounded sweet.

Still there is one exception we must own,
Whom all conspire to praise, and one alone;
One on whose living brow we plant the wreath,
And almost deify on this side death:
He in the plaudits of the present age
Already reads his own historic page,
And, though pre-eminence is under heav'n
The last of crimes by man to be forgiv'n,
Justice her own vicegerent will defend,
The orphan's father and the widow's friend;
Truth, virtue, genius mingle beams so bright,
Envy is dazzl'd with excess of light:
Detraction's tongue scarce stammers out a fault,
And faction blushes for its own assault.

His is the happy gift, the nameless grace,
That shapes and fits the man to every place,
The gay companion at the social board,
The guide of councils, or the senate's lord,
Now regulates the law's discordant strife,
Now balances the scale of death or life,
Sees guilt engendering in the human heart,
And strips from falsehood's face the mask of art.
Whether, assembled with the wise and great,
He stands the pride and pillar of the State,
With well-weigh'd argument distinct and clear
Confirms the judgment and delights the ear,
Or in the festive circle deigns to sit
Attempering wisdom with the charms of wit—
Blest talent, form'd to profit and to please,
To clothe Instruction in the garb of Ease,
Sublime to rise, or graceful to descend,
Now save an empire and now cheer a friend.

More I could add, but you, perhaps, complain,
And call it mere creation of the brain;
Poets you say will flatter—true, they will;
But I nor inclination have nor skill—
Where is your model, you will ask me, where?
Search your own breast, my lord, you'll find it there.

CHAPTER VI.

Mission to Spain—Occasion and incidents of—Storm at sea—Sea fight—Mr. Lucas—A prize—Sea song—Arrival at Lisbon—Letters to Hillsborough—Visit to Cintra—Sets out for Spain—Incidents of the journey—Appearance of the country—Arrival at Madrid.

It is in this period of my life's history, that by accepting a commission which took me into Spain, I was subjected to events that have very strongly contrasted and changed the complexion of my latter days from that of the preceding ones.

I will relate no other circumstances of this negotiation than I am in honor and strict conscience warranted to make public. For more than twenty years I have been silent, making no appeals at any time but to my official employers, who were pledged to do me justice. What I gained by those appeals, and how far that justice was administered to me, will appear from the detail, which I am now about to give; and though I hope to render this narrative not unentertaining to my readers, yet I do most faithfully assure them that no tittle of the truth shall be sacrificed to description, being resolved to give no color to facts and events, but such as they can strictly bear, nor ever knowingly permit a word to stand in these pages inconsistent with that veracity, to which I am so solemnly engaged.

In the year 1780, and about the time of Rodney's capture of the Caracca fleet, I had opportunities of discovering through a secret channel of intelligence many things passing, and some concerting between the confidential agents of France and Spain (particularly the latter), resident in this country, and in private correspondence with the enemies of it. Of these communications I made that use which my duty dictated, and to my judgment seemed advisable. By these, in the course of their progress, a prospect was opened of a secret negotiation with the Minister Florida Blanca, to which I was personally committed, and of course could not decline the undertaking it. My destination was to repair to the neutral port of Lisbon, there to abide whilst the Abbé Hussey, chaplain to his Catholic Majesty, proceeded to Aranjuez, and by the advice, which he should send me, I was to be governed in the alternative of either going into

Spain for the purpose of carrying my instructions into execution, or of returning home by the same ship that conveyed me thither, which was ordered to wait my determination for the space of three weeks, unless dismissed or employed by me within that period.

I was to take my wife and two daughters Elizabeth and Sophia with me on the pretence of travelling into Italy upon a passport through the Spanish dominions, and having received my instructions and letters of accreditation from the Earl of Hillsborough, Secretary of State, on the 17th day of April, 1780, I took my departure for Portsmouth, there to embark on board his majesty's frigate Milford, which I had particularly asked for, as knowing her character to be that of a remarkable swift sailer. On my arrival at Portsmouth, I found she had gone out upon a short cruise after a French privateer, but was expected every hour. On the 21st she came in from her cruise, and I delivered to her captain, Sir William Burnaby, two letters from the Admiralty, one directing him to receive me and my family on board, the other to be opened when he came off the Start-point.

This frigate, being from long and constant service in a weak and leaky state, on which account Sir William had lately brought her into port, and undergone a court martial in consequence of it, I found him and his officers under some alarm as to the unknown extent of my destination, suspecting that I might be bound to the West Indies, and justly doubting the seaworthiness of the ship for any distant voyage. On this point I could give them no satisfaction, but on the day following her arrival (viz: April 22d), went on board to assist in adjusting the accommodations for the females of my family.

In consequence of strong and adverse winds we remained at Spithead till the 28th, when at eight o'clock in the morning we weighed anchor with the wind at south, and brought to at Cowes. Here I fixed three double-headed shot to the box that contained my papers and instructions, and the wind still hanging in the southwest, foul and unfavorable, it was not till the 2d of May, when, upon its veering to the northeast, we took our departure in the forenoon from Cowes, and upon its dying away, anchored in mid-channel for the night in 20 fathom water, Needle-rocks S. W. by W., Yarmouth S. E. by S.

Being off the Start-point on the 3d instant, Sir William Burnaby opened his orders, and with great satisfaction found his destination to be to Lisbon; we saw a large fleet to westward at the Start-point, which proved to be the Quebec trade outward-bound under convoy. On the 6th, having passed the Land's-end, we found the foremast sprung below the trussel-trees, and by the next day the carpenter had moulded a fish on it, when the gale having freshened with rain and squalls, we struck top-gallants, handed the foresail, and hove to under the mainsail; on the 9th the gale increased, and having reefed and furled the mainsail, we laid to under the main-stay-sail and mizzen-stay-sail; Lat. 49° 4′; Long. 1° 45′, Land's-end.

Our situation now became very uncomfortable, and our safety suspicious, for the sea was truly mountainous, and broke over our low and leaky frigate in a tremendous style, which in the mean while occasionally received such hard and heavy shocks, as caused serious apprehensions even in those to whom danger was familiar. I had, in my passages to Ireland, been in angry seas and blowing weather, but nothing I had seen bore any resemblance to the fury of this gale, nor could anything but the confidence I had reason to place in British seamen, and the exertions which I witnessed on their part, have stood between me and absolute despair. The dreadful sight and deafening uproar of those tremendous seas, that by turns whelmed us under a canopy of water, making darkness at mid-day, and rendering every voice inaudible, were as much as my nerves could bear, and whilst the ship was quivering and settling, as I conceived, upon the point of going down, I thought it high time to set out in search of those beloved objects, who had embarked themselves with me, and were as I supposed suffering the extreme of terror and alarm. How greatly was I mistaken in the calculation of their fortitude! I found my wife, then far gone with child, in her cot within the cabin, the water flowing through it like a sluice, so perfectly collected and composed, that I forbore to speak of the situation we were in, and did not hint at the purpose which brought me to her; but she, who knew too well what was passing, to be deceived as to the motive of my coming to her, said to me: 'You are alarmed, I believe; so am not I. We are in a British ship of war, manned with British seamen, and, if we are in danger, which I conclude we are, I don't doubt but they know how to carry us through it.' Thus divested of my alarm by the intrepidity of the very person who had so great a share in causing it, I made my way with some difficulty to the ward-room, where my daughters had taken shelter, whilst Mr. Lucas the purser was serenading them with what would have been a country dance, if the ship had not danced so violently out of all time and tune. In this moment the Abbé Hussey, who had followed me, upon a sudden pitch of the ship, burst head foremost into the ward-room, and with the momentum of a gun broken loose from its lashings, overturned poor Lucas, demolishing his violin, the table, and everything frangible that his colossal figure came in contact with.

Such was our situation on the 9th of May, and when, upon the morning following, the gale moderated, we set the mizzen and foretop-mast staysail, and swaying the top-gallant-mast up, set mainsail and foresail, working the pumps to keep the ship free, whilst the sea ran very lofty with a heavy swell. This was the last time the Milford frigate ever went to sea, for by the time we anchored in the Tagus her main-deck exhibited sufficient proofs how completely she was broken-backed by straining in the gale.

I will here relate an incident no otherwise interesting or curious but as a mere matter of chance, which tends in some degree to show the credulity of our seafaring countrymen. I had been in the habit of wearing in my pocket a broad silver piece given me as a keep-sake by my son George, who received his death at the siege of Charleston in South Carolina the very day after he had taken command of an armed vessel, to which he was appointed. This piece had been beaten out from a dollar by a marine belonging to the Milford, then on the American station, and presented by him to my son, then a midshipman serving on board: on this piece the artist had engraved the Milford in full sail, and on the reverse my coat of arms, and upon my discovering that this same ingenious marine, now become a sergeant, was on the same quarter-deck with me, I had been talking with him upon the incident, and showing him that I had carefully preserved his present, which to this hour I have done, and am now wearing it in my pocket. This man, though a brave and orderly soldier, had so completely yielded himself up to a kind of religious enthusiasm as to be plunged in the profoundest apathy and indifference towards life ; still he exhibited on this occasion some small show of sensibility at the sight of his own work, and the recollection of an amiable youth, now untimely lost. The wind was adverse to our course, our ship still laboring in a heavy sea, whilst strong and sudden squalls, which every now and then annoyed us, together with the incessant labor of the pumps, denied our people that repose which their past toils demanded; in this gloomy moment the fancy struck me to make trial of the superstition of the man at the helm by laying this silver piece on the face of the compass, as a charm to turn the wind a point or two in our favor, which I boldly promised it would do. I found my gallant shipmate eagerly disposed to confide in the experiment, which he put out of all doubt by clinching his belief in it with a deposition upon oath, quite sufficient to convince me of his sincerity, and something more than necessary for the occasion. Accordingly I laid my charm upon the glass of the compass with all the solemnity I could assume, whilst my friend kept his eyes alternately employed upon that and the dog-vane, till in a few minutes with a second oath, much more ornamented and embroidered than the former, he announced to the conviction of all present a considerable shift of wind in our favor. Credulity now began to circulate most rapidly through the ship; even the officers seemed to have caught some touches of its influence, and my friend the meditative sergeant raised his eyes with some astonishment from his book, where they had been riveted to a few dirty pages, loose and torn, as it seemed, out of Sherlock's volume upon death. My first prediction having succeeded so luckily, I boldly promised them a prize in view, and whimsical as the incident is, yet it so chanced that in a very short time the man at the masthead sung out two ships bearing north standing to the southward; this happened at one o'clock; at half an hour past the sternmost tacked and made sail to the northward; we found our ship gaining fast upon her, and at four hoisted Dutch colors; at three-quarters after hoisted St. George's ensign, and fired a shot at her; at five she hoisted French colors and fired a broadside into us, and at six she struck, and proved to be the Duc de Coigny, private frigate, of 28 guns, Mignionet commander, belonging to Granville; this gallant Frenchman had scarcely pronounced his anathema against the man that should offer to strike his colors, when his head was blown to atoms by one of our cannon balls; the prize lost her second captain also and had 50 of her men killed and wounded; we had two seamen and one marine killed, and four seamen and one marine wounded.

This was a new and striking spectacle to a landsman like me, and though I am dwelling on an incident which to a naval reader may seem trifling, yet as it was my good fortune to be present at an animating scene, which does not occur to every man, who occasionally passes the seas in my situation, I presume I am excusable for my description of it.

When I witnessed the dispatch with which a ship is cleared for action, the silence and good order so strictly observed, and the commands so distinctly given upon going into action, I was impressed with the greatest respect for the discipline and precision observed on board our ships of war. Such coolness and preparatory arrangement seemed to me a security for success and conquest. Our spirited purser, Mr. Lucas, performed better with his musket than his violin, and whilst standing by him on the quarter-deck I plainly saw him pick off a French officer in a green coat, whom he jocularly called the parrot, the last of three whom he had dismissed to their watery graves. My melancholy friend the engraver had his arm shattered by the first fire of the enemy, which he received with the most stoical indifference, and would not be persuaded to leave the quarter-deck till the action was over, when, going down to be dressed as my eldest daughter (now Lady Edward Bentinck) was coming up from below, he gallantly presented that very arm to assist her, and when observing him shrink upon her touching it, she said to him—'Sergeant, I am afraid you are wounded,' he calmly replied—'To be sure I am, Madam, else I should not have been so bold to have crossed you on the stairs.' This was a strain of chivalry worthy of the days of old, and something more than Tom Jones's gallantry to Sophia Western, who only offered her his serviceable arm, and kept the broken one unemployed. One other incident, though of a very different sort, occurred as I was handing her along the main-deck from the bread-room, when, slipping in the blood and brains of a poor fellow who lay dead beside his gun, an insensible brat who was boasting and rejoicing at his own escape, cried out: 'Have a care, Miss, how you tread. Look at this fellow; I stood close by him when he got this knock: the shot went clear over me, and this damn'd fool put his head in the way of it. Wasn't that a droll affair?'

The shifting the prisoners was a task of danger, as the sea ran very high, and they were beastly drunk. In this our people were employed all night: when they had refitted the rigging shot away in the action, and hoisted in the boats, we made sail with the prize in company. The carpenters were employed in repairing the boats, which were stove in shifting the prisoners, of which we took on board 155 French and Americans: Lat. 49° 6′; Long. 1° 45′.

Our surgeon and his assistants being exhausted with their duty on board both ships, my anxiety kept me sleepless through a turbulent night, and I went about the ship to the wounded men, one of whom (James Eaton by name) a quarter-master, and one of the finest fellows I ever saw, expired as I stood by him without any external hurt, having been struck in the side by a splinter. I read the burial service over him the next morning, whilst Abbé Hussey performed that office for the other two, who were Irish and of his communion.

On the 11th we took the prize in tow; we had fresh breezes with dark cloudy weather, and at midnight we wore ship, and in veering having broken the hawser we shortened sail for the prize, but soon after made signal for her to stand about and go into port, which she safely effected. In the course of this day

I wrote a song for my amusement, descriptive of our action, and adapted it to the tune of—

Whilst here at Deal we're lying, boys,
With the noble Commodore.

Our crew were very musically inclined, and we had some passably good singers amongst them, which suggested to me the idea of writing this sea song; we frequently sung it at Lisbon in lusty chorus, but their delicacy would not allow them to let it be once heard till their prisoners were removed; and this was the answer made to me by a common seaman, when I asked why they would not sing it during the voyage: an objection which had escaped me, but which I felt the full force of when stated by him.

The song was as follows, and the circumstances under which it was hastily written must be my apology for inserting it:—

"'Twas up the wind three leagues or more
We spied a lofty sail;
Set your topgallant sails, my boys,
And closely hug the gale.

Nine knots the nimble Milford ran,
Thus, thus, the master cried;
Hull up we brought the chase in view,
And soon were side by side.

Dowse your Dutch ensign, up Saint George!
To quarters now, all hands;
With lighted match beside his gun
Each British hero stands.

Give fire, our gallant captain cries,
'Tis done, the cannons roar;
Stand clear, Mounseers, digest these pills,
And soon we'll send you more.

Our chain-shot whistles in the wind,
Our grape descends like hail—
Hurrah, my souls! three cheering shouts,
French hearts begin to quail.

Rak'd fore and aft her shatter'd hull
Lets in the briny flood,
Her decks are carnag'd with the slain,
Her scuppers stream with blood.

Her French jack shivers in the wind,
Its lilies all look pale;
Down it must come, it must come down,
For Britons will prevail.

And see! 'tis done: she strikes, she yields;
Down, haughty flag of France:
Now board her, boys, and on her staff
The English cross advance!

There, there triumphantly it flies,
It conquers and it saves—
So gayly toss the can about,
For Britons rule the waves.'

During the 12th, 13th, and 14th, we had fresh gales and squally, till on the night of the latter, being then in latitude 44° 2′, longitude 3° 16′, we had light airs and fair weather, when, descrying a frigate under English colors to the southward, standing to the northward, we cleared ship for action, but soon after lost sight of her. The next day, viz: the 15th, we saw a fleet of the enemy to the southward, standing to the westward, forty-five in number, of which were eight sail of the line and three or four frigates. They proved to be the French squadron under the command of Tournay, and having brought to on the starboard tack, dispatched a line-of-battle ship in chase of us; coming down in a slanting course she appeared at first to gain upon us, till half past eight in the evening (our rate being then better than at twelve knots), she left off chase, having given us her lower guns, whilst the prisoners, expecting us to be captured, became so unruly that our men were obliged to drive them down with the hand-spikes.

On the 16th we brought to and took a Portuguese pilot on board, passed the Burlings, and the next day at six in the evening anchored with the best bower in eight fathom water, Belem Castle N. E. Abbé Hussey and I with the second lieutenant landed at the castle, and at eight at night we obtained pratique. We found riding here his majesty's ship Romney, Captain Home, with the Cormorant sloop, Captain John Payne, under the command of Commodore Johnstone.

One of my first employments was to purchase a large stock of oranges for the refreshment of the ship's company, especially the wounded, and of these my friend, the sergeant, condescended to partake, though he had been so extremely occupied with his meditations upon death, as hardly to be persuaded to let his arm be dressed, answering all the kind inquiries of his comrades in the most sullen and oftentimes abusive terms. 'They were wicked wretches, and deserved damnation for presuming to condole with him. It was God's good pleasure to exercise his spirit with pain, and he had supreme satisfaction in bearing it. What business was it of theirs to be troubling him with their impertinent inquiries?' This was in the style of his civilest replies; to some his answers were very short and extremely gross.

The day after our arrival, we weighed and dropped further up the river; at night we discharged the prisoners, and the commodore visited us in his barge. Mr. Hussey prepared for his journey into Spain, and I provided apartments for my family at Mrs. Duer's hotel, at Buenos Ayres. The next day the commodore entertained us at Belem, and the day ensuing he, with Captains Home and Payne, dined with us on board.

My orders were to wait at Lisbon till Mr. Hussey wrote to me from Aranjeuz, and according to the tenor of his report I was to use my discretion as to proceeding onwards, or returning home; and this being a point decisive as to my credit or discredit in the management of the business I was intrusted with, I was most urgent and precise with Mr. Hussey in conjuring him to be extremely careful and correct in his report, by which I was to guide myself, and this he solemnly promised me that he would observe. On the 19th and 20th I prepared my dispatches, and on the 21st delivered them to the packet master, who took his departure that very day.

In the mean time, I understood from Mr. Hussey, that in applying to the Spanish ambassador Count Fernan Nunez for his passport, he had committed himself to a conversation, from which he drew very promising expectations; of this I informed my proper minister Lord Hillsborough, as will appear by the following extract of my letter dated the 19th of May, 1780.

'My Lord: When Mr. Hussey waited on Count Fernan Nunez yesterday for his passport, he would have made his commission for the exchange of prisoners the pretence for his journey into Spain, but the ambassador gave him plainly to understand he was confidential with Count Florida Blanca in the business upon which we are come. This being the case, Mr. Hussey thought it by no means necessary to decline a conversation with the ambassador under proper reserve. He was soon told that his arrival was anxiously expected at Aranjuez. No expression of good will to him, to me, and to the commission I am entrusted with was omitted. It was proposed by the ambassador to pay me the honor of a visit, if acceptable, in any way I liked best; but this Mr. Hussey, without referring to me, very properly and readily prevented.

He entered into many pertinent inquiries as to the state of the ministry, and the manner in which Lord North had been pressed in the House of Commons; he would have stirred the question of an accommodation with France, but was plainly answered by Mr. Hussey that he had no one word to say upon that subject; the channel was open, he observed, but ours was not that channel. * *

The conversation then closed with such assurances of a sincere pacific disposition on the part of Spain, that if Count Fernan Nunez reports fairly and is not imposed on, our business seems to be in an auspicious train.' * * *

My gratitude to Sir William Burnaby and his officers induced me to address the following letter and request to Lord Hillsborough, which I made separate, and sent under cover to the same dispatch.

'*To the Earl of Hillsborough.*

Milford frigate, off Belem, May the 20th, 1780.

My Lord: I cannot let this opportunity go by without expressing to your

Lordship, and through you to Lord Sandwich, my most thankful acknowledgments for indulging my wishes by putting me on board the Milford, under the care and command of Sir William Burnaby, whose unremitted kindness and attention to me and my family, I can neither duly relate nor repay. Throughout a long and an eventful passage, whether we were struggling with a gale, or clearing ship for action, both he and his officers uniformly conducted themselves with that harmony, temper and precision, as seemed to put them in assured possession of success; the men themselves have been so long attached to their officers, and all of them to the ship itself, that the severest duty is here directed without an oath, and obeyed without a murmur. Though we have been encumbered with such a crowd of prisoners, many of whom seemed to possess the spirit of mutiny in full force, our discipline has kept all in perfect quiet, and such humane attention has been paid to their health, that not a single prisoner has sickened or complained.

I take the liberty of intruding upon your lordship with these particulars to introduce a suit to you, which I have most anxiously at heart, and in which I am joined with equal anxiety by my friend Mr. Hussey: it is, my lord, to beseech you to promote the application made by Sir William Burnaby to Lord Sandwich in behalf of his first lieutenant, Mr. William Grosvenor, to be made master and commander; an officer of ten years' standing, well known in the navy and distinguished for activity, sobriety, and professional skill and ability: he went round the world with Admiral Byron, and is highly respected by him; he has been in this ship during the whole war, and assisted in the capture of near fourscore prizes, by which he has acquired very little more than the approbation of his captains, and the love and reverence of the men.

Had our prize been a king's ship, Mr. Grosvenor would have come home in her, and his promotion would most probably have followed in train; however, as she is a very fine new frigate, and will, I dare say, be reported fit for the king's use, the opportunity is judged favorable for recommending Mr. Grosvenor's pretensions, and as the Milford may be said to be now acting under your lordship's orders, I flatter myself you will take her under your protection by granting your good offices with Lord Sandwich in Mr. Grosvenor's behalf; an obligation that I shall ever gratefully carry in remembrance.

I have the honor to be, &c. &c.

R. C.'

This letter produced no advantage to Mr. Grosvenor, nor any other gratification to me except the recollection that I had done my best to serve a meritorious officer.

At Buenos Ayres I was visited by our minister, Mr. Walpole, Commodore Johnstone, Sir John Hort, the consul, Captain Payne, and several gentlemen of the factory. On the 25th instant, the ceremony of the Corpus Christi took place in a day excessively sultry, when the king and prince walked with the patriarch of Lisbon, the religious orders, knights of Christ and nobility of Portugal, in procession through the streets, of which even the ruins were decorated with rich tapestries, silk and velvets, forming at once a splendid and a melancholy scene. I was with my daughters at a house, from which we had a very good view of what was passing, and as they presented themselves at an open window in their English dresses (and I may add, without vanity, in all their native charms), they most evidently arrested the attention of the holy brotherhood in a manner that by no means harmonized with the solemnity of their office; more perfect wolves in sheep's clothing never were beheld. The haughtiness and ill-breeding of the Portuguese nobles is notorious to a proverb. One of these, the son of the minister Pombal, came into the room where I was waiting for the procession above mentioned; turning to me with an air of supercilious protection, very awkwardly assumed, and making a motion with his hand towards a chair, he was pleased to tell me that I might sit down. There was an insolence in the manner of it irresistibly provoking, and I am not ashamed to say my answer was at least as contemptuous as his address was insolent.

Early in the morning of the 30th I went with my daughters and some of our naval friends to Cintra, visiting the palace of Queluz in the way; the terrors of an earthquake are evidently expressed in the construction of this palace, which is nothing more than a long range of pavilions in the Moorish character, very richly furnished and profusely gilt; the heat was quite oppressive, but the shady walks and delicious odor of the orange groves, the refreshing sight of the fountains and exquisite beauty of the flowers in high bloom and boundless abundance recompensed all we suffered by the mid-day violence of the burning sun. In the romantic and more temperate retreat of Cintra, we enjoyed the most charming and enchanting scenes and prospects nature can display. The rock, the cork convent, and the ancient palace of Cintra, are objects that surpass description; from the latter of these the rock and town of Cintra, with all the country about it as far as to the palace of Mafra, till where it is bounded by the sea, form a most superb and interesting scene; the interior of the castle is unfurnished, though the painted tiles, gilded ceilings and arrangement of the apartments, opening to parterres, cut out of the rock in stories and terraces one above the other, is singularly grand and striking. In one of the great chambers the ceiling is ornamented with the scutcheons of all the noble families of Portugal affixed to the necks of stags, of no ordinary painting or design, and, though very ancient, their remarkable freshness bespeaks the extreme softness and dryness of the climate; in this collection the bearings and titles of the noble family of D'Aveiro had a conspicuous station, from which they are now dislodged and their very name expunged.

On our return to Lisbon we passed the remarkable aqueduct of Alcantara so often described, and on the 5th of June, at early morning, I received the expected dispatch from Mr. Hussey, with letters inclosed for the Earl of Hillsborough and Lord George Germain. His letter to me was as follows:—

'*Aranjuez*, 31st May, 1780.

MY DEAR FRIEND: I arrived here three days ago, conversed with the minister of state upon the subject of your journey, and do find that the delays which this business met with, and the different turn which matters have taken, render this negotiation every day exceedingly arduous and difficult. However, as the minister is so very desirous of finding some means to bring it to a happy conclusion, and as you are already so far advanced on your journey, I think it by all means advisable that you come (giving out that you mean to pass through Spain for the benefit of your health), and so give the negotiation a fair trial. You know me too well to suspect that I shall be wanting to cultivate the good wishes of the minister of state, and to incline him towards an accommodation. My servant Daly carries a memorandum of the road and the different places where the relays of carriages are to meet you.

Do not forget to mention to Mrs. Cumberland and the young ladies, theirs and Your affectionate friend, THOMAS HUSSEY.

P. S. His Catholic Majesty's orders are gone to Badajoz, the frontier town, not to examine your baggage.'

Embarrassed by this letter, and doubtful of the part I ought to take, I obeyed my instructions by resorting to our minister Mr. Walpole, and delivered to him a letter from Lord Hillsborough, the contents of which I was privy to, and by which I was directed to be confidential and explicit with him. As there was but one point upon which he hesitated, and which I had good reason to know would not be made a stipulation obstructive to my measures, I was disposed, according to Mr. Hussey's advice, to give the negotiation a trial, though his letter was by no means such as I expected from him, nor so explicit as to give me a safe rule to go by. Nevertheless, upon full consideration of all circumstances, and under the persuasion that delay (which was the utmost that Mr. Walpole suggested) would in effect be tantamount to absolute abandonment, I determined for the journey, and gave my reasons for pursuing the advice of Mr. Hussey, and meeting the advances of the Spanish minister, exemplified by his preparations for receiving me, in the following dispatch, which I transmitted to Lord Hillsborough by Sir William Burnaby, then upon his departure for England:—

'*To the Earl of Hillsborough.*

Lisbon, June 6th, 1780.

MY LORD: In my letter No. 1, I informed your lordship of my arrival here on the 17th of last month, at six in the afternoon, and of Mr. Hussey's departure from Aranjuez on the 19th following, at eleven o'clock in the forenoon. I have now the honor of transmitting to you a letter which I received yesterday morning by express from Aranjuez, addressed to your lordship, and I inclose one also, which I had from Mr. Hussey, of the 31st of last month, by the same conveyance.

The letter of my instructions is explicit for my returning to England, or advancing to Spain, as that Court shall make or not make the cession of Gibraltar the basis of a negotiation.[1] The simple resolution of this question formed the whole purport of Mr. Hussey's journey, and as I well knew it was clearly understood on his part, I expected a reply in the same style of precision with these instructions: the case is now unexpectedly become exceedingly embarrassing and delicate. As he does not say that Spain stipulates for the cession aforesaid, I do not consider myself under orders to return; on the other hand, as he does not tell me that she will treat without it, I am doubtful whether I am warranted to advance. He says the minister is very desirous of finding means of bringing things to a happy conclusion, and I have not only his authority, but good grounds from private information, to give credit to his assertion. I am also furnished with the necessary passports from the Minister of Spain, and from her ambassador at this court. It remains, therefore, a question with me, and a very difficult one I feel it, whether I should wait at Lisbon, and require a further explanation, or proceed without it.

If I take the first part of this alternative, I must expect it will create offence to the punctilio of the Spanish court, who have given me their passport for myself and family, have not only provided me with every convenience of coaches and relays through Spain, but have directed their ambassador here to give me every furtherance from hence that can accommodate me to Badajoz, and I have this day received Count Fernan Nunez's passport, with a letter of recommendation to the Marquis de Ustariz, intendant of Badajoz. By the terms in which Count Florida Blanca has couched my passport, it is set forth that I am travelling through Spain, towards Italy, for the establishment of my health. Under this pretext it is in my power to take my route as a private traveller, and by no means deliver to the minister your lordship's letter, until I have explicit satisfaction in the leading points of my instructions. Should I find the court of Spain acquiescent under these particulars, success will justify a doubtful measure; whereas if I withstand the invitation and advice of Mr. Hussey, sent, no doubt, with the privity of the minister, and expressive of his good wishes and desires for an accommodation, I shall throw everything into heat and ferment, ruin all Mr. Hussey's influence, from which I have so much to expect, and at once blast all his operations, now in so fair a train for success, and which probably have been much advanced since Daly's departure. In short, my lord, I regard this dilemma as a case in which personal caution points to one side, and public service to the other. In this light I view it, and although Mr. Hussey's letter to your lordship (for it was under a flying seal), is as silent on the same material point, as that to me is, I have, after full deliberation, thought it for his majesty's service that I should no longer hesitate to pursue the advice of Mr. Hussey, but resolve to set out upon my journey for Spain.

The high opinion I entertain of Mr. Hussey's understanding weighs strongly with me for this measure, because I know he has intuition to penetrate chicanery, and discretion enough not to expose me to it; and though he does not expressly say there is no obstacle in my way, yet this, I am persuaded, must be his firm assurance and belief before he would commit me to the journey. The verbal message he has sent me by his servant Daly that all is well, is to me a very encouraging circumstance, because it is a concerted token and password between us, agreed upon when we were together in the frigate. The underlined expressions in the memorandum for my journey have not escaped my observation, and I inclose you the original for your inspection. He says, I am impatient to tell you a thousand things which I do not write. This marks to me an embarrassment and reserve in his letter which probably arose from the necessity of his communicating it to the sub-minister Campo, or to the minister himself. The letters to your lordship and me were couched nearly in the same

---

[1] The express condition of Cumberland's advance into Spain, it will be seen, was not observed by him. Spain did not make the cession of Gibraltar the basis of a negotiation; and by thus proceeding against the letter of his instructions, he gave Lord North a pretext for withholding his salary.

words, and these so much out of his style of expression, that they seem either shaped to meet another man's thoughts, or to be of another man's dictating. He tells me in the same memorandum, that at Aranjuez everything else, as well as his heart, will be ready to receive me. These expressions from Mr. Hussey I know to be no trivial indications of his thoughts, and though I am sensible my duty instructs me to take clearer lights for my guidance than side-way hints and insinuations can supply, yet such circumstances may come as aids, though not as principals, in the formation of an opinion.

I think it material to add that I have reason to believe the dispatch, which the Spanish ambassador received from the minister by the hands of Daly, Mr. Hussey's servant, is expressive of the same disposition to a separate accommodation with Great Britain, and accords with what is stated by Mr. Hussey in his letter to your lordship.

Through the same intelligence I have discovered the channel, by which the propositions fabricated in this place were conveyed to the Spanish minister, and am to the bottom made acquainted with that whole intrigue. I can only by this opportunity inform your lordship that it is a discovery of much importance to me in my future proceedings, gives me power over, and possession of, an agent in trust and confidence with the minister of Spain, as well as with the ambassador here, and that the deductions I draw from it strongly operate to incline my judgment to the resolution I have now taken of entering Spain.

I have the honor, &c. &c. R. C.'

Having hired carriages and provided myself with things necessary for my journey to Badajoz, I wrote on the next morning the following letter to the Secretary of State, separate and distinct from the dispatch, inserted as above:—

' *To the Earl of Hillsborough.*

Lisbon, June 7th, 1780. Wednesday morning, 5 o'clock.

My Lord: I am sensible I have taken a step which exposes me to censure upon failure of success, unless the reasons on which I have acted shall be weighed with candor and even with indulgence. In the decision I have taken for entering Spain, I have had no other object but to keep alive a negotiation, to which any backwardness or evasion on my part in the present crisis would, I am persuaded, be immediate extinction. I know where my danger lies, but as my endeavors for the public service and the honor of your administration are sincere, I have no doubt but I shall obtain your protection.

Though I dare not rest my public argument so much on private opinion as I am disposed to confess to you, yet you will plainly see how far I am swayed by my confidence in Mr. Hussey, and this will be the more evident when I must fairly own that Mr. Walpole's opinion is not with me for my immediate journey into Spain. I owe this justice to him, that, if I fail, it may be known he is free from all participation in my error. I have delivered your letter, and in general opened the business to him as I was directed to do, but I have disclosed to him no other instruction, except that on which Mr. Hussey's errand turns. He appears to me totally to discredit the sincerity of Spain towards any accommodation with Great Britain, and this opinion certainly colored his whole argument upon the subject. Had we agreed in this principal position, it is not likely we should have differed in deductions from it.

I have written to Mr. Hussey, and beg leave to send you a copy of my letter. I had fully purposed, in conformity to what I said to your lordship, that my family should not accompany me upon my journey, but the nature of the passport, and the circumstances that have arisen, make it indispensible for me to take them with me, not only as an excuse for my delay upon the road till Mr. Hussey shall meet me, but also as a cover for my pretence of health, should I find it necessary to pass through Spain without an explanation with the minister, &c. &c. R. C.'

At three o'clock in the afternoon of the 8th instant, I took my departure from Lisbon, embarking in one of the queen's barges for Aldea Gallega, whilst my wife and daughters accompanied me in the Milford's cutter with the first lieutenant and master.

The passage to Aldea Gallega is about nine miles up the river, which here forms a magnificent sheet of water. At the wretched Posada in this place we had our first sample of that dirt and loathsomeness, which admit of no description, and which every baiting place throughout Portugal and Spain with little variation presented to us. Men may endure such scenes; to women of delicacy they are, and must be nauseous in the extreme. The policy of these courts agrees in prohibiting the publican from furnishing anything to the traveller but firing: provisions must be purchased by the way, and the kid, whose carcass has dangled on your carriage in the sun and dust, half fried by the one, and more than half basted by the other, must be roasted for your meal by the fagot, that you purchase of your host, which in the mean while if you do not manfully defend, the muleteer and way-faring carrier will take a share of, and incense your poor carrion kid with the execrable fumes of his rank mess of oil and garlic. This rarely fails to stir up strife and fierce contention, which the host takes little or no pains to allay, sometimes ferments, till, if your people cannot drive off the intelopers with a high hand, you call in the peace-officer of the village or town to adjust your rights, which he is in no haste to do till you quicken his tardy sense of justice with a portion of your roast meat. I was once driven to this reference, when my people were outnumbered, and then my defender gave me gravely to understand that his spouse was extremely partial to cold turkey, that alluring object having been incautiously exposed to his eager ken. I tried if he would compound for a leg, but his spouse had a decided preference for the wing, and nothing short of half could move him to give sentence for my right. I had purchased at Lisbon two gray mules for the saddle at a high price; they were beautiful creatures, very fast trotters and perfectly sure-footed, so that I rode occasionally and could make short excursions, when there was anything better than a dreary wilderness to tempt me out of the road.

On the 9th, at three o'clock in the morning, Captain Payne arrived, having been all night on the water; we breakfasted, and having taken leave of our friends, departed from Aldea Gallega, our road lying over a sandy country, interspersed, however, with the olive and cork-tree, and almost covered with myrtle bushes in full bloom. We passed by Vendas Novas, an unfurnished palace of the Queen's, and put up our beds for the night at a lone house near Silveira. On the 10th we passed Montemor, situated on a beautiful eminence, and further on Arrayolas, where there are the remains of a stately castle of Moorish construction, as it should seem, and concluded our day's journey at a lone house, called Venda do Duque. On the 11th, passing through Estremos we came to Elvas, the frontier town of Portugal, within sight of Badajoz, in the plain at three leagues distance. The works erected by Count la Lippe on the hill, which commands the town, and the fortifications of the town itself seemed very extensive and in perfect repair, and the troops well accoutred and in good order, but the more striking sight to me was that of the aqueduct: it is raised on four lofty arches of stone one over the other, and enters the town in a very grand style. The suburbs are finely planted and laid out into walks by Count la Lippe, the projector, to whom Elvas is indebted for those public works, that constitute at once both her ornament and her defence. As our minister at Lisbon had not furnished me with any letter to the governor of Elvas, I was not only put to trouble about my baggage, but evidently became an object of suspicion. The former of these difficulties I got over by a bribe, but the latter subjected me to restraint, for upon attempting to walk out of my inn I found a guard of soldiers with fixed bayonets at the gate, who prevented me from stirring out, and mounted on me through the remainder of the day and the whole night, which I passed there. The next morning, whilst my carriages were in waiting for me, an Irish Benedictine walked into my room, and in a very authoritative and unceremonious style insisted on my staying there all day, and even was proceeding to countermand my carriages. He believed, or pretended to believe, that I was an American agent or negotiator, travelling into Spain, and began to inveigh most virulently against the king and country, of which he was a subject born: if he was employed to sound me (which is not improbable) he executed his office very clumsily, yet his insolent importunity was a considerable interruption and extremely troublesome. His language, in the mean time, was intolerably offensive, and his action worse, for as I reached out my hand to take my pistols from the table, the saucy fellow caught at them, with an action so suspicious, that I was obliged to put him from me, and sending my ladies out of the room before me to the carriages, got in last myself and ordered the postilions to proceed. The pertinacious monk still continued to oppose my going, and even vented his anathemas on the drivers, if they presumed to move. When I saw at the same time that there was a party of dragoons mounted and parading at the gate with drawn swords before the heads of my mules, I doubted whether they were in fact an escort of honor or arrest, but in a few minutes my leading carriage moved, and thus guarded I passed the barriers, whilst the monk, keeping his hand upon my carriage, and vociferating without intermission, never left me till we had passed through all the out-posts, and fairly entered the plain in sight of Badajoz.

It was not pleasant, and I did not think that the proper precautions had been taken for me. When I had got rid of my monk (the guard having taken no notice of his insolent behavior), in about a league and a half's driving a foot's pace we came to a small stream, which divides the territories of Portugal from Spain. He we watered the mules, whilst on the opposite bank I perceived a party of Spanish infantry, waiting, as it seemed, to receive and escort me. My Portuguese dragoons in perfect silence wheeled about and departed, and no sooner had I touched the Spanish soil than the party presented arms, and a messenger in the livery of the king, with his badge of office on his sleeve, signified to me that coaches were in waiting for me at Badajoz, and that he had his Catholic majesty's commands to attend upon me through my journey. During this, my Portuguese postilions, finding themselves in my power, and apprehending, no doubt, that their hesitation in obeying me against the denunciations of the aforesaid Benedictine, might justly have offended me, fell on their knees in the most abject manner, kissing the skirts of my coat, and imploring pardon and forgiveness. Having ordered them to mount and proceed, we soon reached Badajoz, and were received into the garrison with all the honors they could show us. As a town, Badajoz has nothing to engage the traveller, and as a fortified place stands in no degree of comparison with Elvas. The troops, being mostly invalids, made a very indifferent appearance, but the windows and balconies were thronged with spectators, who bestowed every mark of favor and good-will upon us as we passed the streets.

Here I found a coach and six mules in waiting, and after some stay set forward at midnight, the gates being opened for me, and a guard turned out by order of the governor, and we proceeded to Miajada, where a fresh relay was in readiness. The province of Estremadura is miserably barren, producing nothing to relieve the eye but cork-trees thinly scattered, and here and there a few distorted olive-trees. The like disconsolate aspect of a country, where neither cattle nor habitations were to be seen, prevailed through the whole of our next stage to Truxillo, where we halted on the night of the 14th instant.

In this stage we were warned by our attendant messenger to be upon our guard against robbers, and in truth the country furnished most appropriate scenes and inviting opportunities for such adventurers. I had three English servants and two men hired in Lisbon, besides the messenger above mentioned, and my English servants and myself in particular were excellently armed and ammunitioned. My Englishmen consisted of Mr. Hussey's man Daly, a London hair-dresser of the name of Legge, whom I took for the convenience of my wife and daughters, and my own faithful servant Thomas Camis, of tried courage and attachment, who had lived with me from the age of ten years. In the middle of the night, when we were in the depth of the forest, or rather wilderness, the Spaniard rode up to my coach window, and telling me we were then in the most suspicious part of our road, recommended it to me to collect my people about me and keep them together. Daly indeed was not far behind, but in a state of absolute intoxication, and sleeping on his mule; my hair-dresser pretty much in the same state, but totally disabled from excess of cowardice, of which he had given some unequivocal and most ridiculous tokens before and during our action in the frigate; I had not much reliance on my Portuguese, one of whom was a black fellow, and in the mean time my brave and trusty servant Camis was not to be found, nor did he answer to any call. Distressed with apprehension lest some fatal accident had befallen this most valuable man, I got out of my coach determined not to move from the spot without him, and sent the Spanish messenger and two other men in search of him. During their absence I heard a trampling of horses, and soon discovered through the dusk of night two men armed with guns, which they carried under the thigh, who rode smartly up to the carriage and proved to be archers on the patrole. This confirmed the report that the road was infested by robbers, and whilst this was passing I had the satisfaction to be joined by my servant Thomas Camis on foot, his mule having sunk under him, exhausted with fatigue. He now mounted behind the coach, and the men dispatched in search for him having come in, we pursued our route and arrived in safety at Truxillo.

From Truxillo we passed a very rugged and mountainous tract of country to Venta del Lugar Nuevo on the banks of the Tagus. This is a very romantic station, and the bridge a curious and most striking object, passing from one rock to another upon two very lofty Roman arches, the river flowing underneath at a prodigious depth.

On the 16th we passed through La Calzada to Talavera la Reina, a town in New Castile of considerable population and extent. A silk fabric is here established under the king's especial patronage. Here the following letter from Mr. Hussey met me:—

From Mr. Hussey to me.

'*Aranjuez*, Wednesday morning, 14th June, 1780.

My Dearest Friend: How could you suspect that I would send for you if I found the obstacle in my way, which makes you so uneasy? But it was always my intention to go part of the way from Aranjuez to meet you, to indulge my affection by personally attending you and your family as soon as possible; but as you do not mention what delay you intended to make in Badajoz, I cannot precisely guess the day of your arrival here, and therefore I dispatch this letter to meet you at Talavera la Reina, that I may know it more exactly, which will be by returning a line to me, informing me of the day, and whether you think it will be in the morning or evening. As the distance between Talavera and Aranjuez is too great for one day's journey with the same mules, I have ordered a fresh set to be posted for you seven leagues from this place, at La Venta de Olias, two leagues and a half from that part of the Tagus called Las Barcas de Azecar, where you cross the water, and probably you will meet me; otherwise you will come on and meet me on the road. This fresh set of mules was absolutely necessary, because you could find no place to sleep in between Talavera and Aranjuez. You do not come through Toledo. I long to embrace you and my amiable friends, and open my mind to your satisfaction, as well as my pleasure. Adieu! T. H.'

To this letter I answered as follows:—

To Mr. Hussey.

'*Talavera la Reina*, Friday, 16th June, half past 5, evening.

My Dearest Friend: Your consolatory letter meets me at the end of a long and laborious journey, and like a magical charm puts all my cares to rest at once. Say not, however, how could I suspect. Had that been the case, how could I advance? Yet I am come at every risk upon the reliance, which I am fixed to repose in your honor and friendship upon all occasions.

I have entered on an arduous service without any conditions, and, I fear, without securing to myself that sure support, which they, by whom and for whom I am employed, ought to hold forth to me; but you know full well who is, and who is not, my corresponding minister, and if success does not bear me through in this step, which I have taken, my good intentions will not stand me in much stead. Still, when I saw that my reluctance would affect your situation, dash every measure you had laid, and annihilate all chance of rendering service to my country in this trying crisis, I did not hesitate to risk this journey, even against the advice of Mr. W.

We are not long since arrived, after a most sultry stage, and have been travelling all night without a halt. I dare not but give Mrs. Cumberland an hour or two's repose, and shall not take my departure from hence till midnight. I shall stop at La Venta de Olias, to relieve my party from a few hot hours, and shall be there to-morrow morning about ten or eleven. I shall set out from thence at seven o'clock in the evening, at latest, and reach the ferry at Las Barcas de Azecar at nine that evening. There, if we meet, or whenever else more convenient to yourself, it will, I trust in God, be remembered as one of the happy moments that here and there have sparingly checkered the past life of your Affectionate R. C.'

From Talavera on the 17th instant we came to the little village of Olias, about half way, where we took the necessary relief of rest, and as the weather was now intolerably hot, my wife and daughters being almost exhausted with fatigue, we lay by for the whole of the day. Here the Alcayde of the village very hospitably sent me refreshments, and called on me at my inn, offering his house and whatever it afforded. I returned his visit, and found the good old man surrounded by his children and grand-children, a numerous family, grouped in their degrees, and sitting in their best apartment ready to receive me. After chocolate had been served, the guitar was introduced, and the younger parties danced their sequedillas. When they had animated themselves with this dance, the player on the guitar began to sound the notes of the fandango: I had seated myself by the old grandfather, a feeble, nerveless creature, and observed, with some concern, a paralytic motion vibrating in all his limbs and muscles, when at once, unable to keep his seat, he started up in a kind of ecstasy, and began snapping his fingers like castanets, and dancing the fandango to my surprise and amusement. This was the first time I had seen it performed, and I ceased to wonder at the extravagant attachment which the Spaniards show for that national tune and dance.

On Sunday the 18th of June, at five o'clock in the morning, we arrived at Aranjuez, and were most affectionately welcomed by Mr. Hussey. He delivered a paper to me dictated by the minister, and first appearances argued favorably for my negotiation. The day following I was visited by the subminister Campo, Anduaga and Escarano (belonging to the minister's department), also by the Duc d'Almodovar, Abbé Curtis, and others, and in the evening of that day I had my first interview with the Count Florida Blanca.

CHAPTER VII.

News of Lord George Gordon's riots—Influence of on the court of Spain—Progress of negotiations—Count D'Estaing—Florida Blanca—Galvez—Uncomfortable situation—Mr. Hussey—Departure of D'Estaing—Character of Hussey—Thrown from his mule—His surgeons—Anecdote—Patrick Curtis—Letter from Del Campo—Return of Hussey to England—Letters of Brutus—Visit to the Escurial—Paintings—Interview with the king.

I SHALL not enter upon local descriptions; it is neither to my purpose, nor can it edify the reader, who will find all this done so much better by writers who have travelled into Spain, and been more at leisure for looking about them than I ever was. My thoughts were soon distressfully occupied by the account, which met me, of the riots and disturbances in London by what was called Lord George Gordon's mob, which all but quite extinguished my hopes of success in the very outset of my business. I had repeated interviews with the minister, whom I visited by night, ushered by his confidential valet through a suit of five rooms, the door of every one of which was constantly locked as soon as I had passed it. The description of those dreadful tumults was given to the Spanish court by their ambassador at Paris, Count d'Aranda, and faithfully given without exaggeration. The effect it had upon the King of Spain was great indeed, and for me most unfortunate, for I had no advices from my court to qualify or oppose it. How this intelligence operated on the mind of his Catholic Majesty can only be conceived by such as were acquainted with his character, and knew to what degree he remained affected by the insurrection, then not long passed, in his own capital of Madrid. I will only say that my treaty was in shape, and such as my instructions would have warranted me to transmit and recommend. Spain had received a recent check from Admiral Rodney, Gibraltar had been relieved with a high hand, she was also upon very delicate and dubious terms with France. The crisis was decidedly in my favor; my reception flattering in the extreme; the Spanish nation was anxious for peace, and both court, ecclesiastics and military, professedly anti-gallican. The minister did not lose an hour after my arrival, but with much apparent alacrity in the cause immediately proceeded to business. I never had any reason, upon reflection, to doubt the sincerity of Count Florida Blanca at this moment, and verily believe we should have advanced the business of the preliminaries, if the fatal news of the riots had not most critically come to hand that very day, on which, by the minister's own appointment, we were to meet for fair discussion of the terms, while nothing seemed to threaten serious difficulty or disagreement between us.

According to appointment I came to him, perfectly ignorant of what had come to pass in my own country: I had prepared myself to the best of my capacity for a meeting and discussion which it behooved me to manage with discretion and address, and which, according to my view of it, promised to crown my mission with success. We were to write, and Campo was to be present, so that when I entered the minister's inner chamber, and saw only a small table with a single candle, no Campo present and no materials for writing, I own my mind misgave me. I did not wait more than two minutes before Florida Blanca came out of his closet, and in a lamentable tone sung out the downfall of London; king, ministers, and government whelmed in ruin, the rebellion of America transplanted to England, and heartily as he condoled with me, how could he, under such circumstances, commit his court to treat with me? I did not take the whole for truth, and was too much on my guard to betray any astonishment or alarm, but left him to lament the unhappy state of my wretched country, and affected to treat the narrative as a French exaggeration of the transitory tumults of a London mob. In the mean time, I could not fail to see that nothing was to be done on my part, but to yield to the moment and wait for information upon which I might rely. All that I did in the interim was to address a letter to the minister, and confidently risk a prediction that the tumult would be quashed so speedily and completely, as to add dignity to the king's government and stability to his ministers. He gave for answer that both his Catholic Majesty and himself trembled for the king, but of the extermination of the ministry no question could be made. I renewed my assertions in terms more confident than before, not so much upon conviction as from desperation, well knowing that if I was undone by the event, it was of little importance that I was disgraced by my over-confidence and presumption.

In the course of a very few days my prediction was happily verified, for on the 24th I was informed by Escarano, that the rioters were quelled, Lord George Gordon committed to the Tower, and indemnification ordered to the sufferers in the tumult, and on the day following the minister sent me the letter he had received from Count d'Aranda, to explain why he had delayed to inform me of the news from London. I availed myself of this happy change, by every means in my power for bringing back the negotiation to that state of forwardness, in which it stood before it was interrupted; but the minds and understandings of those with whom I had to deal, were not easy to be cured of alarms once given, or prejudices once received. It is not necessary for me to discuss the characters with whom it was my lot to treat; it is enough to say that during more than a year's abode in Spain, I believe no moment occurred so favorable to the business I had in hand, as that of which ill fortune had deprived me in the very outset of my undertaking. There was a gloomy being, out of sight and inaccessible, whose command as Confessor over the royal mind was absolute, and whose bigotry was disposed to represent everything in the darkest colors against a nation of heretics, whose late enormities afforded too good a subject for his spleen to descant upon; and in the mind, where no illumination, no elasticity resides, impressions will strike strongly and sink deep.

On the 26th I had completed my dispatches, in which I gave a full and circumstantial detail of my proceeding, the hopes I had entertained and the interruption I had met with, the conferences and correspondences I had held with the minister, and the measures I had pursued for reviving the negotiation, and reconducting it according to the tenor of my instructions. In this dispatch I observe to the Secretary of State, 'that although I relied upon his lordship's kind interpretation of my motives for leaving Lisbon, yet it was no inconsiderable anxiety that I suffered till my doubts were satisfied upon the points which Mr. Hussey's letter had not sufficiently explained. As it appeared to me a case where I might use my discretion, and in which the inconveniences incidental to my disappointment, bore no proportion to the good that might result from my success, I decided for the journey, which I had now performed, and flattered myself his lordship would see no cause to regret the step I had taken.'

'Had I not made ready use of my passports and relays, I had good reason to believe my hesitation would have proved decisive against any treaty; whereas, now I had the satisfaction of seeing many things point to a favorable and friendly issue.'

Speaking of a probability of detaching Spain, antecedent to the news of the disturbances in London, I tell the Secretary of

State—'That the moment for detaching Spain is now peculiarly favorable. She is upon the worst terms with France; not only the King of Naples, but the Queen of Portugal have written pressingly to his Catholic Majesty to make peace with England, and since my arrival a further influence is set to work to aid the friends of peace, and this is the Duc de Losada, who, on behalf of his nephew, the Duc d'Almodovar, has actually solicited the embassy to England, and been favorably received. These and many other circumstances conspire to press the scale for peace; in the opposite one we may place their unretrieved disgrace in the relief of Gibraltar, their hopes in the grand armament from Cadiz, of the 28th of April, their overrated successes in West Florida, and their belief that your expeditions to the South American continent are dropped, and that Sir Edward Hughes's condition disables him from attempting any enterprise against the Manillas.' I then recite the circumstance that gave a check to my negotiation, state the measures I had since taken for resuming it, and transmit a summary of such points in requisition as require answers and instructions, and conclude with suggesting such a mode of accommodating these to the punctilio of the Spanish court, as in my opinion cannot fail to bring the treaty to a successful issue. 'If this is conveyed,' I observe, 'in mild and friendly terms towards Spain, who submits the mode to the free discretion of Great Britain, and requests it only as a salvo, I think I have strong grounds to say her family compact will no longer hold her from a separate peace with Great Britain.'

On the 27th I removed with my family to Madrid, where I took a commodious house in an airy situation, and on the 1st of July the king and royal family arrived from Aranjuez. Though I had frequent communications with Count Florida Blanca through the subminister Campo, which occasioned me to dispatch letters on the 6th instant, yet I had no appointed interview till the 15th; our treaty paused for the expected answer to my transmission before mentioned, and it was clear to me that the Spanish minister, under the pretence of sounding the sincerity of the British cabinet, was in effect manœuvring upon the suspicion of their stability. Nevertheless, in this conversation, which he held on the 15th instant, he expressly declares, 'that if Great Britain sends back any answer, which shall be couched in mild and moderate terms towards Spain, he will then proceed upon the treaty with all possible good-will, and give me his ideas without reserve, endeavoring to adjust some expedient satisfactory to both parties; but he fears that our ministry is so constituted as to deceive my hopes in the temper and quality of their reply.'

During this interval, whilst I remained without an answer to my dispatch, the court removed to San Ildefonso, where Count D'Estaing arrived, specially commissioned to traverse my negotiation, and detach the Spanish court from their projected treaty with Great Britain. France, in the mean time, sacrificed her whole naval campaign in the harbor of Cadiz, where a combined force of sixty line-of-battle ships was assembled, whilst the British fleet, under the successive commands of Geary and Derby, did worse than nothing, and the capture of our great East and West Indian convoy by the Spanish squadron completed their triumph and our discomfiture.

A mind so fluctuating and feeble as that of the Spanish minister was not formed to preserve equanimity in success, or to persist in its resolutions against the counter-action of opinions. He was at this period[1] absolutely intoxicated, not only by the capture of our trading ships, but by the alluring promises of D'Estaing, and surrendered himself to the self-interested counsels of Galvez, minister of the Indies, for the continuance of the war. That minister (the creature of France to all intents and purposes), had, like himself, been raised to high office from the humble occupation of a petty advocate, and by early habits of intimacy, as likewise by superiority of intellect, acquired a power over his understanding little short of absolute ascendency.

Through the influence of this man and by the intrigues of Count D'Estaing, my situation at this period became as critical as possible; my house was beset with spies, who made report of everything they could collect or impute; I was proscribed from all my accustomed friends and visitors, whilst no one ventured publicly to enter my doors but the empress's ambassador, Count Kaunitz, whom no circumstances ever separated from me, and a few religious, whose visits to me were more than suspicious. The most insidious means were practised to break Mr. Hussey from me, but though they had their effect for a short time, his good sense soon discovered the contrivance and prevented its effects.

Finding myself thus beset, I attached to my service certain confidential agents, who were extremely useful to me, and amongst these, a gentleman in the employ of one of the northern courts, the ablest in that capacity, and of the most consummate address I ever became acquainted with; by his means I possessed

[1] The summer of 1780.

myself of authentic papers and documents, and was enabled to expose and effectually to traverse some very insidious and highly important manœuvres much to my own credit and to the satisfaction of the cabinet, before whom they were laid by my corresponding minister.

I now received the long expected answer to my first dispatch. It served little more than to cover a letter to Count Florida Blanca, and that letter found him now in the hands of D'Estaing, and more than half persuaded that the co-operation of France would put him in possession of Gibraltar, that coveted fortress, which I would not suffer him even to name, and for which Spain would almost have laid the map of her islands, and the keys of her treasury at my feet. I must confess this letter, which I had looked to with such hope, was more suited to gratify his purposes than mine, for if quibble and evasion were what he wished to avail himself of at this moment, he certainly found no want of opportunity for the accomplishment of his wish.

But if the inclosed letter was not altogether what I hoped for, the covering letter was most decidedly what I had not deserved, for it conveyed a more than half implied reproof for my having written to the Spanish Minister on the matter of the riots, and at the same time acknowledges that my paper was cautiously worded, and that I had most certainly succeeded in my argument. Why I was not to write to the minister, who had first written to me, especially when I wrote so cautiously and argued so successfully, I could never comprehend. When I was surprised by a very alarming and unpleasant piece of intelligence, conveyed to my knowledge through the channel of my country's enemy, not of my country's minister, what could I do more conformable to my duty than attempt to soften the impressions it had created? I had not been five minutes arrived before the minister's letter and proposals were put into my hands. What could occur to me so natural both in policy and politeness as to write to him, especially on a subject so deeply interesting, so imperiously demanding of me an appeal, that to have sunk under it in silence would have been disgraceful in the extreme?

In the same letter I am reminded: That I was instructed not even to converse upon any particular proposition, until I was satisfied of the willingness of the Court of Spain to treat at all. Of this willingness his lordship professes to doubt, and grounds that doubt upon what he gathers from my report of the change which seemed to have been wrought in the disposition of the minister by the intelligence of the disturbances in London; whereas, the conversation which he alludes to was held before that intelligence arrived, when the willingness to treat was put out of all doubt by the very progress made in that treaty, and which was only not completed by the check which that intelligence gave to it. If when the premier of Spain assured himself of the total overthrow of our ministry he hesitated to proceed in treating with the agent of that ministry, it is nothing wonderful; but it would have been wonderful, if, when I had such proofs of his willingness, I had not been satisfied with them, because something totally unforeseen might come to pass to thwart the business we were then engaged in. By parity of reason I might as well have been made responsible for the riots themselves, as for the consequences that resulted from them. It is a pity that his lordship did not advert to the order of time laid down in my dispatch by which he could not have failed to discover, that in one part of it I was reporting conversation held when all was well, and in the other part, remarking upon embarrassments naturally produced by unforeseen events of the most alarming nature.

That I had been careful enough to have satisfactory proofs of a willingness to treat before I committed myself to conversation is sufficiently clear from the circumstance above mentioned of the overtures presented to me in the very instant of my arrival, before I had seen the minister, or he had seen my letter of accreditation. Willingness more unequivocal hardly can be conceived, and when I did present that letter upon my first interview, I reported to my secretary of state the sum total of my conversation, which, consisting only of the following words, copied verbatim from the transcript of my letter to Lord Hillsborough, could not much edify his excellency, or divulge any secrets I was instructed to be reserved upon. I tell his lordship, in my letter of the 26th of June, 1780: 'That after the first civilities, I put into the minister's hands his lordship's letter, which I desired he would consider a conveying in the language of sincerity the mind of a most just and upright king, who in his love of peace rejoices to meet similar sentiments in the breast of his Catholic Majesty, and who has been graciously pleased to send me to confer with his excellency, not from my experience in negotiation, but as one confidential to the business in all its stages, and zealously devoted to conduct it to an issue.' I proceed to say: That 'as this visit passed wholly in expressions of civility, I shall observe no further to your lordship upon it, than that I was perfectly well pleased with my reception.'

If in any one part of my conduct or conversation I had advanced a step beyond the line of my instructions, or varied from them in a single instance, I should not have sought to shelter myself under the peculiar difficulties of my situation, I must have met the reproof I merited, and was certain to receive; but when I was arraigned for giving credit to sincerity, when it did exist, and being doubtful of it, when it wavered, as I was not conscious of an error, I was not moved by a reproof; but without entering into any argumentation, unprofitable and extraneous, applied my utmost diligence to the business I was upon, and continued to dictate to Mr. Hussey my dispatches for England, when I was disabled from writing them by a fractured arm.

The instant I was able to endure the motion of my coach, I attended upon the minister Florida Blanca at San Ildefonso; D'Estaing was there, in high favor and much caressed; Hussey was not permitted to accompany me; I was alone, and closely watched. It was the most unfavorable moment that I passed during my whole residence in Spain. Florida Blanca, instead of taking up his negotiation where he left it, gave little credit or attention to the letter of Lord Hillsborough, but evasively adverted to certain propositions which he had made before I came into Spain and transmitted through the hands of Mr. Hussey, to which propositions he observed our ministry had returned no answer. 'I admitted that no answer had been given to the propositions he alluded to, because they were formed upon the suggestions of Commodore Johnstone, at Lisbon, without any authority; it was a matter I had in charge to disavow those overtures in the most direct terms; they neither originated with the cabinet nor were ever before it; but if he could stand in need of any proof to satisfy his doubts as to the disposition of my court towards peace, I desired him to recollect that I had been sent into Spain for that express purpose, without any interchange on his part, and against the formal practice of states in actual war.' He acknowledged that my observation was fair, and that he admitted it, but he again reverted to Commodore Johnstone, observing, 'That although he might take on himself to make unauthorized propositions (which, by the way, he must think was strange presumption, and still more strange that it was passed over with impunity), yet he said that he answered with authority; his propositions had the sanction of his court, and as such he hoped they merited an answer from mine.' It was now clear to me, when he was driven to allude to these unaccreditated propositions, that evasion was his only object.

'Did he now refer to them,' I asked, 'as the actual basis of a treaty?'

He saw no reason to the contrary.

'They contained,' I said, 'an article for the cession of Gibraltar.'

They did.

'How then did such a stipulation accord with his word given, that I should be subjected to no requisition on that point?'

He was now evidently embarrassed, and turning aside to the subminister Campo, held some conversation with him apart: he then resumed his discourse, but in a desultory way, and being one of the most irritable men living, was so entirely off his guard, as to let out nearly the whole of Count D'Estaing's intrigue, and plainly intimated that Gibraltar was an object, for which the king, his master, would break the Family Pact and every other engagement with France, which he exemplified by stamping the very paper itself under his feet upon the marble floor; when, recollecting himself after awhile, and composing his countenance, that had been distorted with agitation, he said, 'That if I would bind him to his word it must be so. However, if the article for Gibraltar was inadmissible, what prevented our taking the remaining propositions into consideration?'

I told him, and with truth, that I had seen his propositions, but was not in possession of them. 'Would he put them down afresh, and join me in discussing them?'

'The Abbé Hussey had his original, and he had taken no copy.'

As I recollected enough of these propositions to know myself restrained from treating upon them, it occurred to me, as the only expedient left to keep the treaty alive, to consent to his sending them over by Mr. Hussey, who was now become heartily sick of his situation, and catching at every possible plea for his returning home. Still I was resolved that the proposal of sending over propositions of that sort by Mr. Hussey, should not originate with me, though I was perfectly willing to acquiesce in it, as giving my ministers the chance of getting out of a war, which I thought good policy would rather have sought to narrow in its extent than to widen, and which, ever since I had been in Spain, presented nothing but a succession of disasters.

This expedient of getting Mr. Hussey to be sent home by the minister with propositions, which, though upon a broader scale of treaty than my instructions allowed me to embrace, were yet, in my opinion of them, by no means inadmissible, appeared to me the best I could resort to in the present moment. With this idea in my thoughts, I asked Count Florida Blanca if he knew the mind of France, and whether he was prepared with any overtures on her part, which could be transmitted? I put this question experimentally, for I had obtained pretty full information of what D'Estaing had been about.

He had by this time recovered his serenity, and with great deliberation made answer to me, as nearly as it can be rendered, (for he always spoke in his own mother tongue), to this effect: 'We have no overtures to make on the part of France; France, as well as all the other courts which have representatives here resident, has been very inquisitive touching your business in this place; the only answer given on our part has been, that the Catholic King is an honorable monarch, and will faithfully observe all his engagements; on the faith of this single assertion the whole matter rests. If your court is sincere for peace, let her now set to work upon that business, which, sooner or later, must be the business of all parties. We will honestly and ardently second her endeavors; we do not put her to anything which may revolt her dignity; we acknowledge and conceive the degree of sensibility (call it, if you please, indignation) which she must harbor against a state in actual alliance with the rebel subjects of her empire; let her act with that dignity which is her due constantly in sight; but let her meet his Catholic Majesty in his disposition for finishing a war which can only exhaust all parties; and as she best knows what her own interests will admit, let her suggest such terms as she would receive were France the proponent, and let her couple them with terms for Spain, and if these be fair and reasonable on both sides, and such as Spain in her particular can possibly accede to, the Catholic King will close with her on his own behalf, and exert all his influence with his ally to make the peace general. This is an arduous and delicate business; let us cordially unite our endeavors to bring it forward. I shall be at all times ready to confer with you freely and without disguise, and let no difference of opinion affect our personal good understanding.'

The day following this conference Mr. Hussey arrived at San Ildefonso, and having communicated to him what had passed and my wish for his going to England with the minister's propositions, he readily agreed to it, and before that day passed the subminister Campo came to my house to sound me on this very expedient, managing, as he conceived, with great finesse to induce me to consent to what in fact I much desired, and expressing, as from the minister, his earnest hope that I would not quit Spain in the interim. Unpleasant as my situation was now become, still I was unwilling to abandon the negotiations, as I knew that D'Estaing was on his departure for Cadiz, where I had good reason to believe he would lose his influence and forfeit his popularity. I then availed myself of his informers, and through their channel gave out what I knew would come to his ears, and induce him to think that my negotiation was totally desperate: accordingly I departed from San Ildefonso, leaving Mr. Hussey to settle propositions with the minister, and the day following my return to Madrid, D'Estaing set out for his command at Cadiz. Florida Blanca offered to communicate to me copies of what he transmitted by Mr. Hussey, but for obvious reasons I declined his offer.

D'Estaing at Cadiz soon lost all the interest he had gained at Court. He put to sea with his fleet against the protest of the Spanish admiral, and with circumstances that rendered him completely unpopular. The British fleet under Admiral Darby was at sea in his track; the French ships were in the worst condition imaginable, but our fleet did not avail itself of the opportunity for bringing them to action, and they reached their port without exchanging a shot. How justifiable this was on our part I will not doubt, how disappointing even to Spain, whose wishes had by this time turned about, and how derogatory in her opinion to the credit of our arms, I can truly witness.

I had now manœuvred the Abbé Hussey into a mission, the most acceptable to him that could be devised, as it took him out of Spain, and liberated him from the necessity of acting a part, which he could not longer have sustained with any credit to himself; for it was only whilst the treaty was in train with the sincere good-will of Spain that he could be truly cordial in the cause; when unforeseen events occurred to check and interrupt the progress of it, his sagacity did not fail to discover that he could no longer preserve a middle interest with both parties, but must be hooked into a dilemma of choosing his side; which that would have been when duplicity must have been thrown off, was a decision he did not wish to come to, though I perhaps can conjecture where it would have led him. He had no great prejudices for England; Ireland was his native country, but even that and the whole world had been renounced by him, when he threw himself into the oblivious convent of La Trappe, and was only dragged from out his cell by force and the emancipating authority of the Pope himself. Whilst he was here digging his own grave, and consigning himself to perpetual taciturnity, he was a very young man, high in blood, of athletic strength, and built as if to see a century to its end. It was not the enthusiasm of devotion, no holy raptures, that inspired him with this desperate resolution: it was the splenetic effect of disappointed passion; and such was the change, which a short time had wrought in him, that Father Robinson, the worthy priest with whom he afterwards cohabited, told me that when he attended the order for his deliverance, he could hardly ascertain his person, especially as he persisted to asseverate in the strongest terms that he was not the man they were in search of.

When he came forth again into the world, with passions rather suspended than subdued, I am inclined to think he considered himself as forced upon a scene of action, where he was to play his part with as much finesse and dissimulation as suited his interest, or furthered his ambition; and this he probably reconciled to his conscience by a commodious kind of casuistry, in which he was a true adept.

He wore upon his countenance a smile sufficiently seductive for common purposes and cursory acquaintance: his address was smooth, obsequious, studiously obliging, and at times glowingly heightened into an impassioned show of friendship and affection. He was quick enough in finding out the characters of men, and the openings through which they were assailable to flattery; but he was not equally successful in his mode of tempering and applying it; for he was vain of showing his triumph over inferior understandings, and could not help coloring his attentions oftentimes with such a florid hue as gave an air of irony and ridicule, that did not always escape detection; and thus it came to pass that he was little credited (and perhaps even less than he deserved to be) for sincerity in his warmest professions, or politeness in his best attempts to please.

As I am persuaded that he left behind him in his coffin at La Trappe no one passion, native or engrafted, that belonged to him when he entered it, ambition lost no hold upon his heart, and of course I must believe that the station which he filled in Spain, and the high-sounding titles and dignities which the favor of his Catholic Majesty might so readily endow him with, were to him such lures, as, though but feathers, outweighed English guineas in his balance: for of these I must do him the justice to say he was indignantly regardless; but to the honors that his church could give, to the mitre of Waterford, though merely titular, it is clear to demonstration he had no repugnance.

He made profession of a candor and liberality of sentiment, bordering almost upon downright Protestantism, whilst in heart he was as high a priest as Thomas à Becket, and as stiff a Catholic, though he ridiculed their mummeries, as ever kissed the cross. He did not exactly want to stir up petty insurrections in his native country of Ireland, but to head a revolution that should overturn the church established, and enthrone himself primate in the cathedral of Armagh, would have been his brightest glory and supreme felicity: and in truth he was a man, by talents, nerves, ambition, intrepidity, fitted for the boldest enterprise.

After he had negotiated my introduction into Spain, and set the treaty on foot, the very first check, which it received by the disturbances in London, left me very little hope of further help from him; but when the prospect was darkened by accumulated clouds, and he discovered nothing through the gloom of my embarrassed situation but a tottering ministry, a discontented people, an unquiet capital, our trading fleets captured, and our fighting fleets no longer worthy of the name; when he saw Spain assume a proud and conquering attitude, and (buoyed up by the promises of France) blockading Gibraltar and preparing for the actual siege of it, he began to perceive he had engaged himself in a most unpromising intrigue, and readily lent his ear to those that were at hand and ready to intrigue him out of it. He was assiduous in his homage to the Archbishop of Toledo, and in the closest intimacy and communication with the minister of the Elector of Treves, and all at once, without the smallest cause of offence, or any reason that I could possibly divine, changed his behavior as an inmate of my family, and from the warmest and most unreserved attachment, that man ever professed to man, took up a character of the severest gloom and sullenness, for which he would assign no cause, but to all my inquiries, all my remonstrances, was either obstinately silent, or evasively uncommunicative. He would stay no longer, he was resolved to demand his passports, and actually wrote to Del Campo to that purpose. To this demand an answer was returned, refusing him the passports until he had leave from Lord Hillsborough for quitting Spain, which it was at the same time observed to him could not be for his reputation to do in the depending state of the business on which he came. Upon this he proceeded to write a short letter to Lord Hillsborough, demanding leave to return: he was not hardy enough to dispatch this letter without communicating it to me for my opinion: I gave it peremptorily against his sending it: I stated to him my reasons why I thought both the measure and the mode decidedly improper and dishonorable; he grew extremely warm, and so intemperate, that I found it necessary to tell him, if he persisted in demanding his return of the secretary of state in those terms, that it would oblige me to write home in my own justification, and also to enter upon explanations with the Spanish minister, who might else impute his conduct to a cabal with me, though it was so directly against my judgment and my wishes. I declared to him that I had not written a line, or taken a step without his privity, and that no one word had ever passed my lips, but what was dictated by sincere regard and consideration for him, and this was solemnly and strictly true: I said that I observed he had altered his behavior towards me and my family, which he could not deny, and I added that this proceeding must not only ruin him with the minister of Spain, but was such as might be highly prejudicial to my business, unless I took every prudent precaution to explain and avert the mischief it was pregnant with. The consequence of this conversation was, that he did not send his letter to Lord Hillsborough, but as he was not explicit on that point, I prepared myself with a letter to Lord Hillsborough, and another to Del Campo, explanatory of his conduct, which, upon his assuring me on our next meeting that he would not write to England, I also forbore to send. Upon the following day, without any cause assigned or explanation given, my late sullen associate met me with a smiling countenance, and was as perfectly an altered man, as if he had come a second time out of the cloisters of La Trappe. He was in fact a most profound casuist, and a confessor of the highest celebrity.

I cannot say this caprice of Mr. Hussey gave me much concern, or created in me any extraordinary surprise, though I could never thoroughly develop the cause of it; yet at that very time my life was brought into imminent danger by the unskilfulness of the surgeons, who attended upon me in consequence of my having received a very serious injury by a fall from one of my Portuguese mules. I was riding on the Pardo road, when the animal took fright, and in the act of stopping him the bit broke asunder in his mouth. In this state, being under no command, he ran with violence against an equipage drawn by six mules that was passing along the road in a train with many others. In the concussion I came to the ground; the carriage fortunately stopped short, and I was lifted into it stunned with the shock, and for a time insensible. I was bleeding at the elbow, where the skin was torn, and upon recovering my senses I found myself supported by my wife in her chariot, and probably indebted to her drivers for my life. Though I had cause to tremble for the consequences of the violent alarm I had given her, as she was now very near her time, yet in other respects it was a fortunate and extraordinary chance, that my accident should have thrown me immediately into her protection, who lost not an instant of time in conveying me home. Two surgeons, such as Madrid could furnish, were called in and speedily arrived, but for no other purpose, as it seemed, except to dispute and wrangle with each other upon the question if the arm was fractured at the shoulder or at the elbow, whilst each alternately twisted and tortured it as best suited him in support of his opinion. In the height of their controversy a third personage made his appearance in the uniform of the Guardes de Corps, being chief surgeon of that corps, and sent to me by authority. This gentleman silenced both, but agreed with neither, for he pronounced the bone to be split longitudinally from the shoulder to the elbow, and finding it by this time extremely swelled and inflamed, very properly observed that no operation could be performed upon it in that state. He proceeded, therefore, to bathe it liberally with an embrocation, which he affirmed was sovereign for the purpose, but if his object was to reduce the swelling and assuage the inflammation, the learned gentleman was most egregiously mistaken, for the fiery spirit of the rum, with which he fomented it, soon increased both to so violent a degree with such a raging erysipelas as in a few days had every symptom of a mortification actually commencing, when the case being pressing, my wife, whose presence of mind never deserted her in danger, took the prudent measure of dismissing the whole trio of ignoramuses, and calling to her assistance a modest, rational practitioner in our near neighborhood, who, under the sign of a brass basin, professed the sister arts of shaving and surgery conjointly, by reversing the practice so injurious and applying the bark, rescued me from their hands, and, under Providence preserved, my life.

Here I must take leave to digress a little from the tenor of my tale, whilst I record an anecdote, in itself of no other material interest except as it enables me to state one amongst the many reasons which I have to love and revere the memory of a deceased friend, who devoted to me the evening of every day without the exception of one, which I passed during my residence in Madrid. This excellent old man, Patrick Curtis by name, and by birth an Irishman, had been above half a century settled in Spain, domestic priest and occasionally preceptor to three successive dukes of Osuna. In this situation he had been expressly the founder of the fortunes of the Premier Florida Blanca, by recommending him as advocate to the employ and patronage of that rich and noble house. The Abbé Don Patricio Curtis was of course looked up to as a person of no small consideration; he was also not less conspicuous and universally respected, for his virtues, for his high sense of honor, his bold sincerity of speech, and generous benignity of soul; but this good man at the same time had such an over-abundant portion of the *amor patriæ* about him, was so marked a devotee to the British interest, and so unreserved an opponent to that of France, that it seemed to demand more circumspection than he was disposed to bestow for guarding himself against the resentment of a party; whose principles he arraigned without mitigation, and whose power he set at open defiance without caution or reserve. Though considerably past eighty, his affections were as ardent and his feelings as quick as if he had not reached his twentieth year. When I was supposed to be out of chance of recovery, this affectionate creature came to me in an agony of grief to take his last farewell. He told me he had been engaged in fervent prayer and intercession on my behalf, and had pledged before the altar, his most earnest and devoted services for the consolation and protection of my beloved wife and daughters, if it should please Heaven to remove me from them, and reject his humble supplications for my life: he lamented that I had no spiritual assistant of my own church to resort to; he did not mean to obtrude his forms, to which I was not accustomed, but on the contrary, came purposely to tender me his services according to my own; and was ready, if I would furnish him with my prayer-book, and allow him to secure the doors from any that might intrude or overhear to the peril of his life, to administer the sacrament to me exactly as it is ordained by our church, requesting only that I would reach the cup with my own hand, and not employ his to tender it to me. All this he fulfilled, omitting none of the prayers appointed, and officiating in the most devout impressive manner (though at times interrupted and overcome by extreme sensibility), to my very great comfort and satisfaction. Had the office of Inquisition, whose terrific mansion stood within a few paces of my gates, had report of this which passed in my heretical chamber, my poor friend would have breathed out the short remnant of his days between two walls, never to be heard of more. From six o'clock in the afternoon till ten at night, he never failed to occupy the chair next to me in my evening circle, and though I saw with infinite concern, that his constitution was rapidly breaking up for the last six or seven weeks of my stay, no persuasion could keep him from coming to me and exposing his declining health to the night air; at last, when I was recalled and had fixed the day for my departure, dreading the effect which the act of parting forever might have upon his exhausted frame, I endeavored to impose upon him a later hour of the morning than I meant to take for my setting out, and enjoined strict secrecy to all my party; but these precautions were in vain; at three o'clock in the morning, when I entered the receiving room, I found my poor old friend alone and waiting, with his arms extended to embrace me and bathed in tears, scarcely able to support himself on his tottering legs, now miserably tumefied, a spectacle that cut my heart to the quick, and perfectly unmanned me. He had purchased a number of masses of some pious mendicants, which he hoped would be efficacious and avail for our well-doing; he had no great faith in amulets, he told me, yet he had brought me a ring of Mexican workmanship and materials, very ancient, and consecrated and blessed by a venerable patriarch of the Indies, since canonized for his miracles; which ring had been highly prized by the late Duchess of Osuna for its efficacy in preserving her from thunder and lightning, and though he did not presume to think that I would place the slightest confidence in its virtue, yet he hoped I would let him bestow it on the person of the infant daughter, which was born to me in Spain, whom I then gave into his arms, whilst he invoked a thousand blessings upon her. He brought a very fine crucifix cut in ivory; he said he had put up his last prayers before it, and had nothing more to do but lie down upon his bed and die, which as soon as I departed he was prepared to do, sensible that his last hour was near at hand, and that he should survive our separation a very few days. I prevailed with him to retain his crucifix, but I accepted an exquisite Ecce Homo by El Divino Morales, and exchanged a token of remembrance with him; I saw him led out of my house to that of the Duke of Osuna near at hand, and whilst I was yet on my journey the intelligence reached me of his death, and may the God of mercy receive him into bliss!

When I had so far advanced in my recovery as to be able to wear my arm in a sling, and endure the motion of a carriage, I dispatched my servant Camis to San Ildefonso, and proposed to the minister a conference with him there upon the supposed mediation of Russia, on which he had thought fit to sound me. My servant returned, bringing a letter from the subminister Campo, in which he signifies the minister's wish that I would consent to defer my visit, but adds that 'if I think otherwise I shall always be welcome.' I well knew to whom and to what I was indebted for this letter, and naturally was not pleased with it, yet I thought it best and most prudent to answer it as follows:—

'*To Senor Don Bernardo Del Campo.*

DEAR SIR: My servant returned with your letter of this day in time to prevent my setting out for San Ildefonso.

When I tell you that it is with pleasure I accommodate myself to the wishes of Count Florida Blanca, I not only consult my own disposition, but I am persuaded I conform to that of my court, and of the minister under whose immediate instructions I am acting. The reconciliation of our respective nations is an object which I look to with such cordial devotion, that I would on no account interpose myself in a moment unacceptable to your court, for any consideration short of my immediate duty. I am persuaded there is that honor and good faith in the councils of Spain, and in the minister who directs them, that I shall not suffer in his esteem by this proof of my acquiescence, and I know too well the sincerity of my own court to apprehend for the part I have taken.

At the same time that I signify to you my acquiescence as above stated, I think my predicament thereby becomes such as to require an immediate report to my court, and I desire you will request of his excellency Count Florida Blanca to send me a blank passport, to be filled up by me with the name of such person as I may find convenient to dispatch to England by the way of Lisbon. I am, &c. &c. R. C.'

This letter produced a most courteous invitation, and thence ensued those conferences already described, which separated Mr. Hussey from me, and sent him home with propositions, which my instructions did not allow me to discuss. By this chasm in the business I was upon, I found myself so far at leisure, that I was tempted to indulge my curiosity by a visit to the Escurial, and accordingly set out for that singular place with a letter from the minister to the Prior, signifying the king's pleasure that I should have free access to the manuscripts, and every facility, that could be given to my researches of whatever description. I had been informed by Sir John Dalrymple of a curious manuscript, purporting to be letters of Brutus, to which he could not get access; these letters are written in Greek, and are referred to by Doctor Bentley in his controversy with Boyle as notoriously spurious, fabricated by the sophists, of which there can be no doubt.. I obtained a sight of the manuscript, and the fathers favored me with a copy of the Greek original, and also of the Latin translation by Petrarch. I have them by me, but they are good for nothing, and bear decided evidence of an imposture. This the worthy father, who introduced himself to me as librarian and professor of the learned languages, discovered by a very curious process, observing to me that these could not be the true letters of Brutus, forasmuch as they profess to have been written after the death of Julius Cæsar, which he had found out to be a flagrant anachronism, assuring me that Brutus, having died before Cæsar, could not be feigned to have written letters after the decease of the man who survived him. When I apologized for my hesitation in admitting his chronology, and asked him if Brutus was not suspected of having a hand in the murder of Cæsar, he owned that he had heard of it, but that it was a mere fable, and, hastening to his cell, brought me down a huge folio of chronology, following me into the court, and pointing out the page, where I might read my own conviction. I thanked him for his solicitude, and assured him that his authority was quite sufficient for the fact, and recollecting how few enjoyments he probably had in that lugubrious mansion, left him in possession of his victory and triumph.

I took nobody with me to the Escurial but my servants and a Milanese traiteur, who opened an empty hotel, and provided me with a chamber and my food. There were indeed myriads of annoying insects, who had kept uninterrupted possession of their quarters, against whom I had no way of guarding myself but by planting my portable crib in the middle of the room, with its legs immersed in pails of water. The court was expected, but not yet arrived, and the place was a perfect solitude, so that I had the best possible opportunity of viewing this immense edifice at my ease and leisure. I am not about to describe it; assuredly it is one of the most wonderous monuments that bigotry has ever dedicated to the fulfilment of a vow. Yet there is no grace in the external, which owes its power of striking to the immensity of its mass: the architect has been obliged to sacrifice beauty and proportion to security against the incredible hurricanes of wind, which at times sweep down from the mountains that surround it; of a scenery more savage, nature hardly has a sample to produce upon the habitable globe: yet within this gloomy and enormous receptacle, there is abundant food for curiosity in paintings, books, and consecrated treasures exceeding all description. There is a vast and inestimable collection of pictures, and the great masters, whose works were in my poor judgment decidedly the most prominent and attractive, are Raphael, Titian, Rubens, Velasquez and Coello, of which the two last were natives of Spain and by no means unworthy to be classed with the three former. Of Raphael there are but four pre-eminent specimens, of which the famous Perla is one, but hung very disadvantageously; of Titian there is a splendid abundance; of Rubens not many, but some that show him to have been a mighty master of the passions, and speak to the heart with incredible effect; they throw the gauntlet to the proudest of the Italian schools, and seem to leave Vandyke behind him almost out of sight; of Velasquez, if there was none other than his composition of Jacob, when his sons are showing him the coat of Joseph, it would be enough to rank him with the highest in his art; Coello's fame may safely rest upon his inimitable altar-piece in the private chapel. Were it put to me to single out for my choice two compositions, and only two, from out the whole inestimable collection, I would take Titian's Last Supper in the refectory for my first prize, and this altar-piece of Coello's for my second, leaving the Perla and Madona del pesce of Raphael, the Dead Christ of Rubens, and the Joseph of Velasquez with longing and regret, but leaving them notwithstanding.

The Court removed from San Ildefonso to the Escurial in a

few days after I had been there, and I was invited to bring my family thither, which accordingly I did. My reception here was very different from what I had experienced at San Ildefonso. The king, one of the best tempered men living, was particularly gracious; in walking through his apartments in the Escurial, I surprised him in his bed-chamber; the good man had been on his knees before his private altar, and upon the opening of the door, rose; when seeing me in the act of retiring, he bade me stay, and condescended to show me some very curious South American deer, extremely small and elegantly formed, which he kept under a netting; and amongst others a little green monkey, the most diminutive and most beautiful of its species I had ever seen. He also showed me the game he had shot that morning of various sorts from the bocafica to the vulture. He was alone, and seemed to take peculiar pleasure in gratifying our curiosity. No monarch could well be more humbly lodged, for his state consisted in a small camp-bed, miserably equipped with curtains of faded old damask, that had once been crimson, and a cushion of the same by his bedside, with a table, that held his crucifix and prayer-book, and over that a three-quarters picture of the *Mater-dolorosa* by Titian, which he always carried with him for his private altar-piece; of which picture I was fortunate enough to procure a very perfect copy by an old Spanish master (Coello as I suspect) upon the same sized cloth, and very hardly to be distinguished from the original. This picture I brought home with me, and it is now in my possession. His majesty's dress was, like his person, plain and homely; a buff leather waistcoat, breeches of the same, and old-fashioned boots (made in Pall Mall), with a plain drab coat, covered with snuff and dust, a bad wig and a worse hat, constituted his wardrobe for the chase, and there were very few days in the year when he denied himself that recreation.

CHAPTER VIII.

The Prince of Asturias—His pavilion—Present of horses—Anecdote of Cumberland's daughter—Honors to the English monarch—The Princess Asturias—Mode of life at Madrid—Count Kaunitz—Giusti—Pallavicini—Foreign ambassador—His visitors—Tiranna—The Duke of Osuna—Anthony Smith—Recalled—Generous offer of the Spanish king—Bills dishonored—Bad treatment—Memoirs—Official letters.

THE Prince of Asturias, now the reigning sovereign, was always so good as to notice the respect I duly paid him, with the most flattering and marked attention. He spoke of me and to me with distinguished kindness, and caused it to be signified to me, that he was sorry circumstances of etiquette did not allow him to show me those more pointed proofs of his regard, by which it was his wish to make appear the good opinion he was pleased to entertain of me. Such a testimony from a prince, of his reserved and distant cast of character, was to be valued for its sincerity. On my way from San Ildefonso to Segovia, one morning at an early hour, as I was mounting a hill, that opened that extensive plain to my view, I discovered a party of horsemen and the prince considerably advanced before them, at the full speed of his horse; I had just time to order my chariot out of the road, and halt it under some cork-trees by the way-side, and, according to my custom, I got out to pay him my respects. The prince stopped his horse upon the instant, and with his hat in his hand, wheeled him about to come up to me, when the high-spirited animal, either resenting the manœuvre, or taking fright, as it seemed, at the gleamy reflection of my gray mules, half covered with the cork branches, reared and wheeled upon his hinder legs, in a most alarming manner. The prince appeared to me in such imminent danger, that I was about to seize the bit of his bridle, but he was much too complete a cavalier to accept of assistance, and after a short but pretty severe contest, brought his horse up to me in perfect discipline, and with many handsome acknowledgments for the anxiety I had shown, on his account, in a very gracious manner took his leave, and pursued his road to San Ildefonso. He was a man of vast bodily strength, and a severe rider: the fine animal, one of the most beautiful I had seen in

Spain, showed the wounds of the spur, streaming with blood down his glossy-white sides, from the shoulder to the flank.

This prince had a small but elegant pavilion, at a short distance from the Escurial, which in point of furniture and pictures was a perfect gem. He did me and my family the honor to invite us to see it; at the appointed hour we found it prepared for our reception, with a table set out and provided with refreshments; some of the officers of his household were in waiting; the Dukes of Alva, Granada, Almodovar, and others of high rank, accompanied us through the apartments, and when I returned to my hotel, at the Escurial, the prince's secretary called on me, by command, to know my opinion of it. There could be no difficulty in delivering that, for it really merited all the praise that I bestowed upon it. In a very short time after, the same gentleman returned and signified the prince's express desire to know if there was anything in the style of furniture that struck me as defective, or anything I could suggest for its improvement. With the like sincerity I made answer, that in my humble opinion the fitting of the principal room in the Chinese style, though sufficiently splendid, was not in character with the rest of the apartments, that were hung round with some of the finest pictures of the Spanish and Italian masters, where a chaster style, in point of ornament, had been preserved.

I heard no more of my critique for some days, and began to suspect that I had made my court very ill by risking it, when another message called me to review the complete change which that apartment had undergone, to the exclusion of every atom of Japan work, in consequence of my remark.

It was on this occasion that the minister, Florida Blanca, in the moment of that favor and popularity which I then enjoyed, addressed me in a very different style from any he had ever used, and with an air of mock solemnity, charged me with having practised upon the heir apparent of the crown of Spain by some secret charm, or love-powder, to the engagement of his affections, 'which,' said he, 'I perceive you are so exclusively possessed of, that I must throw myself on your protection, and request you to preserve to me some place in his regard.' As I had found his excellency, for the first time, in the humor for raillery, I endeavored to keep up the spirit of it by owning to the love-powder; in virtue of which I had gained that power over the prince, as to seize the bridle of his horse, and arrest him on the road, which led me to relate the anecdote of our rencounter on the way to Segovia above described. He listened to me with great good humor, appearing to enjoy my narrative of the adventure, and at the conclusion observed to me, that my life was forfeited by the laws of Spain; but as he supposed I had no evil design against the prince himself, but only wanted to possess myself of so fine a charger, as an offering to my excellent and royal master, whose virtues made his life and safety dear to all the world, he would, in confidence, disclose to me, that order was given out by his Catholic Majesty, to select from his stud, in the Mancha, ten, the noblest horses that could be chosen, and out of those, upon trial of their steadiness and temper, to select two, which I might tender as my offering to the acceptance of my sovereign; and this, he observed, was a present never before made to any crowned head in Europe, but of his majesty's own immediate family, alluding to the King of Naples.

A few days after my return to Madrid this gracious promise was fulfilled, and two horses of the royal stud, led by the king's grooms, and covered by cloths on which the royal arms, &c., were embroidered, were brought into the inner court of my house, and there delivered to me. I flatter myself they were such horses as had not been brought out of Spain for a century before, and not altogether unworthy of the acceptance of the illustrious personage who condescended to receive them. I was at dinner when they arrived, and Count Kaunitz, the imperial ambassador, was at the table with me. I had not spoken to him, or any other person, of this expected present, and his astonishment at seeing that which had been the great desideratum of many ambassadors, and himself amongst the number, thus voluntarily and liberally bestowed upon me (the secret and untitled agent of a court at war with Spain), surprised him into some comments, which had the only tincture of jealousy that I ever discovered in him. A crowd had followed these horses to the gates which inclosed my courts; one of these opened to the Plazuela de los Affligidos, and the other to the street of the Inquisition; I caused these gates to be thrown open, and when the people saw the horses with their royal coverings upon them led into my stable, they gave a shout expressive of their pleasure and applause. If my very amiable friend Kaunitz was not quite so highly gratified by these occurrences as I was, he was perfectly excusable.

I kept these horses in my stables at Madrid, and should not have used them but at the special requisition of the royal donor; when that was signified to me, my daughters and myself rode them, as occasion suited, and as a proof how noble they were by nature, the following instance will suffice. As my eldest daughter was passing a small convent, not a mile from the gate of San

Bernandino, a large Spanish mastiff of the wolf-dog kind rushed out of the convent, and seizing her horse by the breast, hung there by his teeth, whilst the tortured animal rushed onwards at full speed, showing no manner of vice, and only eager to shake off his troublesome encumbrance. In this situation she was perceived and rescued by a Spanish officer on foot, who presenting himself in the very line of the horse's course, gave him the word and signal to stop, when, to my equal joy and astonishment (for I saw the action), the generous animal obeyed, the dog dropped his hold, and the lady, still firm and unshaken in her seat, though alarmed and almost breathless, was seasonably set free by the happy presence of mind of her deliverer, and the very singular obedience of her royal steed, whose generous breast long retained the marks of his ignoble and ferocious assault.

When I had received my recall, I sent these horses before me under the care of two Spaniards, father and son, of the name of Valasco, who led them from Madrid through Paris to Ostend, walking on foot, and sleeping by them in their stables every night; and taking their passage from Ostend to Margate, arrived with them at my door in Portland Place, and delivered them without spot or blemish in perfect order and condition to his majesty's grooms at the royal Mews.

If my gratitude to the memory of the late benevolent sovereign, who was pleased by this and many other favors graciously to mark the sincere, though ineffectual efforts of an humble individual, defeated in his hopes by unforeseen events, which he could not control, and afterwards abandoned to distress and ruin by his employers for want of that success, which he could not command; if my gratitude (I repeat it) to the deceased King of Spain causes me to be too particular, or prolix, in recording his goodness to me, it is because I naturally must feel it with the greater sensibility from the contrast, which I painfully experienced, when I returned bankrupt, broken-hearted and scarce alive to my native country. But of this more at large in its proper place.

I have hinted at the surprise which my friend Count Kaunitz expressed upon the present of the royal horses; it was again his chance to experience something of the like nature, when he did me the honor to dine with me upon the 4th of June, when, with a few cordial friends, I was celebrating my beloved sovereign's birth-day, in the best manner my obscurity and humble means allowed of. On this occasion I confess my surprise was as great as his, when the music of every regiment in garrison at Madrid, not excepting the Spanish guards, filed into my court-yard, and afforded me the exquisite delight of hearing those who were in arms against my country, unite in celebrating the return of that day which gave its monarch birth.

I frequently visited the superb collection of paintings in the palace at Madrid; the king was so good as to give orders for any pictures to be taken down and placed upon the easel, which I might wish to have a nearer view of; he also gave direction for a catalogue to be made out at my request, which I have published and attached to my account of the Spanish painters; he authorized me to say, that if the king, my master, thought fit to send over English artists to copy any of the pictures in his collection, either for engravings or otherwise, he would give them all possible facility, and maintain them at free cost, whilst they were so employed; this I made known on my return. He gave direction to his architect, Sabbatini, to supply from the quarries in Spain any blocks or slabs of marble, according to the samples which I brought over to the amount of above a hundred, whenever any such should be required for the building or ornamenting the royal palaces in England.

I bear in my remembrance many other favors, which, after what I have related, are not necessary to enumerate. They were articles to which his grace and goodness gave a value, and exactly such as I could with perfect consistency of character accept. The present of Viguna cloth from the royal manufactory, which he had given to the ambassador, Lord Grantham, in the same proportion was bestowed upon me. The superior properties of the Spanish pointer are well known, and dogs of the true breed are greatly coveted; the king understood I was searching after some of this sort, and was pleased to offer me the choice of any I might wish to have from out his whole collection; but I had already possessed myself of two very fine ones, which his majesty saw, and thought them at least equal to any of his own; I therefore, thankfully acknowledged his kind offer, but did not avail myself of it.

The Princess of Asturias, now reigning Queen of Spain, had taken an early opportunity of giving a private audience to my wife and daughters, and gratifying their curiosity with a sight of her jewels, most of which she described to be of English setting. She condescended to take a pattern of their riding habits, though they were copied from the uniform of our guards, and, when apprised of this, replied that it was a further motive with her for adopting the fashion of it; I remember, however, that she caused a broad gold lace to be carried round the bottom of the skirt. She also condescended to send for several other articles of their dress, as samples, whilst they were conforming to the costume of Spain to the minutest particular, and wearing nothing but silks of Spanish fabric, rejecting all the finery of Lyons, and every present or purchase, however tempting, of all French manufactures whatever. This lure for popularity succeeded to such a degree, that when these young Englishwomen, habited in their Spanish dresses (and attractive, as I may presume to say they were by the bloom and beauty of their persons), passed the streets of Madrid, their coach was brought to frequent stops, and hardly found its passage through the crowd. A Spanish lady, when she rides, occupies both sides of her palfrey, and is attended by her lacqueys on foot, her horse, in the mean time, *movens, sed non promovens*, brandishing his legs, but advancing only by inches. When my wife and daughters, on the contrary, who were all admirable riders, according to the English style and spirit, put their horses to their speed, it was a spectacle of such novelty, and oftentimes drew such acclamations, particularly from the Spanish guards whilst we were at the Escurial, as might have given rise to some sensations, if persisted in, which in good policy made it prudent for me to remand them to Madrid.

Here I considered myself bound in duty to adapt my mode of life to the circumstances of my situation, and the undefined character in which I stood. I was not restricted from receiving my friends, but I made no visits whatsoever, and the journal of any one day may serve for a description of the whole. The same circle assembled every afternoon at the same minute, and with the same regularity broke up. The ladies had a round table of low Pope-Joan, and I had a party of sitters-by. My house was extremely spacious, and that space by no means choked up with furniture; I had fourteen rooms on the principal floor, and but one fireplace; in this, during the winter months, I burnt pieces of wood, purchased of a coach maker, many of them carved and gilt, the relics of old carriages, and it was no uncommon thing to discover fragments of arms and breasts of Careatides, who had worn themselves out in the service of some departed Grandee, who had left them, like the wreck of Pharaoh's chariots, to their disgraceful fate. I found my mansion in the naked dignity of brick floors and white walls; upon the former I spread some mats, and on the other I pasted some paper. I farmed my dinners from a Milanese traiteur, exorbitantly dear and unpardonably bad; but I had no resource: they came ready cooked to my house, and were heated up afresh in my stoves. The lacqueys, that I hired, had two shillings per day, and dieted themselves; my expense in equipage was very great, for the mules appropriate to my town use could not go upon the road; others were to be hired for posting, and less than six had been against all rule. I had a stable full of capital Spanish horses, exclusive of the king's, three of which were lent to me for the use of the ladies, and two given to me by Count Kaunitz; one of these, a most beautiful creature of the under-size, and a favorite of my wife's, I brought to England: the other was an aged horse, milk-white, the victor over nine bulls, and covered in his flanks and sides with honorable scars; he had been devoted to the amphitheatre under suspicion of having the glanders, but he outlived the imputation, and, in the true character of the Spanish horse, carried himself in the proudest style of any I ever saw, possessing the sweetest temper with the noblest spirit, and when in the possession of the great Grandee Altamira, had been prized and admired above all other horses of his day. My eldest daughter seldom failed to prefer him, but, thinking him too old to undergo any great fatigue, I did not risk the bringing him to England, but returned him to the noble donor.

This amiable personage, son to the Imperial Minister, Count Kaunitz, had been ambassador to Russia, and was now filling that distinguished station at the court of Spain. When I had been but a few days in Madrid, whilst I was in my box at the comedy, with my wife and daughters, he asked leave to enter, and placed himself in a back seat: the drama, as far as I could understand it, seemed to be grounded on the story of Richardson's Pamela, and amongst the characters of the piece there was one who meant to personate a British sea-captain. When this representative of my countryman made his entrance on the stage, Kaunitz, who perhaps discovered something in my countenance, which the ridiculous dress and appearance of the actor very possibly excited, leaning forwards and addressing himself to me for the first time, said: 'I hope, sir, you will overlook a small mistake in point of costume, which this gentleman has very naturally fallen into, as I am convinced he would have been proud of presenting himself to you in his proper uniform, could he have found, amongst all his naval acquaintance, any one, who could have furnished him with a sample of it.' This apology, at once so complimentary and ingenious, set off by his elegant manner of address, led us into conversation, and from that evening I can hardly call to mind one, in which he failed to honor me with his company. In his features he bore a striking resemblance to the portrait, which he gave me of his father; in his manners, which were those of a perfect gentleman, he was correctly fitted to the situation that he filled, and for that situation his talents, though not pre-eminently brilliant, were doubtless all-sufficient. He was not unconscious of those high pretensions to which his birth and station entitled him, but it was very rarely indeed that I could discover any symptoms in his behavior, that betokened other than a proper and becoming sensibility towards his honor and his office. With a constitution rather delicate, he possessed a heart extremely tender, and how truly and entirely that heart was devoted to the elder of my daughters, I doubt not but he severely felt, when, frustrated in his honorable and ardent wishes to be united to her, he saw her depart out of Spain, and after one day's journey in our company took his melancholy leave forever; for after the revolution of a few months, when it may be presumed he had conquered his attachment, and reconciled himself to his disappointment, this amiable young man, being then upon his departure for his native country, sickened and died at Barcelona.

There were two other gentlemen of the imperial party, who very constantly were pleased to grace my evening circle; the one Signor Giusti, an Italian, secretary of the embassy; the other, General Count Pallavicini, a man not more ennobled by the splendor of his birth, than by the services he had performed, and the fame he had acquired. In the short war between Austria and Prussia, this gallant officer, by a very brilliant coup-de-main, had surprised a fortress and made prisoners the garrison, which covered him with glory and the favors of his sovereign; he was now making a military tour by command and at the charge of the Empress Queen, and came into Spain, consigned (as I may say) to Count Kaunitz, for the purpose of being passed into the Spanish lines, then investing Gibraltar. Into this fortress he was anxiously solicitous to obtain admission, and when no accommodation could be granted to his wishes through the influence of Count Kaunitz, I gave him letters to Mr. Walpole, which he carried to him at Lisbon, and by a route which that minister pointed out, assisted by his and my introduction to General Elliot, succeeded in his wishes, and I believe no man entertained a higher respect for the brave defenders of that fortress, or a warmer sense of the gratifying indulgence, which they granted to him in so liberal a manner. Count Pallavicini was in the prime of life, of a noble air and high-born countenance; tall, finely formed, gay, natural, open-hearted; his spirit was alive in every feature; it did not need the aid of suscitation; no dress could hide the soldier, or disguise the gentleman. He had a happy flow of comic humor at command, unobtrusive, however, and only resorted to at times and seasons; of the suavity and pomposity of the Castilian character, he seemed to have taken up a very contemptible impression, and would no otherwise fall in with any of their habits and customs, than for the purpose of ridiculing them by imitations designedly caricatured. There are twenty ways of arranging the Spanish Capa; he never would be taught any one of them, though he underwent a lecture every night at parting, but in an one-and-twentieth way of his own hung it on his shoulders, and marched off most amusingly ridiculous. I think it never was my lot to make acquaintance with a man, for whom my heart more rapidly warmed into friendship, than it did towards this engaging gallant hero; he continued to me his affectionate correspondence, till, turning out against the Turks, and ever foremost in the field of glory, his head was sabred from his body at a stroke, and he died, as he had lived, in the very arms of victory; his ardent courage, though it turned the battle, did not serve him to ward off the blow.

From this lamented friend, whose memory will be ever dear to me, I have now in my possession letters, written from Prague, where he had a separate command of eight thousand men, by which letters, though he could not prevail with either of my daughters (for he successively addressed himself to each) to change their country and forsake their parents and connections, yet I trust he was assured and satisfied from the answers he received, that it was because they could not detach themselves from ties like these, and not because they were insensible to his merits, when in their humble station they felt themselves compelled to reject those offers, that would have conferred honor on them, had they ranked amongst the highest.

The Nuncio Colonna, cardinal elect, paid me some attentions, and the Venetian ambassador favored me with his visits. The Saxon minister, Count Gerstoff, was frequently at our evening parties, and the Danish minister, Count Reventlau, seldom failed. The former of these was an animated lively man, and a most agreeable companion; Reventlau had been in a diplomatic character at the court of London, and had brought with him the language, manners, and habitudes of an Englishman of the first fashion. His partiality to our native country created in me and my family a reciprocal partiality for him, and so interesting was this elegant young Dane in person, countenance, and address, that the eye which could have contemplated him with indifference, must have held no correspondence with the heart. We passed the whole evening before our departure with this engaging and affectionate friend; the parting was to all most painful, but by one in particular more acutely felt than I will attempt to describe. Reventlau was one, and not the eldest of a very numerous and noble family; his father had been minister, but his hereditary property was by no means large, and the purity of his principle disdained the accumulation of any other advantages or rewards, than those which attached themselves to his reputation, and were rigidly consistent with the character of a patriot.

Colonel O'Moore, of the Walloons, a very worthy and respectable man, and Signor Nicolas Marchetti, of the corps of Engineers, a Sicilian, were constant parties in our friendly circle. There were other Irish officers in the Spanish service, some religious also of that nation, and some in the commercial line, who frequently resorted to me; but to the generous and benevolent Marchetti in particular, who accompanied me through the whole of my disastrous journey from Madrid, by the way of Paris, I am beholden for the means that enabled me to reach my native country, as will appear hereafter.

Count Pietra Santa, lieutenant-colonel of the Italian band of body guards, was my most dear and intimate friend; by that name in its truest and most appropriate sense I must ever remember him (for he is now no more), and though the days that I passed with him in Spain did not outnumber those of a single year, yet in every one of these I had the happiness to enjoy so many hours of his society, that in his case, as in that of the good old Abbé Curtis, whilst we were but young in acquaintance, we might be fairly said to be old in friendship. It is ever matter of delight to me, when I can see the world disposed to pay tribute to those modest unassuming characters, who exact no tribute, but in plain and pure simplicity of heart recommend themselves to our affections, and borrowing nothing from the charms of wit, or the display of genius, exhibit virtue—in itself how lovely. Such was my deceased friend, a man whom everybody, with unanimous assent, denominated the good Pietra Santa, whom everybody loved, for he that ran could read him, and who, together with the truest courage of a soldier, and the highest principles of honor, combined such moral virtues with such gentle manners and so sweet a temper, that he seemed destined to give the rare example of a human creature, in whom no fault could be discovered.

In this society I could not fail to pass my hours of relaxation very much to my satisfaction without resorting to public places or assemblies, in which species of amusement Madrid was very scantily provided, for there was but one theatre for plays, no opera, and a most unsocial gloomy style of living seemed to characterize the whole body of the nobles and grandees. I was not often tempted to the theatre, which was small, dark, ill-furnished, and ill-attended, yet when the celebrated tragic actress, known by the title of the Tiranna, played, it was a treat which I should suppose no other stage then in Europe could compare with. That extraordinary woman, whose real name I do not remember, and whose real origin cannot be traced, till it is settled from what particular nation or people we are to derive the outcast race of gypsies, was not less formed to strike beholders with the beauty and commanding majesty of her person, than to astonish all that heard her, by the powers that nature and art had combined to give her. My friend Count Pietra Santa, who had honorable access to this great stage heroine, intimated to her the very high expectation I had formed of her performances, and the eager desire I had to see her in one of her capital characters, telling her at the same time that I had been a writer for the stage in my own country; in consequence of this intimation she sent me word that I should have notice from her, when she wished me to come to the theatre, till when, she desired I would not present myself in my box upon any night, though her name might be in the bill, for it was only when she liked her part, and was in the humor to play well, that she wished me to be present.

In obedience to her message I waited several days, and at last received the looked-for summons; I had not been many minutes in the theatre before she sent a mandate to me to go home, for that she was in no disposition that evening for playing well, and should neither do justice to her own talents, nor to my expectations. I instantly obeyed this whimsical injunction, knowing it to be so perfectly in character with the capricious humor of her tribe. When something more than a week had passed, I was again invited to the theatre, and permitted to sit out the whole representation. I had not then enough of the language to understand much more than the incidents and action of the play, which was of the deepest cast of tragedy, for in the course of the plot she murdered her infant children, and exhibited them dead on the stage lying on each side of her, whilst she, sitting on the bare floor between them (her attitude, action, features, tones, defying all description), presented such a high-wrought picture of hysteric frenzy, 'laughing wild amidst severest woe,' as placed her in my judgment at the very summit of her art; in fact I have no conception that the powers of acting can be carried higher, and such was the effect upon the audience, that whilst the spectators in the pit, having caught a kind of sympathetic frenzy from the scene, were rising up in a tumultuous manner, the word was given out by authority for letting fall the curtain, and a catastrophe, probably too strong for exhibition, was not allowed to be completed.

A few minutes had passed, when this wonderful creature, led in by Pietra Santa, entered my box; the artificial paleness of her cheeks, her eyes, which she had dyed of a bright vermilion round the edges of the lids, her fine arms bare to the shoulders, the wild magnificence of her attire, and the profusion of her dishevelled locks, glossy black as the plumage of the raven, gave her the appearance of something so more than human, such a Sibyl, such an imaginary being, so awful, so impressive, that my blood chilled as she approached me not to ask but to claim my applause, demanding of me if I had ever seen any actress that could be compared with her, in my own or any other country. 'I was determined,' she said, 'to exert myself for you this night; and if the sensibility of the audience would have suffered me to have concluded the scene, I should have convinced you that I do not boast of my own performances without reason.'

The allowances which the Spanish theatre could afford to make to its performers, were so very moderate, that I should doubt if the whole year's salary of the Tiranna would have more than paid for the magnificent dress in which she then appeared; but this and all other charges appertaining to her establishment were defrayed from the coffers of the Duke of Osuna, a grandee of the first class and commander of the Spanish Guards. This noble person found it indispensably necessary for his honor to have the finest woman in Spain upon his pension, but by no means necessary to be acquainted with her, and at the very time of which I am now speaking, Pietra Santa seriously assured me, that his excellency had indeed paid large sums to her order, but had never once visited, or even seen her. He told me at the same time that he had very lately taken upon himself to remonstrate upon this want of curiosity, and having suggested to his excellency how possible it was for him to order his equipage to the door, and permit him to introduce him to this fair creature, whom he knew only by report and the bills she had drawn upon his treasurer, the duke graciously consented to my friend's proposal, and actually set out with him for the gallant purpose of taking a cup of chocolate with his hitherto invisible mistress, who had notice given her of the intended visit. The distance from the house of the grandee to the apartments of the gypsy was not great, but the lulling motion of the huge stage-coach, and the softness of the velvet cushions had rocked his excellency into so sound a nap, that when his equipage stopped at the lady's door, there was not one of his retinue bold enough to undertake the invidious task of troubling his repose. The consequence was, that after a proper time was passed upon the halt for this brave commander to have waked, had nature so ordained it, the coach wheeled round, and his excellency having slept away his curiosity, had not, at the time when I left Madrid, ever cast his eyes upon the person of the incomparable Tiranna. I take for granted my friend Pietra Santa drank the chocolate, and his excellency enjoyed the nap. I will only add, in confirmation of my anecdote, that the good Abbé Curtis, who had the honor of having educated this illustrious sleeper, verified the fact.

When Count Pallavicini left Madrid and went to Lisbon in the hope of getting into Gibraltar through the introduction that I gave him to the minister, Mr. Walpole, and others of my correspondents in that city, I availed myself of that opportunity for conveying my dispatches of the 12th of December, 1780, to the Secretary of State, Lord Hillsborough. They embraced much matter and very many particulars, interesting at that time, but now so long since gone by, that the insertion of them here could answer no purpose but to set forth my own unwearied assiduity and good fortune in procuring intelligence, which, in the event, proved perfectly correct. On the 3d of the month following, viz: January, 1781, I inform Lord Hillsborough that, 'having found means to obtain copies of some state papers, the authenticity of which may be relied upon, I have the honor to transmit them to your lordship by express to Lisbon.' These were all actual dispatches of the minister, Florida Blanca, secret and confidential, to the Spanish envoy at the court of Petersburg, and developed an intrigue, of which it was highly important that my court should be apprised. This project it was my happy chance to lay open and defeat by the acquisition of these papers, through the agency of one of the ablest and most efficient men that ever was concerned in business of a secret nature. Had my corresponding minister listened to the recommendation I gave of this gentlemen, I could have taken him entirely into the pay and service of my court, and the advantages to be derived from a person of his talents and address were incalculable. He served me faithfully and effectually on this and some other occasions, and it was not without the most sensible regret I found myself constrained to leave him behind me.

When I had sent my faithful servant, Camis, express with this important dispatch, I received the following letter from the Earl of Hillsborough:—

'*St. James's*, 9th December, 1780.

SIR: I have duly received your letters from No. 7 to No. 12 inclusive, and laid them before the king. The last number was delivered to me by Mr. Hussey.

That gentleman has communicated to me the purport of Count Florida Blanca's conversation with him, for which purpose alone he appears to me to have returned to London. The introduction of Gibraltar, and the American rebellion into that conversation, convinces me that there is no intention in the court of Spain to make a separate treaty of peace with us. I do not, however, as yet signify to you the king's command for your return, though I see little utility in your remaining at Madrid.

If you should obtain any further intelligence concerning the mediation, which you informed me you understood had been proposed by the Empress of Russia, I desire you will acquaint me with it.

Mr. Hussey undertakes to deliver this letter to you. I have nothing further to add, but to repeat to you, that the king expects from you the strictest adherence to your instructions, without any deviation whatsoever, during the remainder of the time you shall continue at Madrid.

I am, with great truth and regard, sir,
Your most obedient humble servant,
MR. CUMBERLAND, (Signed) HILLSBOROUGH.'

This was sufficient authority for me to believe that my mission was fast approaching to its conclusion, and I prepared myself accordingly. In the mean time, Mr. Hussey, who undertook to deliver this letter to me, was stopped at Lisbon and not permitted to continue his journey into Spain; for, in fact, the train which my minister had now contrived to throw the negotiation into, was not acceptable to the Spanish court, and the rigor with which I was enjoined to adhere to my instructions, operated so effectually against the several overtures which were repeatedly made to me on the part of Florida Blanca, that I must ever believe the negotiation was lost on our part by transferring it to one with whom Spain was not inclined to treat, and tying up my hands with whom there seemed every disposition to agree. In fact, we parted merely on a punctilio, which might have been qualified between us with the most consummate ease; they wanted only to talk about Gibraltar, and I was not permitted to hear it named; the most nugatory article would have satisfied them; and if I had dared to have given in writing to the Spanish minister the salvo that I suggested in conversation, after my receiving the letter above referred to, I have every reason to be confident that the business would have been concluded, and the object of a separate treaty accomplished without any other sacrifice than that of a little address and accommodation in the matter of a mere punctilio.

When some conferences had passed, in which, fettered as I was by my instructions, I found it impossible to put life into our expiring negotiation, favored, though I was, by the court and minister to the last moment of my stay, I wrote to Lord Hillsborough as follows:—

'*Madrid*, January 18th, 1781.

No. 19. MY LORD: In consequence of a letter which Mr. Hussey will receive by this conveyance from Count Florida Blanca, I am to conclude that he will immediately return to England, without coming to this court. In the copy of this letter which his excellency has communicated to me, he remarks that, in case the negotiation shall break off upon the answer now given, my longer residence at Madrid will become unnecessary; and as I am persuaded that your lordship and the cabinet will agree with the minister of Spain in this observation, I shall put myself in readiness to obey his majesty's recall. In the mean time, I beg leave to repeat to your lordship that I shall strictly adhere to his majesty's commands, trusting that you will have the goodness to represent to his majesty my faithful zeal and devotion, how ineffectual soever they may have been, in the fairest light.

Understanding that the king had been pleased to accept from the late Prince Masserano, a Spanish horse, which was in great favor, and hoping that it might be acceptable to his majesty, if occasion offered of supplying his stables with another of the like quality, I desired permission of the minister to take out of Spain a horse, which I had in my eye, and his excellency having reported this my desire to the King of Spain, his Catholic Majesty was so good as to give immediate direction for twelve of the best horses in Andalusia, of his breed of royal Caribaneers, to be drafted out, and from these two of the noblest and steadiest to be selected, and given to me for the above purpose. I have accordingly received them, and, as they fully answer my expectations both in shape and quality, and are superior to any I have seen in this kingdom, I hope they will be approved of by his majesty, if they are fortunate in a safe passage, and shall arrive in London without any accident.

Don Miguel Louis de Portugal, ambassador from her most faithful majesty to this court, died a few days ago of a tedious and painful decay. The Infanta of Spain is sufficiently recovered to remove from Madrid to the Pardo, where the court now resides.

I have the honor to be, &c. &c. R. C.'

Whilst the court was at the Pardo, a complaint, founded on the grossest misrepresentations, was started and enforced upon me by the minister respecting the alleged ill treatment of the Spanish prisoners of war in England. I traced this complaint to the reports of a certain Captain Nunez, then on his parole and lately come from England; with this gentleman there came a nephew of my friend the Abbé Curtis, who had been chaplain on board Captain Nunez's frigate, when she was taken, and who was now liberated, having brought over with him a complete copy of the minutes of Parliament, in which the matter in complaint was fully and completely inquired into, and the allegations in question confuted upon the clearest evidence, Captain Nunez himself being present at the examination, and testifying his satisfaction and entire conviction upon the result of it. These documents the worthy nephew of my friend very honorably put into my hands, and, armed with these, I proved to the court of Spain that, upon a sickness breaking out amongst the Spanish prisoners from their own uncleanliness and neglect, our government, with a benevolence peculiar to the British character, had made exertions wholly out of course, furnishing them with entire new bedding at a great expense, supplying them with medicines and all things needful, whilst in attendance on the deceased more than twenty surgeons (I speak from memory, and I believe I am correct) had sacrificed their lives. If, in the refutation of a charge so grossly unjust and injurious as this, I lost my patience, and for a short time forgot the management befitting my peculiar situation, I can truly say it was the only error I committed of that sort, though it was by no means the only instance that occurred to provoke me to it, as the following anecdote will demonstrate.

There was a young man, by name Anthony Smith, a native of London, living at Madrid upon a small allowance, paid to him upon the decease of his father, who had been watchmaker to the King of Spain. I took this young man into my family upon the recommendation of the Abbé Curtis, and employed him in transcribing papers, arranging accounts, and other small affairs, in which his knowledge of the language rendered him very useful. One day, about noon, the criminal judge with his attendants walked into my house, and seizing the person of this young man took him to prison, and shut him up in a solitary cell without assigning any cause for the proceeding, or stating any crime, of which he was suspected. I took the course natural for me to take, and from the effect which my remonstrance and appeal to the minister instantly produced, I had no reason to think him privy to the transaction, for late in the evening of the next day Anthony Smith was brought to my gates by the officers of justice, from whom I would not receive him, but sent him back till the day following, when I required him to be delivered to me at the same hour and in the same public manner as they had chosen to take him from me, and further insisted that the same criminal judge with his attendants should be present at the surrender of their prisoner. All this was exactly complied with, and the foolish magistrate was hooted at by the populace in the most contemptuous manner. It seemed that this wise judge was in search of an assassin, who was described as an old, black-complexioned fellow with a lame foot, whereas Smith was a very fair young man, with red hair, and perfectly sound and active on his legs. What were the motives for this wanton act of cruelty I never could discover; I brought him with me to England, but the terrors he had suffered during his short but dismal confinement haunted him through every stage of his journey, till we passed the frontiers of Spain. When we arrived in London, I recommended him to my friend Lord Rodney, as Spanish clerk on board his flag ship, but poor Smith's spirit was so broken, that he declined the service, and found a more peaceful occupation in a merchant's counting-house.

I was now in daily expectation of my recall, and as my own immediate negotiation was shifted, for a time, into other hands,

I availed myself of those means which, by my particular connections I was possessed of, for collecting such a body of useful information as might safely be depended upon, and this I transmitted to my corresponding minister in my dispatches No. 20 of the 31st of January, and No. 21 of the 3d of February, 1781. I had now no longer any hope of bringing Spain into a separate treaty, whilst my court continued to receive overtures, and return answers, through the channel of Mr. Hussey, then at Lisbon, and Florida Blanca having imparted to me a dispatch, which he affected to call his ultimatum, I plainly saw extinction to the treaty upon the face of that paper, for he would still persist in the delusive notion that he could insinuate articles and stipulations for Gibraltar in his communications through Mr. Hussey, though I by my instructions could not pass a single proposition in which it might be named. When he had written this letter, which he called his ultimatum, it seems to have occurred to him to communicate it to me rather too late for any good purpose, inasmuch as he had taken his Catholic Majesty's pleasure upon it, and made it a state paper, before he put it into my hands. He, nevertheless, was earnest with me to give him my opinion of it, and I did not hold myself in any respect bound to disguise from him what I thought of it, neither did I scruple to suggest to him the idea, which I had formed in my mind, of an expedient, that might have conciliated both parties, and would at all events have obviated those consequences, to which his unqualified requisition could not fail to lead. It will suffice to say that he candidly declared his readiness to adopt my idea, and form his letter anew in conformity to it, if he had not, by laying it before the king, made it a state paper, and put it out of his power to alter and new-model it, without a second reference to the royal pleasure. This, however, he was perfectly disposed to do, provided I would give him my suggestions in writing, as a producible authority for reconsidering the question. Here my instructions stood so irremovably in my way, that, although he tendered me his honor that my interference should be kept secret, I did not venture to commit myself, nor could he be brought to consider conversation as authority.

Upon the failure of this, my last effort, I regarded the negotiation as lost, and, reflecting upon what had passed in the conference above referred to, when I had finished my letter No. 20, of the 31st of January, 1781, I attached to it the following paragraph, viz:—

'Since Count Florida Blanca dispatched his express to Lisbon, I have not heard from Mr. Hussey, neither do I know any thing of his commission, but what Count Florida Blanca's answer opens to me, and as I must, believe that in great part, a finesse, I cannot but lament that it had not been prepared by discussion.'

As the court of Spain was now become the centre of some very interesting and important intrigues, by which she was attempting to impose the project of a general pacification, under the pretended mediation of Russia only, and to substitute this project in the place of the separate and exclusive treaty, now on the point of dissolution, I felt myself justified in taking every measure which my judgment dictated, and my connections gave me opportunity to pursue, for bringing that event to pass, of which I apprise Lord Hillsborough in the following paragraph of my letter No. 20, viz:—

'An express from Vienna, brought to Count Kaunitz, in the evening of the 27th instant, the important particulars, relative to the mediation of his imperial majesty, jointly with the Empress of Russia. This court being at the Pardo, the Ambassador Kaunitz took the next day for communicating with Count Florida Blanca, and yesterday a courier arrived from Paris, with the instructions of that court, to Count Montmorin, on the subject.

'When the minister of Spain shall deliver the sentiments of his Catholic Majesty to the imperial ambassador, which will take place on the day after to-morrow, they will probably be found conformable to those of France, of which I find Count Kaunitz is already possessed. I shall think it my duty to apprise your lordship of any particulars that may come to my knowledge, proper for your information.'

In my letter No. 21, of the 3d of February, I acquaint Lord Hillsborough that 'the answer of Spain to the proposition of the emperor's mediation was made on the day mentioned in my letter No. 20, and as I then believed it would conform to that of France, so in effect it happened, with this further circumstance, that in future reference is to be made to the Spanish ambassador, at Paris, who, in concert with the minister of France, is to speak for his court, being instructed in all cases for that purpose.'

Upon this arrangement, I observe that it is made, 'as well to soothe the jealousy of the French court, who, in their answer, glanced at the separate negotiation here carrying on with Great Britain, as for other obvious reasons.' In speaking of the emperor's proposed mediation, I explain the reason that prevailed with me for expressing my wishes in a letter, No. 8, of the 4th of August. 'That the good offices of the imperial court might maintain their precedency, before those of any other, and that I am well assured it was owing to the knowledge Russia had of these overtures, made by the imperial court, that she put her propositions to the belligerent powers in terms so guarded and so general, as should not awaken any jealousy in the first proponent,' and I add, 'that I know the instructions of Monsieur de Zinowieff, the Russian ambassador, to have been so precise, on this head, so far removed from all idea of the formal overture, pretended by the Spanish minister, that I think he would hardly have been induced to deliver, in any writing, as Monsieur Simolin did in London, although it had been so desired.'

I shall obtrude upon my readers only one more extract from this letter, in which, 'I beg leave to add a word, in explanation of what I observe, at the conclusion of my letter No. 20, touching the answer made to Mr. Hussey, viz: that it were to be wished it had been preceded by a discussion; this, I said, my lord, because the answer was no sooner settled, and given to the king, than a disposition evidently took place, to have reconsidered and modified the stipulation for Gibraltar, now so glaringly inadmissible; but this, and every other observation touching our negotiation, traversed by so many unforeseen events, will, for the future, as I hope, find its course in a more general and successful channel.'

I make no other comment upon the good or ill policy of laying me under those restrictions, but that I could else have prevented the transmission of that article, which gave the deathblow to my negotiation.

For this I was prepared, and after the revolution of a few days received his majesty's recall, communicated to me in the following letter:—

'*St. James's*, 14th February, 1781.

Sir: I am sorry to find from your last letter, No. 19, and from that written from Count de Florida Blanca to Mr. Hussey, which the latter received at Lisbon, that an entire stop is put to the pleasing expectation, which had been formed from your residence in Spain. Had I been as well informed of the intentions of the Court of Madrid, when you went abroad, as I now am, you would certainly not have had the trouble and fatigue of so long a voyage and journey.

There remains nothing now for me but to acquaint you that I am commanded by the king to signify to you his majesty's pleasure, that you do immediately return to England: when I say immediately, it is not intended that your departure should have the appearance of resentment, or that you should be deprived of the opportunity of expressing a just sense of the marks of civility and attention which Mr. Cumberland has received since his arrival in Madrid.

I am, with great truth and regard, sir,
Your most obedient humble servant,
(Signed) HILLSBOROUGH.'

I had now his majesty's commands, signified to me as above, for my return to England, and his lordship's interpretation of them to direct my behavior in avoiding all appearance of resentment which I did not feel, and expressing that sense of gratitude which I did feel, for the many marks of civility and attention which I had received in the person of Mr. Cumberland, since his arrival in Madrid. To these excellent rules of conduct I was prepared to pay the most correct and cheerful obedience.

For the favor of his lordship's information, that he would have spared me the trouble and fatigue of my long journey, if he had been aware that there was no occasion for my taking it, I could not but be duly thankful, and I am most sincerely sorry that nobody could be found with prescience to inform his lordship what the intentions of the court of Madrid would be for a whole year to come, nor to apprise me what my recompense would be upon the expiration of it. If such inspiration had been vouchsafed to both, I think I can guess who would have been the greater gainer of the two.

Had any kind, good-natured incendiary been so confidential as to have told me that it was his intention to set fire to London as soon as I was well out of it; or had Count Florida Blanca had the candor to have premised that his invitation of me into Spain had no other object in view but to give me the amusement of a tour, and himself the pleasure of my company, it would, perhaps, have been very flattering to my vanity, but I don't think it would have suited my principle to have passed it off for a negotiation, and I am quite convinced it would not have suited my finances to have paid his excellency the visit, and sacrificed my fortune to the amusement of it.

It certainly would be extremely convenient if we could always see to the end of an experiment before we undertake it. I could not see to the end of the riots in London when they were reported to be so terrible, yet I predicted as truly as if I had foreseen it, and was reprimanded notwithstanding; if then I acted wrong by guessing right at the only favorable occurrence that happened whilst I was in Spain, how should I have escaped a severer reproof if I had been as successful in foretelling the many evil occurrences of that disastrous year, during the whole course of which I kept alive a treaty, which was never lost till it was taken out of my hands?

If here I seem to speak too vainly of my unsuccessful services, I have to appeal to the testimony of that great and able minister, Prince Kaunitz, who, together with his tender of the mediation of the imperial court, communicated to the British cabinet, suggests a wish that I may be included in the commission, if such shall be appointed, at the general congress;

and is pleased to give for his reason the favorable impressions which his correspondence with Spain had given him of my conduct there in carrying on a very arduous business, which many circumstances contributed to embarrass. This I should never have had the gratification to know had it not been communicated to me by a friend after my return to England, who, concluding I had been informed of it, was complimenting me upon it. Thus I went abroad to find friendship and protection, and came home to meet injustice and oppression.

If the following fact, which is correctly true, and which I now for the first time make public, shall prove that those whom I could not put at peace with my country, were yet at perfect peace with me, I hope I shall not be suspected of having overstrained the privilege allowed me by my letter of recall, and carried my complaisance too far upon my farewell visit to the Spanish minister at the Pardo. I certainly harbored no resentment in my heart, and having free leave to avoid the appearance of it, had no object but to express, as well as I was able, the grateful sense I entertained of the many favors which the king and court of Spain had condescended to bestow upon me and mine. In replying to these acknowledgments, so justly due, Count Florida Blanca, assuming an air of more than ordinary gravity, and delivering himself slowly and distinctly, as one who wishes that a word should not be lost, addressed the following speech to me, which, according to my invariable practice, I wrote down and rendered into English in my entry book, whilst it was yet fresh in my memory; and from that record I have transcribed not only this, but every other speech that I have given as authentic in these Memoirs:—

'Sir, the king my sovereign has been entirely satisfied with every part of your conduct during the time you have resided amongst us. His majesty is convinced that you have done your duty to your own court, and exerted yourself with sincere good will to promote that pacification, which circumstances out of your reach to foresee, or to control, seem for the present to have suspended. And now, sir, you will be pleased to take in good part what I have to say to you with regard to your claims for indemnification on the score of your expenses, in which I have reason to apprehend you will find yourself abandoned and deceived by your employers. I have it therefore in command to tell you, that the king my sovereign has taken this into his gracious consideration, and tenders to you through me full and ample compensation for all expenses which you have incurred by your coming into Spain; being unwilling that a gentleman, who has resorted to his court, and put himself under his immediate protection, without a public character, honestly endeavoring to promote the mutual good and benefit of both countries, should suffer, as you surely will do, if you withstand the offer, which I have now the honor to make known to you.'

What I said in answer to this generous, but inadmissible offer, I shall make no parade of; it is enough to say that I did not accept a single dollar from the King of Spain, or any in authority under him, which, as far as a negative can be proved, was made clear, when upon my journey homewards my bills were stopped, and my credit so completely bankrupt, that I might have gone to prison at Bayonne, if I had not borrowed five hundred pounds of my friendly fellow-traveller Marchetti, which enabled me to pay my way through France and reach my own country.

How it came to pass that my circumstances should be so well known to Count Florida Blanca is easily accounted for, when the dishonoring of my bills by Mr. Devisme at Lisbon, through whose hands the Spanish banker passed them, was notorious to more than half Madrid, and could not be unknown to the minister. The fact is, that I had come into Spain without any other security than the good faith of government, upon promise, pledged to me through Mr. Robinson, secretary of the treasury, that all bills drawn by me upon my banker in Pall Mall, should be instantly replaced to my credit, upon my accompanying them with a letter of advice to the said secretary Robinson. This letter of advice I regularly attached to every draft I made upon Messrs. Crofts, Devaynes and Co., but from the day that I left London to the day that I returned to it, including a period of fourteen months, not a single shilling was replaced to my account with my bankers, who persisted in advancing to my occasions with a liberality and confidence in my honor, that I must ever reflect upon with the warmest gratitude. If I was improvident in relying upon these assurances, they who made them were inexcusable in breaking them, and betraying me into unmerited distress. I solemnly aver that I had the positive pledge of treasury through Mr. Robinson for replacing every draft I should make upon my banker, and a very large sum was named, as applicable at my discretion, if the service should require it. I could explain this further, but I forbear. I had one thousand pounds advanced to me upon setting out; my private credit supplied every farthing beyond that; for the truth of which I need only to refer the reader to the following letter:—

'*To John Robinson, Esquire, &c.*

Madrid, 8th of March, 1781.

SIR: My banker informs me of a difficulty which has arisen in replacing the bills which I have had occasion to draw upon him for the expenses of my commission at this court.

As I have not had the honor of hearing from you on this subject, and as it does not appear that he had seen you, when he wrote to me, the alarm which such an event would else have given me, is mitigated by this consideration, as I am sure there can be no intention in government to disgrace me at this court in a commission, undertaken on my part without any other stipulation than that of defraying my expenses. I flatter myself, therefore, that you have before this done what is needful in conformity to what was settled on our parting. Suffer me to add, that by the partition I have made of my office with the gentleman who executes it, by the expenses preparatory to my journey, all which I took on myself, and by many others since my departure, which I have not thought proper to put to the public account, I have greatly burdened my private affairs during my attendance on the business I am engaged in.

That I have regulated my family here for the space of near a twelvemonth, with all possible economy upon a scale in every respect as private, and void of ostentation as possible, is notorious to all who know me here; but a man must also know this court and country to judge what the current charges of my situation must inevitably be; what the occasional ones have been can only be explained by myself; and as I can clearly make it appear that I have neither misapplied the money nor abused the trust of government in any instance, I cannot merit, and I am persuaded I shall not experience any misunderstanding or unkindness.

I have the honor to be, &c. &c. R. C.'

I might have spared myself the trouble of this humiliating appeal. It produced just what it should produce—nothing; for it was addressed to the feelings of those who had no feelings; and called for justice, where no justice was, no mercy, no compassion, honor or good faith.

I wearied the door of Lord North till his very servants drove me from it. I withstood the offer of a benevolent monarch, whose munificence would have rescued me; and I embraced ruin in my own country to preserve my honor as a subject of it; selling every acre of my hereditary estate, jointured on my wife by marriage settlement, who generously concurred in the sacrifice, which my improvident reliance upon the faith of government compelled me to make.

But I ought to speak of these things with more moderation, so many years having passed, and so many of the parties having died, since they took place. In prudence and propriety these pages ought not to have seen the light, till the writer of them was no more; neither would they, could I have persisted in my resolution for withholding them, till that event had consigned them into other hands; but there is something paramount to prudence and propriety, which wrests them from me—

My poverty, but not my will, consents.

The copyright of these Memoirs produced to me the sum of five hundred pounds, and if, through the candor and protection of a generous public, they shall turn out no bad bargain to the purchaser, I shall be most sincerely thankful, and my conscience will be at rest—but I look back, and find myself still at Madrid, though on the point of my departure. On the 15th of March I write to the Earl of Hillsborough as follows, viz:—

'My Lord: On the 11th instant I had the honor of your lordship's letter, dated the 14th of February, and in obedience to his majesty's commands, therein signified, I took occasion on the same day of demanding my passports of the minister of Spain. Agreeably to the indulgence granted me by His Majesty, I yesterday took leave of Count Florida Blanca, at the Pardo, and this day my family presented themselves to the Princess of Asturias, at the convent of Santo Domingo el Real, who received their parting acknowledgments with many expressions of kindness and condescension. I am to see the King of Spain on Sunday, and expect to leave Madrid on Tuesday or Wednesday next.

The ambassador of France having in the most obliging manner given me a passport, and your lordship's letter containing no directions to the contrary, I propose to return by Bayonne and Bourdeaux, to which route I am compelled by the state of my health, and that of part of my family.

I have the honor to be, &c. &c. R. C.

I hope your lordship has received my letter No. 18, also those numbered 20 and 21, which conclude what I have written.'

To the sub-minister Campo, who had been confidential throughout, and present at almost every conference I had held with the Premier, I wrote as follows:—

'*Madrid*, March 20th, 1781.

You have done all things, my dear sir, with the greatest kindness and the politest attention. I have your passports, and as my baggage is now ready to be inspected, I wait the directions of the Minister Musquiz, which I pray you now to dispatch. To-morrow, in the forenoon, at 11 o'clock, or any other hour more convenient to the officers of the customs, will suit me to attend upon them.

You tell me that no more could be done for me, were I an ambassador. I am persuaded of it, for being, as I am, a dependant on your protection, and intrusted to you by my country, how can I doubt but that the Spanish point of honor will concede to me not less (and I should not wonder if it granted more), than any ambassador can claim by privilege.

I have never ceased to feel a perfect confidence in my situation, nor ever wished for any other title to all the rights of hospitality and protection than what I derive from the trust, which my court has consigned to me, and that which I repose in yours.

I bring this letter in my pocket to the Pardo, lest you should not be visible at the hour I shall arrive. I beg to recommend to you the cause of the English prisoners, who have undersigned the inclosed paper.

I hope to set out on Friday: be assured I shall carry with me a lasting remembrance of your obliging favors, and I shall ardently seize every occasion in my future life of expressing a due sense of them.

If your leisure serves to favor us with another visit at Madrid, we shall be happy to see you, and I shall be glad to confer with you on the subject of the Spanish prisoners, and apprise you of the language I shall hold on that topic upon my return home.

On all occasions, and in every place I shall conscientiously adhere to truth. Let me say, for the last time I shall speak of myself, that no man ever entered Spain with a more conciliating disposition, and I hope I leave behind me some proof of patience.

Farewell! ever faithfully yours, R. C.'[1]

---

[1] In perusing Cumberland's narrative of his mission to Spain, the reader cannot fail to be struck with his evident anxiety to have it redound to the benefit of his country. His great mistake was in advancing into Spain at all, inasmuch as, under the circumstances, it was a violation of the letter of his instructions. He acted, however, as he conceived, for the advantage of his country. His error was of the head; and the ministry's refusal of payment for his services was a harsh and cruel return for all his sacrifices and endeavors. The mission to Spain, honorable in itself, was disastrous in its consequences, and embittered the remainder of Cumberland's life.

In addition to the causes which he assigns for its failure, the disturbances in London, and other untoward circumstances, it must not be forgotten that, amid all the tortuosities of Spanish diplomacy, and notwithstanding all its protestations and propositions, there was a strong desire to see British power humbled, and British supremacy overthrown. At the same time, the opinion prevailed that the American Revolution was a bad example to the Spanish colonies, and dangerous to Spain, as the United States, if they should become ambitious, and be seized with the spirit of conquest, might aim at Mexico and Peru. The court of Spain seem to have acted on the principle, either to make no treaty with the United States, until they had accomplished their independence, or to make important concessions to them the *conditio sine qua non* of a treaty, and consequent aid.

When Cumberland arrived at Madrid, he found there, as minister from the United States, John Jay, who had resigned his post of President of Congress, to accept this mission. The disclosures of Jay and Cumberland exhibit in a very striking light the craft and duplicity of Florida Blanca, and, indeed, of all the Spanish officials connected with the foreign office. While Cumberland was received and caressed in the manner he has described, 'it was given out, and Jay was officially informed, that Cumberland and his family were desirous of passing through Spain, to Italy; that the journey was undertaken on account of the ill health of a daughter, to whom the Duke of Dorset was much attached; that the opposition made by his friends to the marriage had affected her health, &c. The minister assured Jay that whatever proposals Mr. Cumberland might make, should be candidly communicated to him. It is needless, perhaps, to add that no such communication was made. . . . . The people, said Mr. Jay, supposed Cumberland's errand to be secret overtures for peace, and, as far as he could judge, were very glad of it. In truth, the war with England was very unpopular with the Spaniards. 'They appear to me,' wrote Jay, 'to like the English, hate the French, and to have prejudices against us.' —*Flanders' Lives and Times of the Chief Justices*, p. 298.

Whatever the sentiments of the Spanish people, the Spanish court had different objects to accomplish. They cajoled and deceived Cumberland, and their conduct towards Jay was marked by treachery and duplicity. With the desire to curtail British power, was associated the fear that the independence of America might be prejudicial to Spain. But whatever might betide, the Spanish ministry were anxious so to shape their conduct that Spain should profit from whatever turn affairs might take.

CHAPTER IX.

Leaves Spain—Madrid—Progress and incidents of his homeward journey.

On the 24th of March, 1781, having taken a last painful leave of the worthy Abbé Curtis and the rest of my friends, at half past ten in the forenoon I set out upon my journey. My party consisted of my wife, my two eldest daughters, and my infant daughter, born in Spain, at the breast of a Spanish nurse, a wild but affectionate creature, native of San Andero; the good Marchetti and the poor redeemed prisoner Anthony Smith accompanied us, and we had three English servants, two of which (Thomas Camis and Mary Sampson) had been in my family from their earliest years, and have never since served any other master. Two Spanish coaches, drawn by six mules each, with mules for our out-riders, constituted our travelling equipage, and I contracted for their attending upon us to Bayonne. They are heavy clumsy carriages, but they carry a great deal of baggage, and if the traveller has patience to put up with their very early hours and slow pace, there is nothing else to complain of.

Madrid, which may be considered as the capital of Spain, though it is not a city, disappoints you if you expect to find suburbs, or villas, or even gardens when you have passed the gates, being almost as closely environed with a desert as Palmyra is in its present state of ruin. The Spaniards themselves have no great taste for cultivation, and the attachment to the chase, which seems to be the reigning passion of the Spanish sovereigns, conspires with the indolence of the people in suffering every royal residence to be surrounded by a savage and unseemly wilderness. The lands, which should contribute to supply the markets, being thus delivered over to waste and barrenness, are considered only as preserves for game of various sorts, which includes everything the gun can slay, and these are as much *res sacræ* as the altars, or the monks, who serve them. This *solitudo ante ostium* did not contribute to support our spirits, neither did the incessant jingling of the mules' bells relieve the tedium of the road to Guadarama, where we were agreeably surprised by the Counts Kaunitz and Pietra Santa, who passed that night in our company, and next morning with many friendly adieus departed for Madrid, never to meet again—

> Animas queis candidiores
> Nusquam terra tulit.

The next day we passed the mountains of Guadarama by a magnificent causeway, and entered Old Castile. Here the country began to change for the better; the town of Villa Castin presents a very agreeable spectacle, being new and flourishing, with a handsome house belonging to the Marchioness of Torre-Manzanares, who is in part proprietor of the town. This illustrious lady was just now under a temporary cloud for having been party in a frolic with the young and animated Duchess of Alva, who had ventured to exhibit her fair person on the public parade in the character of postilion to her own equipage, whilst Torre-Manzanares, mounted the box as coachman, and other gallant spirits took their stations behind as footmen, all habited in the splendid blue and silver liveries of the house of Alva. In some countries a whim like this would have passed off with eclat, in many with impunity, but in Spain, under the government of a moral and decorous monarch, it was regarded in so grave a light, that, although the great lady postilion escaped with a reprimand, the lady coachman was sent to her castle at a distance from the capital, and doomed to do penance in solitude and obscurity.

We were now in the country for the Spanish wool, and this place being a considerable mart for that valuable article, is furnished with a very large and commodious shearing-house. We slept at a poor little village called San Chidrian, and being obliged to change our quarters on account of other travellers, who had been beforehand with us, we were fain to put up with the wretched accommodations of a very wretched posada.

The third day's journey presented to us a fine champaign country, abounding in corn, and well peopled. Leaving the town of Arebalo, which made a respectable appearance, on our right, we proceeded to Almedo, a very remarkable place, being surrounded with a Moorish wall and towers in very tolerable preservation; Almedo also has a fine convent and a handsome church.

The fourth day's journey, being March the 27th, still led us through a fair country, rich in corn and wine. The river Adaga runs through a grove of pines in a deep channel very romantic, wandering through a vast tract of vineyards without fences. The weather was serene and fresh, and gave us spirits to enjoy the scenery, which was new and striking. We dined at Valdestillas, a mean little town, and in the evening reached Valladolid, where bigotry may be said to have established its head-quarters. The gate of the city, which is of modern construction, consists of three arches of equal span, and that very narrow; the centre of these is elevated with a tribune, and upon that is placed a pedestrian statue of Carlos III. This gate delivers you into a spacious square, surrounded by convents and churches, and passing this, which offers nothing attractive to delay you, you enter the old gate of the city, newly painted in bad fresco, and ornamented with an equestrian statue of the reigning king with a Latin inscription, very just to his virtues, but very little to the honor of the writer of it. You now find yourself in one of the most gloomy, desolate and dirty towns, that can be conceived, the great square much resembling that of the Plaza-mayor in Madrid, the houses painted in grotesque fresco, despicably executed, and the whole in miserable condition. I was informed that the convents amount to between thirty and forty. There is both an English and a Scottish college; the former under the government of Doctor Shepherd, a man of very agreeable, cheerful, natural manners; I became acquainted with him at Madrid through the introduction of my friend Doctor Geddes, late Principal of the latter college, but since Bishop of Mancecos, Missionary and Vicar General at Aberdeen. I had an introductory letter to the Intendant, but my stay was too short to avail myself of it; and I visited no church but the great cathedral of the Benedictines, where mass was celebrating, and the altars and whole edifice were arrayed in all their splendor. The fathers were extremely polite, and allowed me to enter the sacristy, where I saw some valuable old paintings of the early Spanish masters, some of a later date, and a series of Benedictine Saints, who, if they are not the most rigid, are indisputably the richest, order of Religious in Spain.

Our next day's journey advanced us only six short leagues, and set us down in the ruinous town of Duenas, which, like Olmedo, is surrounded by a Moorish fortification, the gate of which is entire. The Calasseros, obstinate as their mules, accord to you in nothing, but in admitting indiscriminately a load of baggage, that would almost revolt a wagon, and this is indispensible, as you must carry beds, provisions, cooking vessels, and every article for rest and sustenance, not excepting bread, for in this country an inn means a hovel, in which you may light a fire, if you can defend your right to it, and find a dunghill called a bed, if you can submit to lie down in it.

Our sixth day's stage brought us to the banks of the Douro,

which we skirted and kept in sight during the whole day from Duenas through Torrequemara to Villa Rodrigo. The stone-bridge at Torrequemara is a noble edifice of eight and twenty arches. The windings of this beautiful river and its rocky banks, of which one side is always very steep, are romantic, and present fine shapes of nature, to which nothing is wanting but trees, and they not always. The vale through which it flows, inclosed within these rocky cliffs, is luxuriant in corn and wine; the soil in general of a fine loam mixed with gravel, and the fallows remarkably clean; they deposit their wine in caves hollowed out of the rocks. In the mean time, it is to the bounty of nature rather than to the care and industry of man, that the inhabitant, squalid and loathsome in his person, is beholden for that produce, which invites exertions that he never makes, and points to comforts that he never tastes. In the midst of all these scenes of plenty you encounter human misery in its worst attire, and ruined villages amongst luxuriant vineyards. Such a bountiful provider is God, and so improvident a steward is his vicegerent in this realm.

It should seem, that in this valley, on the banks of the fertilizing Douro, would be the proper site for the capital of Spain; whereas, Madrid is seated on a barren soil, beside a meagre stream, which scarce suffices to supply the washer-women, who make their troughs in the shallow current, which only has the appearance of a river when the snow melts upon the mountains, and turns the petty Manzanares, that just trickles through the sand, into a roaring and impetuous torrent. Of the environs of Madrid I have already spoken, and the climate on the northern side of the Guadaramas is of a much superior and more salubrious quality, being not so subject to the dangerous extremes of heat and cold, and much oftener refreshed with showers, the great desideratum, for which the monks of Madrid so frequently importune their poor helpless saint Isidore, and make him feel their vengeance, whilst for months together the unrelenting clouds will not credit him with a single drop of rain.

Upon our road this day we purchased three lambs at the price of two pisettes (shillings) a piece, and, little as it was, we hardly could be said to have had value for our money. Our worthy Marchetti, being an excellent engineer, roasted them whole, with surprising expedition and address, in a kitchen and at a fire, which would have puzzled all the resources of a French cook, and which no English scullion would have approached in her very worst apparel. A crew of Catalunian carriers at Torrequemara disputed our exclusive title to the fire, and with their *arroz a la Valenciana*, would soon have ruined our roast, if our gallant proveedór had not put aside his capa, and displayed his two epaulets, to which military insignia the sturdy interlopers instantly deferred.

There is excellent morality to be learned in a journey of this sort. A supper at Valla Rodrigo is a better corrective for fastidiousness and false delicacy than all that Seneca and Epictetus can administer, and if a traveller in Spain will carry justice and fortitude about him, the Calasseros will teach him patience, and the Posadas will enure him to temperance; having these four cardinal virtues in possession, he has the whole; all Tully's offices can't find a fifth.

On the seventh day of our travel we kept the pleasant Douro still in sight. Surely this river plays his natural sovereign a slippery trick; rises in Galicia, is nourished and maintained in his course through Spain, and as soon as he is become mature in depth and size for trade and navigation, deserts and throws himself into the service of Portugal. This is the case with the Tagus also: this river affords the Catholic King a little angling for small fry at Aranjuez, and at Lisbon becomes a magnificent harbor to give wealth and splendor to a kingdom. The Oporto wines, that grow upon the banks of the Douro in its renegado course, find a ready and most profitable vent in England, whilst the vineyards of Castile languish from want of a purchaser, and in some years are absolutely cast away, as not paying for the labor of making them into wine.

The city and castle of Burgos are well situated on the banks of the river Relancon. Two fine stone bridges are thrown over that stream, and several plantations of young trees line the roads as you approach it. The country is well watered, and the heights furnish excellent pasture for sheep, being of a light downy soil. The cathedral church of Burgos deserves the notice and admiration of every traveller, and it was with sincere regret I found myself at leisure to devote no more than one hour to an edifice that requires a day to examine it within side and without. It is of that order of Gothic which is most profusely ornamented and enriched; the towers are crowned with spires of pierced stone-work, raised upon arches, and laced all through with open-work like filligree: the windows and doors are embellished with innumerable figures, admirably carved in stone, and in perfect preservation; the dome over the nave is superb, and behind the grand altar there is a spacious and beautiful chapel, erected by a Duke of Frejas, who lies entombed with his duchess, with a stately monument recumbent with their heads resting upon cushions, in their robes and coronets, well sculptured in most exquisite marble of the purest white. The bass-reliefs at the back of the grand altar, representing passages in the life and actions of our Saviour, are wonderful samples of sculpture, and the carrying of the cross in particular is expressed with all the delicacy of Raphael's famous Pasma de Sicilia. The stalls of the choir in brown oak are finely executed, and exhibit an innumerable group of figures: whilst the seats are ludicrously inlaid with grotesque representations of fauns and satyrs, unaccountably contrasted with the sacred history of the carved work that incloses them. The altars, chapels, sacristy and cloisters are equally to be admired, nor are there wanting some fine paintings, though not profusely bestowed. The priests conducted me through every part of the cathedral with the kindest attention and politeness, though mass was then in high celebration.

When I was on my departure, and my carriages were in waiting, a parcel of British seamen, who had been prisoners of war, most importunately besought me that I would ask their liberation of the Bishop of Burgos, and allow them to make their way out of the country under my protection. This good bishop, in his zeal for making converts, had taken these fellows upon their word into his list of pensioners, as true proselytes, and allowed them to establish themselves in various occupations and callings, which they now professed themselves most heartily disposed to abandon, and doubted not but I should find him as willing to release them, as they were to be set free. Though I gave little credit to their assertions, I did not refuse to make the experiment, and wrote to the bishop in their behalf, promising to obtain the release of the like number of Spanish prisoners if he would allow me to take these men away with me. To my great surprise, I instantly received his free consent and permit under his hand and seal to dispose of them as I saw fit. This I accordingly did, and by occasional reliefs upon the braces of my carriages marched my party of renegadoes entire into Bayonne, where I got leave, upon certain conditions, to embark them on board a neutral ship bound to Lisbon, and consigned them to Commodore Johnstone, or the commanding officer for the time being, to be put on board, and exchanged for the like number of Spanish prisoners, which accordingly was done with the exception of one or two, who turned aside by the way. I have reason to believe the good bishop was thoroughly sick of his converts, and I encountered no opposition from the ladies, whom two or three of them had taken to wife.

We pursued our eighth day's journey over a deep rich soil,

with mountains in sight covered with snow, which had fallen two days before. There was now a scene of more wood, and the face of the country much resembled parts of England. We advanced but seven leagues, the river Belancon accompanying us for the last three, where our road was cut out of the side of a steep cliff, very narrow, and so ill defended, that in many places the precipice, considering the mode in which the Spanish Calasseros drive, was seriously alarming. The wild woman of San Andero, who nursed my infant, during this day's journey was at high words with the witches, who twice pulled off her redecilla, and otherwise annoyed her in a very provoking manner till we arrived at Breviesca, a tolerable good Spanish town, where they allowed her to repose, and we heard no more of them.

From Breviesca we travelled through a fine picturesque country, of a rich soil, to Pancorvo, at the foot of a steep range of rocky mountains, and passing through a most romantic fissure in the rock, a work of great art and labor, we reached the river Ebro, which forms the boundary of Old Castile. Upon this river stands the town of Miranda, which is approached over a new bridge of seven stone arches, and we lodged ourselves for the night in the posada at the foot of it: a house of the worst reception we had met in Spain, which is giving it as ill a name as I can well bestow upon any house whatever.

A short stage brought us from Breviesca to the town of Vittoria, the capital of Alaba, which is one portion of the delightful province of Biscay. We were now for the first time lodged with some degree of comfort. We showed our passport at the custom-house, and the administrator of the post-office having desired to have immediate notice of our arrival, I requested my friend Marchetti to go to him, and in the mean time poor Smith passed a very anxious interval of suspense, fearing that he might be stopped by order of government in this place (a suspicion I confess not out of the range of probabilities), but it proved to be only a punctilio of the subminister Campo, who had written to this gentleman to be particular in his attentions to us, inclosing his card, as if in person present to take leave; this mark of politeness on his part produced a present from the administrator of some fine asparagus, and excellent sweetmeats, the produce of the country, with the further favor of a visit from the donor, a gentleman of great good manners and much respectability.

The Marquis Legarda, Governor of Vittoria, to whom I had a letter from Count D'Yranda, the Marquis D'Allamada, and other gentlemen of the place, did us the honor to visit us, and were extremely polite. We were invited by the Dominicans to their convent, and saw some very exquisite paintings of Ribeira and Murillo. At noon we took our departure for Mondragone, passing through a country of indescribable beauty. The scale is vast, the heights are lofty without being tremendous, the cultivation is of various sorts, and to be traced in every spot, where the hand of industry can reach; a profusion of fruit trees in blossom colored the landscape with such vivid and luxuriant tints, that we had new charms to admire upon every shift and winding of the road. The people are laborious, and the fields being full of men and women at their work (for here both sexes make common task), nothing could be more animated than the scenery; 'twas not in human nature to present a stronger contrast to the gloomy character and squalid indolence of the Castilians. And what is it, which constitutes this marked distinction between such near neighbors, subjects of the same king, and separated from each other only by a narrow stream? It is because the regal power, which in Castile is arbitrary, is limited by local laws in Catalunia, and gives passage for one ray of liberty to visit that happier and more enlightened country.

From Mondragone we went to Villa Franca, where we dined, and finished our twelfth day's journey at Tolosa; the country still presented a succession of the most enchanting scenery, but I was now become insensible to its beauties, being so extremely ill that it was not without much difficulty, so excruciating were my pains, that I reached Tolosa. Here I stayed three days, and when I found my fever would not yield to James's powder, I resolved to attempt getting to Bayonne, where I might hope to find medical assistance, and better accommodation.

On the seventeenth day, after suffering tortures from the roughness of the roads, I reached Bayonne, and immediately put myself under the care of Doctor Vidal, a Huguenot physician. Here I passed three miserable weeks, and though in a state of almost continued delirium throughout the whole of this time, I can yet recollect that, under Providence, it is only owing to the unwearied care and tender attentions of my ever-watchful wife (assisted by her faithful servant Mary Samson) that I was kept alive; from her hands I consented to receive sustenance and medicine, and to her alone, in the disorder of my senses, I was uniformly obedient.

It was at this period of time that the aggravating news arrived of my bills being stopped, and my person subjected to arrest. I was not sensible to the extent of my danger, for death hung over me, and threatened to supersede all arrests but of a lifeless corpse; the kind heart, however, of Marchetti had compassion for my disconsolate condition, and he found means to supply me with five hundred pounds, as I have already related. It pleased God to preserve my life, and this seasonable act of friendship preserved my liberty. The early fruits of the season, and the balmy temperature of the air in that delicious climate, aided the exertions of my physician, and I was at length enabled to resume my journey, taking a day's rest in the magnificent town of Bourdeaux, from whence, through Tours, Blois and Orleans, I proceeded to Paris, which, however, I entered in a state as yet but doubtfully convalescent, emaciated to a skeleton, the bones of my back and elbows still bare and staring through my skin.

I had both Florida Blança's and Count Montmorin's passports, but my applications for post-horses were in vain, and here I should in all probability have ended my career, as I felt myself relapsing apace, had I not at length obtained the long-withheld permission to pass onwards. They had pounded the King of Spain's horses also for the space of a whole month, but these were liberated when I got my freedom, and I embarked them at Ostend, from whence I took my passage to Margate, and arrived at my house in Portland Place, destined to experience treatment which I had not merited, and encounter losses I have never overcome.

I will here simply relate an incident without attempting to draw any conjectures from it, which is, that whilst I lay ill at Bayonne, insensible, and, as it was supposed, at the point of death, the very monk, who had been so troublesome to me at Elvas, found his way into my chamber, and upon the alarm given by my wife, who perfectly recognized his person, was only driven out of it by force. Again when I was in Paris, and about to sit down to dinner, a salad was brought to me by the lacquey who waited on me, which was given to him for me by a red-haired Dominican, whose person, according to his description, exactly tallied with that of the aforesaid monk; I dispatched my servant Camis in pursuit of him, but he had escaped, and my suspicion of the salad being poisoned was confirmed by experiment on a dog.

I shall only add that somewhere in Castile, I forget the place, but it was between Valladolid and Burgos, as I was sitting on a bench at the door of a house, where my calasseros were giving water to the mules, I tendered my snuff-box to a grave elderly man, who seemed of the better sort of Castilians, and who appeared to have thrown himself in my way, sitting down beside me as one who invited conversation. The stranger looked steadily in my face, and after a pause, put his fingers into my box, and taking a very small portion of my snuff between them, said to me: 'I am not afraid, sir, of trusting myself to you, whom I know to be an Englishman, and a person in whose honor I may perfectly repose. But there is death concealed in many a man's snuff-box, and I would seriously advise you on no account to take a single pinch from the box of any stranger, who may offer it to you; and if you have done that already, I sincerely hope no such consequences as I allude to will result from your want of caution.' I continued in conversation with this stranger for some time; I told him I had never before been apprised of the practices he had spoken of, and being perfectly without suspicion, I might, or might not, have exposed myself to the danger he was now so kind as to apprise me of, but I observed to him, that however prudent it might be to guard myself against such evil practices in other countries, I should not expect to meet them in Castile, where the Spanish point of honor most decidedly prevailed. 'Ah! Senor,' he replied, 'they may not all be Spaniards, whom you have chanced upon, or shall hereafter chance upon, in Castile.' When I asked him how this snuff operated on those who took it, his answer was, as I expected, 'on the brain.' I was not curious to inquire who this stranger was, as I paid little attention to his information at the time, though I confess it occurred to me, when after a few days I was seized with such agonies in my head as deprived me of my senses; I merely give this anecdote as it occurred; I draw no inferences from it.

I have now done with Spain, and if the detail, which I have truly given of my proceedings, whilst I was there in trust, may serve to justify me in the opinion of those who read these Memoirs, I will not tire their patience with a dull recital of my unprofitable efforts to obtain a just and equitable indemnification for my expenses, according to agreement. The evidences, indeed, are in my hands, and the production of them would be highly discreditable to the memory of some, who are now no more; but redress is out of my reach; the time for that is long since gone by, and has carried me on so far towards the hour which must extinguish all human feelings, that there can be little left for me to do but to employ the remaining pages of this history in the best manner I can devise, consistently with strict veracity, for the satisfaction of those who may condescend to peruse them, and to whom I should be above measure sorry to appear in the character of a querulous, discontented, and resentful old man; I rather hope that when I shall have laid before them a detail of literary labors, such as few have executed within a period of the like extent, they will credit me for my industry, at least, and allow me to possess some claim upon the favor of posterity as a man, who, in honest pride of conscience, has not let his spirit sink under oppression and neglect, nor suffered his good-will to mankind, or his zeal for his country's service and the honor of his God, to experience intermission or abatement, nor made old age a plea for insolence, or an apology for ill humor.

Nevertheless, as I have charged my employers with a direct breach of faith, it seems necessary for my more perfect vindication, to support that charge by an official document, and this consideration will, I trust, be my sufficient apology for inserting the following statement of my claim:—

'*To the Right Honorable Lord North, &c. &c. &c.*

The humble memorial of Richard Cumberland sheweth:—

That you memorialist in April, 1780, received his majesty's most secret and confidential orders and instructions to set out for the court of Spain, in company with the Abbé Hussey, one of His Catholic Majesty's chaplains, for the purpose of negotiating a separate peace with that court.

That to render the object of this commission more secret, your memorialist was directed to take his family with him to Lisbon, under the pretence of recovering the health of one of his daughters, which he accordingly did, and having sent the Abbé Hussey before him to the court of Spain, agreeably to the king's instructions, your memorialist and his family soon after repaired to Aranjuez, where his Catholic Majesty then kept his court.

That your memorialist, upon setting out on this important undertaking, received by the hands of John Robinson, Esquire, one of the secretaries of the treasury, the sum of one thousand pounds on account, with directions how he should draw, through the channel of Portugal, upon his banker in England, for such further sums as might be necessary (particularly for a large discretionary sum to be employed as occasion might require in secret services), and your memorialist was directed to accompany his drafts by a separate letter to Mr. Secretary Robinson, advising him what sum or sums he had given order for, that the same might be replaced to your memorialist's credit with the bank of Messieurs Crofts & Co., in Pall Mall.

That your memorialist, in the execution of this commission, for the space of nearly fourteenth months, defrayed the expenses of the Abbé Hussey's separate journey into Spain, paid all charges incurred by him during four months' residence there, and supplied him with money for his return to England, no part of which has been repaid to your memorialist.

That your memorialist, with his family, took two very long and expensive journeys (the one by way of Lisbon and the other through France), no consideration for which has been granted to him.

That your memorialist, during his residence in Spain, was obliged to follow the removals of the court to Aranjuez, San Ildefonso, the Escurial, and Madrid, besides frequent visits to the Pardo; in all which places, except the Pardo, he was obliged to lodge himself, the expense of which can only be known to those who, in the service of their court, have incurred it.

That every article of necessary expense, being inordinately high in Madrid, your memorialist, without assuming any vain appearance of a minister, and with as much domestic frugality as possible, incurred a very heavy charge.

That your memorialist, having no courier with him, nor any cypher, was obliged to employ his own servant in that trust, and the servant of Abbé Hussey, at his own proper cost, no part of which has been repaid to him.

That your memorialist did at considerable charge obtain papers and documents containing information of a very important nature, which need not here be enumerated, of which charge so incurred no part has been repaid.

That upon the capture of the East and West India ships by the enemy, your memorialist was addressed by many of the British prisoners, some of whom he relieved with money, and in all cases obtained the prayer of their memorials. Your memorialist also, through the favor of the Bishop of Burgos, took with him out of Spain some valuable British seamen, and restored them to his majesty's fleet; and this, also, he did at his own cost.

That your memorialist, during his residence in Spain, was indispensably obliged to cover these, his unavoidable expenses, by several drafts upon his banker to the amount of £4,500, of which not one single bill has been replaced, nor one farthing issued to his support during fourteen months' expensive and laborious duty in the king's immediate and most confidential service; the consequence of which unparalleled treatment was, that your memorialist was stopped and arrested at Bayonne by order from his remittancers at Madrid; in this agonizing situation your memorialist, being then in the height of a most violent fever, surrounded by a family of helpless women in an enemy's country, and abandoned by his employers, on whose faith he had relied, found himself incapable of proceeding on his journey, and destitute of means for subsisting where he was; under this accumulated distress he must have sunk and expired, had not the generosity of an officer in the Spanish service, who had accompanied him into France, supplied his necessities with the loan of five hundred pounds, and passed the King of Great Britain's bankrupt servant into his own country, for which humane action this friendly officer (Marchetti by name) was arrested at Paris, and by the Count D'Aranda remanded back to Madrid, there to take his chance for what the influence of France may find occasion to devise against him.

Your memorialist, since his return to England, having, after innumerable attempts, gained one only admittance to your lordship's person, for the space of more than ten months, and not one answer to the frequent and humble suit he has made to you by letter, presumes now, for the last time, to solicit your consideration of his case, and as he is persuaded it is not, and cannot be, in your lordship's heart to devote and abandon to unmerited ruin an old and faithful servant of the crown, who has been the father of four sons (one of whom has lately died, and three are now carrying arms in the service of their king), your memorialist humbly prays that you will give order for him to be relieved in such manner as to your lordship's wisdom shall seem meet.

All which is humbly submitted by
Your lordship's most obedient
And most humble servant,
RICHARD CUMBERLAND.'

This memorial, which is perhaps too long and loaded, I am persuaded Lord North never took the pains to read, for I am unwilling to suppose that, if he had, he would have treated it with absolute neglect. He was upon the point of quitting office when I gave it in, and being my last effort, I was desirous of summing up the circumstances of my case so, that if he had thought fit to grant me a compensation, this statement might have been a justification to his successor for the issue; but it produced no compensation, though I should presume it proved enough to have touched the feelings of one of the best tempered men living, if he would have devoted a very few minutes to the perusal of it.

CHAPTER X.

Secretary Robinson—Lord North—Lord George Germain—Sir Edward Sackville—Duelling—Loses his situation at the Board of Trade—Removes to Tunbridge Wells—The men of Kent—Description of his house—Merciful to animals—His children—His books—'The Observer'—'Anecdotes of eminent painters in Spain'—Offence to Sir Joshua Reynolds—'The Walloons'—'The Mysterious Husband'—Henderson—'The Observer'—Habits of composition—'The Clouds'—Anecdote of Henderson—'The Arab'—Garrick—Anecdote of Dr. Johnson—Reynolds—Romney—Lines to.

It is not possible for me to call to mind a character in all essential points so amiable as that of this departed minister, and not wish to find some palliation for his oversights; but if I were now to say that I acquit him of injustice to me, it would be affectation and hypocrisy; at the same time I must think, that Mr. Secretary Robinson, who was the vehicle of the promise, was more immediately bound to solicit and obtain the fulfilment of it, and this I am persuaded was completely in his power to do: to him, therefore, I addressed such remonstrances, and enforced them in such terms, as no manly spirit ought to have put up with; but anger and high words make all things worse; and language, which a man has not courage to resent, he never will have candor to forgive.

When in process of time I saw and knew Lord North in his retirement from all public affairs, patient, collected, resigned to an afflicting visitation of the severest sort, when all but his illuminated mind was dark around him, I contemplated an affecting and an edifying object, that claimed my admiration and esteem; a man, who, when divested of that incidental greatness, which high office for a time can give, self-dignified and independent, rose to real greatness of his own creating, which no time can take away; whose genius gave a grace to everything he said, and whose benignity shed a lustre upon everything he did; so richly was his memory stored, and so lively was his imagination in applying what he remembered, that after the great source of information was shut against himself, he still possessed a boundless fund of information for the instruction and delight of others. Some hours (and those not few) of his society he was kind in bestowing upon me; I eagerly courted, and very highly apprized them.[1]

[1] The unbroken good humor, the conciliating and amiable qualities, the extensive information, excellent sense, unflinching courage, ready and powerful talents of Lord North, have been alike applauded by those who approved and those who condemned his public conduct. He incurred great odium in America from being the responsible advocate of the ill-starred policy towards the colonies; and the American war, as Lord Brougham justly observes, is the great blot upon his fame. It is now well known that he perceived the folly of the American contest, and was only kept at the helm, advocating a line of conduct which he disapproved, 'by constant entreaties, by monthly expostulations, by the most vehement protestations of the misguided prince. . . . But although we may thus explain, we are not the better enabled to excuse the minister's conduct. When he found that he could no longer approve the policy which he was required to pursue, and of course to defend, he was bound to quit the councils of his obstinate and unreasonable sovereign.'—*Lord Brougham's Sketches.*

Lord North was the eldest son of the Earl of Guilford, and born in 1733. He was educated at Eton and Oxford, and then proceeded to the Continent, where he remained three years. In addition to his classical knowledge, which was extensive and accurate, he had made himself master of French, German, and Italian. On coming of age he was returned to Parliament, and soon became the recipient of ministerial favors. Lord of the Treasury, joint paymaster of the forces, and chancellor of the exchequer; these were the posts bestowed on him before he had attained his thirty-fifth year. But through all these promotions, says Lord Mahon, 'it may be said with truth, that he did not seek honors; it was rather that honors sought him. He was by no means of an eager and aspiring temper, nor ever feeling tempted to deviate from principle in quest of popularity. . . . . Of outward advantages,' says the same authority, 'Lord North was altogether destitute. His figure was overgrown and ungraceful, and his countenance gave little promise of ability. He was extremely near-sighted; a great obstacle in the way of Parliamentary eminence, which has never, perhaps, been wholly overcome, except by himself, and in our own time by Lord Derby. A few days only before he became prime minister, one of his keenest opponents, Mr. Burke, thus described him in the House of Commons: 'The noble lord who spoke last, after extending his right leg a full yard before his left, rolling his flaming eyes, and moving his ponderous frame, has at length opened his mouth.' But Mr. Burke might have added, though he did not, that no sooner was that mouth opened, than it made ample amends for every defect of form or gesture. Out there came, fresh at each emergency, a flow of good sense and sterling information, enlivened by never-failing pleasantry and wit. During his long and, for the most part, disastrous administration, it was frequently his fate to maintain almost alone, a contest with some of the ablest orators whom the world had ever seen. Yet by his natural and acquired gifts of mind, conjoined with high character and with sturdy courage, he was enabled to stand firm, during so many years, against all the efforts of Fox and Burke, of Dunning, Savile, and Barré, and at last the younger Pitt. Unequal as he might be to some, at least, of these in powers of eloquence, he far surpassed them, and indeed all men of his time, in his admirable mildness and placidity of temper. So cheerful was ever his mien, and so unruffled his composure, that it seemed scarcely an effort to him to wage the warfare of debate even against such adversaries. Indeed, his great difficulty during the violent volleys of attacks that were often poured upon him as he sat upon the treasury bench, was to keep himself awake! Many a keen opponent, charging him to his face with the heaviest crimes and misdemeanors, must have felt not a little disconcerted at seeing opposite the object of all his vehemence dropping by de-

I experienced no abatement in the friendship of Lord George Germain; on the contrary, it was from this time chiefly to the day of his death, that I lived in the greatest intimacy with him. Whilst he held the seals I continued to attend upon him both in public and in private, rendering him all the voluntary service in my power, particularly on his levee-days, which he held in my apartment in the Plantation office, though he had ceased to preside at the Board of Trade, and here great numbers of American loyalists, who had taken refuge in England, were in the habit of resorting to him: it was an ardous and delicate business to conduct: I may add it was also a business of some personal risk and danger, as it engaged me in very serious explanations upon more occasions than one. Upon Lord George's putting into my hands a letter he had received from a certain naval officer, very disrespectful towards him, and most unjustifiably so to me, for having brought him an answer to an application, which he was pleased to consider as private and confidential, I felt myself obliged to take the letter with me to that gentleman, and require him to write and sign an apology of my own dictating: whatever was his motive for doing what I peremptorily required, so it was, that to my very great surprise he submitted to transcribe and sign it, and when I exhibited it to Lord George, he acknowledged it to be the most complete revocation and apology he had ever met with.

There were other situations still more delicate, in which I occasionally became involved, but which I forbear to mention; but in those unpleasant times men's passions were inflamed, and in every case, when reasoning would not serve to allay intem-

grees into a gentle doze, and only roused by his neighbor's elbows into starts of watchfulness. . . . . This sweetness of temper in Lord North was by no means confined to public life; it was no less manifest, and no less delightful in his domestic circle. . . . . As an upright public servant, the character of Lord North stands above all suspicion or reproach; indeed, but for the wardenship of the Cinque Ports, which the king's spontaneous act bestowed upon him, as afterwards upon Mr. Pitt, he would have left office a poorer man than he had entered it. On all occasions his feelings as his manners were those of an honorable and high-bred gentleman. He had great sagacity in unravelling, and great quickness in maturing the most intricate details of public business. But in conducting that business it cannot be denied that he lacked something of energy, of firmness, of fixed and resolute will. These qualities—needful to a statesman at all times, but doubly needful at a period so fraught with difficulties as the American contest—never certainly shone forth in this too amiable, too complying prime minister. It is his main reproach, as he stands before the tribunal of history, nor can history absolve him from the charge, that he frequently yielded his own deliberate judgment to the persuasion of his sovereign or friends.'—*History of England*, vol. v. p. 255, *et seq.* *Vide*, also, the supplement to this volume.

perance, and explanation was lost upon them, I never scrupled to abide the consequence.

When Lord George Germain resigned the seals, the king was graciously pleased, in reward for his services, to call him to the House of Lords by the title of Viscount Sackville. The well-known circumstance,[1] that occurred upon the event of his elevation to the peerage, made a deep and painful impression on his feeling mind, and if his seeming patience under the infliction of it should appear to merit in a moral sense the name of virtue, I must candidly acknowledge it as a virtue that he had no title to be credited for, inasmuch as it was entirely owing to the influence of some, who overruled his propensities, and made themselves responsible for his honor, that he did not betake himself to the same abrupt, unwarrantable mode of dismissing this insult, as he had resorted to in a former instance. No man can speak from a more intimate knowledge of his feelings upon this occasion than I can, and if I was not on the side of those who no doubt spoke well and wisely when they spoke for peace, it is amongst the many errors and offences which I have yet to repent of.

There was once a certain Sir Edward Sackville, whom the world has heard of, who probably would not have possessed himself with so much calmness and forbearance as did a late noble head of his family, whilst the question I allude to was in agitation, and he present in his place. It was by the medium of this noble personage that the Lord Viscount Sackville meditated to send that invitation he had prepared, when the interposition and well-considered remonstrances of some of his nearest friends (in particular of Lord Amherst) put him by from his resolve, and dictated a conduct more conformable to prudence, but much less suited to his inclination.

The law that is sufficient for the redress of injuries does not always reach to the redress of insults; thus it comes to pass that many men, in other respects wise, and just, and temperate, not having resolution to be right in their own consciences, have

[1] Lord George Germain had been convicted by a court martial of disobedience of orders at the battle of Minden, and when it was reported that he had been created Viscount Sackville, the Marquis of Caermarthen moved in the Peers that to recommend to the crown, for such a dignity, any person laboring under so heavy a sentence of a court martial, was derogatory to the honor of the House of Lords. And the same motion was renewed when he took his seat. This is the 'well-known circumstance' to which Cumberland refers. The attack of Caermarthen was deemed disgustful, and without justification. 'Lord Caermarthen made himself odious; and Lord George found at least that mankind were not so abandoned as to enjoy such wanton malevolence.'—*Memoirs of the Reign of George III.*, vol. ii. p. 296, note.

set aside both reason and religion, and, in compliance with the evil practice of the world about them, performed their bloody sacrifices, and immolated human victims to the idol of false honor. Truth obliges me to confess that the friend, of whom I am speaking, though possessing one of the kindest hearts that ever beat within a human breast, was with difficulty diverted from resorting a second time to that desperate remedy, which modern empirics have prescribed for wounds of a peculiar sort, oftentimes imaginary, and always to be cured by patience.

When Lord North's administration was overturned, and the Board of Trade, of which I was Secretary, dismissed under the regulations of what is commonly called Mr. Burke's Bill,[1] I found myself set adrift upon a compensation, which, though much nearer to an equivalent than what I had received upon my Spanish claims, was yet in value scarce a moiety of what I was deprived of. By the operation of this reform, after I had sacrificed the patrimony I was born to, a very considerable reduction was made even of the remnant that was left to me; I lost no time in putting my family upon such an establishment as prudence dictated, and fixed myself at Tunbridge Wells.

This place, of which I had made choice, and in which I have continued to reside for more than twenty years, had much to recommend it, and very little that in any degree made against it. It is not altogether a public place, yet it is at no period of the year a solitude. A reading man may command his hours of study, and a social man will find full gratification for his philanthropy. Its vicinity to the capital brings quick intelligence of all that passes there; the morning papers reach us before the hour of dinner, and the evening ones before breakfast the next day; whilst between the arrival of the general post and its departure there is an interval of twelve hours; an accommodation in point of correspondence that even London cannot boast of. The produce of the neighboring farms and gardens, and the supplies of all sorts for the table are excellent in their

[1] The laudable spirit manifested by Burke in his celebrated bill, has been the subject of much and deserved praise. Unlike most reformers, he did not press forward to his object with undiscriminating zeal. His speech, when bringing forward his motion, was pronounced by Lord North one of the ablest he had ever heard, 'a speech,' he said, 'such as no other member could have made.' It has been said, indeed, that his ideas of reform were too extensive, and not sufficiently matured; that subsequently, when invested with the responsibilities of office, he seceded from a large portion of his scheme. But, 'the high statesmanlike ability with which Burke, in his speech, pleads for all the wise and temperate—wise, because temperate—principles on which he argues, is such as to claim the most careful perusal, and the most respectful mention, so long as the British Parliament or the British people may endure.'—*Lord Mahon, History of England*, vol. vii. p. 5.

quality; the country is on all sides beautiful, and the climate pre-eminently healthy, and in a most peculiar degree restorative to enfeebled constitutions. For myself, I can say that through the whole of my long residence at Tunbridge Wells I never experienced a single hour's indisposition that confined me to my bed, though I believe I may say with truth, that till then I had encountered as many fevers, and had as many serious struggles for my life, as have fallen to most men's lots in the like terms of years.

Some people can sit down in a place, and live so entirely to themselves and the small circle of their acquaintance, as to have little or no concern about the people amongst whom they reside. The contrary to this has ever been my habit, and wheresoever my lot in life has cast me, something more than curiosity has always induced me to mix with the mass, and interest myself in the concerns of my neighbors and fellow subjects, however humble in degree; and from the contemplation of their characters, from my acquaintance with their hearts and my assured possession of their affections, I can truly declare that I have derived, and still enjoy, some of the most gratifying sensations that reflection can bestow. The Men of Kent, properly so called, are a peculiar race, well worthy of the attention and study of the philanthropist. There is not only a distinguishing cast of humor, but a dignity of mind and principle about them, which is the very clue that will lead you into their hearts, if rightly understood; but, if mistaken or misused, you will find them quick enough to conceive, and more than forward enough to express their proud contempt and resolute defiance of you. I have said in my first volume of 'Arundel,' page 220, that they are 'a race distinguishable above all their fellow subjects for the beauty of their persons, the dignity of their sentiments, the courage of their hearts, and the elegance of their manner.' Many years have passed since I gave this testimony, and the full experience I have now had of the men of Kent, ever my kind friends, and now become my comrades and fellow soldiers, confirms every word that I have said, or can say, expressive of their worthiness, or my esteem.

The house which I rented of Mr. John Fry, at that time master of the Sussex Tavern, was partly new and partly attached to an old foundation; it was sufficient for my family, and when I had fitted it up with part of my furniture, and all my pictures from Portland Place, it had more the air of comfort and less the appearance of a lodging-house than most in the place; it was by no means the least of its recommendations, that it was well appointed with offices and accommodations for those old and faithful domestics, who continued in my service. There was a square patch of ground in front, of about half an acre, fenced and planted round with trees, which I converted into a flower garden and encircled with a sand walk; it had now become the only lot of English terra firma over which I had a legal right, and I treated it with a lover-like attention; it soon produced me excellent wall-fruit of my own rearing, and at last I found a little friendly spot, the only one as yet discovered, in which my laurels flourished. My true and trusty servant, Thomas Camis (more than ever attached, because more than ever necessary to me), had a passion for a flower-garden, and he quickly made it a bed of sweets, and a display of beauty. It was now, unhappily for me, too evident that the once excellent constitution of my beloved wife, my best friend, and, under Providence, the preserver of my life, was sinking under the effects which her late sufferings and exertions in attending upon me had entailed upon her; I had tried the sea-coast, and other places before I settled here, but in this climate only could she breathe with freedom and experience repose; the boundary of our little garden was in general the boundary of her walk, and beyond it her strength but rarely suffered her to expatiate; so long as she could have recourse to her horse, she made a struggle for fresh air and exercise, but when she had the misfortune to lose her favorite Spaniard, so invaluable and so wonderfully attached to her, she despaired of replacing him, and I can well believe there was not in all England an animal that could. He had belonged to the King of Spain, and came, by what means I have forgot, into the possession of Count Joseph Kaunitz, who gave him to Mrs. Cumberland; he was a most perfect war-horse, though upon the scale of a galloway, and whilst his eyes menaced everything that was fiery and rebellious, nothing living was more sweet and gentle in his nature; he could not speak, for he had not the organs of speech, but he had dog-like sagacity, and understood the words that were addressed to him, and the caresses that were bestowed upon him. Being *entire*, and of course prohibited from passing out of Spain, I am persuaded some villanous measures were practised on the frontiers towards him in his journey, for he died in agonies under so inveterate a strangury, that though I applied all the remedies that an excellent surgeon could suggest for his relief, nothing could save him, and he expired, whilst resting his head on my shoulder, his eyes being fixed upon me with that intelligent and piteous expression, which seemed to say: Can you do nothing to assuage my pain? I thank God I never angrily and unjustifiably chastised but one horse to my remembrance, and that creature (a barb given to me by Lord

Halifax), never whilst it had life forgave me, or would be reconciled to let me ride it in any peace, though it carried my wife with all imaginable gentleness. I disdain to make any apology for this prattle, nor am willing to suppose it can be uninteresting to a benevolent reader; for those who are not such, I have no concern. The man who is cruel to his beast is odious, and I am inclined to think there may be cruelty expressed even in the treatment of things inanimate; in short, I believe that I am destined to die, as I have lived, with all that family weakness about me, which will hardly suffer me to chastise offence, or tell a fellow creature he is a rascal, for fear the intimation should give him pain. I have been wrongfully and hardly dealt with; I have had my feelings wounded without mercy; I declare to God I never knowingly wronged a fellow creature, or designedly offended; if, whilst I am giving my own history, I am to give my own character, this in a few words is the truth; I am too old, too conscientious, too well persuaded and too fearful of a judgment to come, to dare to go to death with a lie in my mouth; let the censors of my actions, and the scrutinizers of my thoughts confute me if they can.[1]

The children, who were inmate with me, when I settled at Tunbridge Wells, were my second daughter Sophia, and the infant Marianne, born to me in Spain; my three surviving sons, Richard, Charles, and William, were serving in the 1st regiment of guards, the 10th foot, and the royal navy. My eldest daughter, Elizabeth, had married the Lord Edward Bentinck, brother to the Duke of Portland, and at that time member for the county of Nottingham; of him were I to attempt at saying what my experience of his character and my affection for his person would suggest, I should only punish his sensibility, and fall far short of doing justice to my own. He is too well esteemed and beloved to need my praise, and how truly and entirely I love him is, I trust, too well known to require professions.[2]

[1] We do not always see ourselves as others see us. And while we may give Cumberland credit for sincerity, in this general exculpation of his character, it is proper to mention that while he was esteemed both for his honorable and benevolent principles, it was known that he was apt to be detractive; a reputation by no means desirable, and under which Cumberland was very restive.

[2] It is said to have been one of Cumberland's weaknesses, and who is without them, to regard the higher ranks with overweening veneration. Sir Walter Scott, it is well known, and lamented by the most eminent admirers of his literary labors, unlike Johnson, who always asserted his own dignity, as a man and scholar, but, like Cumberland, evinced something more than proper deference to blood and rank. 'The first time that I was in company with Mr. Cumberland,' says Taylor, 'was at the Chaplain's table, in St. James's Palace. Among the party was Dr. or Mr. Jackson, one of his majesty's chaplains. Jackson, whose character resembled that of Mr. Cumberland in veneration for

I was now within an hour's ride of Stonelands, where Lord Sackville resided for part of the year, and as this was amongst the motives that led me to locate myself at Tunbridge Wells, so it was always one of my chief gratifications to avail myself of my vicinity to so true and dear a friend.

Being now dismissed from office, I was at leisure to devote myself to that passion which, from my earliest youth, had never wholly left me, and I resorted to my books and my pen, as to friends who had animated me in the morning of my day, and were now to occupy and uphold me in the evening of it. I had happily a collection of books, excellent in their kind, and perfectly adapted to my various and discursive course of reading. In almost every margin I recognized the hand-writing of my grandfather, Bentley, and wherever I traced his remains, they were sure guides to direct and gratify me in my fondness for philological researches. My mind had been harassed in a variety of ways, but the spirit that, from resources within itself, can find a never-failing fund of occupation, will not easily be broken by events that do not touch the conscience. That portion of mental energy which nature had endowed me with, was not impaired; on the contrary, I took a larger and more various range of study than I had ever done before, and collaterally, with other compositions, began to collect materials for those essays, which I afterwards completed and made public under the title of 'The Observer.' I sought no other dissipation than the indulgence of my literary faculties could afford me, and, in the mean time, I kept silence from complaint, sensible how ill such topics recommend a man to society in general, and how very nearly most men's show of pity is connected with contempt.

I had already published, in two volumes, my 'Anecdotes of Eminent Painters in Spain.' I am flattered to believe it was an interesting and curious work, to readers of a certain sort, for there had been no such regular history of the Spanish school

the higher ranks, began with asking how Lord Edward Bentinck was, that nobleman having married a daughter of Mr. Cumberland. Mr. Cumberland expatiated upon the health of his lordship, and nothing was heard but about his lordship for some time, his lordship's title adorning every inquiry, and closing every answer. At length, when his lordship had sufficiently wearied the company, Lady Edward was introduced in turn, and engrossed nearly as much of the conversation as his lordship, with as much repetition of her ladyship's title. When these subjects were exhausted, it became Mr. Cumberland's turn to inquire; and as Jackson was patronized by the Duke of Leeds, Mr. Cumberland, of course, thought it his duty to inquire after his grace. His grace then was echoed over the table as frequently as had been his lordship and her ladyship.' —*Records of my Life*, p. 327.

in our language, and when I added to it the authentic catalogue of the paintings in the royal palace at Madrid, I gave the world what it had not seen before, as that catalogue was the first that had been made, and was by permission of the King of Spain, undertaken at my request, and transmitted to me after my return to England.

When these 'Anecdotes' had been for some short time before the public, I was surprised to find myself arraigned for having introduced a passage, in my second volume, grossly injurious to the reputation of Sir Joshua Reynolds, and, I am sorry to add, that I had reason to believe that the misconception of my motives for the insertion of that passage was adopted by Sir Joshua himself. The charge consists in my having quoted a passage from a publication of Azara's, which, but for my noticing it, might have never met the observation of the English reader. I own I thought this charge too ridiculous to merit any answer, for I had not gone out of my way to seek Azara's publication; it was in the shops at London, and there I chanced upon it and purchased it. Azara was the friend of Mengs, and treats professedly of his character and compositions. A work of this sort was in no degree likely to preserve its incognito, neither had it so done before it came into my hands.

The following extract from my 2d vol. p. 206, comprises every word that has any reference to Sir Joshua Reynolds, and I am persuaded it cannot fail to acquit me in the judgment of every one, who reads it, most clearly and completely—this it is—'Whether Mengs really thought with contempt of art, which was inferior to his own, I will not pretend to decide; but that he was apt to speak contemptuously of artists superior to himself, I am inclined to believe. Azara tells us that he pronounced of the academical lectures of our Reynolds, that they were calculated to mislead young students into error, teaching nothing but those superficial principles, which he plainly avers are all that the author himself knows of the art he professes—*Del libro moderno del Sr Reynold, Ingles, decia que es una obra, que puede conducir los Juvenes al error; posque se queda en los principios superficiales, que conoce solamente a quel autor.* Azara immediately proceeds to say that Mengs was of a temperament *colerico y adusto*, and that his bitter and satirical turn created him *infinitos agraviados y quejosos.* When his historian and friend says this, there is no occasion for me to repeat the remark. If the genius of Mengs had been capable of producing a composition equal to that of the tragic and pathetic Ugolino, I am persuaded such a sentence as the above would never have passed his lips; but flattery made him vain, and sickness rendered him peevish; he found himself at Madrid in a country without rivals, and, because the arts had travelled out of his sight, he was disposed to think they existed nowhere but on his own pallet.'

If this be not sufficient for my justification, I could wish any of my readers, who has my book within his reach, would refer himself to the page in question, and read onwards till I dismiss the subject of Mengs with the following strictures on his talents, dictated no doubt in that spirit of resentment, which Azara's anecdote above recorded had most evidently inspired: for what more highly tinctured with asperity could be said of Mengs, than—'that he was an artist, who had seen much, and invented little; that he dispenses neither life nor death to his figures, excites no terror, rouses no passions, and risks no flights; that by studying to avoid particular defects, he incurs general ones, and paints with tameness and servility; that the contracted scale and idea of a painter of miniatures (as which he was brought up) is to be traced in all or most of his compositions, in which a finished delicacy of pencil exhibits the hand of the artist, but gives no emanations of the soul of the master? If it is beauty, it does not warm; if it is sorrow, it excites no pity: that when the angel announces the salutation to Mary, it is a messenger, that has neither used dispatch in his errand, nor grace in his delivery of it; that although Rubens was by one of his oracular sayings condemned to the ignominious dulness of a Dutch translator, Mengs was as capable of painting 'Rubens' Adoration,' as he was of creating the star in the east, that ushered the Magi. But these are questions above my capacity; I resign Mengs to abler critics and Reynolds to better defenders; well contented that posterity should admire them both, and well assured that the fame of our countryman is established beyond the reach of envy or detraction.'

If I had been aiming to employ the authority of Mengs against the reputation of Reynolds, I think it would not have been my part to take such pains for lessening the importance of it, and disappointing my own purpose. I cannot doubt but I am fairly open to reproach for these invectives against the fame of Mengs, but if there is any edge in the weapon I have wielded, I may say to his shade—

> ——Pallas te hoc vulnere, Pallas
> Immolat.

In the second volume, p. 8, where I am speaking of the great luminary of the Spanish school, Velasquez, I observe that, amongst other studies more immediately attached to his art, he perfected himself in the propositions of Euclid—'Elements that prepare the mind in every art and every science, to which the human faculties can be applied; which give a rule and measure for everything in life, dignify things familiar and familiarize things abstruse; invigorate the reason, restrain the licentiousness of fancy, open all the avenues of truth, and give a charm even to controversy and dispute.' I insert this extract because it is in proof to show that my opinion with respect to the importance of an academical education was at this period of life altogether as strong in favor of the mathematical studies, as I have expressed it to be in the former part of these Memoirs.

If it were not a ridiculous thing for an author to give his own works a good word, I should be tempted to risk it in the instance of these two volumes of anecdotes; forasmuch as I bear them in grateful remembrance, as having cheered some of my heaviest hours, and as being the first production sent by me into the world after my return out of Spain; from which period to the present hour, when I review the mass of those many and various works which my literary labors have struck out, I will venture to say, that if I have merited any chance of living in the remembrance of posterity, it is in these my latter years I am to look for it.

Before I settled myself at Tunbridge Wells, I had written my comedy of 'The Walloons,' brought out at Covent Garden Theatre, where my friend Henderson exhibited a most inimitable specimen of his powers in the character of Father Sullivan. If some people were ingenious enough to discover any likeness of the Abbé Hussey in that sketch, they imputed to me a design that was never in my thoughts. It was Henderson, with whom I was living in the greatest intimacy, who put me upon the project of writing a character for him in the cast of Congreve's Double Dealer. 'Make me a fine bold-faced villain,' he said, 'the direst and the deepest in nature I care not, so you do but give me motives strong enough to bear me out, and such a prominence of natural character, as shall secure me from the contempt of my audience; whatever other passions I can inspire them with will never sink me in their esteem.' Upon the same principle I conceived the character of Lord Davenant for him in 'The Mysterious Husband,' and in that he was not less conspicuously excellent.

He was an actor of uncommon powers, and a man of the brightest intellect, formed to be the delight of society, and few indeed are those men of distinguished talents, who have been more prematurely lost to the world, or more lastingly regretted. What he was on the stage, those who recollect his Falstaff, Shylock, Sir Giles Overreach, and many other parts of the strong cast, can fully testify; what he was at his own fireside and in his social hours, all, who were within the circle of his intimates, will not easily forget. He had an unceasing flow of spirits, and a boundless fund of humor, irresistibly amusing; he also had wit, properly so distinguished, and from the specimens which I have seen of his sallies in verse, levelled at a certain editor of a public print, who had annoyed him with his paragraphs, I am satisfied he had the talents at his command to have established a very high reputation as a poet. I was with him one morning when he was indisposed, and his physician, Sir John Elliot, paid him a visit. The doctor, as is well known, was a merry little being, who talked pretty much at random, and oftentimes with no great reverence for the subjects which he talked upon; upon the present occasion, however, he came professionally to inquire how his medicines had succeeded, and in his northern accent demanded of his patient—'Had he taken the *palls* that he sent him.' 'He had.' 'Well, and how did they agree? What had they done?' 'Wonders,' replied Henderson; 'I survived them.' 'To be sure you did,' said the doctor, 'and you must take more of 'em, and live for ever; I make all my patients immortal.' 'That is exactly what I am afraid of, doctor,' rejoined the patient. 'I met a lady of my acquaintance yesterday; you know her very well; she was in bitter affliction, crying and bewailing herself in a most piteous fashion; I asked her what had happened; a melancholy event; her dearest friend was at death's door.' 'What is her disease?' cried the doctor. 'That is the very question I asked,' replied Henderson; 'but she was in no danger from her disease; 'twas very slight; a mere excuse for calling in a physician.' 'Why, what the devil are you talking about,' rejoined the doctor, 'if she had called in a physician, and there was no danger in the disease, how could she be said to be at death's door?' 'Because,' said Henderson, 'she had called in you; everybody calls you in; you dispatch a world of business, and, if you come but once to each, your practice must have made you very rich.' 'Nay, nay,' quoth Sir John, 'I am not rich in this world; I lay up my treasure in heaven.' 'Then you may take leave of it for ever,' rejoined the other, 'for you have laid it up where you will never find it.'

Henderson's memory was so prodigious, that I dare not risk the instance which I could give of it, not thinking myself entitled to demand more credit than I should probably be disposed to give. In his private character many good and amiable qualities might be traced, particularly in his conduct towards an aged mother, to whom he bore a truly filial attachment; and in laying up a provision for his wife and daughter he was at least sufficiently careful and economical. He was concerned with the elder Sheridan in a course of public readings; there could not be a higher treat than to hear his recitations, from parts and passages in Tristram Shandy; let him broil his dish of sprats, seasoned with the sauce of his pleasantry, and succeeded by a dessert of Trim and my Uncle Toby, it was an entertainment worthy to be enrolled amongst the *noctes cœnasque Divûm*. I once heard him read part of a tragedy, and but once; it was in his own parlor, and he ranted most outrageously; he was conscious how ill he did it, and laid it aside before he had finished it. It was clear he had not studied that most excellent property of pitching his voice to the size of the room he was in; an art, which so few readers have, but which Lord Mansfield was allowed to possess in perfection. He was an admirable mimic, and in his sallies of this sort he invented speeches and dialogues, so perfectly appropriate to the characters he was displaying, that I don't doubt but many good sayings have been given to the persons he made free with, which, being fastened on them by him in a frolic, have stuck to them ever since, and perhaps gone down to posterity amongst their memorabilia. If there was any body now qualified to draw a parallel between the characters of Foote and Henderson, I don't pretend to say how the men of wit and humor might divide the laurel between them, but in this all men would agree that poor Foote attached to himself very few true friends, and Henderson very many, and those highly respectable, men virtuous in their lives, and enlightened in their understandings. Foote, vain, extravagant, embarrassed, led a wild and thoughtless course of life, yet when death approached him, he shrunk back into himself, saw and confessed his errors, and I have reason to believe was truly penitent. Henderson's conduct through life was uniformly decorous, and in the concluding stage of it exemplarily devout.[1]

I have said he played the part of Lord Davenant in my drama of 'The Mysterious Husband.' I believe it was upon the last night of its representation, the king and queen being present, when Henderson's exertions in the concluding scene, where he dies upon the stage, occasioned certain agitations, which have thenceforward rendered spectacles of that sort very properly ineligible. The late Mrs. Pope was very successful and impressive in the character of Lady Davenant, which I am inclined to consider as the best female part which I have ever tendered to

[1] See *ante*, pp. 198, 199, for a notice of Henderson.

the stage; but as the play is printed, and before the public, the public judgment will decide upon it.

Though I continued to amuse my fancy with dramatic composition, my chief attention was bestowed upon that body of original essays which compose the volumes of 'The Observer.' I first printed two octavos experimentally at our press in Tunbridge Wells; the execution was so incorrect that I stopped the impression as soon as I engaged my friend, Mr. Charles Dilly, to undertake the reprinting of it. He gave it a form and shape fit to meet the public eye; and the sale was encouraging. I added to the collection very largely, and it appeared in a new edition of five volumes; when these were out of print, I made a fresh arrangement of the essays, and, incorporating my entire translation of 'The Clouds,' we edited the work, thus modelled, in six volumes, and these being now attached to the great edition of the British Essayists, I consider the 'Observer' as fairly enrolled amongst the standard classics of our native language.

This work, therefore, has obtained for itself an inheritance; it is fairly off my hands, and what I have to say about it will be confined to a few simple facts. I had no acknowledgments to make in my concluding essay, for I had received no aid or assistance from any man living; every page and paragraph, except what is avowed quotation, I am singly responsible for. My much esteemed friend, Richard Sharp, Esquire, now of Mark Lane, had the kindness, during my absence from town, to correct the sheets as they came from the press. Had that judicious friend corrected them before they went to the press, they would have been profited by the reform of many more than typographical errors; but the approbation he was pleased to bestow upon that portion of the work which passed under his inspection was a very sensible support to me in the prosecution of it, for though I was aware what allowances I had to make for his candid disposition to commend, I had too much confidence in his sincerity to suppose him capable of complimenting me against his judgment or his conscience.

I have been suspected of taking stories out of Spanish authors, and weaving them into some of these essays as my own, without acknowledging the plagiarism. One of my reviewers instances the story of 'Nicolas Pedrosa,' and roundly asserts that, from internal evidence, it must be of Spanish construction, and from these assumed premises leaves me to abide the odium of the inference; to this, I answer, with the most solemn appeal to truth and honor, that I am indebted to no author whatever, Spanish or other, for a single hint, idea, or suggestion of an incident in the story of Pedrosa, nor in that of the Misanthrope, nor in any other which the work contains. In the narrative of the Portuguese, who was brought before the Inquisition, what I say of it, as being matter of tradition, which I collected on the spot, is a mere fiction to give an air of credibility and horror to the tale; the whole, without exception of a syllable, is absolute and entire invention.

I take credit to myself for the character of Abraham Abrahams. I wrote it upon principle, thinking it high time that something should be done for a persecuted race. I seconded my appeal to the charity of mankind by the character of Sheva, which I copied from this of Abrahams. The public prints gave the Jews credit for their sensibility in acknowledging my well-intended services; my friends gave me joy of honorary presents, and some even accused me of ingratitude for not making public my thanks for their munificence. I will speak plainly on this point. I do most heartily wish they had flattered me with some token, however small, of which I might have said, *This is a tribute to my philanthropy*, and delivered it down to my children, as my beloved father did to me his badge of favor from the citizens of Dublin; but not a word from the lips, not a line did I ever receive from the pen of any Jew, though I have found myself in company with many of their nation, and in this perhaps the gentlemen are quite right, whilst I had formed expectations that were quite wrong, for if I have said for them only what they deserve, why should I be thanked for it? But if I have said more, much more than they deserve, can they do a wiser thing than hold their tongues?

It is reported of me, and very generally believed, that I compose with great rapidity. I must own the mass of my writings (of which the world has not seen more than half) might seem to warrant that report; but it is only true in some particular instances, not in the general—if it were, I should not be disinclined to avail myself of so good an apology for my many errors and inaccuracies, or of so good a proof of the fertility and vivacity of my fancy. The fact is, that every hour in the day is my hour for study, and that a minute rarely passes in which I am absolutely idle; in short, I never do nothing. Nature has given me the hereditary blessing of a constitutional and habitual temperance, that revolts against excess of any sort, and never suffers appetite to load the frame; I am accordingly as fit to resume my book or my pen the instant after my meal as I was in the freshest hours of the morning. I never have been accustomed to retire to my study for silence and meditation; in fact, my book-room at Tunbridge Wells was occupied as a bed-room, and what books I had occasion to consult, I brought down to the common sitting-room, where, in company with my wife and family (neither interrupting them, nor interrupted by them, I wrote 'The Observer,' or whatever else I had on hand.

I think it cannot be supposed but that the composition of those essays must have been a work of time and labor; I trust there is internal evidence of that, particularly in that portion of it which professes to review the literary age of Greece, and gives a history of the Athenian stage. That series of papers will, I hope, remain as a monument of my industry in collecting materials, and of my correctness in disposing them; and when I lay to my heart the consolation I derive from the honors now bestowed upon me, at the close of my career, by one who is only in the first outset of his, what have I not to augur for myself, when he who starts with such auspicious promise has been pleased to take my fame in hand, and link it to his own? If any of my readers are yet to seek for the author to whom I allude, the *Comicorum Graecorum fragmenta quaedam* will lead them to his name, and him to their respect.

If I cannot resist the gratification of inserting the paragraph (page 7) which places my dim lamp between those brilliant stars of classic lustre, Richard Bentley and Richard Porson, am I to be set down as a conceited vain old man? Let it be so! I can't help it, and in truth I don't much care about it. Though the following extract may be the weakest thing that Mr. Robert Walpole, of Trinity College, Cambridge, ever has written, or ever shall write, it will outlive the strongest thing that can be said against it, and I will therefore arrest and incorporate it as follows: *Aliunde quoque haud exiguum ornamentum huic volumini accessit, siquidem Cumberlandius nostras amicè benevolèque permissit, ut versiones suas quorundam fragmentorum, exquisitas sane illas, mirâque elegentiâ conditas et commendatas huc transferrem.*

If there is any man, who has reached my age, and written as much as I have with as little recompense for it, who can seriously condemn me, to his sentence I submit; as for the sneerers and subcritics, who can neither write themselves, nor feel for those who do, they are welcome to make the most of it.

My publisher informs me that inquiries are made of him, if I have it in design to translate more comedies of Aristophanes, and that these inquiries are accompanied by wishes for my undertaking it. I am flattered by the honor which these gentlemen confer upon me, but the version of 'The Clouds' cost me much time and trouble; I have no right to reckon upon much more time for anything, and it is very greatly my wish to collect and revise the whole of my unpublished, and above all of my unacted dramas, which are very numerous; I have also a work far advanced, though put aside during the writing of these Memoirs, which, if life is granted to me, I shall be anxious to complete. I must further observe that there is but one more comedy in our volume of Aristophanes, viz: 'The Plutus,' which I could be tempted to translate.

As I hope I have already given a sufficient answer to those who were offended with my treatment of Socrates, I have nothing more to say of 'The Observer,' or its author.

Henderson acted in one other play of my writing for his benefit, and took the part of the Arab, which gave its title to the tragedy. I have now in my mind's eye the look he gave me, so comically conscious of taking what his judgment told him he ought to refuse, when I put into his hand my tributary guineas for the few places I had taken in his theatre—'If I were not the most covetous dog in creation,' he cried, 'I should not take your money; but I cannot help it.' I gave my tragedy to his use for one night only, and have never put it to any use since. His death soon followed, and he was hurried to the grave in the vigor of his talents, and the meridian of his fame.

The late Mrs. Pope, then Miss Young, performed a part in 'The Arab,' and I find an epilogue, which I presume she spoke, though of this I am not certain. I discovered it amongst my papers, and as I flatter myself there are some points in it not amiss, I take the liberty of inserting it.

'*Epilogue to the Arab.*

MISS YOUNG.

Yes 'tis as I predicted. There you sit
Expecting some smart relisher of wit.
Why, 'tis a delicacy out of season—
Sirs, have some conscience! ladies, hear some reason!
With your accustom'd grace you come to share
Your humble actor's annual bill of fare;
But for wit, take it how he will, I tell you,
All have not Falstaff's brains that have his belly.
Wit is not all men's money; when you've bought it,
Look at your lot. You're trick'd. Who could have thought it?
Read it, 'tis folly; court it, a coquette;
Wed it, a libertine—you're fairly met.
No sex, age, country, character, nor clime,
No rank commands it; it obeys no time;
Fear'd, lov'd, and hated; prais'd, ador'd, and curs'd,
The very best of all things, and the worst;
From this extreme to that forever hurl'd,
The idol and the outlaw of the world,
In France, Spain, England, Italy, and Greece,
The joy, plague, pride, and foot-ball of caprice.
  Is it in that man's face, who looks so wise
With lips half-opened, and with half-shut eyes?

Silent grimace!—Flows it from this man's tongue,
With quaint conceits and punning quibbles hung?
A nauseous counterfeit!—Hark! now I hear it—
Rank infidelity!—I cannot bear it.
See where her tea-table Vanessa spreads!
A motley group of heterogeneous heads
Gathers around; the goddess in a cloud
Of incense, sits amidst the adoring crowd,
So many smiles, nods, simpers she dispenses
Instead of five, you'd think she'd fifteen senses;
Alike impatient all at once to shine,
Eager they plunge in wit's unfathom'd mine:
Deep underneath the stubborn ore remains,
The paltry tin breaks up, and mocks their pains.
Ask wit of me! O monstrous, I declare
You might as well ask it of my Lord Mayor:
Require it in an epilogue! a road
As track'd and trodden as a birth-day ode;
Oh, rather turn to those malicious elves,
Who see it in no mortal but themselves;
Our gratitude is all we have to give,
And that we trust your candor will receive.'

Garrick died also, and was followed to the Abbey by a long extended train of friends, illustrious for their rank and genius, who truly mourned a man, so perfect in his art, that nature hath not yet produced an actor worthy to be called his second.[1] I saw old Samuel Johnson standing beside his grave, at the foot of Shakspeare's monument, and bathed in tears: a few succeeding years laid him in the earth, and though the marble shall preserve for ages the exact resemblance of his form and features, his own strong pen has pictured out a transcript of his

[1] Garrick died on the 20th of January, 1779. Goldsmith's delineation of his character, in his poem called 'Retaliation,' is deemed a masterly summary of his mingled faults and virtues:—

'Here lies David Garrick, describe him who can,
An abridgment of all that was pleasant in man;
As an actor, confest without rival to shine;
As a wit, if not first, in the very first line;
Yet, with talents like these, and an excellent heart,
The man had his failings, a dupe to his art.
Like an ill-judging beauty, his colors he spread,
And beplastered with rouge his own natural red.
On the stage he was natural, simple, affecting;
'Twas only that when he was off he was acting.
With no reason on earth to go out of his way,
He turn'd and he varied full ten times a day:
Though secure of our hearts, yet confoundedly sick,
If they were not his own by finessing and trick:
He cast off his friends, as a huntsman his pack,
For he knew when he pleased he could whistle them back.
Of praise a mere glutton, he swallowed what came,
And the puff of a dunce, he mistook it for fame.'
&c. &c.

mind, that shall outlive that and the very language, which he labored to perpetuate. Johnson's best days were dark, and only when his life was far in the decline, he enjoyed a gleam of fortune long withheld. Compare him with his countryman and contemporary last mentioned, and it will be one instance amongst many, that the man who only brings the Muse's bantlings into the world has better lot in it than he who has the credit of begetting them.

Reynolds, the friend of both these worthies, had a measure of prosperity amply dealt out to him; he sunned himself in an unclouded sky, and his Muse, that gave him a pallet dressed by all the graces, brought him also a cornucopia rich and full as Flora, Ceres, and Bacchus, could conspire to make it. His hearse was also followed by a noble cavalcade of mourners, many of whom, I dare believe, left better faces hanging by the wall, than those they carried with them to his funeral. When he was lost to the world, his death was the dispersion of a bright and luminous circle of ingenious friends, whom the elegance of his manners, the equability of his temper, and the attraction of his talents, had caused to assemble round him as the centre of their society. In all the most engaging graces of his heart; in disposition, attitude, employment, character of his figures, and above all in giving mind and meaning to his portraits, if I were to say Sir Joshua never was excelled, I am inclined to believe so many better opinions would be with me, that I should not be found to have said too much.[1]

Romney, in the mean time, shy, private, studious and contemplative; conscious of all the disadvantages and privations of a very stinted education; of a habit naturally hypochondriac, with aspen nerves, that every breath could ruffle, was at once in art the rival, and in nature the very contrast of Sir Joshua. A man of few wants, strict economy, and with no dislike to money, he had opportunities enough to enrich him even to satiety, but he was at once so eager to begin, and so slow in

[1] 'In painting portraits,' Burke finely observes, 'he appeared not to be raised upon that platform, but to descend to it from a higher sphere.' His paintings illustrated his lessons, and his lessons seemed to be derived from his paintings.'

In person, Reynolds is described as rather under the middle size, with a florid complexion, round, blunt features, and altogether a pleasing countenance. All accounts concur as to his manners; they were those of the polished gentleman.

As an artist, he achieved an enduring fame. His portraits, his historical painting, and lectures, are the legacies he bequeathed to posterity, as monuments of his power and taste. As a portrait painter he is said, by his admirers, to have combined the mellowness of Titian, the simplicity and delicacy of Vandyke, and the force and splendor of Rembrandt.

finishing his portraits, that he was forever disappointed of receiving payment for them by the casualties and revolutions in the families they were designed for, so many of his sitters were killed off, so many favorite ladies were dismissed, so many fond wives divorced, before he would bestow half an hour's pains upon their petticoats, that his unsalable stock was immense, whilst with a little more regularity and decision, he would have more than doubled his fortune, and escaped an infinitude of petty troubles that disturbed his temper. At length, exhausted rather by the languor than by the labor of his mind, this admirable artist retired to his native country in the North of England, and there, after hovering between life and death, neither wholly deprived of the one, nor completely rescued by the other, he continued to decline, till at last he sunk into a distant and inglorious grave, fortunate alone in this, that his fame is consigned to the protection of Mr. Hayley, from whom the world expects his history; there, if he says no more of him, than that he was at least as good a painter as Mr. Cowper was a poet, he will say enough; and if his readers see the parallel in the light that I do, they will not think that he shall have said too much.

When I first knew Romney, he was poorly lodged in Newport Street, and painted at the small price of eight guineas for a three-quarters portrait: I sat to him, and was the first who encouraged him to advance his terms, by paying him ten guineas for his performance. I brought Garrick to see his pictures, hoping to interest him in his favor; a large family piece unluckily arrested his attention; a gentleman in a close-buckled bob-wig and a scarlet waistcoat laced with gold, with his wife and children (some sitting, some standing), had taken possession of some yards of canvas very much, as it appeared, to their own satisfaction, for they were perfectly amused in a contented abstinence from all thought or action. Upon this unfortunate group when Garrick had fixed his lynx's eyes, he began to put himself into the attitude of the gentleman, and turning to Mr. Romney—'Upon my word, sir,' said he, 'this is a very regular well-ordered family, and that is a very bright well-rubbed mahogany table, at which that motherly good lady is sitting, and this worthy gentleman in the scarlet waistcoat is doubtless a very excellent subject to the state (I mean if all these are his children), but not for your art, Mr. Romney, if you mean to pursue it with that success which I hope will attend you.' The modest artist took the hint, as it was meant, in good part, and turned his family with their faces to the wall. When Romney produced my portrait, not yet finished—It was very well,

Garrick observed: 'That is very like my friend, and that blue coat with a red cape is very like the coat he has on, but you must give him something to do; put a pen in his hand, a paper on his table, and make him a poet; if you can once set him down well to his writing, who knows but in time he may write something in your praise?' These words were not absolutely unprophetical: I maintained a friendship for Romney to his death; he was uniformly kind and affectionate to me, and certainly I was zealous in my services to him. After his death I wrote a short account of him, which was published in a magazine; I did my best, but must confess I should not have undertaken it, but at the desire of my excellent friend Mr. Green, of Bedford Square, and being further urged to it by the wishes of two other valuable friends, Mr. Long, of Lincoln's Inn Fields, and Mr. Daniel Braythwaite, whom I sincerely esteem, it was not for me to hesitate, especially as I was not then informed of Mr. Hayley's purpose to take that work upon himself.

Here I am tempted to insert a few lines, which about this time I put together, more perhaps for the purpose of speaking civilly of Mr. Romney than for any other use that I could put them to; but as I find there is honorable mention made of Sir Joshua Reynolds also, I give the whole copy as a further proof, that neither in verse or prose did I ever fail to speak of that celebrated painter but with respect so justly due.

'When Gothic rage had put the arts to flight
And wrapt the world in universal night,
When the dire northern swarm with seas of blood
Had drowned creation in a second flood,
When all was void, disconsolate, and dark,
Rome in her ashes found one latent spark,
She, not unmindful of her ancient name,
Nurs'd her last hope and fed the secret flame;
Still as it grew, new streams of orient light
Beamed on the world and cheered the fainting sight;
Rous'd from the tombs of the illustrious dead
Immortal science rear'd her mournful head;
And mourn she shall to time's extremest hour
The dire effects of Omar's savage power,
When rigid Amrou's too obedient hand
Made Alexandria blaze at his command;
Six months he fed the sacrilegious flame
With the stor'd volumes of recorded fame:
There died all memory of the great and good,
Then Greece and Rome were finally subdu'd.
  Yet monkish ignorance had not quite effac'd
All that the chisel wrought, the pencil trac'd;
Some precious relics of the ancient hoard
Or happy chance, or curious search restor'd;
The wondering artist kindled as he gaz'd,
And caught perfection from the work he prais'd.

Of painters then the celebrated race
Rose into fame with each attendant grace;
Still, as it spread, the wonder-dealing art
Improv'd the manners and reform'd the heart;
Darkness dispers'd, and Italy became
Once more the seat of elegance and fame.
Late, very late, on this sequester'd isle
The heaven-descended art was seen to smile;
Seldom she came to this storm-beaten coast,
And short her stay, just seen, admir'd and lost;
Reynolds at length, her favorite suitor, bore
The blushing stranger to his native shore;
He by no mean, no selfish motives sway'd
To public view held forth the liberal maid,
Call'd his admiring countrymen around,
Freely declar'd what raptures he had found;
Told them that merit would alike impart
To him or them a passage to her heart.
Rous'd at the call, all came to view her charms,
All press'd, all strove to clasp her in their arms;
See Coats and Dance and Gainsborough seize the spoil,
And ready Mortimer that laughs at toil;
Crown'd with fresh roses, graceful Humphrey stands,
While beauty grows immortal from his hands;
Stubbs like a lion springs upon his prey,
With bold eccentric Wright that hates the day:
Familiar Zoffany with comic art,
And West, great painter of the human heart.
These and yet more unnam'd that to our eyes
Bid lawns, and groves, and tow'ring mountains rise,
Point the bold rock or stretch the bursting sail,
Smooth the calm sea, or drive th' impetuous gale:
Some hunt 'midst fruit and flowery wreaths for fame,
And Elmer springs it in the feather'd game.
Apart and bending o'er the azure tide,
With heavenly Contemplation by his side,
A pensive artist stands—in thoughtful mood,
With downcast looks he eyes the ebbing flood;
No wild ambition swells his temperate heart,
Himself as pure, as patient as his art,
Nor sullen sorrow, nor intemperate joy
The even tenor of his thoughts destroy,
An undistinguish'd candidate for fame,
At once his country's glory and its shame:
Rouse then, at length, with honest pride inspir'd,
Romney, advance! be known and be admir'd."[1]

---

[1] See *ante*, p. 195, for a sketch of Romney.

CHAPTER XI.

His dramas—Mrs. Siddons—Kemble—Reflections on theatrical fame—Controversy with the Bishop of Llandaff—With Dr. Parr—Mr. Dilly—Boswell—Rogers—Lines to Richard Sharpe—Sir James Bland Burges—Miss Farren—John Palmer—Lord Sackville—His interview with Lord Mansfield—His death—'The Impostor'—'Arundel'—Principles on which a novel should be conducted—'Paradise Lost'—'Calvary'—'Tristram Shandy'—'Junius'—Burke's reflections on the French Revolution—Variety of Cumberland's writings—His dramatic labors—'The Jew'—Bannister—Dowton—Mrs. Bludworth—Fugitive compositions.

I PERCEIVE I must resume the immediate subject of these Memoirs; it is truly a relief to me, when I am called off from it, for unvaried egotism would be a toil too heavy for my mind. When I attempt to look into the mass of my productions, I can keep no order in the enumeration of them; I have not patience to arrange them according to their dates; I believe I have written at least fifty dramas, published and unpublished. Amongst the latter of these there are some which, in my sincere opinion, are better than most which have yet seen the light; they certainly have had the advantages of a more mature correction. When I went to Spain I left in Mr. Harris's hands a tragedy on the subject of 'The Elder Brutus;' the temper of the times was by no means suited to the character of the play; I have never written any drama so much to my own satisfaction, and my partiality to it has been flattered by the judgment of several, who have read it. I have written dramas on the stories of 'False Demetrius,' of 'Tibereus in Capreæ,' and a tragedy on a plot purely inventive, which I entitled, 'Torrendal;' these, with several others, may, in time to come, if life shall be continued to me, be formed into a collection and submitted to the public.

About the time at which my story points, my tragedy of 'The Carmelite' was acted at Drury Lane, and most ably supported by Mrs. Siddons, who took the part of the Lady of Saint Valori, and also spoke the Epilogue. She played inimitably, and in those days, when only men and women trod the stage, the public were contented with what was perfect in nature, and of course admired and applauded Mrs. Siddons;

they could then also see merit in Mr. Kemble, who was in the commencement of his career, and appeared in the character of the youthful Montgomeri. The audiences of that time did not think the worse of him because he had reached the age of manhood, and appeared before them in the full stature and complete maturity of one of the finest forms, that probably was ever exhibited upon a public stage.[1] A revolution since then has taken place, a caprice, as ridiculous as it is extraordinary, and a general act of superannuation has gone forth against every male performer, that has a beard. How I am to style this young child of fortune, this adopted favorite of the public, I don't rightly know; the bills of Covent Garden announce him as Master Betty, those of Drury Lane as the young Roscius. Roscius, as I believe upon the authority of Shakspeare, was an actor in Rome, and Cicero, who admired him, made a speech in his praise. All this, of course, is very right on both sides, and exactly as it should be. Mr. Harris announces him to the old women in the galleries in a phrase that is familiar to them; whilst Mr. Sheridan, presenting him to the senators in the boxes by the style and title of Roscius, fails perhaps in his little representative of the great Roman actor, but perfectly succeeds in his own similitude to the eloquent Roman orator. In the mean time, my friend Smith, of Bury, with all that zeal for merit, which is natural to him, marries him to Melpomene, with the ring of Garrick, and strewing roses of Parnassus on the nuptial couch, crowns happy master Betty, alias Young Roscius, with a never-fading chaplet of immortal verse:—

> And now, when death dissolves his mortal frame,
> His soul shall mount to heav'n, from whence it came,
> Earth keep his ashes, verse preserve his fame.

How delicious to be praised and panegyrized in such a style; to be caressed by dukes, and (which is better), by the daughters of dukes, flattered by wits, feasted by aldermen, stuck up in

[1] When Kemble appeared for the first time in London, at Drury Lane Theatre, on the 30th Sept. 1783, he had attained the age of twenty-six. His Hamlet was universally applauded. In Taylor's poem, entitled 'The Stage,' will be found a critical estimate of his talents as an actor.

> 'To close in order due our long career,
> See *Kemble* march, majestic and severe;
> Fraught with uncommon pow'rs of form and face,
> He comes the pomp of Tragedy to grace.
> Fertile in genius, and matur'd by art,
> Not soft to steal, but stern to seize, the heart;
> In mould of figure, and in frame of mind,
> To him th' heroic sphere must be assigned.'
> &c. &c.

21

the windows of the print-shops, and set astride, as these eyes have seen him, upon the cut-water of a privateer, like the tutelary genius of the British flag.

What encouragements doth this great enlightened nation hold forth to merit? What a consolatory reflection must it be to the superannuated yellow admirals of the stage, that when they shall arrive at second childhood, they may still have a chance to arrive at honors second only to these! I declare I saw with surprise a man, who led about a bear to dance for the edification of the public, lose all his popularity in the street, where this exquisite gentleman has his lodging; the people ran to see him at the window, and left the bear and the bear-leader in a solitude. I saw this exquisite young gentleman, whilst I paced the streets on foot, wafted to his morning's rehearsal in a vehicle that, to my vulgar optics, seemed to wear upon its polished doors the ensign of a ducal crown; I looked to see if haply John Kemble were on the braces, or Cooke perchance behind the coach; I saw the lacqueys at their post, but Glenalvon was not there. I found John Kemble sick at home—I said within myself—

> Oh! what a time have you chose out, brave Caius,
> To wear a kerchief? Would you were not sick!

We shall have a second influx of pigmies; they will pour upon us in multitudes innumerable as a shoal of sprats, and when at last we have nothing else but such small fry to feed on, an epidemic nausea will take place.

There are intervals in fevers; there are lucid moments in madness; even folly cannot keep possession of the mind for ever. It is very natural to encourage rising genius, it is highly commendible to foster its first shoots; we admire and caress a clever school-boy, but we should do very ill to turn his master out of his office and put him into it. If the theatres persist in their puerilities, they will find themselves very shortly in the predicament of an ingenious mechanic, whom I remember in my younger days, and whose story I will briefly relate, in hopes it may be a warning to them.

This very ingenious artist, when Mr. Rich the Harlequin was the great dramatic author of his time, and wrote successfully for the stage, contrived and executed a most delicious serpent for one of those inimitable productions, in which Mr. Rich, justly disdaining the weak aid of language, had selected the classical fable, if I rightly recollect it, of Orpheus and Eurydice, and having conceived a very capital part for the serpent, was justly anxious to provide himself with a performer who could support a character of that consequence with credit to himself and his author. The event answered his most ardent hopes; nothing could be more perfect in his entrances and exits, nothing ever crawled across the stage with more accomplished sinuosity, than this enchanting serpent; every soul was charmed with its performance; it twirled, and twisted, and wriggled itself about in so divine a manner, the whole world was ravished with the lovely snake; nobles and non-nobles, rich and poor, old and young, reps and demi-reps flocked to see it and admire it. The artist, who had been the master of the movement, was intoxicated with his success; he turned his hands and head to nothing else but serpents; he made them of all sizes, they crawled about his shop as if he had been chief snake-catcher to the furies; the public curiosity was satisfied with one serpent, and he had nests of them yet unsold; his stock lay dead upon his hands, his trade was lost, and the man was ruined, bankrupt, and undone.

Here it occurs to me that in one of my preceding pages I have promised to address a parting word to my brethren and contemporaries in the dramatic line. If what I have been now saying coincides with their opinions, I have said enough; if it does not, what I might add to it would be all too much, and the experience of gray hairs would be in vain opposed to the prejudices of green heads. May success attend them in their efforts, whenever they shall seriously address them to the study of the legitimate drama, and the restoration of good taste! There is no lack of genius in the nation: I therefore will not totally despair, old as I am, of living still to witness the commencement of a brighter era.

About this time I undertook the hardy task of differing in opinion with one of the ablest scholars and finest writers in the kingdom, and controverted the proposal of the Bishop of Llandaff for equalizing the revenues of the hierarchy and dignitaries of the church established. I still think I had the best of the argument, and that his lordship did a wiser thing in declining the controversy than in throwing out the proposal. I have read a charge of the bishop's to the clergy of his diocese for enforcing many points of discipline, and enjoining residence. As his lordship neither resides in his diocese, nor executes the important duty of Regius Professor of Divinity in person, I am not informed whether his clergy took their rule of conduct from his precept or from his example; but I take for granted that those whose poverty confined them to their parsonages, did not stray from home, and that those whose means enabled them to visit other places, did not want a precedent to refer to for their apology.

As I have dealt extremely little in anonymous publications, I may as well confess myself in this place the author of a pamphlet entitled 'Curtius rescued from the Gulph.' I conceived that Doctor Parr had hit an unoffending gentleman too hard, by launching a huge fragment of Greek at his defenceless head.[1] The subject was started, and the exterminating weapon produced at one of my friend Dilly's literary dinners; there were several gentlemen present better armed for the encounter than myself, but the lot fell upon me to turn out against Ajax. I made as good a fight as I could, and rummaged my indexes for quotations, which I crammed into my artillery as thick as grape shot, and in mere sport fired them off against a rock invulnerable as the armor of Achilles. It was very well observed by my friend Mr. Dilly, upon the profusion of quotations which some writers affectedly make use of, that he knew a Presbyterian parson who for eighteen pence would furnish any pamphleteer with as many scraps of Greek and Latin, as would pass him off for an accomplished classic. I simply discharge a debt of gratitude, justly due, when I acknowledge the great and frequent gratifications I have received at the hospitable board of the worthy friend last mentioned, who, whilst he conducted upon principles of the strictest integrity the extensive business carried on at his house in the Poultry, kept a table ever open to the patrons and pursuers of literature, which was so administered as to draw the best circles together, and to put them most completely at their ease. No man ever understood this better, and few ever practised it with such success, or on so large a scale; it was done without parade, and in that consisted the peculiar air of comfort and repose which characterized those meetings; hence it came to pass that men of genius and learning resorted to them with delight, and here it was that they were to be found divested of reserve, and in their happiest moments. Under this roof the biographer of Johnson, and the pleasant tourist to Corsica and the Hebrides, passed many jovial joyous hours; here he has located some of the liveliest scenes and most brilliant passages in

[1] Parr's pretensions as a man of letters, says a writer in Blackwood's Magazine, 'were splendid, and fitted, under a suitable guidance, to have produced a more brilliant impression on his own age than they really did, and a more lasting one in the next age than they ever will.' In his lifetime, it is true, the applauses of his many pupils, and his great political friends, to a certain extent made up for all deficiencies on his own part; but now, when these vicarious props are withdrawn, the disproportion is enormous, and hereafter will appear to be more so, between the talents that he possessed, and the effects that he accomplished.'

his entertaining anecdotes of his friend Samuel Johnson, who yet lives and speaks to him. The book of Boswell is ever, as the year comes round, my winter evening's entertainment; I loved the man; he had great convivial powers and an inexhaustible fund of good humor in society; nobody could detail the spirit of a conversation in the true style and character of the parties more happily than my friend James Boswell, especially when his vivacity was excited, and his heart exhilarated by the circulation of the glass, and the grateful odor of a well-broiled lobster.[1]

To these parties I can trace my first impressions of esteem for certain characters whose merits are above my praise, and of whose friendship I have still to boast. From Mr. Dilly's hospitality I derive not only the recollection of pleasure past, but the enjoyment of happiness yet in my possession. Death has not struck so deep into that circle, but that some are left, whose names are dear to society, whom I have still to number amongst my living friends, to whom I can resort and find myself not lost to their remembrance. Our hospitable host, retired from business, still greets me with a friendly welcome; in the company of the worthy Braythwaite I can enjoy the contemplation of a man universally beloved, full indeed of years, but warm in feeling, unimpaired in faculties and glowing with benevolence.

I can visit the justly-admired author of 'The Pleasures of Memory,' and find myself with a friend who, together with the brightest genius, possesses elegance of manners and excellence of heart. He tells me he remembers the day of our first meeting at Mr. Dilly's; I also remember it, and though his modest unassuming nature held back and shrunk from all appearances of ostentation and display of talents, yet even then I take credit for discovering a promise of good things to come, and suspected him of holding secret commerce with the Muse, before the proof appeared in shape of one of the most beautiful and harmonious poems in our language. I do not say that he has not ornamented the age he lives in, though he were to stop where he is, but I hope he will not so totally deliver himself over to the Arts as to neglect the Muses; and I now publicly call upon Samuel Rogers to answer to his name, and stand forth in the title page of some future work that shall be in substance greater, in dignity of sub-

[1] 'It is a wonder,' says Taylor, 'that Mr. Boswell was universally well received. He was full of anecdote, well acquainted with the most distinguished characters, good humored, and ready at repartee. There was a kind of jovial bluntness in his manner, which threw off all restraint, even with strangers, and immediately kindled a social familiarity.'—*Records of my Life*, p. 127.

ject more sublime, and in purity of versification not less charming than his poem above mentioned.[1]

My good and worthy friend Mr. Sharpe has made himself in some degree responsible to the public, for having been the first to suggest to me the idea of writing this huge volume of my Memoirs; he knows I was not easily encouraged to believe my history could be made interesting to the readers of it, and in truth, opinion less authoritative than his would not have prevailed with me to commit myself to the undertaking. Neither he nor I, however, at that time had any thought of publishing before my death; in proof of which I have luckily laid my hand upon the following lines amongst the chaos of my manuscripts, which will show that I made suit to him to protect this and other relics of my pen, when I had paid the debt of nature:—

'*To Richard Sharpe, Esquire, of Mark Lane.*

'If rhyme e'er spoke the language of the heart,
Or truth employ'd the measur'd phrase of art,
Believe me, Sharpe, this verse, which smoothly flows,
Hath all the rough sincerity of prose.
False flattering words from eager lips may fly,
But who can pause to harmonize a lie?
Or e'er he make the jingling couplet chime,
Conscience would start and reprobate the rhyme.
If then 'twere merely to entrap your ear
I call'd you friend, and pledg'd myself sincere,
Genius would shudder at the base design,
And my hand tremble as I shap'd the line.
Poets ofttimes are tickled with a word,
That gayly glitters at the festive board,
And many a man, my judgment can't approve,
Hath trick'd my foolish fancy of its love;
For every foible natural to my race
Finds for a time with me some fleeting place;
But occupants so weak have no control,
No fix'd and legal tenure in my soul,
Nor will my reason quit the faithful clue,
That points to truth, to virtue, and to you.
In the vicissitudes of life we find
Strange turns and twinings in the human mind,
And he, who seeks consistency of plan,
Is little vers'd in the great map of man;
The wider still the sphere in which we live,
The more our calls to suffer and forgive:

---

[1] On the 18th of December, 1855, half a century after Cumberland penned these lines, Rogers died, at his house in St. James's Place, at the great age of ninety-three. Whether his 'Columbus,' 'Jacqueline,' 'Human Life,' and 'Italy,' will stand the test of future criticism, and give the Banker Bard an enduring place among the favored sons of Parnassus, all-decisive time will determine. That his wealth and position in London literary society have much enhanced his contemporary reputation, he who is familiar with the world will not be disposed to question.

But from the hour (and many years are past),
From the first hour I knew you to the last,
Through every scene, self-centr'd and at rest,
Your steady character hath stood the test,
No rash conceits divert your solid thought,
By patience foster'd and with candor fraught;
Mild in opinion, but of soul sincere,
And only to the foes of truth severe,
So unobtrusive is your wisdom's tone,
Your converts hear and fancy it their own,
With hand so fine you probe the festering mind,
You heal our wounds, and leave no sore behind.
  Now say, my friend— but e'er you touch the task,
Weigh well the burden of the boon I ask—
Say, when the pulses of this heart shall cease,
And my soul quits her cares to seek her peace,
Will your zeal prompt you to protect the name
Of one not totally unknown to fame?
Will you, who only can the place supply
Of a lost son, befriend my progeny?
For when the wreck goes down there will be found
Some remnants of the freight to float around,
Some that long time hath almost snatch'd from sight,
And more unseen, that struggle for the light;
And sure I am the stage will not refuse,
To lift her curtain for my widow'd Muse,
Nor will her hearers less indulgent be,
When that last curtain shall be dropt on me.'

I have fairly given the reasons that prevailed with me for publishing these Memoirs in my lifetime, and I believe every man, that knows them, will acknowledge they are reasons sufficiently cogent. My friend Sharpe very kindly acceded to the suit above made; Mr. Rogers has since joined him in the task, and Sir James Bland Burges, of whose friendship I have had many and most convincing proofs, has, with the candor that is natural to an enlightened mind, generously engaged to take his share in selecting and arranging the miscellaneous farrago, that will be found in my drawers, after my body has been committed to the earth. To these three friends I devote this task, and upon their judgment I rely for the publication or suppression of what they may find amongst my literary relics; they are all much younger men than I am, and I pray God that death, who cannot long spare me, will not draw those arrows from his quiver, which fate has destined to extinguish them, till they have completed a career equal at least in length to mine, crowned with more fame, and graced with much more fortune and prosperity. I know that they will do what they have said, and faithfully protect my posthumous reputation, as I have been a faithful friend to them and to their living works.

The heroic poem of 'Richard the First' is truly a very extraordinary work. I am a witness to the extreme rapidity with which my friend the author wrote it. It far exceeded the supposed rate at which Pope translated Homer, which being at fifty lines per day, Samuel Johnson hesitates to give credit to. If to this we take into account the peculiar construction of the stanza, every one of which involves four, three, and two terminations in rhyme, and which must naturally have enhanced the labor of the poet in a very considerable degree, I am astonished at the facility with which Sir James has triumphed over the difficulties that he chose to impose upon himself, and must confess his Muse moves gracefully in her fetters. I was greatly pleased to see that the learned and judicious Mr. Todd, in his late edition of Spenser, has spoken of this poem in such handsome terms, as I can never meet a stronger confirmation of my own opinion, than when I find it coinciding with that of so excellent a critic. The era in which my friend has placed his poem, the hero he has chosen, and the chivalric character with which he has very properly marked it, are circumstances that might naturally prevail with him for modelling it upon the stanza of the Fairy Queen, which, though it has not so proud a march as the heroic verse, has certainly more of the knightly prance in it, and of course more to the writer's purpose than the rhyming couplet. Perhaps the public at large have not yet formed a proper estimate of the real merit of this heroic poem. Its adoption of a stanza, obsolete and repetitionary on the ear, is a circumstance that stamps upon it the revolting air of an imitation, which in fact it is not, and deters many from reading it, who would else find much to admire, and instead of discovering any traces of the Fairy Queen, would meet enough to remind them of a nobler model in the Iliad of Homer. In the mean time, it gives me great satisfaction to know that the author of Richard has since paid loyal service to the dramatic Muse, and when a mind so prompt in execution, and so fully stored with the knowledge both of men and books, shall address its labors to the stage, I should be loath to doubt but that the time will come when classic writing shall expel grimace.

I hope I shall in nowise hurt the feelings of a lady who now most worthily fills a very elevated station, if, in speaking of my humble productions in the course of my subject, I cannot avoid to speak of one of the most elegant actresses that ever graced the stage. When I brought out my comedy of 'The Natural Son,' I flattered myself that in the sketch of Lady Paragon I had conceived a character not quite unworthy of the talents of Miss Farren;[1] it is saying little in the way of praise, when I acknow-

[1] 'With this actress,' says Taylor, 'I never had the pleasure of being personally acquainted, but I met her one morning with Lord Derby, at the house

ledge the partiality I still retain for that particular part, and indeed for that play in general. It was acted and published in the same season with the 'Carmelite,' and though I did not, either in that instance or in any other, to my knowledge, obtrude myself upon the public to the exclusion of a competitor, still it was so that the town was pleased to interpret my second appeal to their candor, and the newspapers of the day vented their malignancy against me in the most opprobrious terms. So exquisite was the style in which Miss Farren gave her character its best display, and so respectable were her auxiliaries in the scene, particularly Mr. John Palmer,[1] that they could never deprive the comedy of favorable audiences, though their efforts too frequently succeeded in preventing them from being full ones. It was a persecution most disgraceful to the freedom of the press, and the performers resented it with a sensibility that did them honor; they traced some of the paragraphs to their dirty origin, but upon minds entirely debased shame has no effect.

I now foresaw the coming-on of an event, that must inevitably deprive me of one of the greatest comforts which still adhered to me in my decline of fortune. It was too evident that the constitution of Lord Sackville, long harassed by the painful visitation of that dreadful malady, the stone, was decidedly giving way. There was in him so generous a repugnance against troubling his friends with any complaints, that it was from external evidence only, never from confession, that his sufferings could be guessed at. Attacks, that would have confined most people to their beds, never moved him from his habitual punctuality. It was curious, and probably in some men's eyes would, from its extreme precision, have appeared ridiculously minute and formal, yet in the movements of a domestic establishment

of the late Mr. Kemble. She seemed to be lively and intelligent, with less affectation than might reasonably be expected in a fine lady who had a prospect of elevated rank. According to report, she was the daughter of a military officer, who died when she was young, and left his widow in distress. . . . It would be unbecoming in me to enter into a criticism on her talents, as they are so well known, and were so justly admired by the public. She was lively and elegant, and only wanted the satirical point and spirit of Mrs. Abington, which, after all, is perhaps a vulgar quality; but she had what Mrs. Abington never possessed, and that was pathos. . . . . At length, like Miss Fenton, the first Polly in 'The Beggar's Opera,' she was destined to assume a high rank, which by all accounts she supported as if she had been 'to the manor born,' and was esteemed as one of the chief ornaments in the circle of nobility.' —*Records of my Life*, p. 235.

[1] Sheridan is said to have delineated Palmer's real character, in his 'Joseph Surface.' In certain characters, such as Brush in the 'Clandestine Marriage,' Brass, or Dick, in the 'Confederacy,' Palmer was unrivalled as an actor.

so large as his, it had its uses and comforts, which his guests and family could not fail to partake of. As sure as the hand of the clock pointed to the half-hour after nine, neither a minute before nor a minute after, so sure did the good lord of the castle step into his breakfast room, accoutred at all points according to his own invariable costume, with a complacent countenance, that prefaced his good-morning to each person there assembled; and now, whilst I recall these scenes to my remembrance, I feel gratified by the reflection, that I never passed a night beneath his roof, but that his morning salutation met me at my post. He allowed an hour and a half for breakfast, and regularly at eleven took his morning's circuit on horseback at a foot's pace, for his infirmity would not admit of any strong gestation; he had an old groom, who had grown gray in his service, that was his constant pilot upon these excursions, and his general custom was to make the tour of his cottages to reconnoitre the condition they were in, whether their roofs were in repair, their windows whole, and the gardens well cropped and neatly kept; all this it was their interest to be attentive to, for he bought the produce of their fruit-trees, and I have heard him say with great satisfaction that he has paid thirty shillings in a season for strawberries only to a poor cottager, who paid him one shilling annual rent for his tenement and garden; this was the constant rate at which he let them to his laborers, and he made them pay it to his steward at his yearly audit, that they might feel themselves in the class of regular tenants, and sit down at table to the good cheer provided for them on the audit day. He never rode out without preparing himself with a store of six-pences in his waistcoat pocket for the children of the poor, who opened gates and drew out sliding bars for him in his passing through the inclosures; these barriers were well watched, and there was rarely any employment for a servant; but these six-pences were not indiscriminately bestowed, for as he kept a charity school upon his own endowments, he knew to whom he gave them, and generally held a short parley with the gate-opener as he paid his toll for passing. Upon the very first report of illness or accident relief was instantly sent, and they were put upon the sick list, regularly visited, and constantly supplied with the best medicines administered upon the best advice; if the poor man lost his cow, or his pig, or his poultry, the loss was never made up in money, but in stock. It was his custom to buy the cast-off liveries of his own servants as constantly as the day of clothing came about, and these he distributed to the old and worn-out laborers, who turned out daily on the lawn and paddock in the Sackville livery to pick up boughs and sweep up leaves, and in short do just as much work as served to keep them wholesome and alive.

To his religious duties this good man was not only regularly but respectfully attentive: on the Sunday morning he appeared in gala, as if he was dressed for a drawing-room; he marched out his whole family in grand cavalcade to his parish church, leaving only a sentinel to watch the fires at home, and mount guard upon the spits. His deportment in the house of prayer was exemplary, and more in character of times past than of time present: he had a way of standing up in sermon time for the purpose of reviewing the congregation, and awing the idlers into decorum, that never failed to remind me of Sir Roger de Coverly, at church: sometimes, when he has been struck with passages in the discourse, which he wished to point out to the audience as rules for moral practice worthy to be noticed, he would mark his approbation of them with such cheering nods and signals of assent to the preacher, as were often more than my muscles could withstand; but when to the total overthrow of all gravity, in his zeal to encourage the efforts of a very young declaimer in the pulpit, I heard him cry out to the Reverend Mr. Henry Eatoff in the middle of his sermon—'Well done, Harry!' it was irresistible; suppression was out of my power: what made it more intolerably comic was, the unmoved sincerity of his manner, and his surprise to find that anything had passed that could provoke a laugh so out of time and place. He had nursed up with no small care and cost in each of his parish churches a corps of rustic psalm-singers, to whose performances he paid the greatest attention, rising up, and with his eyes directed to the singing gallery, marking time, which was not always rigidly adhered to, and once, when his ear, which was very correct, had been tortured by a tone most glaringly discordant, he set his mark upon the culprit by calling out to him by name, and loudly saying, 'Out of tune, Tom Baker!' Now this faulty musician Tom Baker happened to be his lordship's butcher, but then in order to set names and trades upon a par, Tom Butcher was his lordship's baker; which I observed to him was much such a reconcilement of cross partners as my illustrious friend George Faulkner hit upon, when in his Dublin Journal he printed—'Erratum in our last—For His Grace the Duchess of Dorset, *read* Her Grace the Duke of Dorset.'

I relate these little anecdotes of a man whose character had nothing little in it, that I may show him to my readers in his private scenes, and be, as far as I am able, the intimate and true transcriber of his heart. While the marriage-settlement of his eldest daughter was in preparation, he said to the noble person then in treaty for her, 'I am perfectly assured, my lord, that you have correctly given in a statement of your affairs, as you in honor and in conscience religiously believe them to be; but I am much afraid they have been estimated to you for better than they really are, and you must allow me, therefore, to apprise you, that I shall propose an alteration in my daughter's fortune, more proportioned to what I now conceive to be the real valuation of your lordship's property.' To this, when the generous and disinterested suitor expressed his ready acquiescence, my friend replied (I had the anecdote from his own mouth), 'I perceive your lordship understands me as proposing a reduction from my daughter's portion; not so, my lord; my purpose is to double it, that I may have the gratification of supplying those deficiencies in the statement, which I took the liberty of noticing, and which, as you were not aware of them, might else have disappointed and perhaps misled you.' When he imparted this circumstance to me in the words, as nearly as I can remember, but correctly, in the spirit of those words, he said to me: 'I hope you don't suppose I would have done this for my eldest daughter, if I had not assured myself of my ability to do the same for the other two.'

It was in the year 1785, whilst he was at Stoneland, that those symptoms first appeared, which gradually disclosed such evidences of debility as could not be concealed, and showed to demonstration that the hand of death was even then upon him. He had prepared himself with an opinion deliberately formed upon the matter of the Irish Propositions, and when that great question was appointed to come on for discussion in the House of Lords, he thought himself bound in honor and duty to attend in his place. He then for the first time confessed himself to be unfit for the attempt, and plainly declared he believed it would be his death. He paused for a few moments, as if in hesitation how to decide, and the air of his countenance was impressed with melancholy: we were standing under the great spreading tree, that shelters the back entrance to the house; the day was hot; he had dismounted heavily from his horse; we were alone, and it was plain that exercise, though gentle, had increased his languor; he was oppressed both in body and spirit; he did not attempt to disguise it, for he could no longer counterfeit: he sat down upon the bench at the tree-foot, and composing his countenance, as if he wished to have forced a smile upon it, had his suffering given him leave. 'I know,' said he, 'as well as you can tell me, what you think of me just now, and that you are convinced if I go to town upon this Irish business, I go to my death; but I also know you are at heart not against my undertaking it, for I have one convincing proof forever present to me, how much more you consult my honor than my safety. And after all what do I sacrifice, if with the sentence of inevitable death in my hand, I only lop off a few restless hours, and in the execution of my duty meet the stroke? In one word, I tell you I shall go: we will not have another syllable upon the subject; don't advise it, lest you should repent of it, when it has killed me; and do not oppose it, because it would not be your true opinion, and if it were, I would not follow it.'

It was in that same day, after dinner, as I well remember, the evening being most serene and lovely, we seated ourselves in the chairs that were placed out upon the garden grass-plat, which looks towards Crowberry and the forest. Our conversation led us to the affair of Minden; my friend most evidently courted the discussion; I told him I had diligently attended the whole process of the trial, and that I had detailed it to Mr. Doddington; I had consequently a pretty correct remembrance of the leading circumstances as they came out upon the evidence. But I observed to him that it was not upon the questions and proceeding agitated at that court, that I could perfect my opinion of the case; there must be probably a chain of leading causes, which, though they could not make a part of his defence in public court, might, if developed, throw such lights on the respective conduct of the parties, as would have led to conclusions different from those which stood upon the record.

To this he answered that my remark was just; there were certain circumstances antecedent to the action, that should be taken into consideration, and there were certain forbearances, posterior to the trial, that should be accounted for. The time was come when he could have no temptation to disguise and violate the truth, and a much more awful trial was now close at hand, where he must suffer for it if he did. He would talk plainly, temperately, and briefly to me, as his manner was, provided I would promise him to deal sincerely, and not spare to press him on such points as stuck with me for want of explanation. This being premised, he entered upon a detail, which, unless I could give as taken down from his lips, without the variation of a word, so sacred do I hold the reputation of the dead intrusted to me, and the feelings of the living, whom any error of mine might wound, that I shall forbear to speak of it except in general terms. He appeared to me, throughout his whole discourse, like a man who had perfectly dismissed his passions; his color never changed, his features never indicated embarrassment, his voice was never elevated, and being relieved at times by my questions and remarks, he appeared to speak without pain, and in the event his mind seemed lightened by the discharge. When I compare what he said to me in his last moments (not two hours before he expired), with what he stated at this conference, if I did not from my heart and upon the most entire conviction of my reason and understanding, solemnly acquit that injured man, now gone to his account, of the opprobrious and false imputations, deposed against him at his trial, I must be either brutally ignorant, or wilfully obstinate against the truth.

At the battle of Fontenoy, at the head of his brave regiment, in the very front of danger and the heat of action, he received a bullet in his breast, and being taken off the field by his grenadiers, was carried into a tent belonging to the equipage of the French King, and there laid upon a table, whilst the surgeon dressed his wound; so far had that glorious column penetrated in their advance towards victory, unfortunately snatched from them. Let us contemplate the same man, commanding the British cavalry in the battle of Minden, no longer in the front of danger and the heat of action, no longer in the pursuit of victory, for that was gained, and can we think with his unjust defamer, that such a man would tremble at a flying foe? It is a supposition against nature, a charge that cannot stand, an imputation that confutes itself.

Perhaps I am repeating things that I have said in my account of him, published after his death, but I have no means of referring to that pamphlet, and have been for some time writing at Ramsgate, where I have not a single book to turn to, and very few papers and minutes of transactions to refresh my memory.

Lord Sackville attended Parliament, as he said he would, and returned, as he predicted, a dying man. He allowed me to call in Sir Francis Millman, then practising at Tunbridge Wells: all medical assistance was in vain; the saponaceous medicines, that had given him intervals of ease, and probably many years of existence, had now lost their efficacy, or by their efficacy worn their conductors out. He wished to take his last leave of the Earl of Mansfield, then at Tunbridge Wells; I signified this to the earl, and accompanied him in his chaise to Stoneland; I was present at their interview. Lord Sackville, just dismounted from his horse, came into the room, where we had waited a very few minutes, and staggered as he advanced to reach his hand to his respectable visitor; he drew his breath with palpitating quickness, and, if I remember rightly, never rode again: there was a death-like character in his countenance, that visibly affected and disturbed Lord Mansfield, in a manner that I did not quite expect, for it had more of horror in it than a firm man ought to have shown, and less perhaps of other feelings than a friend, invited to a meeting of that nature, must have discovered, had he not been frightened from his propriety.

As soon as Lord Sackville had recovered his breath, his visitor remaining silent, he began by apologizing for the trouble he had given him, and for the unpleasant spectacle he was conscious of exhibiting to him in the condition he was now reduced to; 'but my good lord,' he said, 'though I ought not to have imposed upon you the painful ceremony of paying a last visit to a dying man, yet so great was my anxiety to return you my unfeigned thanks for all your goodness to me, all the kind protection you have shown me through the course of my unprosperous life, that I could not know you was so near me, and not wish to assure you of the invariable respect I have entertained for your character, and now in the most serious manner to solicit your forgiveness, if ever in the fluctuations of politics or the heats of party, I have appeared in your eyes at any moment of my life unjust to your great merits, or forgetful of your many favors.'

When I record this speech, I give it to the reader as correct; I do not trust to memory at this distance; I transcribe it: I scorn the paltry trick of writing speeches for any man, whose name is in these Memoirs, or for myself, in whose name these Memoirs shall go forth, respectable at least for their veracity; for I certainly cannot wish to present myself to the world in two such opposite and incoherent characters as the writer of my own history, and the hero of a fiction.

Lord Mansfield made a reply perfectly becoming and highly satisfactory: he was far on in years, and not in sanguine health or a strong state of nerves; there was no immediate reason to continue the discourse; Lord Sackville did not press for it; his visitor departed, and I stayed with him.[1] He made no other

[1] It was reported that Lord Sackville was the author of Junius, and it has been supposed that he intended by a dying declaration to disabuse Lord Mansfield's mind of any suspicion of that kind. If Lord Mansfield was affected and disturbed by his interview with Lord Sackville, it was an exception to his general impassiveness on such occasions. In the memorable scene in the House of Lords, when the illustrious Chatham had swooned, and lay, as it seemed, in the very agonies of death, Mansfield alone, of all the peers, retained his seat, and looked with slight unconcern on the fall of his former rival;

observation upon what had passed than that it was extremely obliging in Lord Mansfield, and then turned to other subjects.

In him the vital principle was strong, and nature, which resisted dissolution, maintained at every outpost, that defended life, a lingering agonizing struggle. Through every stage of varied misery—extremes by change more fierce—his fortitude remained unshaken, his senses perfect, and his mind never died, till the last pulse was spent, and his heart stopped forever.

In this period intelligence arrived of the Propositions being withdrawn in the Irish House of Commons; he had letters on this subject from several correspondents, and one from Lord Sydney, none of which we thought fit then to give him. I told him in as few words, and as clearly as I could, how the business passed, but requested he would simply hear it, and not argue upon it. 'I am not sorry,' he said, 'that it has so happened. You can witness that my predictions are verified; something might now be set on foot for the benefit of both countries. I wish I could live long enough to give my opinion in my place; I have formed my thoughts upon it; but it is too late for me to do any good; I hope it will fall into abler hands; and you forbid me to argue. I see you are angry with me for talking, and indeed it gives me pain. I have nothing to do in this life, but to obey and be silent.' From that moment he never spoke a word upon the subject.

As I knew he had been some time meditating on his preparations to receive the sacrament, and death seemed near at hand, I reminded him of it; he declared himself ready and at peace with all mankind; in one instance only he confessed it cost him a hard struggle. What that instance was he needed not to explain to me, nor am I careful to explain to any. I trust, according to the infirmity of man's nature, he is rather to be honored for having finally extinguished his resentment, than condemned for having fostered it too long. A Christian saint would have done it sooner: how many men would not have done it ever!

'almost as much unmoved,' Lord Camden writes, 'as the senseless body itself.' —*Mahon's History of England*, vol. vi. p. 231.

Lord Mansfield had two serious defects; he lacked moral courage, and he wanted *heart*. 'He had,' says his biographer, 'no warmth of affection; he formed no friendships; and he neither made exertions nor submitted to sacrifices purely for the good of others. The striking fact to prove that he *reasoned* rather than *felt* is, that he never visited his native land, from the time when he first crossed the border, riding a Highland pony, on his way to Westminster; although he left behind him his father and mother, who survived many years, and were buried in the church at Scone.'—*Campbell's Lives of the Chief Justices*, vol. ii. p. 436. (Amer. ed.)

The Reverend Mr. Sackville Bayle, his worthy parish priest and ever faithful friend, administered the solemn office of the sacrament to him, reading at his request the prayers for a communicant at the point of death. He had ordered all his bed-curtains to be opened and the sashes thrown up, that he might have air and space to assist him in his efforts; what they were, with what devotion he joined in those solemn prayers, that warn the parting spirit to dismiss all hopes that centre in this world, that reverend friend can witness; I also was a witness and a partaker; none else was present at that holy ceremony.

A short time before he expired, I came by his desire to his bedside, when, taking my hand, and pressing it between his, he addressed me for the last time in the following words: 'You see me now in those moments when no disguise will serve, and when the spirit of a man must be proved. I have a mind perfectly resigned, and at peace within itself. I have done with this world, and what I have done in it, I have done for the best; I hope and trust I am prepared for the next. Tell not me of all that passes in health and pride of heart; these are the moments in which a man must be searched, and remember that I die, as you see me, with a tranquil conscience and content.'[1] I have

[1] Lord George Sackville, afterwards Germain, was the youngest son of the first Duke of Dorset, and born in 1716. He was a man, says Walpole, 'of very sound parts, of distinguished bravery, and of an honorable eloquence, but hot, haughty, ambitious, obstinate.'—*Memoir of the Reign of George II.*, vol. i. p. 279.

'He had served on several foreign expeditions'—we are quoting Mahon—'without disparagement, at least, if not without distinction; he had been secretary for Ireland during his father's viceroyalty; he had taken on many occasions a forward and able part in debate.'—*History of England*, vol. iv. p. 178.

At the battle of Minden, he commanded the whole English, and some German cavalry on the right wing of the Allies. In the crisis of the battle, when the French were in disorder, and when a cavalry charge would have completed their destruction, and when Lord George had positive orders from Prince Ferdinand, who commanded the Allies, to bring up the cavalry, he hesitated, and the opportune moment was thrown away. The outcry against him, both in England and Germany, was loud and fierce. He resigned his command and returned home. 'On arriving in England . . . he found himself received by the nation with scarcely less abhorrence, or less clamor, than Byng. . . . . . He was at once dismissed from all his employments—the command of a regiment, a post in the ordnance, and the rank of general.'—*Ibid.* He was tried by a court-martial, convened at his own request, found guilty of disobeying Prince Ferdinand's orders, and declared unfit to serve his majesty in any military capacity whatever. His conduct on the trial was bold and undaunted. 'Nothing was timid—nothing humble in his behavior. His replies were quick and spirited. He prescribed to the court, and they acquiesced. An instant of such resolution at Minden had established his character forever.'—*Walpole.*

It is generally conceded that the decision of the court-martial was equitable. The important point, so far as it concerns the character of Lord George is, whether he was swayed by one of those fancies to which men of quick genius

reason to know I am correct in these expressions, because I transcribe them word for word from a copy of my letter to the Honorable George Damer, now Earl of Dorchester, written a few days after his uncle Lord Sackville's death, and dated September 13th, 1785.

To that excellent and truly noble person I recommend and devote this short but faithful sketch of his relation's character, conscious how highly he deserved, and how entirely he possessed, the love and the esteem of the deceased.

It may to some appear strange that I do not rather address myself to the present lord, the eldest son of his father and the inheritor of his title. He, who knows he has no plea for slighting the friend, who has loved him, knows that he has put it out of my power, and that I must be of all men most insensible, if I did not poignantly feel and feelingly lament his unmerited neglect of me. If the foregoing pages ever meet his eyes, I hope the record of his father's virtues will inspire him to imitate his father's example.

I put in my plea for pardon in the very first page of my book with respect to errors in the dates of my disorderly productions. I should have mentioned my comedy of 'The Impostor,' and the publication of my novel of 'Arundel,' in two volumes, which I hastily put together whilst I was passing a few idle weeks at Brighthelmstone, where I had no books but such as a circulating novel-shop afforded. I dispatched that work so rapidly, sending it to the press by parcels, of which my first copy was the only one, that I really do not remember what moved me to the undertaking, nor how it came to pass that the *cacoëthes scribendi nugas* first got hold of me. Be this as it may, I am not about to affect a modesty which I do not feel, or to seek a shelter from the sin of writing ill, by acknowledging the folly of writing rapidly, for I believe that 'Arundel' has entertained as many readers, and gained as good a character in the world as most heroes of his description, not excepting the immaculate Sir

are sometimes prone, or by an envy of Prince Ferdinand's greatness, and a desire to leave the victory of his rival incomplete. The latter motive, says Lord Mahon, is alleged by several writers. He admits that his own opinion inclines to the former.—*History of England*, vol. iv. p. 181.

A man of such spirit, of such indomitable energy as Sackville, could not be borne down by such a disgrace as had fallen upon him. He again aspired to high honors and employments, and he obtained them. He was restored to the Privy Council, made Secretary of State, and raised to the peerage as Viscount Sackville. His plans and counsels during the American contest had an unprosperous issue; and his life, on the whole, was marked by misfortune. In his duel with Governor Johnstone, he fought with a coolness 'that with almost all men justly palliated or removed the imputation on his spirit.'—*Walpole.*

Charles Grandison, in whose company I have never found myself without being puzzled to decide whether I am most edified by his morality or disgusted by his pedantry. 'Arundel,' perhaps, of all the children which my brain has given birth to, had the least care and pains bestowed upon his education, yet he is a gentleman, and has been received as such in the first circles, for though he takes the wrong side of the question in his argument with Mortlake upon duelling, yet there is hardly one to be found, who thinks with Mortlake, but would be shamed out of society if he did not act with Arundel. In the character of the Countess of G. I confess I have set virtue upon ice; she slips, but does not fall; and if I have endowed the young ladies with a degree of sensibility that might have exposed them to danger, I flatter myself I have taken the proper means of rescuing them from it by marrying them respectively to the men of their hearts.

The success, however, which by this novel I obtained without labor, determined me to write a second, on which I was resolved to bestow my utmost care and diligence. In this temper of mind I began to form to myself in idea what I conceived should be the model of a perfect novel; having, after much deliberation, settled and adjusted this to the best of my judgment, I decided for the novel in detail; rejecting the epistolary process, which I had pursued in 'Arundel,' and also that in which the hero speaks throughout, and is his own biographer; though in putting both these processes aside I felt much more hesitation in the last-mentioned case than in the first.

Having taken Fielding's admirable novel of Tom Jones as my pattern in point of detail, I resolved to copy it also in its distribution into chapters and books, and to prefix prefatory numbers to the latter, to the composition of which I addressed my best attention. In some of these I have taken occasion to submit those rules for the construction of a novel, which I flattered myself might be of use to future writers in that line, less experienced than myself. How far I have succeeded is not for me to say, but if I have failed, I am without excuse, for I had this work in hand two full years, and gave more polish and correction to the style, than ever I bestowed upon any of my published works before. The following few rules which I laid down for my own guidance, and strictly observed, I still persuade myself are such as ought to be observed by others.

I would have the story carried on in a regular uninterrupted progression of events, without those dull recitals, that call the attention off from what is going on, and compel it to look back, perhaps in the very crisis of curiosity, to circumstances antecedent to, and not always materially connected with, the history in hand. I am decidedly adverse to episodes and stories within stories, like that of the Man of the Hill in Tom Jones, and in general all expedients of procrastination, which come under the description of mere tricks to torture curiosity, are in my opinion to be very sparingly resorted to, if not totally avoided. Casualties and broken bones, and faintings and high fevers, with ramblings of delirium and rhapsodies of nonsense, are perfectly contemptible. I think descriptive writing, properly so distinguished, is very apt to describe nothing, and that landscapes upon paper leave no picture in the mind, and only load the page with daubings, that in the author's fancy may be sketches after nature, but to the reader's eye offer nothing but confusion. A novel, professing itself to be the delineation of men and women as they are in nature, should in general confine itself to the relation of things probablé, and though in skilful hands it may be made to touch upon things barely possible, the seldomer it risks those experiments, the better opinion I should form of the contriver's conduct; I do not think quotations ornament it, and poetry must be extremely good before I can allow it is of any use to it. In short, there should be authorities in nature for everything that is introduced, and the only case I can recollect in which the creator of the fictitious man may and ought to differ from the biographer of the real man, is, that the former is bound to deal out his rewards to the virtuous and punishments to the vicious, whilst the latter has no choice but to adhere to the truth of facts, and leave his hero neither worse nor better than he found him.

Monsters of cruelty and crime, monks and Zelucos, horrors and thunderings and ghosts are creatures of another region, tools appropriated to another trade, and are only to be handled by dealers in old castles and manufacturers of romances.

As the tragic drama may be not improperly described as an epic poem of compressed action, so I think we may call the novel a dilated comedy; though Henry Fielding, who was pre-eminently happy in the one, was not equally so in the other: *non omnia possumus omnes.* If the readers of Henry have agreed with me in the principles laid down in those prefatory chapters, and here again briefly touched upon, I flatter myself they found a novel conducted throughout upon those very principles, and which in no one instance does a violence to nature, or resorts to forced and improbable expedients to excite surprise; I flatter myself they found a story regularly progressive, without any of those retrogradations or counter-marches which break the line and discompose the arrangement of the fable; I hope they found me duly careful to keep the principal characters in sight, and above all if I devoted myself *con amore* to the delineation of Zachary Cawdle, and in a more particular manner to the best services I could perform for the good Ezekiel Daw, I warmly hope they did not think my partiality quite misapplied, or my labor of love entirely thrown away.

If in my zeal to exhibit virtue triumphant over the most tempting allurements, I have painted those allurements in too vivid colors I am sorry, and ask pardon of all those who thought the moral did not heal the mischief.

If my critics have not been too candid, I am encouraged to believe that, in these volumes of 'Henry,' and in those of 'The Observer,' I have succeeded in what I labored to effect with all my care—a simple, clear, harmonious style; which, taken as a model, may be followed without leading the novitiate either into turgidity or obscurity, holding a middle tone of period, neither swelling into high-flown metaphor, nor sinking into inelegant and unclassical rusticity. Whether or not I have succeeded, I certainly have attempted, to reform and purify my native language from certain false pedantic prevalencies, which were much in fashion when I first became a writer. I dare not say with those whose flattery might mislead me, that I have accomplished what I aimed at, but if I have done something towards it, I may say with Pliny—*Posteris an aliqua cura nostri, nescio. Nos certe meremur ut sit aliqua; non dicam ingenio; id enim superbum; sed studio, sed labore, sed reverentia posterorum.*

The mental gratification which the exercise of the fancy in the act of composition gives me, has, with the exception only of the task I am at present engaged in, led me to that inordinate consumption of paper, of which much has been profitless, much unseen, and very much of that which has been seen, would have been more worthy of the world had I bestowed more blotting upon it before I committed it to the press; yet I am now about to mention a poem not the most imperfect of my various productions, of which the first manuscript copy was the only one, and that perhaps the fairest I had ever put out of my hands. Heroic verse has been always more familiar to me, and more easy in point of composition, than prose: my thoughts flow more freely in metre, and I can oftentimes fill a page with less labor and less time in verse of that description, than it costs me to adjust and harmonize a single period in prose to my entire satisfaction.

The work I now allude to is my poem of 'Calvary,' and the gratification of which I have been speaking, mixed, as I trust, with worthier and more serious motives, led me to that undertaking. It had never been my hard lot to write, as many of my superiors have been forced to do, task-work for a bookseller; it was therefore my custom, as it is with voluptuaries of another description, to fly from one pursuit to another for the greater zest, which change and contrast gave to my intellectual pleasures. I had as yet done nothing in the epic way, except my juvenile attempt, of which I have given an extract, and I applied myself to the composition of 'Calvary,' with uncommon ardor; I began it in the winter, and, rising every morning some hours before daylight, soon dispatched the whole poem of eight books, at the average of full fifty lines in a day, of which I kept a regular account, marking each day's work upon my manuscript. I mention this, because it is a fact; but I am not so mistaken as to suppose that any author can be entitled to take credit to himself for the little care he has bestowed upon his compositions.

It was not till I had taken up Milton's immortal poem of 'Paradise Lost,' and read it studiously, and completely through, that I brought the plan of 'Calvary' to a consistency, and resolved to venture on the attempt. I saw such aids in point of character, incident, and diction, such facilities held out by the sacred historians, as encouraged me to hope I might aspire to introduce my humble Muse upon that hallowed ground without profaning it.

As for the difficulties which, by the nature of his subject, Milton had to encounter, I perceived them to be such as nothing but the genius of Milton could surmount: that he has failed in some instances cannot be denied, but it is matter of wonder and admiration that he has miscarried in so few. The noble strucure he has contrived to raise with the co-operation of two human beings only, and those the first created of the human race, strikes us with astonishment; but, at the same time, it forces him upon such frequent flights beyond the bounds of nature, and obliges him in so great a degree to depend upon the agency of supernatural beings, of whose persons we have no prototype, and of whose operations, offices, and intellectual powers we are incompetent to form any adequate conception, that it is not to be wondered at, if there are parts and passages in that divine poem that we either pass over by choice, or cannot read without regret.

Upon a single text in Scripture he has described a Battle in Heaven, in most respects tremendously sublime, in others painfully reminding us how impossible it is for man's limited imagination to find weapons for immortal spirits, or conceive an army of rebellious angels employing instruments of human invention upon the vain impossible idea, that their material artillery could shake the immaterial throne of the One Supreme Being, the Almighty Creator and Disposer of them and the universe. Accordingly, when we are presented with the description of Christ, the meek Redeemer of mankind, going forth in a chariot to the battle, brilliant although the picture is, it dazzles, and we start from it revolted by the blaze. But when the poet, deeming himself competent to find words for the Almighty, contrives a conference between the First and Second Persons in the Trinity, we are compelled to say with Pope—

'That God the Father turns a school-divine.'

I must entreat my readers not so to misconceive my meaning as to suppose me vain enough to think, that by noticing these spots in Milton's glorious sun, I am advancing my dim lamp to any the most distant competition with it. I have no other motive for mentioning them but to convince the patrons of these Memoirs, that I did not attempt the composition of a sacred epic, where he must for ever stand so decidedly pre-eminent, till by comparing the facilities of my subject with the amazing difficulties of his, I had found a bow proportioned to my strength, and did not presume to bend it till I was certified of its flexibility.

It could not possibly be overlooked by me, that, in taking the Death of Christ for my subject, I had the advantage of dating my poem at a point of time the most awful in the whole history of the world, the most pregnant with sublime events, and the most fully fraught with grand and interesting characters; that I had those characters, and those events, so pointedly delineated and so impressively described by the inspired historians, as to leave little else for me to do, but to restrain invention, and religiously to follow in the path that was chalked out to me. Accordingly I trust there will be found very little of the audacity of fancy in the composition of 'Calvary,' and few sentiments or expressions ascribed to the Saviour, which have not the sanction and authority of the sacred record. When he descends into Hades, I have endeavored to avail myself of what has been revealed to us for those conjectural descriptions, and I hope I have not far outstripped discretion, or heedlessly indulged a wild imagination; for though I venture upon untouched ground, presuming to unfold a scene which mystery has involved in darkness, yet I have the visions of the Saint at Patmos to hold up a light to me, and assist me in my efforts to pervade futurity.

My first publication of 'Calvary' in quarto had so languid a sale, that it left me with the inconvenient loss of at least one hundred pounds, and the discouraging conviction that the public did not concern itself about the poem or the poem-maker; I felt at the same time a proud indignant consciousness, that it claimed a better treatment, and whilst I called to mind the true and brotherly devotion I had ever borne to the fame of my contemporaries, I was stung by their neglect; and having laid my poem on the death of my Redeemer at the feet of my sovereign, which, for aught that ever reached my knowledge, he might, or might not, have received by the hand of his librarian, I had nothing to console me but the reflection that there would, perhaps, be a tribunal that would deal out justice to me when I could not be a gainer by it, and speak favorably of my performance when I could not hear their praises.

I shall now take leave of 'Calvary' after acknowledging my obligations to my publishers for their speculation of a new edition, and also to the purchasers of that edition for their reconcilement to a book, which, till it was reduced to a more portable size, they were little disposed to take away with them.

I consider 'Tristram Shandy' as the most eccentric work of my time, and 'Junius' the most acrimonious; we have heard much of his style; I have just been reading him over with attention, and I confess I can see but little to admire. The thing to wonder at is, that a secret, to which several must have been privy, has been so strictly kept; if Sir William Draper, who baffled him in some of his assertions, had kept his name out of sight, I am inclined to think he might have held up the cause of candor with success. The publisher of 'Junius,' I am told, was deeply guaranteed; of course, although he might not know his author, he must have known whereabouts to look for him. I never heard that my friend Lord George Germain was amongst the suspected authors, till by way of jest he told me so not many days before his death: I did not want him to disavow it, for there could be no occasion to disprove an absolute impossibility. The man who wrote it had a savage heart, for some of his attacks are execrable; he was a hypocrite, for he disavows private motives, and makes pretensions to a patriotic spirit. I can perfectly call to mind the general effect of his letters, and am of opinion that his malice overshot its mark. Let the anonymous defamer be as successful as he may, it is but an unenviable triumph, a mean and cowardly gratification, which his dread of a discovery forbids him to avow.

As for 'Tristram Shandy,' whose many plagiarisms are now detected, his want of delicacy is unpardonable, and his tricks have too much of frivolity and buffoonery in them to pass upon the reader; but his real merit lies not only in his general conception of character, but in the address with which he marks them out by those minute, yet striking touches of his pencil, that make his descriptions pictures, and his pictures life; in the pathetic he excels, as his story of Lefevre witnesses, but he seems to have mistaken his powers, and capriciously to have misapplied his genius.

I conceive there is not to be found in all the writings of my day, perhaps I may say not in the English language, so brilliant a cluster of fine and beautiful passages in the declamatory style, as we are presented with in Edmund Burke's inimitable tract upon the French Revolution. It is most highly colored and most richly ornamented, but there is elegance in its splendor, and dignity in its magnificence. The orator demands attention in a loud and lofty tone, but his voice never loses its melody, nor his periods their sweetness. When he has roused us with the thunder of his eloquence, he can at once, Timotheus-like, choose a melancholy theme, and melt us into pity; there is grace in his anger; for he can inveigh without vulgarity; he can modulate the strongest bursts of passion, for even in his madness there is music.

I was so charmed with the style and matter of this pamphlet that I could not withstand the pleasure of intruding upon him with a letter of thanks, of which I took no copy, but fortunately have preserved his answer to it, which is as follows:—

'*Beconsfield*, November 13th, 1790.

DEAR SIR: I was yesterday honored with your most obliging letter. You may be assured that nothing could be more flattering to me than the approbation of a gentleman so distinguished in literature as you are, and in so great a variety of its branches. It is an earnest to me of that degree of toleration in the public judgment, which may give my reasonings some chance of being useful. I know, however, that I am indebted to your politeness and your good nature, as much as to your opinion, for the indulgent manner in which you have been pleased to receive my endeavor. Whether I have described our countrymen properly, time is to show: I hope I have, but at any rate it is perhaps the best way to persuade them to be right by supposing that they are so. Great bodies, like great men, must be instructed in the way in which they will be best pleased to receive instruction; flattery itself may be converted into a mode of counsel: *laudando admonere* has not always been the most unsuccessful method of advice. In this case moral policy requires it, for when you must expose the practices of some kinds of men, you do nothing if you do not distinguish them from others.

Accept once more my best acknowledgments for the very handsome manner in which you have been pleased to consider my pamphlet, and do me the justice to believe me with the most perfect respect,

Dear sir,
Your most faithful
And obliged humble servant,
EDM. BURKE.'

Am I, or am I not to regret that this fine writer devoted himself so professedly to politics? I conceive there must be two opinions upon this question amongst his contemporaries, and only one that will be entertained by posterity. Those who heard his parliamentary speeches with delight, will not easily be induced to wish that he had spoken less; whilst those who can only read him, will naturally regret that he had not written more. The orator, like the actor, lives only in the memory of his hearers, and his fame must rest upon tradition; Mr. Burke in Parliament enjoyed the triumph of a day, but Mr. Burke on paper would have been the founder of his own immortality.

Amongst the variety of branches, to which Mr. Burke is pleased so flatteringly to allude, and which certainly are more in number than the literary annals of any author in my recollection can exhibit, I reflect with satisfaction that I have devoted much time and thought to serious subjects, and been far from idle or lukewarm in the service of religion. I have written at different times as many sermons as would make a large volume, some of which have been delivered from the pulpits; I have rendered into English metre fifty of the psalms of David, which are printed by Mr. Strange, of Tunbridge Wells, and upon which I flatter myself I have not in vain bestowed my best attention. I have for some years been in the habit of composing an appropriate prayer of thanksgiving for the last day in the year, and of supplication for the first day in the succeeding year. I published, by Messrs. Lackington & Co., a religious and argumentative tract, entitled 'A few Plain Reasons for Believing in the Evidences of the Christian Revelation;' and this tract, which I conceive to be orthodox in all its points, and unanswerably demonstrative as a confutation of all the false reasoners according to the new philosophy, I presented with all due deference to the Bishop of London, who was pleased to honor me with a very gracious acknowledgment by letter, and likewise to the late Archbishop of Canterbury, who was not pleased to acknowledge it in any way whatever. But I had no particular right to expect it; all regulars are not equally candid to the volunteer, as I have good reason to know.

I have selected several passages from the Old Testament, and turned them into verse; they are either totally lost, or buried out of sight in the chaos of my manuscripts; I find one only amongst the few loose papers I have with me, and I take the liberty of inserting it:—

'*Judges, Chapter the 5th.*

Hear, all earth's crowned monarchs, hear!
Princes and judges to my song give ear:
To Israel's God my voice I'll raise,
And joyful chant Jehovah's praise.

Lord, when in Edom's glorious day
Thou wentest forth in bright array,
Earth to her inmost centre shook,
The mountains melted at thy look,
The clouds drop't down their wat'ry store,
Rent with the thunder's loud tremendous roar.

Must I remember Shamgar's gloomy days,
And that sad time when Jael rul'd our coast?
No print of foot then mark'd our public ways,
Waste horror reign'd, the human face was lost.
Then I, I Deborah, assum'd command,
The nursing mother of the drooping land;
Then was our nation alien from the Lord,
Then o'er our heads high wav'd the hostile sword,
Nor shield, nor spear, was found to arm for fight,
And naked thousands turn'd their backs in flight.

But now awake, my soul, and thou arise,
Barak; to thee the victory is giv'n;
Let our joint song ascend the skies,
And celebrate the majesty of heav'n.
On me, the priestess of the living Lord,
The care of Israel was bestow'd:
Ephraim and Benjamin obey'd my word,
The Scribes of Zebulon allegiance show'd,
And Issachar, a princely train,
With glittering ensigns dazzled all the plain.
But oh! what sad divisions keep
Reuben inglorious 'midst his bleating sheep?
Gilead in Jordan his asylum seeks,
Dan in his ships, and Asher in his creeks,
Whilst Naphthali's more warlike sons expose
Their gallant lives, and dare their country's foes.
Then was the battle fought by Canaan's kings
In Taänach beside Megiddo springs;
The stars themselves 'gainst Sisera declare;
Israel is heaven's peculiar care.
Old Kishon stain'd with hostile blood,
Roll'd to the main a purple flood;
The neighing steed, the thund'ring car
Proclaim'd the terrors of the war;
But high in honor 'bove the rest
Be Jael, our avenger, blest,
Blest above women! to her tent she drew
With seeming friendship Jabel's mighty chief;
Fainting with heat and toil he sought relief,
He slept, and in his sleep her weary guest she slew.
The workman's hammer in this hand she took,
In that the fatal nail, then boldly struck;
Through both his temples drove the deadly wound,
Transfix'd his brain and pinn'd him to the ground.
Why stays my son, his absent mother cries;
When shall I welcome his returning car,
Loaded with spoils of conqu'ring war?
Ah, wretched mother, hide thine eyes;
At Jael's feet a headless trunk he lies.
So Sisera fell, and God made wars to cease,
So rested Israel, and the land had peace.'

Of my dramatic pieces I must say in the gross, that if I did not always succeed in entertaining the audience, I continued to amuse myself. I brought out a comic opera in three acts, founded on the story of 'Wat Tyler,' which being objected to by the Lord Chamberlain, I was obliged to new model, and produce under the title of the 'Armorer.' When I had taken all the comedy out of it, I was not surprised to find that the public were not very greatly edified by what was left.

I also brought out a comedy called 'The Country Attorney,' at the summer theatre, when it was under the direction of the elder Mr. Colman. At the same theatre, under the auspices of the present candid and ingenious superintendent, I produced my comedy of 'The Box-Lobby Challenge,' and my drama of 'Don Pedro.'

When the new and splendid theatre of Drury Lane was opened, my comedy of 'The Jew' was represented, and if I am not mistaken (I speak upon conjecture), it was the first new piece exhibited on that stage. I am ashamed to say with what rapidity I dispatched that hasty composition, but my friend Bannister, who saw it act by act, was a witness to the progress of it; in what degree he was a promoter of the success of it I need not say; poor Suett also, now no more, was an admirable second.

The benevolence of the audience assisted me in rescuing a forlorn and persecuted character, which till then had only been brought upon the stage for the unmanly purpose of being made a spectacle of contempt, and a butt for ridicule. In the success of this comedy I felt of course a greater gratification than I had ever felt before upon a like occasion.

The part of Sheva presented Mr. Bannister to the public in that light, in which he will always be seen, when nature fairly drawn and strongly charactered is committed to his care. Let the poet give him the model, and his animation will give it the action and the life.

It has also served as a stepping-stone to the stage for an actor who, in my judgment (and I am not afraid of being singular in that opinion), stands amongst the highest of his profession; for if quick conception, true discrimination, and the happy faculty of incarnating the idea of his poet, are properties essential in the almost undefinable composition of a great and perfect actor, these and many more will be found in Mr. Dowton. Let those, who have a claim upon his services, call him to situations not unworthy of his best exertions, and the stage will feel the value of his talents.

'The Wheel of Fortune' came out in the succeeding season, and 'First Love' followed close upon its steps. They were successful comedies, and very powerfully supported by the performers of them in every part throughout. I was fortunate in the plot of the first; for there is dignity of mind in the forgiveness of injuries, which elevates the character of Penruddock, and Mr. Kemble's just personification of it added to a lucky fiction all the force and interest of a reality. When so much belongs to the actor, the author must be careful how he arrogates too much to himself.

Of 'First Love' I shall only say, that when two such exquisite actresses conspired to support me, I will not be so vain as to presume I could have stood without their help.

I think, as I am now so near the conclusion of these Memoirs, I may as well wind up my dealings with the theatres before I proceed any further. I am beholden to Covent Garden for accepting my dramas of 'The Days of Yore' and 'False Impressions.' To Drury Lane for 'The Last of the Family,' 'The Word for Nature,' 'The Dependent,' 'The Eccentric Lover,' and for 'The Sailor's Daughter.' My life has been a long one, and my health of late years uninterrupted; I am very rarely called off by avocations of an undomestic kind, and the man who gives so very small a portion of his time to absolute idleness as I have done, will do a vast deal in the course of time, especially if his body does not stand in need of exercise, and his mind, which never knows remission of activity, incessantly demands to be employed.

I was in the practice of interchanging an annual visit with Mrs. Bludworth, of Holt, near Winchester, the dearest friend of my wife. When I was upon those visits, I used to amuse myself with trifles that required no application to my books. A few from amongst many of these fugitive compositions appear to me not totally unworthy of being arrested and brought to the bar as petty-larceny pilferers of the sonnet-writing style, of which some elegant sisters of the Muses have published such ingenious originals, as ought to have secured them against interlopers, who have nothing better to produce than some such awkward imitations as the following:—

WIT.

No. 1.

'How shall I paint thee, many-color'd Wit?
Where are the pallet's brilliant tints to vie
With the bright flash of thine electric eye?
Nor can I catch the glance; nor wilt thou sit
Till my slow copying art can trace
One feature of thy varying face.

Soul of the social board, thy quick retort
Can cut the disputatious quibbler short,
Stop the dull pedant's circumstantial saw,
And silence ev'n the loud-tongu'd man of law.

The solemn ass, who dully great
Mistakes stupidity for state,
Unbends his marble jaws, and brays
Involuntary, painful praise.

Thou, Wit, in philosophic eyes
Can'st make the laughing waters rise;
Proud Science vails with bended knee
His academic cap to thee,
And though thy sallies fly the test
Of truth, she titters at the jest.

Thrice happy talent, could'st thou understand
Virtue to spare and buffet vice alone,
Would'st thou but take discretion by the hand,
The world, O Wit, the world would be thine own.'

AFFECTATION.

No. 2.

'Why, Affectation, why this mock grimace?
Go, silly thing, and hide that simpering face;
Thy lisping prattle and thy mincing gait,
All thy false mimic fooleries I hate;
For thou art Folly's counterfeit, and she,
Who is right foolish, hath the better plea;
Nature's true idiot I prefer to thee.

Why that soft languish? Why that drawling tone?
Art sick, art sleepy? Get thee hence, begone!
I laugh at all those pretty baby tears,
Those flutterings, faintings, and unreal fears.

Can they deceive us? Can such mumm'ries move,
Touch us with pity, or inspire with love?
No, Affectation, vain is all thine art,
Those eyes may wander over every part;
They'll never find their passage to the heart.'

VANITY.

No. 3.

'Go, Vanity, spread forth the painted wing;
I'll harm thee not, gay flutterer, not I;
Poor innocent, thou hast no sting,
Pass on unhurt! I war not with a fly.
But if the Muse in sportive style
Banters thy silly freaks awhile,
Fear not—she'll lash thee only with a smile.
If thou art heard too loud of tongue,
And thy small tap of wit runs out
Too fast, and bubbles all about,
'Twere charity, methinks, to stop the bung.
If when thou should'st be staid and sage,
Thou'lt take no warning from old age,
But still run riot, and spread sail
In all the colors of the peacock's tail:
If, with too hollow cheeks bedaub'd with red,
The ostrich plume nods on thy palsied head,

And with soft glances from lack-lustre eyes
Thou aim'st to make our hearts thy beauty's prize,
Then, then, Dame Vanity beware;
Look to thyself—beshrew me if I spare.'

AVARICE

No. 4

'A little more, and yet a little more—
Oh, for the multiplying art
To heap the still increasing store,
Till it make Ossa like a wart!

Oh Avarice, thou rage accurst,
Insatiate dropsy of the soul,
Will nothing quench thy sordid thirst?
Were the sea gold, would'st drink the whole?

Lo! pity pleads—What then? There's none.
The widow kneels for bread. Begone—
Hark, in thine ears the orphan's cry;
They die of famine—let them die.

Oh scene of wo; heart-rending sight;
Can'st thou turn from them? Yes, behold:
From all those heaps of hoarded gold
Not one, one piece to save them? Not a mite.
Pitiless wretch, such shall thy sentence be
At the last day, when Mercy turns from thee.'

PRUDERY.

No. 5.

'What is that stiff and stately thing I see?
Of flesh and blood like you and me,
Or is it chisel'd out of stone,
Some statue from its pedestal stept down?

'Tis one and both—a very prude
Of marble flesh and icy blood;
Dead and alive at once—behold,
It breathes and lives; touch it, 'tis dead and cold.
Look how it throws the scowling eye
On Pleasure, as she dances by;
Quick flies the sylph, for long she cannot bear
The damping rigor of its atmosphere,
Chill as the eastern fog that blights
Each blossom upon which it lights.

Say, ye that know what virtue is, declare,
Is this the form her votaries must wear?
Tell me in time; if such it needs must be,
Virtue and I shall never more agree.'

ENVY.

No. 6.

(See 'The Observer,' vol. iv. No. 94.)

PRIDE.

No. 7.

'Curst in thyself, O Pride, thou canst not be
More competently curst by me.
Hence, sullen, self-tormenting, stupid sot,
Thy dullness damps our joys ; we want thee not.
Round the gay table side by side
Social we sit ; there is no room for Pride ;
We cannot bear thy melancholy face ;
The company is full ; thou hast no place.

Man, man, thou little grovelling elf,
Turn thine eyes inward—view thyself;
Draw out thy balance, hang it forth,
Weigh every atom thou art worth,
Thy peerage, pedigree, estate,
(The pains that fortune took to make thee great),
Toss them all in—stars, garters, strings,
Heap up the mass of tawdry things,
The whole regalia of kings.
Now watch the beam, and fairly say
How much does all this trumpery weigh ?
Give in the total ; let the scale be just,
And own, proud mortal, own thou art but dust.'

HUMILITY.

No. 8.

'Oh sweet Humility, can words impart
How much I love thee, how divine thou art?
Nurse us not only in our infant age,
Conduct us still through each successive stage
Of varying life, lead us from youth's gay prime
To the last step of man's appointed time.

Wit, Genius, Learning—What are these ?
The painter's colors or the poet's lays,
If without thee they cannot please,
If without thee we cannot praise ?

Why do I call my lov'd Eliza fair ?
Why do I dote upon her faded face ?
Nor rosy health, nor blooming youth is there ;
Humility bestows the angel grace.

Where should a frail and trembling sinner lie,
How should a Christian live, how should he die,
But in thine arms, conscious Humility ?

'Twas in thy form the world's Redeemer came,
And condescended to his human birth,
With thee he met revilings, death and shame,
Though angels hail'd him Lord of heav'n and earth.'

CHAPTER XII.

Military preparations—Major commandant—Drills—Presented with a sword—The volunteer system—His family—Lines to the Princess Amelia—Conclusion.

WHEN the consequences resulting from the French revolution had involved us in a war, our country called upon its patriotic volunteers to turn out and assemble in its defence. I was still resident at Tunbridge Wells, and, though not proprietor of a single foot of land in the county of Kent, yet I found myself in the hearts of my affectionate friends and fellow subjects; they immediately volunteered to mount and form themselves under my command as a troop of yeomen cavalry; I was diffident of my fitness to head them in that capacity, and, declining their kind offer, recommended to them a neighboring gentleman, who had served in the line, and held the rank of field officer upon half pay. Men of their principles and spirit could not fail to be respectable, and they are now serving with credit to their captain and themselves under the command of the Lord Viscount Boyne, who resides at Tunbridge Wells, and together with the duties attendant on his commission, as commander of this respectable corps, executes the office of a magistrate for the county, not less amiable and honorable in his private character, than useful and patriotic in his public one.

Some time after this, when certain leading gentlemen of the county began to make their tenders to government for raising corps of volunteer infantry, I no longer hesitated to obey the wishes of the loyal and spirited young men, who offered to enrol themselves under my command, and finding them amount upon the muster to two full companies, properly officered, I reported them to our excellent Lord Lieutenant of the county, the Earl of Romney, and received his Majesty's commission to command them with the rank of Major Commandant. I had instant proof that the zeal they had shown in turning out in their king and country's cause did not evaporate in mere professions, for to their assiduity and aptitude, to their exemplary and correct observance of discipline, and strict obedience to their officers, the warmest testimony that I could give would only do them justice. It was winter when we first enrolled, and every evening after striking work, till ten o'clock at night, we were incessantly at the drill, and after we had been practised in the manual, sometimes turning out for the march by moonlight, sometimes by torch-light. I had not a private that was not in the vigor of his youth; their natural carriage was erect and soldier-like, they fell readily into the attitude and step of a soldier on the march, for they were all artisans, mechanics, or manufacturers of Tunbridge ware, and I had not one who did the work of a mere laboring peasant amongst them, whilst every officer submitted to the rule I laid down, and did the duty and learned the exercise of a private in the line before he stood out and took command in his proper post.

Our service being limited to the district of the counties of Kent, Sussex, and Surry, no sooner were my companions fit for duty, than, at their unanimous desire, I reported them to the Secretary of State as ready and willing to serve in any part of England, and this their loyal tender being laid before the King, His Majesty was graciously pleased to signify to us his royal approbation of our zeal through his Secretary of State.

When the volunteer infantry were dismissed at the peace of Amiens, my men requested leave to hold their arms and serve without pay. At the same time they were pleased to honor me with the present of a sword by the hands of their serjeant-major, to the purchase of which every private had contributed, and which they rendered infinitely dear and valuable to me by engraving on the hilt of it—'That it was a tribute of their esteem for their beloved commander.'

The renewal of hostilities has again put them under my command, and I trust the warmth and sincerity of my unalterable attachment to them has now no need of appealing to professions. We know each other too well, and I am persuaded that there is not one amongst them, but will give me credit for the truth when I declare, that as a father loves his children, so do I love them. We have now augmented our strength to four companies, and from the experience I have repeatedly had of their conduct, when upon permanent duty, I am convinced, that if ever the necessity shall occur for calling them out upon actual service, they will be found steady in the hour of trial, and perfectly resolved never to disgrace the character of Men of Kent, or tarnish that proud trophy, which they inscribe upon their colors.

I humbly conceive that if we take into our consideration the prodigious magnitude and extent of the volunteer system, we shall find it has been productive of more real use, and less incidental embarrassment to government, than could have been expected.

We must make allowances for those who have been accustomed to look for the strength and resources of the nation only in its disposable force, if they are apt to undervalue the importance of its domestic army. But after the proofs, which the capital and country have given of the spirit, discipline, and good order of their volunteers, both cavalry and infantry, it is not wise or politic, or liberal to disparage them as some have attempted to do; there are indeed but few who have so done; the wonder is that there are any; but that a man should be so fond of his own dull jest as to risk it upon one, who has too much wit of his own not to spy out the want of it in others, is perfectly ridiculous; and I am persuaded, that a man of Colonel Birch's acknowledged merit as an officer, and established character for every good quality that denotes and marks the gentleman, would infinitely rather be the object of such a pointless sarcasm, than the author of it.

The man who lives to see many days, must look to encounter many sorrows. My eldest son, who had married the eldest daughter of the late Earl of Buckinghamshire, and sister of the present, died in Tobago, where he went to qualify for a civil employment in that island; and, some time after, death bereft me of my wife. Their virtues cannot need the ornament of description, and it has ever been my study to resign myself to the dispensations of Providence with all the fortitude I can summon, convinced that patience is no mark of insensibility, nor the parade of lamentation any evidence of the sincerity or permanency of grief.

My two surviving sons are happily and respectably married, and have families; I have the care, under chancery, of five children, relicts of the late William Badcock, Esquire, who married my second daughter, and died in my house at Tunbridge Wells, and I have the happiness to number nineteen grandchildren, some of whom have already lived to crown my warmest wishes, and I see a promise in the rest, that flatters my most sanguine hopes. These are comforts that still adhere to me, and whilst I have the kindness of my children, the attachment of my friends, and the candor of the public to look up to, I have ample cause to be thankful and contented.

Charles, the elder of my surviving sons, married the daughter of General Mathew, a truly noble and benevolent gentleman, loved and honored by all who know him, and who will be ever gratefully remembered by the island he has governed, and the army he has commanded.

William, the youngest, married Eliza, daughter of Mrs. Burt, and, when commanding His Majesty's ship the La Pique, in the

West Indies, being seized with the fever of the country at Saint Domingo, was sent home, as the only chance of saving him, and constrained to forfeit the command of that very capital frigate. When the young and amiable Princess Amelia was residing at Worthing for the benefit of the sea and air, my son, then commander of the Fly sloop of war, kept guard upon that station, prepared to accommodate her Royal Highness with his boats or vessels in any excursions on the water, which she might be advised to take. I came to Worthing, whilst he was there upon duty, and was permitted to pay my homage to the Princess. It was impossible to contemplate youth and beauty suffering tortures with such exemplary patience, and not experience those sensations of respect and pity, which such a contemplation naturally must inspire. When my daughter-in-law, Lady Albinia Cumberland, took her turn of duty as lady of the bed-chamber, I took the liberty through her hands to offer the few stanzas which are here inserted:—

'How long, just heav'n, shall Britain's royal maid
With meek submission these sad hours sustain?
How long shall innocence invoke thine aid,
And youth and beauty press the couch of pain?

Enough, dread pow'r, unless it be decreed,
To reconcile thee in these evil times,
That one pure victim for the whole should bleed,
And by her sufferings expiate our crimes.

And sure I am, in thine offended sight
If nothing but perfection can atone,
No wonder thy chastising rod should light
On one who hath no errors of her own.

But spare, Ah spare this object of our love,
For whose dear sake we're punish'd in our fears;
Send down thy saving angel from above,
And quench her pangs in our repentant tears.

Yes, they shall win compassion from the skies,
Man cannot be more merciful than heav'n:
Thy pangs, sweet saint, thy patience shall suffice,
And at thy suit our faults shall be forgiv'n.

And if, whilst every subject's heart is rack'd,
Our pious king presents a father's plea,
What heav'n with justice might from us exact
Heaven's mercy will remit to him and thee.

Nor will I doubt if thy dear mother's prayer,
Breath'd from her sorrowing bosom, shall prevail;
The sighs of angels are not lost in air,
Can then Amelia's sister-suitors fail?

Come then, heart-healing cherub, from on high,
Fresh dipt in dew of Paradise descend,

Bring tender sympathy with tearful eye,
  Bring Hope, bring Health, and let the Muse attend.

Stretch'd on her couch, beside the silent strand,
  Whose skirt's old Ocean's briny billows lave,
From the extremest verge of British land
  The languid fair one eyes the refluent wave.

Was ever suffering purity more meek,
  Was ever virgin martyr more resign'd?
  ark how the smile, yet gleaming on her cheek,
  Bespeaks her gentlest, best of human kind.

Around her stand the sympathising friends,
  Whose charge it is her weary hours to cheer,
Each female breast the struggling sigh distends,
  Whilst the brave veteran drops the secret tear.

And he, whose sacred trust it is to guard
  The fairest freight that ocean ever bore,
He shall receive his loyalty's reward
  In laurels won from Gallia's hostile shore.

Now let thy wings their healing balm distil,
  Celestial cherub, messenger of peace.
'Tis done; the tortur'd nerve obeys thy will,
  And with thy touch its angry throbbings cease.

Light as a sylph, I see the blooming maid
  Spring from her couch. O may my votive strain
Confirm'd evince, that neither I have pray'd,
  Nor thou, my Muse, hast prophesied in vain.'

I have now completed what occurred to me to say of an old man, whose writings have been very various, whose intentions have been always honest, and whose labors have experienced little intermission. I put the first pen to these Memoirs at the very close of the last year, and I conclude them in the middle of September. I had promised myself to the undertaking, and I was to proportion my dispatch to the measure of the time upon which, without presumption, I might venture to reckon. As many of my readers as may have staggered under the weight of such a bulky load, will have a fellow feeling for me, even though I shall have sunk under it: but if I have borne it through with tolerable success, and given an interest to some of the many pages which this volume numbers, I hope they will not mark with too severe a censure errors and inaccuracies—

Quas aut incuria fudit,
Aut humana parum cavit natura.

I have through life sincerely done my best according to my abilities for the edification of my fellow creatures and the honor of my God. I pretend to nothing, whereby to be commended or distinguished above others of my rate, save only for that good-will and human kindness which descended to me from my ancestors, and cannot properly deserve the name of virtue, as they cost no struggle for the exertion of them. I am not exempt from anger, but I never let it fasten on me till it harden into malice or revenge. I cannot pass myself off for better than I have been where I am about to go, and if before my departure I were now to take credit for merits which I have not, the few which I have would be all too few to atone for the deceit; but I am thoroughly weary of the task of talking of myself, and it is with unfeigned joy I welcome the conclusion of my task and my talk.

I have now only to devote this last page of my book, as it is probable I shall the last hour of my life, to the acknowledgments which are due to that beloved daughter, who, ever since the death of her mother, has been my inseparable companion and the solace of my age—

Extremum hunc, Arethusa, mihi concede laborem.

Frances Marianne, the youngest of my children, was born to me in Spain. After many long and dangerous returns of illness, it has pleased Providence to preserve to me the blessing of her life and health. In her filial affection I find all the comforts, that the best of friends can give me; from her talents and understanding I derive all the enjoyments that the most pleasing of companions can communicate. As she has witnessed every step in the progress of this laborious work, and cheered every hour of relaxation whilst I have rested from it, if these pages, which contain the Memoirs of her father's life, may happily obtain some notice from the world, by whomsoever they are read, by the same this testimony of my devotion to the best of daughters shall also be read; and, if it be the will of God, that here my literary labors are to cease for ever, I can say to the world for the last time, that this is a dedication, in which no flattery is mixed, a tribute to virtue, in which fiction has no part, and an effusion of gratitude, esteem and love, which flows sincerely from a father's heart.

CHAPTER XIII.

Supplement—Reasons for writing—Difficulties in speaking of living characters—His unpublished writings—Anecdote of his son and the seaman—Collision with Mr. Hayley—Cowper—Dr. Bentley—Pitt—Cicero—Lines to Pitt—Nelson—Lord Collingwood—Commemorates the victory and death of Nelson—Sharon Turner—Earl of Dorchester—Reform in the newspapers—Love of books—His health at Tunbridge Wells—Rev. Martin Benson—The men of Kent—Volunteer companies—Captain of infantry—Residents at Tunbridge Wells—Death of friends—Mr. Badcock—His children—Erskine—Answers to letters—Lord Mansfield—Anecdote of Charles Townshend—Conversational talents of Mansfield—Andrew Stuart—Lord North—Primate Robinson—Cathedral of Armagh—Sir William Robinson—Archbishop Moore—Doctor Moss—Anecdote of—Consequences of old age—Sir James Bland Burges—Moore—Sir William Spencer—Eccentricities of eminent men—Edinburgh reviewers—Rodney's nautical manœuvre—Rev. Mr. Higgs—Doctor Drake—Epic poem—The Exodiad—His wife—His daughter—Apology to Mr. Smith—Drury Lane and Covent Garden—Garrick—The stage—The profession of actor—Death of Fox—Mr. Higgs—Mistakes in his 'Memoirs'—Sir William Pepys—'A Hint to Husbands'—Napoleon—Conclusion.

February the 19th, 1806.

I AM this day seventy-four years old, and having given to the world an account of what I have been employed upon since I have belonged to it, I thought I had said quite enough of an humble individual, and that I might have been acquitted of my task, and dismissed to my obscurity; but certain friends, upon whose judgment and sincerity I have all possible reliance, tell me that I have disappointed their expectations in the narrative of what I have been concerned in since I came from Spain; a period which, being more within their own time, might, as they conceive, have been made more interesting to them, and to the rest of my readers.

It may be so; nay, I have reason to believe it is so, for I am conscious that I was impatient to conclude my work, and was intimidated by the apprehension of offending against that modesty of discourse, which becomes me to hold when I have no better subject to talk upon than myself.

In deference to their judgment I shall now attempt to fill up that chasm, which they have pointed out, in my imperfect work; but the volume, which is in the hands of the first purchasers, and which I have disposed of to them with all its errors,

I consider myself in honor bound to abide by; as I hold it not correctly fair to recommend a second edition by any means, that may contribute to degrade the first: I therefore leave untouched all which the liberal patrons of my book are already possessed of, and now tender to them a few additional pages, which they may, or may not, attach to their volume, as they shall see fit.

There are considerations, that will weigh with every writer, when his subject leads him to discourse of living characters; there is at once temptation to indulge his friendly prejudices, and motives to deter him from exposing all his free opinions. Hence it comes to pass, that, being checked by truth on one side, and by delicacy on the other, he finds his only safe resource in silence or an inoffensive tame neutrality.

If therefore I have written indolently of this latter period of my life, it was not because I had been more indolent in it, for I might have said, without offence to modesty, that I have been much more active as a literary man since I have ceased to be busied as an official one; but it was because I had fallen into heavy roads, and like the traveller, who, wearied by the tediousness of the way, puts four horses to his chaise for the concluding stage, so did I hasten to terminate my task, shutting my eyes against those objects that would have operated to prolong it.

I will only say in general, that there is a multiplicity of my unpublished productions, written since I came from Spain, which, to those who shall search for them and find them, will evince my industry. The world has such an amiable partiality to dead men's doings, that, perhaps, when these embryos shall see the light, and my eyes shall be forever closed against it, I may look to receive a vast deal of mercy and some praise, when I can no longer be the better for either. If our resurrection critics shall persist to rummage amongst the graves, and carry their eyes like the hare, who sees distinctly only what is behind her, they may probably spy out my shade in the background, and bring it into notice. It is naturally to be presumed that, if they would come manfully forward for a living author, the living author would be better pleased; but this he must not expect; the temple of their praise is reared with dry bones and skulls, and till he is a skeleton he cannot be their hero; in this, however, they are more generous than the legislature, who have given so short a date to the tenure of his copyright, that, till that is out, the circulation of his works can scarce commence. Now although this mode of dealing may not exactly suit the living man's occasions, yet there is a kind of posthumous justice in it, as it leads him to expect a consideration for what he does some time or other, notwithstanding he shall have done it so much the worse for the discouragement which he met with whilst he was about it. It also warns him what he is to expect from the company he lives with, and apprises him of the luxury he is to enjoy when he is out of their society.

My youngest son, now a post-captain in the royal navy, had a lazy, pilfering rascal in his ship, though all the while a prime seaman; when he had seized him up to the gun for some enormity, he liberated him without a stroke, and reminding him of his capacity to perform his duty with credit to himself and good service to his country, appointed him at a word to be captain of the forecastle. Reformation instantly took place in the man's mind; promotion roused his pride; pride inspired honesty, and he thenceforth acquitted himself as an excellent and trustworthy seaman, and was pointed out to me from his quarter-deck as such. Now, according to the moral of my story, we may imagine a young beginner to set out lazily on his first start into authorship: he may, like the seaman, have good stores in his own capacity, but through indolence or something else prefer the shorter process of plagiarism to the laborious efforts of invention. I humbly apprehend that his reviewing officer, instead of flogging him round the fleet of critics, may come sooner to his point, if the object of correction be amendment, by copying the humane experiment of the gallant officer, whom I have taken the liberty to instance, and have the honor of being allied to.

I flatter myself I have through life been not unmindful of the rule, which I have been so frequently importunate to recommend; and I must own in some instances I have had no better reason for my praise and commendation of a brother author than because he was alive; for I was perfectly convinced he would not mend upon discouragement, and I conceived perhaps it was as easy for him to be better, as it was for me to persuade myself that he was not bad.

In these endeavors I have sometimes been defeated, and an instance has occurred since the publication of my Memoirs, which proves how little certainty there is that fair intentions shall be fairly understood. I have unfortunately for myself given offence to Mr. Hayley, and put him to the trouble of stopping the press, whilst advancing peaceably towards the completion of its labor, merely to make room for me in his supplementary pages to the life of Cowper, and with no other cause in view, that I can comprehend, but to show the world that he can be angry without cause. The passages he alludes to in my

Memoirs are in the hands, if not in the recollection, of my readers. As they gave umbrage to him, I wish I could extinguish them; but that is not in my power, and he has made them necessary for my exculpation; to them of course I must appeal; to his pages there is no need that I should make any reference, for all the world will read what Mr. Hayley writes. Still I must think that in the judgment of all men, who have read us both, I shall stand acquitted of any purpose to affront Mr. Hayley; for surely I may hope there cannot be a chance that any man besides himself can so misconstrue and pervert the compliment I meant to pay him.

He doubts if I deserve the praise he gave me; I doubt so too, and my doubts were prior to his. I believe he also doubts if I am justified in publishing his verses. I confess I am at his mercy upon that account; yet he gives me reason to hope he cannot be very angry with me, when I can quote his own authority in extenuation of my fault, for he says—that 'the praise of Cowper is so singularly valuable from the reserve and purity of his disposition, that it would almost seem a cruel injury to suppress a particle of it, when deliberately or even cursorily bestowed'—(page 4 Add. Pages). Now, why it should be 'almost a cruel injury' to suppress Mr. Cowper's praise, and anything like an offence to publish Mr. Hayley's, I do not comprehend; I have ever paid my testimony both publicly and in private to Mr. Hayley's genius, and how then can I be supposed insensible to his praise? Though I should profess myself even as vain of his applause as I could have been of Mr. Cowper's, there is one man at least in the world, who methinks might in his heart be moved to pardon and excuse my error. I must confess, however, that if Mr. Hayley had treated me no better than his hero has treated his three kittens in the 'Colubriad,' I should not have esteemed myself justified in exposing his *lusus poeticus* to the ridicule of the reader.

I had not the happiness to know the hero of Mr. Hayley, and I am not quite sure that I have a clear conception of his character from his biographer's description of it; for when I am told in one page of the reserve and purity of his disposition, and in another, close ensuing, of his unsuspecting innocence and sportive gayety, I am rather puzzled how to reconcile these seeming contrarieties; especially when I am again informed of a peculiarity in his character, a gay and tender gallantry, perfectly distinct from amorous attachment—a reserve of this nature was indeed a peculiarity in the character of this gentleman; and whilst the ladies had nothing to apprehend from his gay and tender gallantry, his male acquaintance, who enjoyed the unsuspecting innocence and sportive gayety of his disposition, very possibly overlooked the reserve of it, and found him a very pleasant companion with the property most decisively characteristic of a very dull one.

Now I want all that respect for the gay reserve of the departed poet, which should cause me to appreciate his praise above that of the living one; and with all the reverence that I can summon, for a gallantry so perfectly distinct from amorous attachment, I cannot bring myself to honor Cowper as a poet one whit the more for his non-amorous gallantry, or Mr. Hayley, in the same light, one atom the less, though any one should officiously suggest that his gallantry may be of a different complexion. I have nothing more to offer in my own defence.

On the part of Doctor Bentley I shall hope that Mr. Hayley describes his character with no better precision than he does the reserve of Mr. Cowper, when he stigmatizes him as an arrogant critic, subject to fits of dogmatical petulance, an imperious Patagonian polemic. These would be hard words in some men's mouths, but I would fain convince the author of 'The Triumphs of Temper,' that I have not been less edified than delighted by his poem; and as the natural suavity of his disposition has induced him to promise that my grandfather shall rest in peace for the present, I can assure Mr. Hayley that I should credit him for his mercy, if I could feel any horror of his vengeance; but when I know he cannot disturb that rest, over which he presumes to arrogate a dispensing power, I must put the best interpretation on his language that it will bear, and calmly tell him—if it was not nonsense, it would be something worse.

But when Mr. Hayley, after venting these invectives against Doctor Bentley, is pleased to announce to the world that he meditates to pay his respects to him again, if Heaven allows him life and leisure to write such a preface as he wishes to prefix to the 'Milton' of Cowper—it seems to me that if this ingenious gentleman had not stopped the press at all, or only stopped his pen before he wrote this vaunting and inveterate paragraph, it would have been a rescue to his reputation. Let the public now decide betwixt the station which Mr. Hayley fills in literature and that which my ancestor once held, and say if I have cause to tremble at the flourish of this proud challenger's trumpet: No: I am well aware that although a gnat can sound a loud horn, it is but a little insect; and I am confident that arrogance and petulance, when charged upon my ancestor by one so open to the rebound, will neither penetrate nor fix, but return back to the place from whence they came.

In the mean time I hope that Mr. Hayley, who piously refers his purpose to the will of Heaven, may have life and leisure allowed to him for all worthy undertakings, and wisdom to abstain from all ridiculous ones; and as for this meditated preface, which he brandishes over the ashes of dead Bentley, I hope he will wish to write nothing but what will do himself credit, and then I hope it will be just such a one as he wishes to prefix; but if it shall be his pleasure to attack him with a repetition of hard names and foul language, and calls that paying his respects, I trust there will be found some friend to truth and good manners, some temperate defender of the real character of that good and benevolent man, who will bring his rash assailant to a better sense by convincing him how very little oil will serve to suffocate a wasp.

Mr. Hayley calls Doctor Bentley the god of my infantine idolatry. I have simply related what I knew of him as a boy; I hope there was nothing fulsome or extravagant in my puerile anecdotes, and trust I have neither made him a god, nor myself an idolater. I do not charge that upon the biographer of Mr. Cowper, though in me as an infant such weakness would be more excusable than in him as a man. Still I own myself impressed with a warm and heartfelt respect for the memory of my grandfather, but it is a respect 'on this side of idolatry,' and when I said of Mr. Hayley, that he was one of the last men living who should disparage Bentley, it was because I regarded him as one of the best classical scholars of his day.

In conclusion, I declare that I never meant to give offence to Mr. Hayley, and as I think he had no shadow of a right to take offence, I cannot consider myself bound to apologize.

I seldom hear the present era spoken of as I think it ought to be, for sure I am that it has been brilliantly distinguished for a variety of characters great in science, arts, and arms. Should I venture to pronounce upon it as the most luminous in the annals of our country, I am not sure that any man would be able to confute the assertion, but I will throw down no such gauntlet to the champions of past times; yet, although instances may not occur of individual pre-eminence so striking as some, which record could supply, still the general diffusion of talents is so very much increased, that it operates as a leveller, which nothing less than first-rate genius can surmount.

I have lived to see Pitt, Nelson, and Cornwallis struck out of the number of the living, yet neither eloquence, valor or integrity are buried in their ashes.

Cicero published studied orations; Pitt uttered unpremeditated speeches; yet who is prepared to say that the eloquence of the

English senator was inferior to the eloquence of the Roman pleader? Cicero wrote innumerable epistles, crammed with praises of himself; I believe there is no Atticus in existence, who can produce such specimens of the vanity of the modern. Cicero humbled himself to Lucceius, and made abject suit even to his partiality, imploring him to write a panegyric on his consulship; Pitt has never been accused of paying court to any man as the historian of his administration, but on the contrary carried himself too loftily towards men of talents, for any such to be in much good humor with him. Cicero had many objects that attracted his ambition, his mind was stored with various kinds of knowledge, and ardently attached to various studies and pursuits; one passion only, untainted by self-interest, unseduced by pleasure, took early possession of Pitt's whole heart, and only left it in the moment when it ceased to beat. If I were now living in times as tumultuous as those when the partisans of Antony stuck up the head of Cicero in the forum, I might be afraid to venture an opinion as to what I take that ruling passion to have been; but under correction of those who, from their knowledge of Mr. Pitt, are better able to judge of his motives and impressions, I conceive that a true and zealous love for his country accompanied him through life to death, and was paramount to every other object in his thoughts.

I am giving my conception of his feelings as a man; of his character as a statesman I do not presume to speak. Those respectable persons, who regularly opposed his public measures as Minister, could not well give countenance to the honors that were decreed to him at his public funeral; but when some, who had efficiently coincided with them in the policy of those measures, coincided also in the condemnation of them, it must have been a strong case, either of conscience or of party spirit, which compelled them, by arraigning him, to criminate themselves. This is rather an awkward alternative for them, as I am afraid the world is not always disposed to put the best interpretation on a doubtful case. At the same time, it is a little difficult to understand the principle of a resolution, in which both old and new opponents united, to discharge his debts out of the public purse, which to my vulgar apprehension seems like complimenting the extravagance of a man in whom they would not acknowledge a single merit that could tend to atone for his bad economy. If he was not in their opinion a useful servant to the public, why should they consent to make him an expensive one? All this perhaps can be readily unravelled, but how he should be entitled to be set clear in what he had outrun, when he did not earn what he had received, is a mystery to me of which no doubt there is a very competent solution, though I cannot guess what it is.

I never was in a private room with Mr. Pitt but once, and that was for a few minutes only at Burlington House. I recollect having troubled him with three several letters at distant periods; but he did not trouble himself to answer any one of them. In the first of these I tendered myself as a candidate for a literary office with a salary so very small, as could of itself be no gentleman's object, in the solicitation: I dare say I did not deserve the office, but I must think that I deserved an answer.

The second letter was very thoroughly considered, for I wrote it at the suggestion of a common friend to us both, who examined and approved of it. It contained a short and modest recital of my services and sufferings, and in general terms humbly prayed to be recommended for some small bounty from the crown in alleviation of my case. I trust it is not too much to say, that justice, humanity, and the manners of a gentleman dictated some reply to this unassuming petition: none was given; not a single word was ever vouchsafed.

The last letter, which I addressed to Mr. Pitt, was upon the question of some proposed arrangements with respect to volunteers, when he was out of office and commanding in person the Cinque-Ports volunteer battalions. I had the honor to command a corps of some years longer standing than his own, and it was a communication which, for the matter it contained, and the terms in which it was couched, ought not to have been overlooked by a gentleman engaged in the same service, and serving in the same county. It imposed no trouble; it solicited no favor; nay, I may venture to say (as it was written with the concurrence and assistance of my brother officers) that it conferred a favor. I took care, in my respect for them, that it should reach his hands; it received no answer.

I have thought it not improper to detail these circumstances, because I would not pass myself upon the reader as a man who had been in the favor of Mr. Pitt, or as if I were making a display of my gratitude; when in fact I have no such feeling in my heart, and only remember him as a man who spurned my humble applications from him with a degree of contempt, which could not fail to divest me of every motive to admire him, save what his great endowments and the compulsive power of his superior genius absolutely extorted from me.

As for the brief delineation of his character, so far as it might be traced by one who viewed him at a distance, I conceive I have not greatly mistaken features, which were so continually in the eyes of the public that he may be said to have sat for his portrait every day of his life. He had so few offsets and ramifications from the one great rooted passion of his mind, that we need not search deeply into his private history or habits for the discovery of those fine and finishing touches which in some instances constitute the whole spirit of the likeness.

A statue in brass was the highest honor the Athenians could decree to a mortal, and many of their minor deities were not accounted worthy to receive it. Upon the presumption that it may be in contemplation to devote a public monument to the memory of this great orator, I take the liberty to insert a few lines, not with the most distant idea of recommending them to the sculptor, but simply to assign to them a short and transient habitation on this perishable page—

'To thee, great orator, whose early mind,
Broke forth with splendor that amaz'd mankind,
To thee, whose lips with elegance were fraught,
By which the aged and the learn'd were taught,
To thee, the wonder of Britannia's isle,
A grateful senate rears this marble pile,
Convinc'd that after ages must approve
This pious token of a nation's love.

Here though the sculptor simply graves thy name,
He gives thy titles and records thy fame;
Thy great endowments had he aim'd to trace,
The swelling catalogue had wanted space.

Though vast the range of thine expansive soul,
Thy God and country occupied the whole:
In that dread hour, when ev'ry heart is tried,
The Christian triumph'd whilst the mortal died;
In the last gasp of thine expiring breath
The pray'r yet quiver'd on the lip of death:
Hear this, ye Britons, and to God be true,
For know that dying pray'r was breath'd for you."[1]

---

[1] Pitt, throughout his career, was an object of unbounded pride and attachment to the most powerful classes of his countrymen. They relied on his great capacity during the stormy times in which he held the reins of authority, with unfaltering trust. Yet an eminent living statesman, whose popularity at one time rose to almost as high a pitch as ever did Pitt's, but whose character inspires much less respect, has declared that, excepting the union with Ireland, which was forced upon him by a rebellion, and which was both corruptly and imperfectly carried, so as to produce the smallest possible benefit to either country, Pitt 'has not left a single measure behind him for which the community, whose destinies he so long swayed, has any reason to respect his memory; while, by want of firmness, he was the cause of an impolity and extravagance, the effects of which are yet felt, and will oppress us beyond the life of the youngest now alive.'—*Brougham's Sketches of Statesmen of the Time of George III.*

A difference of opinion, however, still divides politicians as to Pitt's merits as a statesman; and there are those who, in this respect, applaud him as highly as Brougham condemns him. A generous critic, who steers a middle

As for the illustrious naval hero, who fell in the glorious action of Trafalgar, his fame is exalted on a pedestal, which envy cannot scale, and his funeral triumph carried with it to his grave the hearts of the whole nation. I walked about the streets of the capital on the night of the intelligence, which reached us of his victory and of his death; I remarked with peculiar satisfaction the divided feelings of the common people; they knew not how to rejoice, yet they wanted a triumph; the occasion demanded it, but they were unfitted for enforcing and disqualified from enjoying it: I was charmed with their dilemma.

Great things have been done for the family of this departed hero, and the nation has a right to something more from the present inheritor of his titles and rewards than the mere fortuitous merit of being the vehicle to transmit his name and honors to posterity; I hope he will not tarnish them in their passage by anything that is not congenial with the spirit of his predecessor. In the mean time it appears to me, who am only a looker-on, that the meritorious services of Lord Collingwood in the action itself, and during those disastrous duties that resulted from it, constitute a claim and establish a reputation, hardly secondary to those of his commanding admiral; but this is a subject not properly under my contemplation in these memoirs; a scene not within the short horizon of my humbler prospect; I did, however, say a little through the organs of the stage, and was prepared to say more, if I had not been silenced; still I bore my part in the dirges, which my brother poets sung upon that memorable occasion, and wrote the following impromptu, which Mr. Wroughton addressed to the audience at Drury Lane on the evening of the day in which the news arrived:—

'Is there a man who this great triumph hears,
And with his transport does not mingle tears?

---

course between the extremes of opinion, thus remarks on his talents as a minister: 'The difficulties of his situation were of a nature wholly unparalleled in history; a person of great steadiness might well have faltered in his course through such a sea of troubles; and the resources of a very fertile mind might have easily been exhausted by the strange and novel exigencies of the crisis. Nor have we a right severely to blame him who met this demand, rather by extraordinary devices than happy ones. A minister may well be deemed able whom we must allow to have been equal to such novel emergencies; and much of greatness may be attached to the name of Pitt, while we are compelled wholly to reject the extravagant praises which his followers have lavished upon him. In the policy which he pursued during the more ordinary period which preceded the Revolution, far less appears to censure; and, with the exception of the Russian armament and negotiation, his conduct in relation to foreign powers was firm, consistent, and prosperous. The able and successful measures adopted in the affairs of Holland gained the unqualified approbation of all parties, and the French commercial treaty was never impeached with any effect.'

For though Britannia's flag victorious flies,
Who can refrain from grief when Nelson dies?
Stretch'd on his deck amidst surrounding fires,
There, phœnix-like, the gallant chief expires.
Cover'd with trophies let his ashes rest,
His memory lives in every British breast:
His dirge our groans, his monument our praise,
And whilst each tongue this grateful tribute pays,
His soul ascends to heav'n in glory's brightest blaze.'

I also composed a melo-dramatic piece, which was represented on the third night following, and repeated several times after with that effect which the subject naturally inspired.

For this small service I was favored with the present of a gold snuff-box, and hold myself much honored by the gift.

I had not yet ceased from my attempts to commemorate the victory and death of Nelson, but with more deliberation wrote a piece of two short acts, which was to have been performed at Covent Garden Theatre on the evening after his public funeral. The music was composed, the scenes were preparing, and the drama was in rehearsal, when I was informed that the representation was interdicted by authority. The objections, which so palpably bore against the exhibition of that affecting event at the opera house, were in no respect whatever applicable to my composition, and I am to this hour uninformed of the reasons which actuated the Lord Chamberlain for the suppression of it.

I have noticed with great sensibility the very candid and encouraging reception which my volume of memoirs has been favored with by the public, and I am possessed of letters from some men of eminent talents, which have amply overpaid me for the labor of the task.

That which I am honored with from Mr. Sharon Turner, I shall treasure up for my posterity, as a proud memorial of my having gained the approbation of one of the best writers, of the most learned antiquarians, and most enlightened scholars of his time.

I beg leave to offer my most grateful acknowledgments to the writers of the Reviews, who have universally treated me with the greatest liberality, and in several instances bestowed upon my labors those encomiums which (without affecting a consciousness that I do not feel) I am duly sensible are above my deservings; but it is charitable in them to praise the efforts of a worn-out veteran, and fan the sparks of an expiring flame.

From the amiable Earl of Dorchester I have been flattered with a letter, which, amongst the kind expressions it abounds in towards me, pays a tribute to the memory of the deceased Lord

Sackville, truly gratifying to my feelings, and highly honorable to those of his near relation the writer of it.

I can well believe I have dwelt too long upon the narration of what occurred to me in Spain; yet I must think that every man naturally wishes to exculpate his conduct in a transaction, where his efforts are known to have failed of success; and although I was suspicious that the importance of the subject was not sufficient to compensate for the prolixity of it, still I felt a kind of melancholy gratification in the detail, which none need envy and the humane will pardon; let me be acquitted of all trespasses but such as they may forgive, and I will not repine.

Though I have not been at ease in my circumstances since I came from Spain, and probably never shall, I do not regret my going thither, being proudly conscious of having done my duty, and that I can look back upon no period of my past life with a clearer self-acquittal than I can on that. I am past all hope of receiving any recompense for my sacrifices, and I have accommodated myself to all those privations which the circumscription of my means prescribes. Though in my seventy-fifth year, I am even now in the act of levying contributions on my brains, and thanks be to Providence, age has not quite exhausted the resource which nature and acquirement have endowed me with.

I remember the time, when the malevolent personality of the public prints was truly diabolical; I have lived to see more just and manly principles prevail upon the face of them; this is a revolution to rejoice in; their only fault seems now to be that of tantalizing us with too many good dinners, that we do not partake of; and I must think, if they would make one grand and sweeping remove of the whole, their publications would be profited by it. But if it better suits them to record the splendor in which our great men live, let us not be fastidious readers, but let us recollect that every one of us, without exception, is to a certain degree warmed and enlightened by that effulgence, which a luminous and exalted character, like a beacon on an eminence, scatters and disperses all around. If their information does not serve them to report how wittily these great men talk over their tables, let us hear at least how learnedly they eat; for I can give no better reason for the slight respect in which I hold the science of cookery, except that I am too much of an Englishman to instance any one acquirement, in which the genius of our countrymen must truckle to the talents of the French.

When the historians talk to us of the dark ages, they certainly do not mean to insinuate that the sun was less bright, and the sky not so clear in those days as in certain others, but by a figure call that dark which science and the human genius do not illuminate; surely, then, if we wish to live in the light, it is every man's interest to cherish his neighbor's taper, convinced that, should he blow it out, his own will burn no brighter. I know I have said something to this purpose nearly a hundred times over, but as I am nearly a hundred years old, I will say it once more, and perhaps not for the last time. Let me go to my grave with the consciousness of having succeeded in disposing my contemporaries to foster and encourage one another in the spirit of brotherly love and benevolence, and I have not lived in vain.

When I review that period of my time which I have passed since my return from Spain, I cannot but be sensible that, if I shall leave behind me anything worthy the attention of posterity, it must have been chiefly written within that period when I composed the poem of 'Calvary,' the essays in the Observer, and the novel of 'Henry.' In my retreat at Tunbridge Wells, as soon as I had discharged myself from my house in Portland Place, I sat down with my family, and never had an abiding place in town after that. From that hour to the present moment what cause have I not had to bless my God for having endowed me with that untired attachment to my books and to my pen (those never-failing comforters and friends), which has enabled me to meet and patiently to endure many crosses and some misfortunes of no common magnitude. How fortunate am I now, in the winter of my age, that never, in the sunshine of my younger days, when the world comparatively smiled upon me, did I sink into idleness, or surrender myself to any pleasures that could rival those more temperate and permanent resources which education and early habits of study had supplied me with!

There is no sure way of providing against the natural ills that flesh is heir to, but by the cultivation of the mind. The senses can do little for us, and nothing lasting. When they have for a time enjoyed everything they can wish for, they will ultimately be led to wish for what they can no longer enjoy. A man who wants mental powers, wants everything; for though fortune were to heap superfluities of every species upon him, the very overflowings of prosperity would destroy his peace, as an abundance of things without can never compensate for a vacuity within.

More than twenty years I lived at Tunbridge Wells, inhabiting the same house, and cultivating a plot of garden ground, embowered with trees, and amply sufficient for a profusion of flowers, which my old servant Thomas Camis nursed and took delight in: it was then, if only common justice had been rendered to me by government, I should have enjoyed as much tranquillity and content as can fall to the lot of imperfect man; for my mind was emancipated from the shackles of office, and I seemed to have a property in the day, for which I paid no tax to business. Whilst I lived in town I had hardly ever passed a year without a long and dangerous fever, but in this salubrious climate I never once experienced so much indisposition as to confine me to my bed even for a single hour. In possession of a most excellent wife, I had all the happiness that, as a husband, I could enjoy, and I had seen my eldest daughter Elizabeth married to one of the best and most amiable of men: his choice was conspicuously disinterested; for if anything like worldly wisdom could have found admittance to his generous heart, he might, and must, have sought—*fortunam ex aliis*—neither could the lure of affluence and establishment be the motive that induced my child to share the fortunes of Lord Edward Bentinck. No circumstances in life could more clearly evince the purity of affection in both parties. They have been happy in their lives, and I trust, with God's favor, as the promise is so fair, they will be blest in their posterity. To this beloved daughter I dedicated the volumes of the 'Observer,' and in the unabating duty and affection of her benevolent and grateful heart, I never saw, or fancied that I saw, a moment's variation.

Fortunate as I accounted myself in my location at Tunbridge Wells, and gratified by the kindness and good-will of the people, I was not contented to reside in idleness amongst them, but in everything, that concerned their interests, to the best of my power took an active part, and I flatter myself that some opportunities occurred, when my zeal was not without effect.

A service to the souls of men is above all others, and whilst I am entitled to consider myself as the happy instrument of introducing their present exemplary minister, the Reverend Martin Benson, I don't claim to be remembered by them on account of less important services. Unblemished in his morals, correct in the discharge of every duty that his sacred function can involve, this excellent servant of Christ approves himself the faithful shepherd of his flock. I have had the experience of years in contemplating his merits as the friend of the industrious poor, the reformer of the idle and unwary, and the ever-ready intercessor for the truly penitent at the approach of death.

Mr. Benson cannot need this testimony, and perhaps from me he has not looked to receive it; but I am incapable of withholding this tribute to his virtues, which is so justly due, and, without attempting to establish any better interest in his thoughts than I already have experienced, bid him everlastingly farewell.

I call to mind a conversation I held with my ever-kind and respected friend Primate Robinson, upon one of his visits to Tunbridge Wells, soon after Mr. Benson's induction, respecting the number of seceders, who in times of past laxity had fallen off from the established mode of worship, and gone astray after strange and whimsical teachers. Whilst I was describing to him some of these motley congregations, and the unwearied efforts of Mr. Benson for reclaiming them, he said to me, in his plain and pointed way: 'If you wish to get these people back again, you must sing them in; they won't come to your preaching; argument will do nothing with them; but they have itching ears, and will listen to a hymn or an anthem, and as you have an organ, such as it is, you must set to work and assemble the best singers which your place affords.' I need not say this good advice was followed, for it was the very measure we had projected, and our rural choir soon became conspicuous and in credit. In the mean time, Mr. Benson's admonitions, backed by our melodies, thinned the ranks of the seceders, and a certain female apostle was deserted by her closet congregation, and thenceforth devoted her attention to a favorite monkey, who profited more by her caresses, and about as much by her instructions, as the silly souls who had been lectured by her.

The men of Kent, properly so called, have a point of honor, of which they are extremely jealous, and as they in general merit to be trusted, they are not very patient to endure suspicion. They will hold tenaciously and litigiously to their point, so long as you dispute it; but refer it to their honor, and they shall award that demand upon them as too little, which, so long as you enforced it, they contended was too much; of this I could adduce a case most strikingly in point.

Of the characters of the people in and about the spot, where I have so long been resident, I ought to be a judge, for I have mixed with them as fellow subjects, and commanded them as fellow soldiers; and if I were not forward to acknowledge the just cause I have ever had to love them, to contribute to their comforts, to listen to their sorrows and to bestir myself for their interests, I should be a most ungrateful man.

It is no small credit to the loyalty of Tunbridge Wells, that it is the head-quarters of one troop of yeoman cavalry, and four companies of volunteer infantry. What is likely to be the fate of us, who come under the last-mentioned description, it would be highly unbecoming in me even to conjecture, forasmuch as the measures which are to decide upon us are, at the moment of my writing this, only in their progress, but not complete. This, however, I will take the liberty to say in vindication of the good order, aptitude and discipline of the volunteers (not partially applying those properties to the corps which I have the honor to command, but generally to others, which I have had opportunities to observe) that no other possible method could be taken for rendering them that dry stick, which cannot vegetate, but by depriving them of their permanent duty. When that is done, I most devoutly hope that the evil day, that was heretofore so imminent, will be henceforth so entirely out of sight, as to leave no responsibility on the score of prudence, no charge but that of ingratitude with the projector or projectors of those measures, which are so infallibly contrived to divest them of their usefulness and deprive them of their energy.

The first time I was ordered out upon permanent duty, I had men employed upon the king's works at Hythe, who were absent upon leave; every one of these brave lads came in on the evening before I marched, and took their shilling a day with me and their straw at night, in lieu of the high pay which they earned as carpenters and masons. Sorry I am to add, that when I had marched them home, and they went down to their work again, the director sent them back, and treated my most earnest appeal for their re-employment, backed by certificates of their good behavior, with contempt.

Can I suppose that men like these would disgrace their colors, or desert their officers? Their officers, I am sure, will exchange that confidence with them, and I believe there is no commandant, who was not satisfied of the alertness of his men in that crisis, when expectation watched the beacon that was to give the signal for their turning out upon a moment's notice. It was not then the season to inquire from what shops they issued, and the buffoon, who had risked a silly sneer at any man's vocation, would have met about as much applause for his gabble as a goose would for her hissing.

I readily admit that it must be every loyal man's wish to keep alive the martial spirit of the country, but how it can be any rational man's expectation to accomplish that wish by discouraging and revolting the volunteers, is a riddle that defies solution.

I was a captain of infantry in the year 1747, and am perhaps at this time the most aged field officer of volunteers in the kingdom; but if ever it shall be my lot to find myself under the command of the youngest major in the line, I shall not be the less obedient to my superior, though he should issue out his orders to me in the person of my grandson.

Let him who is now master of the fate of hundreds of thousands of his majesty's brave and loyal subjects, yet carrying arms in their king's and country's cause, lower them to what level he sees fit, he cannot take from them the conscious recollection that they have done their duty, and will hold a rank in history, of which it is in no man's power to strip them.

It was no common recommendation to a place of residence, where our summer society could boast of visitors so respectable as the Lord Chief Justice Mansfield, the Ex-Premier Lord North, the Duke of Leeds, the Lord Primate Robinson, the Lord Chancellor Rosslyn, Archbishop Moore, Bishop Moss, and others, who, like them, have paid the debt of nature, and are now no more.

I must confess when these, and some less illustrious, but more near and dearer to my heart, were struck down, it seemed to me as if the place had lost its sunshine, and our walks, so often paced by their steps, had been strewed with their tombs. Within the period of my residence at Tunbridge Wells I have felt the loss of many friends; I have followed Lord Sackville to his vault at Withyham, my lamented wife to her grave in the church of Frant, and there also I caused to be deposited the remains of William Badcock, Esq., the husband of my second daughter, Sophia, and father of five children, awarded to my care by chancery, and looking up to me for the education that is to decide upon their future destinies. My God! can I presume to hope that thou wilt give me life to execute this sacred trust, and train them in the way, poor innocents, wherein they ought to go?

This young man, Mr. Badcock, died a victim to excess in the prime of life, before he had attained the age of thirty. He had received his education at the Charter House and at the University of Oxford. He had good natural parts, an uncommon strength of memory, read much and recited well and copiously from our English poets; he was no contemptible amateur actor upon the model of Kemble, and exhibited himself repeatedly upon the stages of Bath and Tunbridge Wells, in the parts of Hamlet, Richard, Jaffier, and perhaps some others. He had a great share of a peculiar kind of humor, was an admirable mimic, and at times would be extremely pleasant and entertaining in society; but the general turn of his temper and habits was reserved and gloomy, proudly independent, too quick in conceiving himself affronted, and much too slow in regaining his good humor when he had discovered his mistake. I have often found him under the visitation of these sullen fits of discontent, for which I could assign no cause; in this disposition, as it should seem, he had estranged himself from me for a considerable length of time, residing at Bath, till I was informed by a common friend of his being in town, unattended by any servant, and dangerously ill. I found him in the public room of a coffee house, where he had taken his lodging, and most evidently in the last stage of an incurable and confirmed decay. He received me with extreme affection, and seemed greatly penetrated by the attentions which I paid him in his solitary and alarming situation. I called in the assistance of an eminent physician, who, upon a consultation, confirmed my apprehensions that his case was irrecoverable; the country air was, however, recommended, and I received him in my own house at Tunbridge Wells, where he languished for some few days, and with pious resignation, whilst invoking blessings on his children, whom he recommended to my care, closed his short term of life.

Three of these five fatherless relicts are boys, and as I distributed my four sons between the fleet and army, even so, if my life is spared, I meditate to deal with these grandsons, who seem by nature endowed with vigor both of body and of spirit for their destination. The eldest, a boy of brilliant parts, has now completed more than half his training time, and is serving in his majesty's frigate La Loire, under the command of Captain Maitland; that gallant and distinguished officer reports in terms of my young charge, that inspire me with the warmest hopes of his well-doing and as I think I can foresee that we shall have to fight for our altars and our hearths before the present generation shall pass off, I should be sorry at my soul to suppose that any one of my posterity, over whom I have control, were not in train to take his part in that decisive day, whenever it shall come.

In the arrangement of this business, which gives me the superintendence of my grandchildren's education under the authority of the court of chancery, it was my good fortune to find myself in the hands of a most sincere and honorable friend, who conducted the whole with great legal ability, and delivered the children into my care, bringing them from Bath to Tunbridge Wells. To Mr. Henry Fry I am beholden for every comfort that has accrued to me respecting that ill-fated portion of my family; and so many have been the instances which I have experienced of his invariable affection, his correct integrity and disinterested services ever since, that if I could neglect to render him this public mark of my esteem and love, I should be guilty of the worst ingratitude.

When I first enrolled my companies of volunteer infantry, this young and ardent enthusiast in his king's and country's cause, then living at Tunbridge Wells, resorted to me with several recruits which his popularity had attached to him, and from that hour to the present, at which he is now serving as captain of one of the companies under my command, I have had the gratification of witnessing the true and steady services to the corps, and his cordial attachment to me and to his brother officers.

As my friend is happy in a most amiable and excellent wife, and is already the father of four young children, I have induced him to place his son under my eye at the training school, to which I have sent my grandsons, at Ramsgate, till they are all fit to be removed to Westminster; in the mean time, I have the gratification to see him entering on a more extensive field of business with his worthy and respectable partner, Mr. Crutchley, of Clifford's Inn. In this, and everything else, which concerns his honor, interest, or happiness, I must heartily participate; and I hope my Lord Chancellor Erskine is not angry with me for the letter which, in the zeal of friendship for this excellent young man, I took the liberty to address to him, and which in fact being little more than an humble offering of my respectful congratulations, was naturally considered as the tribute of a person too obscure to be entitled to an answer.

I have known a man as nobly born, as highly endowed and as fully occupied as the illustrious personage I allude to, who never suffered a letter to be thrown by unacknowledged. If I were called upon to name that grace which is most endearing, that maxim which is most worldly-wise for men in elevated stations, it would be punctuality in answers and appointments. It sweetens favors, and it softens refusals; it is the most sovereign charm against envy, malice, and those numerous discontents that indispose the minds of men against the great and fortunate. I think I may venture to say, upon my long experience, that I have never known the person who left a great man's presence in an angry and revengeful humor, when he had been patiently heard and politely treated, although his suit had miscarried.[1]

I have named the Lord Chief Justice Mansfield amongst the distinguished persons who were in the habit of resorting to Tunbridge Wells; I was led to state some few particulars in the former part of these memoirs respecting that great man, whose name will stand so prominent in the annals of his time. I was frequently in his company, but have no right to think that I was ever so far in his confidence as to render me a competent

[1] Cumberland complains of both Pitt and Erskine for neglecting to answer his letters, and evinces a good deal of feeling on the subject. Lord North offended many friends by the same negligence; while the Duke of Wellington gratified hundreds by his prompt answers to their communications. Cumberland's remarks on punctuality in answers and appointments are perfectly just.

delineator of his character. Some few features, as they caught my observation, I may venture to trace out, and can say of him what everybody who knew him in his social hours must say, without the risk of a mistake. I cannot recollect the time when, sitting at the table with Lord Mansfield, I ever failed to remark that happy and engaging art which he possessed, of putting the company present in good humor with themselves; I am convinced they naturally liked him the more for his seeming to like them so well; this has not been the general property of all the witty, great, and learned men whom I have looked up to in my course of life.

Some imaginations are so vivid that they who are under their influence are all tongue and no ears. 'What a sensible and agreeable companion is that gentleman who has just left us,' said the famous Charles Townshend to the worthy and sensible Fitzherbert; 'I never passed an evening with a more entertaining acquaintance in my life.' 'What could entertain you? the gentleman never opened his lips.' 'I grant you, my dear Fitz, but he listened faithfully to what I said, and always laughed in the right place.' 'I am answered,' said Fitzherbert. 'A great nation like ours,' said this last named friend to me, 'should have a Charles Townshend in it for show, as a grand menagerie should have an ostrich.'

Johnson, though in another style of volubility, went rolling on, and never stopped to take in the little rills and rivulets, that would have mingled with his cataract: it was at once too rapid to admit their slender offerings, and too sonorous to allow their feeble tinklings to be heard.

Doctor Bentley would readily have listened, but did not always recollect that he was discussing subjects and discoursing in a language, that his company did not understand and probably could not speak: he accordingly took their task on himself, and kindly posted his own answers to the account of those who had no answers to give.

Lord Mansfield (from whom I have digressed) would lend his ear most condescendingly to his company, and cheer the least attempt at humor with the prompt payment of a species of laugh which cost his muscles no exertion, but was merely a subscription, that he readily threw in towards the general hilarity of the table. He would take his share in the small talk of the ladies with all imaginable affability; he was, in fact, like most men, not in the least degree displeased at being incensed by their flattery. He was no great starter of new topics, but easily led into anecdotes of past times; these he detailed with pleasure, but he told them correctly rather than amusingly. I am inclined to think he did not covet that kind of conversation which gave him any pains to carry on: his professional labors were great, and it was natural that he should resort to society more for relaxation and rest of mind than for anything that could put him upon fresh exertions. Even dulness, so long as it was accompanied with placidity, was no absolute disrecommendation of the companion of his private hours; it was a kind of cushion to his understanding.[1]

I agree with the general remark, that he had the art of modelling his voice to the room or space in which he was; but I am not one of those who admired its tone; it was of a pitch too sharp to please my ear, and seemed more tuned to argumentation than urbanity. His attentions, whenever he was pleased to bestow them, were not set off with any noble air, and I would rather call them civil than polite; for the stamp of his profession was upon him, and his deportment wanted gracefulness and ease. Pope, above all the sons of song, was his Apollo; but I suspect he had no real attachment to the Muses, and was merely civil to them in return for the compliments they had paid to him. I remember when the attack was made upon him for his conduct and opinions in the Douglas cause: I was well acquainted with Mr. Andrew Stuart; he was an acute and able man, and I had the opportunity of knowing how glad he would have been to have drawn Lord Mansfield into the fair field of controversy; but I am persuaded there was more sound wisdom in his lordship's silence, than there could have been sound reasoning in his answer, had his spirit led him to accept the challenge.

I have mentioned his last interview with Lord Sackville in the former part of these Memoirs. It was the only opportunity I

[1] 'Lord Mansfield,' says Campbell, 'appeared nowhere to greater advantage than in the social circle. He did not make a display of condescension like a low-bred man, who accidentally reaching an elevated position, wishes kindly to notice his former associates. He did not imitate those who, by the joint exertion of a great memory and a loud voice, quite unconscious of doing anything amiss, put an end to conversation by a perpetual pouring forth of observations and quotations, which may be useful in an encyclopædia, but which are tiresome in a lecture. He always comported himself like a well-bred gentleman among his equals. He considered that men are to gain renown in the field of battle, in the forum, and in the senate, but that society is for relaxation; and instead of making people despise themselves and hate him by the overwhelming proof of superior powers and acquirements, he studied to render others dearer to themselves, and consequently to inspire into them a benevolent feeling towards himself, by giving them an opportunity of contributing to the general amusement, and of bringing out the information which they peculiarly possessed. His general rule was to reward every man's jest with a smile, although he could not conceal his dislike to a bore or a coxcomb. —*Lives of the Chief Justices*, vol. ii. p. 430, Amer. ed.

had of knowing something of the movements of his heart: I caught a glimpse, as it were through a crevice, but it soon shut up, and the exterior remained, as before, *totus teres atque rotundus.*

When I call to mind the hours I passed with Lord North in the darkness of his latter days, there was such a charm in his genius, such a claim upon my pity in the contemplation of his sufferings, that even then, lacerated as I was in my feelings, I could not help saying within myself—The minister indeed has wronged me, but the man atones. His house at Tunbridge Wells was in The Grove: one day he took my arm, and asked me to conduct him to the parade upon the pantiles. 'I have a general recollection of the way,' he said, 'and if you will make me understand the posts upon the foot-path, and the steps about the chapel, I shall remember them in future.' I could not lead blind Gloster to the cliff: I executed my affecting trust, and brought him safely to his family: the ministering and mild daughter of Tiresias received her father from my hands.

I have already touched upon the character of this interesting man, and what little more my pallet can supply, shall be still only touches. I would not raze the skin, nor mar the polish of his brilliant talents for anything that fame can give; and as for that strong food, on which resentment feeds, I have long since perceived my stomach is too weak to relish it.

I do not know the person, to whose society a man of sensibility might have given himself with more pleasure and security than to that of Lord North; for his wit never wounded, and his humor never ridiculed: he was not disposed to make an unmerciful use of the power which superiority of talents endowed him with, to oppress a weaker understanding: he had great charity for dulness of apprehension, and a pert fellow could not easily put him out of patience; there was no irritability in his nature. To his acquaintance and friends he was all complacency; to his family all affection: he was generous, hospitable, open-handed, and loved his ease infinitely too well to sacrifice any portion of it to a solicitude about money.

The vivacity of his natural parts was strikingly contrasted by the heaviness of his appearance; in this particular, and in some others, he would occasionally remind me of Dodington; they were both scholars and lovers of literature and the Muse: both were quick in repartee, but Dodington could be sarcastic, and I am afraid it was too truly said of him, that he kept a tame booby or two about him for the sake of making them his butt; a kind of luxury very little above the gratification of a hog, when he rubs himself against a post. Dodington was too fond of giving ironical turns to serious subjects, by which he possessed himself of other people's opinions, and kept his own in reserve. I do not say but that occasions may sometimes justify a man in point of policy for thus talking under a mask; but I am very sure it cannot well be resorted to too seldom. He would, also, at times, indulge a whim of aping the rusticity of the vulgar, and, with a considerable share of humor, mimic their dialect and assume their manners; it was this whim that induced him to read Jonathan Wild, and the clowns in Shakspeare, to the Ladies Hervey and Safford, when they were visiting him at Eastbury. I remember his asking them if they had seen him in the print shops astride upon the ear of an elephant, with a sunflower in his mouth. I believe no such caricature was in existence, but I have perfect recollection of the old political print, called 'The Motion,' in which he was admirably portrayed as a mastiff between the legs of John, Duke of Argyle, upon the coach-box, with his name Bubb, if I mistake not, upon a collar round his neck; he had a reverence, so truly aristocratical, for great men with great titles, that it was enough for him to be admitted into the group, though in his dog-like caricature, and he took his metamorphosis in perfect good part.

None of these caprices were to be found in Lord North; he bore his part in conversation, and introduced his anecdotes to the full as appositely as Dodington, but I confess he did not set them off with quite the same advantages of manner. They had both the like propensity of slumbering in company with their ears open, and their wits wide awake, which had a very curious effect when the flash broke out on the sudden, in the midst of somnolency, as if the mind had kept watch whilst the body took a nap.

When Lord North lost his sight, he appeared to enjoy a vivid recollection of the pictures he had stored in his memory from men and books, and I have reason to think that, when he ceased to search for fresh supplies, he became the more liberal in dispensing the stock he had in hand, and that was in no danger of being exhausted. He repeatedly expressed a wish to me, that some young man of education might be found, whose business it should be to read to him, and live an inmate in his family: I observed to him that there were many to be found in either university, of whom he might make choice, but the man who had for so many years been minister of this great country, confessed to me that his means were too scanty to provide for that establishment. Like the great Lord Chatham and Mr. Pitt, he kept his own hands clean and empty, and when he applied to his son, who could not afford to keep his favorite mare, that happy quotation:—

> Equam memento rebus in arduis
> Servare,

the son might have filled up the sentence as it stands in the original, and applied it to the father, who, when deprived of sight, could not afford to maintain a reader, though he had administered the revenues of a nation.

The Lord Primate Robinson was my very kind and partial friend; but, more than this, he was the friend of my father. Splendid, liberal, lofty, publicly ambitious of great deeds, and privately capable of good ones, there was an exterior that, to the stranger, did not always hold out an encouraging aspect, but to him that stepped within that barrier, all was mildness, suavity, benevolence. He supported the first station in the Irish hierarchy with all the magnificence of a prince palatine. He made no court to popularity by his manners, but he benefited a whole nation by his public works; he gave plenty of employment to the industrious, and of food to the hungry, but he spread no table for the idle, and made no carousals for the voluptuous. He built a granite palace from the ground, with all its offices, gardens, farm, and demesne; he repaired and beautified his cathedral, built houses for his vicars choral, erected and endowed a very noble public school, and built several parish churches in the neighborhood of Armagh. He lived and died a bachelor, and administered his revenue with great regularity, else his fortune could never have sufficed for the accomplishment of such expensive projects, for he kept an establishment of servants, equipage, and table highly suitable to his rank.

The cathedral church of Armagh stands in full view from the windows of the palace, and at a short distance from it. Whilst I was passing some days with the primate, on my return to England, from Kilmore, I accompanied him on the Sunday forenoon to the cathedral. We went in his chariot, with six horses, attended by three footmen behind, whilst my wife and daughters, with Sir William Robinson, followed in my father's coach, which he lent me for the journey. At our approach, the great western door was thrown open, and my friend (in person one of the finest men that could be seen), entered, like another Archbishop Laud, in high prelatical state, preceded by his officers and ministers of the church, conducting him in files to the robing chamber, and back again to the throne. After divine service, the officiating clergy presented themselves in the hall of his palace to pay their court. I asked him how many were to dine with us: he answered: 'Not one.' He did them kindnesses, but he gave them no entertainments: they were in excellent discipline. I had accustomed myself so lately to admire the mild and condescending character of my benevolent and hospitable father at Kilmore, that I confess the contrast did not please me; but the primate knew—my father loved—mankind. I saw the princely demesne at Armagh covered with a small army of wretched creatures, making hay after the old Irish fashion, in loose great coats, a lazy, ragged, dirty gang: how different was the scene I had contemplated in my father's fields! But the primate left many noble monuments of his munificence in brick and stone—my father left his bounteous tokens in the human heart.

As my wife and daughters were probably the first and only female visitors who had been lodged within the walls of Armagh palace, the ladies of the neighborhood, not knowing how to decide upon the question of coming to them, very properly took no notice of us, and we enjoyed our liberty without restraint.

Sir William Robinson, elder brother of the Primate, accompanied us on our return to England. He was a man of the mildest and most amiable quality; though perfectly unlike his athletic brother in form and constitution, a feeble, infirm man, and a real valetudinarian, yet he followed step by step the same regimen, observed the same diet, took the same physic, swallowed the same number of rhubarb pills, and fought off the bile with raw eggs and mutton broth mixed up with Muscavado sugar, and although this system did not seem by any means suited to his constitution, yet, being adopted by his brother, he was convinced of its being the best and wisest of all possible systems, and faithfully adhered to it. This good man carried his devotion so far as to form many articles of his wearing apparel upon the same scale with those which the Primate wore; this was inconvenient enough in all conscience, and in some cases the disproportion was not a little ridiculous, particularly in the article of shoes, which he piqued himself upon having made on the same last with the Primate's, who, besides being a colossal man, studied his ease by far too much to cramp his feet; my friend, in the mean time, who, with the pleasing consciousness of putting on the same fraternal shoe, had not by many degrees the same foot to put into that enormous case, was fain to shove it on before him like a boat upon dry land; and indeed it was a boat of such size and burden, that the man who wore it ought, by anatomical proportion, to have been a Hercules *ex pede.*

The bile, however, so far got the mastery over this excellent man, on his journey, and the shaking of our coach so disturbed the quiet of his raw eggs and sugared broth, that at Donaghadee, in a wretched inn, he suffered an alarming attack, and had not my good wife been at hand to have rescued him with James's powders, his old enemy would hardly have given way to any remedy less efficacious.

Archbishop Moore was highly to be esteemed for his mild and condescending manner; and Doctor Moss, the Bishop of Bath and Wells, was an amiable and edifying instance how serenely to the latest period of extreme old age a good man can possess his spirit, when supported by religion. I recollect one day, after dining with Lord Mansfield, the good bishop, who was of the party, informed us that he was repairing an almshouse at Wells for the reception of five and twenty women, the widows of clergymen, and, turning to me, asked if I could suggest to him an appropriate inscription. 'Why do you apply to Cumberland,' said Lord Mansfield, 'for an inscription? I'll furnish you with what you want directly: Here are five and twenty women, all kept by the Lord Bishop of Bath and Wells. That's plain English; Cumberland would have puzzled the cause and his brains into the bargain.'

In general, the connections which I formed at Tunbridge Wells were of a sort to favor rather than obstruct my studies; of frivolous acquaintance I had no great stock, and amongst my intimates I had the happiness to number many valuable characters, many candid and ingenious men. Some of these have now withdrawn themselves to other destinations; some, alas! are no more, and a new order has succeeded, with whom I am not as with them.

What a multitude of past friends can I number amongst the dead! It is the melancholy consequence of old age; if we outlive our feelings we are nothing worth; if they remain in force, a thousand sad occurrences remind us that we live too long. For my part I must sojourn amongst strangers, or seek to make acquaintance with the children and grandchildren of my departed friends. Though I can hardly harmonize with their society, still I prefer the making suit to their favor, and am flattered if they endure me; for I have never yet discovered the delights of solitude. I consider it as a singular felicity in my life, and a circumstance to instance for their credit, with whom I have been connected, that when fortune seemed to have deserted me I had not to lament the falling away of friends. Men of the world are drawn off from us by the world; this is too often interpreted as an abandonment, when in fact it is only the result of avocation; when they, in course of time, cease to tread the public road of life, we meet them in the bypaths of retirement, and find our friendship interrupted only, not renounced.

Whilst Sir James Bland Burges inhabited the next house to mine, at Tunbridge Wells, I had ever an intimate and kind friend to resort to. He has always been a studious man, and his knowledge is very various; few men have read to better purpose, and fewer still can boast a more retentive memory, or a happier faculty of narrating what they remember. The early part of his education he received in Scotland, and completed it at Westminster school under Doctor Smith; at the University of Oxford he was the pupil of Sir William Scott; an opportunity that he has greatly profited by, and an honor that he is justly proud of. Upon his leaving Oxford he resided in the Temple, and devoted himself to the study of the law; since then he has served in Parliament, and filled an active and efficient post in public office; from both these duties he is now released, and, with a mind at leisure to pursue its natural bent, has commenced his literary career by devoting those talents, to which his country has no longer any counter-claim, to the more tranquil service of the Muse.

Reading has stored the mind of my friend with such a plenitude of matter, and nature has given him such a facility of expression, that his rapidity has hitherto been so great as hardly to allow fair leisure for his judgment to exert itself. The world, therefore, that has only seen his Richard Cœur de Lion (and in my humble opinion not yet sufficiently estimated the real merit of that extraordinary poem), has better things to expect from him, when his genius shall begin to feel the rein, and practice shall make him sensible that there is a labor as well as a luxury in composition. He is now concerned in a long and arduous work, too weighty to be moved by slight exertions, and too excursive to be circumscribed by rhyme. He must no longer now caparison his Muse, as a Spaniard does his mule, and make her frisk along the road to the eternal jingle of her own bells.

He has in the mean while written some dramas, and if in these he has not exactly struck out what the times are pleased with, it is more than probable he might have struck out something not so good, and pleased them better; for it is but justice to confess that they have all possible consideration for folly, and no great partiality for common sense. It is a gaudy thoughtless age, and they who live up to the fashion of it, live in a continual display of scenery; their pleasures are all pantomimical; their dinners steam along the columns of every daily paper, and their suppers and assemblies, dazzle the guests with tawdry lights and suffocate them with luscious odors—*natio comeda est.* It must be a surprise upon a plain gentleman, when, in consequence of an invitation from his friend, he drives to the door of what he conceives to be an ordinary street house, and upon entering it finds himself in an illuminated temple, formed perhaps upon the model of the concluding scene in a Harlequin entertainment. I ought to believe there is a great deal of good taste in all this, as so many fine people are concerned in it, but till I am better instructed I cannot help seeing it in a very ridiculous light. I am told the spectacle of 'The Forty Thieves' was a delicious treat; I did not hear quite so good an account of the dialogue; in like manner I read of forty honest gentlemen at least, who set out exquisite entertainments, but nobody records a single syllable of their conversation. It is a lucky circumstance for men of low birth, mean talents and confined education, that if they can buy good wine, and hire a good cook with plenty of winter roses, green peas and strawberries out of season, they can refresh the bowels of the old nobility, who will walk into a man's house, form their own parties when they are in it, and take no more notice of the master of it, than they would of the landlord of the inn they take post at, or the keeper of the turnpike-gate that they pass through; but there must be luxury in the glare of lustres to a man who has drudged at his desk by the light of a tallow candle, and how much handsomer must a floor appear to him, when splendidly bechalked by a capital designer, than when besprinkled with a watering pot by a slipshod apprentice!

The whim must have its run, and so long as our public prints have no better anecdotes to amuse us with than what are dated from the kitchen, we must be content to read what they relate, and let 'Hannah Glass' still flourish in the lustre of her fame. We are apt to covet what we can't obtain, and poets, both ancient and modern, have written much in praise of luxuries, which have not fallen to their share; whilst the ladies of Helicon, who should best understand what is fittest for the constitutions of their votaries, never treat them with anything stronger than a draught of pure water. For my part I cannot comprehend how the genius can effect anything worthy of itself amidst the inroads of dissipation, and whoever the man may be, or may have been, who has written a good song in praise of drinking, I must believe he was sober when he wrote it. They charged Cratinus with writing comedies when he was tipsy, but Cratinus soberly denied it.

I could instance a very ingenious contemporary, who is both a poet and a scholar of no common rank, a man withal of modest conversation, and amongst my acquaintance one of the very last to whom I should impute a natural depravity of mind; yet it must be confessed the Muse of Mr. Moore is by no means pure, and he is a writer of love songs much too highly colored. I am not amongst his intimates, yet I have seen enough of him to be persuaded it is not his character to do purposed mischief, but having, together with the gift of poetry, the grace of song, and his style of composition in music being professedly that of the tender and impassioned, he falls into the habit of suiting his words to his strains, and addresses soft love ditties to imaginary mistresses. That he can write gravely, solidly, and sublimely, no critic, who has read his volume, will deny. There are passages, particularly in his epistles, that are conceived in the true and genuine spirit of poetry. Had he been less tenacious of quantity, and thrown aside some loose disreputable trash, that takes from value what it adds to bulk, no critic could have wounded any feelings that a gentleman should own. He gives a reason why he did not do this, which would have disarmed most men of their severity; but if he has really mixed too much of levity with his better matter (which I am afraid is the fact), let him remember that he owes an atonement to candor; and as he has youth for his apology, and genius for his resource, let him urge his Muse upon some nobler undertaking, and when he has subjected his composition to the review of his correct and judicious friend Mr. Rogers, he may surrender himself without fear to the criticism of the world at large.

I might remind him of another friend, than whom I could not name a better in all points of honor; but Mr. William Spencer has in himself such a superabundance of fancy, that he will hardly be on the restrictive side; he figures in so wide a circle, and is so prodigal of his wit, that he disperses it amongst many, who can neither retail it nor retain it. His good sayings are like the blazing splinters that fly off from the hammered iron, and they that would lay hold of them would only burn their fingers: if he would reserve his Greek for those that understand it, he must seek other company; if he would display his stores of classic knowledge to more public use and profit, he must cease for a time to be the ornament of society, and trim his solitary midnight lamp. This he knows, but this he will not do, and will laugh at me for suggesting it.

I suppose the fog of my Cambridge training will never clear up sufficiently for me to see and understand the world, either as it now is, or heretofore has been. Gray, in his long story, says the Lord Chancellor Hatton danced, and Mr. Bentley, in his ornamented edition of that poet's works, has drawn him in the act of cutting capers. Commissioner Whitelocke was as solemn and precise a personage as need be; he tells us in his memoirs of his 'dauncing the brawls' at the court of Sweden, when he was Oliver Cromwell's ambassador to Queen Christina, and, if we may take his account for truth, he seems to have acquitted himself to the admiration of all beholders, unless indeed he mistook his own admiration for that of other people's, which is not quite impossible, for Goldsmith thought himself extremely graceful, Lord Malcombe studied attitudes in his looking-glass, and Soame Jenyns, as I have before remarked, wrote to the full as seriously on the art of dancing as he did upon the origin of evil. Now, though Aristophanes ridiculed a capering poet, modern times have endured a dancing Lord Chancellor, and may endure such antic tricks again.

The world will take its own course. The illustrious personages, who manage its concerns, will continue to manage them after their own way till they are thrown out of their seats, and when they are prostrate, helpless, and at mercy, the critics, who watch them as magpies watch a flock of sheep, will pounce upon them and pick out their eyes.

We are just now, as I before observed, by no means in our former character of philosophers, but rather living, as creatures should live, who are born for no other purpose, and devoted to no other uses, but to consume the fruits of the earth, and leave their names to be carried down to posterity in the culinary records of our public prints. The frivolity of their tables seems in a great degree to have overturned the solidity of their understandings, and by the frequency of their dealings with confectioners and cooks they appear to have contracted certain new, but consentaneous habits of speech, a sort of huffish puff-paste eloquence, which consists in treating grave and serious matters of debate with a vapid kind of levity, affecting quaint conceits and doggerel quotations, which stand very well in 'Mother Goose's Tales,' but are rather out of their latitude in Saint Stephen's Chapel. I am sorely afraid that our deluded senators, who, by the flatulency of their mental diet, have fallen into this laxity of talk, conceive it has some affinity to wit, and think themselves happy in a familiar style, which has all the point of ridicule and the grace of ease. Alas! it has nor point, nor edge, nor grace, nor ease; in fact, it is no style at all; mere gabble, nothing else. One recommendation it may have, which is that of being unanswerable, for who can remember it; and, being quite as flimsy as Ixion's mistress, who can embrace it?

This is no proof to me that there is a real dearth of taste or genius in the age; it only confirms what we knew before, that false taste and false genius are more obtrusive than true. If ever there was a time for this distinguished nation in a more peculiar manner to maintain her dignity and display her virtue, it is now, when the eyes of suffering and degraded Europe are directed towards her, and she has not yet been tempted to lay aside her arms.

There is a northern junto of periodical critics, who have rendered themselves extremely formidable to us poor authors, and to whom such of us, as have viands at command, offer them up, as Indians do their oblations to the devil; whilst they, who know we do not incense them out of love, but fear, receive our knee-worship with indifference and despise us for our meanness. I have not the honor of being personally acquainted with any one of these gentlemen, but I perceive that my sheets amongst others have been taken into their laundry, and have gone through the usual process of mangling. I am truly and sincerely obliged to them for the great consideration they have had for the feeble fabric of my manufacture, on which they have bestowed so very gentle a squeezing as not to break a thread, that was not rotten before they handled it, nor make one hole but what a housewife's hand may darn. In short, though it is so much my wish to be well with them, I cannot compliment them on their sagacity, forasmuch as they have not hit upon a single fault in my imperfect work, that was not much too obvious for any common marksman to have missed.

They say, with a great deal of natural good manners, that they should have been better reconciled to me, if I had talked more of other people and less of myself. This marks a delicate attention to certain feelings which I am proud to find they give me credit for, and I wish as much as they can do, that I could have discovered the happy means of being my own biographer without egotism; but having been induced, by reasons which I have not scrupled to confess, to render an account of my life and writings, whilst I am yet living and personally responsible for the truth of what I have written, I endeavored, to the best of my power, to lighten a dull topic by digressions, wherever I could avail myself of an opportunity; and if these gentlemen found those digressions the more tolerable part of my performance, so did I also. They seem as if they had written for the very purpose of confirming me in my own opinions.

The friends, who know with what hesitation I yielded to their advice and undertook this task, can witness that I did not expect to make my own immediate memoirs entertaining to the public; yet every reviewer, who has condescended to notice them (these of Edinburgh excepted), have had the charity to make me think they had read me with complacency. But they were my countrymen; they could feel for my motives, they could allow for my difficulties; they had too much manliness of nature to endeavor at depressing me, and forbore for a time to be critics for the gratification of exhibiting themselves in the more amiable character of gentlemen.

I understand that these acrimonious North-Britons are young men; I rejoice to hear it, not only for the honor of old age, but in the hope that they will live long enough to discover the error of their ambition, the misapplication of their talents, and that the combination they have formed to mortify their contemporaries is in fact a conspiracy to undo themselves.[1]

I am afraid that, in spite of the plain hint they have given me, I shall not be able to keep myself totally out of sight through the remaining pages of this supplement, especially as they themselves have given me an opportunity of explaining a circumstance of some importance, which had not come to my knowledge when I was employed upon the former part of these Memoirs.

By the anecdote which I related of Admiral Sir George Rodney, whilst he was manœuvring the cherry-stones upon Lord Sackville's table after dinner at Stonelands, I certainly meant to convey to the reader my sincere belief that it was then he first conceived the project of cutting through the enemy's line. I was not at that time, nor till very lately, apprised that there was a man living who could dispute the originality of that manœuvre with him. I now learn that Mr. Clerk had communications with the admiral, and if they were previous to the period of my anecdote, which may be easily ascertained, it will be evident that I mistook those symptoms, which so strongly impressed me and others present with the belief, which I attached to my relation of that anecdote. That I was more particularly attentive to the whole elaborate process of the gallant admiral with his cherry-stones, is a fact that I can well account for, inasmuch as when I perceived Lord Sackville losing his attention to his guest, and wearied with the many leading questions, uninteresting as they seemed to be to the rest of the company, who did not foresee the point they led to, I thought it right in my regard for both parties to give the more earnest heed to what

[1] The Edinburgh Review, at this time, had begun to stir mightily the stagnant waters of criticism, and was regarded by authors with a feeling something akin to that with which the lamb views the fatal approach of the wolf. That periodical has lived long and done much. Some of the most beneficial reforms that have been made in English law, and some of the most important changes in English policy, can, in part, be traced to the powerful advocacy of the Edinburgh Review.

my friend was about, who seemed to travail with some new idea, and in a whisper predicted to his lordship that I was persuaded that something worth his notice would come out at last.

I repeat this as my apology to Mr. Clerk, and the public at large, if, being misled by these indications, I have ascribed originality to the wrong person: nothing could more strongly character the first conception of a new idea. When the Admiral avowed his resolution to make experiment of his plan in action, and heard it treated with something more than doubt, he quoted no authority in support of it, but seemed contented to stand alone in the opinion of its practicability, and persisted in declaring that he would try it.

I must also beg leave to add that my friend Sir Charles Douglas, upon his return to England, expressly declared to me that the merit of cutting the French line rested entirely with his Admiral, and that his own opinion ever went against it. In my assertion of this fact I am strictly correct, and the observation I deduce from it is, that if Mr. Clerk suggested it to Sir Charles Douglas for the Admiral's consideration, it must have been the sagacity of the principal, not that of the second, which discerned the merit of Mr. Clerk's discovery, and in spite of all discouragements carried it resolutely and successfully into operation.

If, after all this discussion, it shall turn out that two men great in naval tactics, struck upon the same idea, where would be the miracle? Whilst I was upon a visit to my old and worthy friend the Reverend Mr. Higgs, at his rectory of Grandisburgh, in the county of Suffolk, I put the last hand to my poem of 'Calvary.' In his hospitable mansion I enjoyed my leisure in complete tranquillity and peace. It does not often come to pass, that two men, who had been intimates in their boyish days at school, and contemporaries in the same college, shall meet, as we did, in our old age, with the consciousness that there had not been a single moment when our friendship felt a check, or a word had passed that we could wish unsaid. Those days of course were to me peculiarly grateful, and I flatter myself if any visitations of my Muse were happy, it was then they were such, when she led me to those regions, which I attempt to describe as the residence of death. I should hardly presume to particularize these passages, had I not the authority of my kind reviewer Doctor Drake to appeal to for my apology, and to him I shall ever hold myself indebted as the one candid critic, who brought that poem out of its obscurity, and obtained for it a place amongst our British classics.

Encouraged by that favor, which was thus obtained for 'Calvary,' I cherished a design of attempting another epic poem on a sacred subject, and of selecting it from the Old Testament, following the example of Milton in his 'Paradise Lost and Regained.' Whilst these thoughts were in my mind, though without any fixed plan, my friend Sir James Burges suggested to me the history of Moses from the period of his leading the Israelites out of Egypt to his death upon Mount Horeb. This he did not propose in a crude and undigested state, but imparted to me a plan deliberately and minutely methodized, and apportioned into Books, ten in number, with the argument of each correctly drawn up; a work of much labor and considerable research. When I had taken this plan into consideration, I found that he had not only traced out the journal of the sacred historian with the most exact fidelity, but had availed himself of maps and books, till then unknown to me, and which seemed to leave little to the pen that followed him, except the task of filling up the outline he had laid down. It appeared to me to be a subject, comprising every property that should unite to constitute a sacred epic poem—a series of supernatural and sublime events, awful and tremendous judgments, forming a perfect and magnificent whole, displaying characters, achievements, incidents and situations, such as the history of no other people upon earth ever did exhibit, exceeding all the powers of mortal agency, yet backed with the authority of holy writ.

My friend, who had taken to himself the whole labor of the plan, consented also to share that of the execution, and we divided our respective portions accordingly. Though we have each been drawn off to other studies, yet we have advanced considerably in the joint work, and I purpose, with the concurrence of my worthy colleague, to submit the first and second books to the public very shortly, and so to publish part by part, if life and health permit, till the whole shall be completed.—We entitle it *The Exodiad.*

I have also planned, and in great part finished, one more novel, upon which I have bestowed much time and care, anxious to leave something behind me in that way, which may interest the scholar as well as the idler; something which gravity may read without contempt, and modesty without a blush; a work of fancy, that may prove I have not quite exhausted my capacity to amuse, nor quite abandoned my endeavors to instruct.

I hope it is not the character of old age to be querulous and dissatisfied; if it is, I trust I have escaped the common lot, for Nature has bestowed on me such strong animal spirits, and I have been blessed with so long a series of health, that I have hitherto found an unfailing source of occupation in solitude, and of pleasure in society. We old fellows should be aware that the young ones will only suffer us whilst we are conformable; the world at large will pay but little reverence to our gray hairs unless we set them off with the graces of good nature.

For some years before the decease of my wife, such was the unhappy state of her exhausted and decayed constitution, that my house was in a manner inaccessible even to my nearest friends and neighbors, her nerves being utterly destroyed, and even her recollection impaired by the effects of the breaking of a bloodvessel, which no art could heal. Every step that approached her threw her into tremors; and it required careful preparation to enable her to support an interview with any of her children who came at times to pay their duty to her.

The daughter, who is now the comfort of my old age, was then the only inmate in my family. Fortunately for her, she had the same resources with myself; from her earliest infancy, books had been her passion, and of these, her choice was directed much more to edification than mere amusement, and so clear was her comprehension, so retentive her memory, that I had the substance of any new publications, in her own language, so well detailed to me that I could reap the fruits of her studies, and pursue my own. So supported, I could not wholly sink; but when she also fell dangerously ill, and death seemed only pausing between objects so infinitely dear where first to point the inevitable blow, it was a trying and distressing crisis. Still, I struggled against base despondency, to which, amidst the wreck of father, mother, sons, and friends, I never yet had yielded; and here (as I am still my own biographer) I must take leave to say, in mitigation of my many failings and infirmities, that want of patience under the dispensation of God's providence is not amongst their number. Let not my readers think I aim to give false colors to my character; I scorn the imputation, and am too sensible how nearly I am approaching to the hour when every idle word must be accounted for to load my conscience with the guilt of an untruth.

Men who have been in situations, and availed themselves of opportunities for conferring favors, are apt, when fortune turns against them, to be loud in their complaints of the ingratitude of mankind. I have had those opportunities, but am not warranted to make those complaints. Whether I have not met with instances of ingratitude, or have outlived the recollection of them, I would not wish to ascertain, if it were in my power. I know that many people torment themselves with conceiving slights, and teaze their hearers with describing them. I can readily call to mind many small services of mine gratefully remembered, and generously overpaid. I have had many true and steady friends, and never found myself cast off by any only because I could no longer keep the station which I held before. When I am within their reach, they welcome me with all the cordiality of former times, and when I am master of a leisure day in London, I can always find a hospitable table and a friendly host;[1] this is at once my consolation and my pride. I have lived beyond the ordinary limits of man's time on earth, and have not forfeited the good-will of those with whom I lived; whilst, with few exceptions from amongst the numbers who are now no more, I can reflect with comfort that I did not lose them till death took them from me.

One instance of injustice and oppression was so interwoven with my history that I could not avoid the recording it; setting that aside, which it now behooves me to do, I have much reason to think well of the world, and, when my time shall come, much good cause to part from it in peace.

In the quarto edition of my memoirs, page 471, I mention a certain tributary present which my old friend, Mr. Smith, of Bury, was pleased to bestow upon the puerile Roscius in the candid spirit of encouragement. If anything that appears upon that page gave my respectable contemporary a moment's pain, I am sincerely sorry; and though I know he has forgiven me, yet before I can be heartily disposed to forgive myself, he must allow me to tender him this, my public apology. We are both far advanced into the vale of years, both pilgrims gray with age, and pressing onward to our journey's end. Time has been when his encouragement put me upon attempts, which his abilities as an actor contributed to support. I met him lately in town; a lucky chance brought him to the hotel, where I had lodgings; I was delighted to see him in such green old age, upright in person, active in limbs, and of a countenance still so animated, as bespoke him apparently as able to perform the part of 'Charles' as in his younger days. I introduced Mr. Alexander Rae to him, and tempted him to the Haymarket Theatre to see him in the character of Mortimer in 'The Iron Chest.' He sat with me in the orchestra, and was highly pleased with the performance of that young and very promising actor, with whose merits I am so intimately acquainted, and for whose success I am so warmly interested.

[1] Cumberland's manners were those of the courtier and gentleman; and his powers of conversation of a high order. 'The want of company,' says Dr. Johnson, in a letter to Mrs. Thrale, 'is an inconvenience, but Mr. Cumberland is a million.'

Since the stages of Drury Lane and Covent Garden have been so enlarged in their dimensions as to be henceforward theatres for spectators rather than playhouses for hearers, it is hardly to be wondered at if their managers and directors encourage those representations to which their structure is best adapted. The splendor of the scenes, the ingenuity of the machinist, and the rich display of dresses, aided by the captivating charms of music, now in a great degree supersede the labors of the poet. There can be nothing very gratifying in watching the movements of an actor's lips, when we cannot hear the words that proceed from them; but when the animating march strikes up, and the stage lays open its recesses to the depth of a hundred feet for the procession to advance, even the most distant spectator can enjoy his shilling's worth of show. What then is the poet's chance? Exactly what the parson's would be, if the mountebank was in the market-place, when the bells were chiming for church.

On the stage of Old Drury, in the days of Garrick, the moving brow and penetrating eye of that matchless actor came home to the spectator. As the passions shifted, and were by turns reflected from the mirror of his expressive countenance, nothing was lost; upon the scale of modern Drury many of the finest touches of his art would of necessity fall short. The distant auditor might chance to catch the text, but would not see the comment that was wont so exquisitely to elucidate the poet's meaning, and impress it on the hearer's heart.

It was never my object to depress the living candidate for fame, but has been uniformly my desire and my endeavor to uphold and cherish genius whilst it lives amongst us, and may be fostered by our commendations. The dead can do no more; they have finished their career, and there is no more use and profit in our praise of them; the living are our property, we have a participation in their talents, and it is no less our interest than our duty to encourage all their efforts for the honor of the era we belong to. How much more gratifying must it be to behold perfection than to hear of it! If I tell a man that Garrick was an inimitable actor, he may, or he may not, take it on my credit; but how does my report edify him unless I could present him with a sample of his style, and be myself in every circumstance of action, voice and feature perfect Garrick? But this I cannot be, and in the mean time nothing is more illusory and vague than my description; I can give the measure of his stature, and perhaps some idea of his person, but that which alone is interesting to be acquainted with, I cannot communicate. The living actor is within our reach.

So long as I have known the stage, so many eminent performers as I have seen pass over it, and so frequent as my concerns with them have been, I should be glad to say something in this place that might manifest my regard for them, and keep me in their remembrance when I am no more; but when I turn to the essay, No. xxix. in the 'Observer,' which I devoted to their use and service, whilst my thoughts were fresher than they are at present, it is but little I can add, and that little will be hardly worthy of their attention in any other light than as a mark of the unvaried good-will which I entertain for them.

As men separated by their profession into a distinct order, I have the satisfaction to see them maintain a more respectable station in society than they did in my early acquaintance with the stage. Though they have produced no writer from amongst themselves equal to the author of 'The Careless Husband,' yet I could instance some who have written, and still write, more prosperously in their day than Cibber did in his. Though none, perhaps, since Garrick trod the stage, can boast such various excellence as he possessed, yet I have seen nature so admirably imitated in particular characters by performers yet amongst us, that I have said within myself: If human powers can reach perfection, I behold it now.

The stage has never, within my knowledge of it, been wholly unprovided with performers of distinguished merit in the tragic line. I have remarked that it is generally the first ambition of the candidate for histrionic fame to be the hero or heroine of a tragedy. It is perfectly in nature that it should be so; the school-boy who is taught to declaim, has his passages selected from the writers in heroic metre; he speaks a soliloquy of Hamlet's to a parcel of people who are predisposed to applaud him, and he conceives himself a second Garrick; he makes love as Romeo and Marc Antony, behold he is another Barry; he recites an extract from Macbeth or Richard, and he is Kemble, Cooke, or any other, who can please you better, if any such there are. Blank verse adheres more easily to the memory than prose; the human passions are more strongly roused by tragedy than comedy, and he becomes a decided votarist of Melpomene; he enrolls himself in the troop of a country theatre, the manager of which pays no attention to his prejudices, no respect to the sublimity of his ideas, but levels him at once with his fellows, and makes him stand in any gap that wants a substitute to fill it up; at length, by frequent lowerings, he discovers to his surprise, but ultimately to his advantage, that he is a low comedian, and that it is much easier for him to provoke a laugh than to extort a tear. Thus it comes to pass that comedy, in its lower, characters, has been always well filled up, but very few indeed have distinguished themselves in the more refined and elegant department; there must be a graceful ease and a highly finished air, which, without an experience that falls to the lot of very few performers, cannot be engrafted even upon the finest and the fairest forms.

The profession of the actor is laborious in the extreme; it is only to be upheld by habitual temperance and incessant study; indolence cannot retain it; dissipation must extinguish it. They, who are forever in the public eye, can surely estimate the value and advantages of private character; they must know how grudgingly applause is given to such as have no title to respect. The increased exertion of the voice alone is now become a task more toilsome than their predecessors underwent, and by how much the present call for novelties exceeds that which is passed, by so much greater must the exercise of the memory be now than heretofore. With these extraordinary demands upon the vital sources of their noblest functions, how cautious should they be to keep those sources pure! Repletion must impede the faculties; ebriety deserves no pardon.

It would be possible for me to bring to my recollection the particular style and manner of many eminent performers, who are now no more, and my description of them might, perhaps, afford amusement to the generality of my readers; but I am not disposed to make the attempt, because I am so averse from all comparisons between the dead and living, that I will not give any one the opportunity of supposing that my praise implies preference. It is more a trick of talking than a truth of judging in those who make a practice of decrying living actors: if they would write but half as well as the performers can act, the stage would be better furnished with new pieces. A silly, witless coxcomb conceives it is a token of superior taste to contemplate everything with cold indifference; whereas his foolish affectation only impresses us with a sure conviction of his dulness, and a shrewd suspicion of his maliciousness. Such a man will tell you there are no good actors now; they are not to be compared with some that he remembers; whereas, he said the same of those then as he does of these now, and, perhaps, with something more like truth and reason. Is he a judge of what an actor should be? Is he competent to distinguish the just and genuine representation of nature from the tricks of art and studied pedantry of declamation? If he were, he would know better where to look for merit, and how to value it when he had discovered it. But I am resolute to credit no man for merit in himself, who can see none in others, and am persuaded that with all his contempt for the sons and daughters of Thespis, there is no strolling master of a troop of spouters, who would admit him into his barn, unless to snuff the candles or to beat a drum.

The living actors can do justice to the living authors, let them write as well as they can, and as much better than they do write, as it shall please Heaven. If their wit provokes them to attempt a comedy, the danger will not be that any part shall be too good for the performer, but that the performer shall think himself too good for the part. I am satisfied it is not in my power to name the time within more than half a century past, when the stages of Drury Lane and Covent Garden have been better furnished with comedians than at the present hour. Perhaps it is to be lamented that their influence is such as to induce an author to make greater sacrifices, and pay more attention to the particular persons whom he has in view to represent the characters of his play, than to the general interests of the play itself; and though I would not be understood to insinuate that an actor or actress should not have the privilege of declining certain parts, that may be tendered to them, yet I am fully warranted to remark, that they exercise that privilege much too frequently, and upon too frivolous objections. They are become exceptions to a degree that the stage in former times had no idea of, and this unaccommodating caprice reduces the author either to sacrifice the harmony of his composition out of flattery to their freaks, or by submitting to the rebuff, put his play upon its trial with the discouraging circumstance attached to it, of having begged its way through the repugnant heroes and heroines of the green-room. It may not be reasonable in some cases to expect compliance, but when the director of the theatre concurs with the author, in deciding on the cast, either the performer must do his duty, or the writer should withdraw his play, and give his reason to the public.

But it is not in this particular only that the conduct of our theatres seems to need some further regulation; there might, in my opinion, be a better mode adopted than what they now pursue in treating writers for the stage, and passing judgment on the manuscripts referred to them. As there can be no premeditated offence in the person who makes suit to be accepted, there should be nothing that can wound his feelings in the manner of rejecting him. He has an equitable right to know the judge that passes sentence on his work, and there cannot be a good reason why that judge should only be heard to speak through the organs of the prompter, and commit the manuscript to be sent back to its owner, with a note from that servant of the side-scene, so uncourteously concise, that it would barely serve to warn an actor to rehearsal.

If it were to be wished that he whose first proposal does not suit, should not be tempted ever to propose again, a more effectual method of accomplishing that end can hardly be devised. The flame of that dramatic passion must be very strong, which the prompter's extinguisher, thus applied, cannot put out: but if an easy intercourse between parties, mutually interested to serve one common cause, ought in all good policy to be furthered, everything that can give disgust and irritation should with caution be avoided; for in every pursuit where ambition is praiseworthy, attempts should be encouraged.

Conducted as the business now is, the ruler of a theatre may well complain of the burden of his office: but if a judicious and respectable person was sought out, and specially appointed for the purpose of receiving, reading, and reporting upon dramatic compositions, tendered for acceptance, all cause of complaint on the part of the *genus irritabile* would be removed, and there would be no accumulation of the obnoxious mass of manuscripts, that occasion so much trouble to the holders, and give such matter of complaint to the authors, who are destined to be tantalized by long expectations, and at length dismissed by short answers. This person, if duly qualified for his office, will readily distinguish such performances as are evidently inadmissible, and in the disposal of these, nothing more will be required than expedition and a courteous manner of declining the offer; whereas now, when manuscripts of this description are suffered to lie upon the shelf, though they have no title to be accepted, their owners have still just reason to complain of inattention and delay.

There will of course be other tenders made with more respectable pretensions, but which, nevertheless, upon the whole it may be judged expedient to decline; in these cases I should conceive it right to qualify their rejection with such general observations and remarks, as may not only soften disappointment, but convey instruction: candor of this sort would inspire ambition, and if there was a spark of genius in the writer of a piece so treated, it would cherish and improve it.

When a drama shall be judged worthy of acceptance, it must still, from the nature of all human compositions, be found capable of improvement: how many novelties are improvidently brought forward, whose general merit is so glaringly defaced by obvious errors, or stifled by disgustful and unnatural excrescences, which in their passage to the stage might and ought to have been corrected and lopped off! It is then, if the author is not deaf to all advice, and unobservant of effect, that in the course of the rehearsals he may give the finishing touches to his production, and how much depends upon the proper conduct and enforcement of those rehearsals I need not observe; they certainly demand attention, and I suspect they need reform; for what between the affected carelessness of some performers, and the real indolence of others, the play is in part kept out of the author's sight, who is told that such and such an actor will be perfect at representation, or in other words that he will get his part when he can no longer put it by, and speak out to his audience in self-defence, though he has muttered and slurred it over to his author at rehearsal through mere laziness or self-conceit. But neither these, nor any other remarks how apposite soever, can be said to be in place, whilst the stage is so preoccupied by spectacle! As a gaudy equipage will attract notice, though it shall carry a dull company withinside of it, so will fine scenery and rich dresses hide the nakedness of nonsense, and sweet melodies impart a grace even to the lamest and most wretched metre.

If nature can hardly be upheld by Mrs. Jordan, or Shakspeare by Mr. Kemble, what author in his senses will attempt a comedy more legitimate than 'The Forty Thieves,' or a tragedy more serious than 'Tom Thumb?'

Whilst I pause here, death has struck down an illustrious victim in the person of Mr. Fox. The time is marked with awful visitations. Mr. Pitt is taken from us, and now the other luminary of our state and senate is extinct: in the moment when his great abilities were drawn out by great occasions into full exertion, we have lost him. His amiable qualities, his steady friendships, his brilliant talents, will be long recorded in the hearts of those who loved and admired him; their sorrow will be proportionable; but it is to be hoped they will avoid that extravagance in their eulogies, which oversteps discretion, nor mingle that despondency with their bewailings, in which there is no wisdom, policy or common sense.[1] We should recollect

[1] If Pitt was born to be admired, Fox was born to be loved. With his consummate powers, blazing with equal splendor in debate, and in office, he combined a placidity, a sweetness of disposition, that attached friends and disarmed foes. 'If you had been called upon to select a friend from the whole human race,' says Dr. Parr, 'where could you have found one endowed as he was with the guileless playfulness of a child, and the most correct and comprehensive knowledge of the world; or distinguished as he was by profound erudition, by well founded reverence for the constitution of his country, and the keenest penetration into the consequences, near or remote, of all public measures?'

'Mr. Fox,' says Sir James Mackintosh, 'united in a most remarkable degree the seemingly repugnant characters of the mildest of men, and the most vehe-

that it is upon the general spirit of our countrymen that we rest our confidence; when Nelson breathed his last, he breathed out nothing but his own brave soul; our fleets are not become less terrible to our enemies because he no longer lives to command them: if it were so, it were time indeed to withdraw from the contest, for there is one at no great distance from us, who is fearfully and anxiously alert to watch our waverings, and engraft his own advantages upon them; but as the courage of our soldiers has recently chastised his arrogance, so I trust that the harmony of our councils will disappoint his artifice, and enable our nation to maintain that attitude, which alone is worthy of its character and consistent with its security.

As I now find myself once more under the hospitable roof of my old friend Mr. Higgs, I am likely to wind up this supplement of my Memoirs in the very spot where, fifteen years ago, I concluded my poem of 'Calvary.' This companion of my youth, though far advanced into the vale of years, is still enjoying the reward of temperance, a sound mind in a healthful body. He performs all the duties of a parish priest in an exemplary manner, executes the laborious office of an acting justice of the peace with that of a director of the poor-house, established at Nacton in this county of Suffolk, an institution of such striking use and benefit, and productive of so great a public saving in the article of poor rates, that it is matter of astonishment why it has not been more generally adopted. When I fell ill at Ramsgate, and he was made acquainted with my situation, he wrote a letter, that convinced me his affection had suffered no abatement by the lapse of years since I had seen him, and he took a journey of a hundred and forty miles to visit me in my convalescence. He was of the same year with me at Trinity, and we have not a senior to us in the college now living.

To the candid reviewers of the first edition of my Memoirs I

ment of orators. In private life he was gentle, modest, placable, kind, of simple manners, and so averse from dogmatism, as to be not only unostentatious, but even something inactive in conversation. . . . . He certainly possessed above all moderns that union of reason, simplicity and vehemence, which formed the prince of orators. He was the most Demosthenean speaker since the days of Demosthenes.' 'I knew him,' says Burke, 'when he was nineteen; since which time he has risen, by slow degrees, to be the most brilliant and accomplished debater the world ever saw.'

If the private life of Fox had been as unblemished as Pitt's, and he had steered clear of that fatal coalition, his influence on the national mind, and on the government, might have been unparalleled. But such had been the habits of his life, and accompanied with such notoriety, that the people 'would never be persuaded to attribute virtue to his character.' But despite this serious drawback in his influence, he did immense good, and deserves the lasting gratitude of his country.

have already paid my acknowledgments, and if in this octavo republication I have omitted to avail myself of some remarks upon a few verbal inaccuracies, which had escaped my notice, I must beg them to believe it is not that I am obstinate against correction, but because I hold it a point of honor to leave that copy untouched, which my first purchasers are in possession of, preferring to acknowledge my faults and ask pardon of the public, rather than make this second copy better by the amendment of a single word than that which they have bought at twice the price. Perhaps I may refine too much in this particular, but it is my idea of fair dealing, and there are objects in my estimation infinitely more worthy my consideration and attention, than anything which can only affect my reputation as a writer.

When this manuscript was going to the press, I was informed by my publisher, Mr. Lackington, that he had been told I was not correct in stating that the 'West Indian,' when first produced, had no after-piece attached to it. If this was a misstatement, I trust I need not say that it was perfectly involuntary.

While I was employed upon my Memoirs, I was inhabiting a furnished house at Ramsgate, where I was literally provided with nothing but the mere materials for writing, having left my books and papers in their packages at Tunbridge Wells, where they still remain. This I hope will in some degree apologize for my mistake in retorting upon Bishop Lowth, by saying I had traced his quotation against Doctor Bentley up to its source in one of the most uncleanly samples in Catullus; it is a palpable error, of which I am very properly reminded, and I thank my kind reviewer in the 'British Critic,' for giving me this opportunity of acknowledging it.

At the same time that I was writing without books, I was living without any literary friend or neighbor to resort to, till the arrival of Sir William Pepys at Ramsgate gave me an opportunity of renewing my acquaintance with one of the best classical scholars of his time, and who, together with his learning, possessed a correct taste, and admirable judgment. When I lived with Johnson, Garrick, Dodington, Jenyns, and the wits of that period; I had the happiness also of living with Sir William Pepys. No man had a better right to be present wherever men of talents held their meetings; for with a very quick comprehension, a ready elocution, and a fund of erudition, this gentleman has a grace and suavity of manners not always to be found in contact with a superior understanding. There are few now left who can be heard with equal profit upon literary topics, for his opinions are delivered with peculiar clearness and a marked precision; they are not such as can puzzle and entangle;

they must either confirm or confute. He attached himself very zealously to Samuel Johnson, for he admired the man, and was more solicitous to elicit his talents than to display his own; on many subjects I have known him follow where he might have led; for if the orbit in which Johnson's mighty genius rolled was wider than his, or probably than any other man's of his time, still, on all points where classical authorities were to be appealed to, and somebody was to be appointed as expounder of those authorities, I should conceive there could be none more fit than him of whom I am speaking. When I had him within a few doors of me, though much the greater part of my work had passed the press, I did not fail to solicit his revision of the few concluding sheets, which I had yet in manuscript; to this request he most kindly accorded, and I must ever regret, not less for the sake of my readers than for myself, that I had so limited an opportunity of availing myself of his judgment.

In the winter season, I produced with Mr. Harris's permission a comedy in five acts, which I entitled 'A Hint to Husbands.' It was originally engaged to take its fate upon the stage of Drury, and was calculated to suit the cast of certain performers belonging to that theatre, particularly Mr. Johnstone, so justly admired for his excellent display of Irish characters. If I had done right, I should have prevailed upon Mr. Harris not to risk his expectations and property upon it, when both Mr. Kemble and Mr. Lewis thought proper to reject the parts which they were solicited to undertake; he was too generous, however, to let their scruples divert him from his protection of the play, and brought it on his stage, where, after the flattering reception of a first night, it languished through a chilling course of five successive snowy evenings, severe enough to have starved a healthier babe than mine. This play has been published, and they, who are pleased to patronize it in their closets, will perceive that I have persisted in making no sacrifice to the ruling fashion of the times, nor studied to contrive any situations which the favorers of farce are likely to be amused with; if it may aspire to any merit, it will be found where I would wish to place it, in the moral; the whole is written in five-footed verse, and perhaps some passages may recommend themselves to the reader as not unworthy of the British stage.

I have now concluded the account I undertook to give of a long life, not often occupied in interesting and important pursuits, but certainly comprising very few periods of indolence and inaction. What further time may be allotted to me I shall devote to the works which I have noticed in this supplement, and I hope the publication of this edition will be speedily followed by that of the first part of 'The Exodiad.' But I apprehend we are fast approaching towards an awful crisis when the minds of men will be too much occupied to spare a thought for literary objects. Perhaps the Destroyer, who has been sent on earth for the chastisement of the nations, has already reached the summit of his power, and, like Apollyon, shadowed out in the Apostle's vision, is verging towards extinction, together with those symbolical locusts, who have him as a king over them, and on their heads as it were crowns like gold; and I doubt not but it will be the destiny of our brave countrymen to convince the rescued world that these vermin are not invincible.

It is a delicate and arduous task I have had in hand, and I trust that now, as heretofore, I shall be read and judged with candor. I have not knowingly transgressed, or even strained, the truth, to which I pledged myself; but fairly and sincerely stated how I have employed my faculties, what I have been, and what I am. Man hath no need, no right, no interest to know of man more than I have enabled every one to know of me. I have no undivulged evil in my heart; but with unabated affection for my friends, and good-will towards my fellow-creatures, I remain the reader's most devoted servant,[1]

RICHARD CUMBERLAND.

[1] But little remains to complete the record of Cumberland's life. 'That a man of such learning,' says one of his contemporaries, 'of such versatility of literary talent, such unquestionable genius, and such sound morality, should, in 'the vale of years' feel the want of what he has lost by his exertions for the public good, must, to every feeling mind, be a subject of keen regret.'—*Biographica Dramatica.* Yet such was the fact. The evening of his day was clouded by pecuniary embarrassments, from which he endeavored in vain to relieve himself by his literary labors. His latter days were spent chiefly in London, where, on the 7th of May, 1811, he expired, after a short illness, at the house of a friend, in Bedford Place, being then in the 79th year of his age.

'Of the personal character of Cumberland, a pretty accurate judgment may be formed from his memoirs. His self-esteem was great, and his vanity overweening, but, although extremely sensitive to criticism, and intolerant of censure, he had not real malignity in his composition, and, like most excitable persons, seems to have been as placable as he was irritable. His temperament was of a kind which, if easily disturbed, as quickly recovered its balance; and there is every reason to believe that the predominant tone of his feelings was alike generous and liberal. On the only occasion of his life when his moral principles were put to the test, they appeared to the very greatest advantage. His conduct respecting the bequest of Mr. Reynolds, who had devised to Mr. Cumberland his estate, to the exclusion of the natural heir, evinced the greatest disinterestedness, and the highest sense of honor and probity. It was his misfortune to have been bred a courtier, and never to have taken his degrees in that school. He evidently wanted the suppleness and versatility necessary to insure success in such a career. In a subordinate station, which merely required attention to formal and technical duties, he acquitted himself indifferently well; but in venturing to act as minister, he found himself wofully deficient in those qualities, without the possession of which genius and talents are of little avail. . . . . In society, his chief aim was to please; and, by the admission of his contemporaries, few men appeared to more advantage in conversation, or evinced a more perfect mastery, when he chose to exercise it, of the art of pleasing. The great faults of his character were a tendency to lavish hollow compliments on those who were present, and a propensity, without provocation or necessity, to indulge in bitter sarcasms against individuals after they had taken their departure. . . . . As a writer, he is more remarkable for the number than for the excellence of his works; but many of them, it should be remembered, were hastily produced, in order to better his income, and some of them are marked by no ordinary degree of intellectual power. In every variety of fortune the drama was his favorite pursuit; and if he has produced much that is perishable or forgotten, he has also evolved orations which have been inregistered as among the finest efforts of genius. The character of Penruddock in 'The Wheel of Fortune,' for example, is a masterpiece, which received a double consecration from the histrionic talents of John Kemble, by whom it was so often, so nobly personated. As a poet he cannot by any means rank high; for, while he had a play of imagination, which unfitted him for the concerns of actual life and business, his warmest admirers can only claim for him the praise of correct versification and elegant sentiment, which, however, has secured for some of his poetical works a considerable share of popularity.'

This brief summary of Cumberland's qualities as a man and author, is taken from the 'Encyclopædia Britannica.' Whether it is altogether charitable, the reader of these memoirs must decide.

THE END.

PUBLICATIONS

OF

PARRY & McMILLAN,

SUCCESSORS TO A. HART, LATE CAREY & HART,

PHILADELPHIA.

August, 1854.

BACON'S COMPLETE WORKS.

The Complete Works of Francis Bacon, Lord Chancellor of England. A new edition, with a Life of the Author. By BASIL MONTAGU, Esq.

In three volumes, royal octavo. Cloth, ... $7 50
Sheep, ... 8 50
Half morocco, ... 9 00
Calf backs, ... 10 00

"Printed from the most accurate as well as complete English edition, and carefully revised, in a form at once compact, elegant, and economical."—*Brother Jonathan.*

THE WAVERLEY NOVELS.

The Waverley Novels, complete in five volumes; containing the whole of the world-renowned Novels of Sir WALTER SCOTT. In the cheapest form ever offered for sale. Paper covers, ... 2 50
Cloth backs, ... 3 50
Full cloth, ... 5 00
Full bound in sheep, ... 6 00

WAVERLEY NOVELS (FINE EDITION).

The Waverley Novels, in five volumes—same type as the last edition—on fine white paper. Cloth, extra gilt, ... 7 50
Calf backs, extra, ... 10 00

Or in twenty-five parts—each Novel complete in one part, in paper binding. Price 25 cents each.

SIR WALTER SCOTT'S COMPLETE WORKS.

The Works of Sir Walter Scott—including the Waverley Novels—all his Prose Works—and all his Poetical Works—with his Life, by J. G. LOCKHART, Esq. Containing the whole of the contents of the Edinburgh edition in ninety-eight volumes. Complete in ten volumes, octavo. Cloth, ... 10 00
Sheep, ... 12 50
Calf backs, ... 15 00

Scott's Poetical Works.

Sir Walter Scott's Poetical Works, complete; including the Minstrelsy of the Scottish Border. One volume, cloth, ... 1 00

Scott's Life of Napoleon.

The Life of Napoleon Bonaparte. By Sir Walter Scott. Complete in one volume, octavo, cloth, ... 1 00

Lockhart's Life of Scott.

The Life of Sir Walter Scott. By his nephew, John G. Lockhart, Esq. Complete in one volume, octavo, cloth, ... 1 00

Mrs. Sigourney's Poems.

Illustrated Poems. By Mrs. L. H. Sigourney. With designs by F. O. C. Darley, engraved by distinguished artists. With a beautiful Portrait of the Author by Cheney, after Freeman. Handsomely bound in cloth, super extra, ... 5 00

Turkey morocco, extra gilt, ... 7 00

List of Illustrations.—The Divided Burden—A Landscape—Oriska—The Ancient Family Clock—Eve—The Scottish Weaver—The Indian Summer—Erin's Daughter—The Western Emigrant—The Aged Pastor—The Tomb—The Drooping Team—The Beautiful Maid.

Sigourney's Select Poems.

Select Poems, by Mrs. L. H. Sigourney. With illustrations. New edition. In one handsome volume, 12mo., cloth, ... 1 25

Cloth, extra gilt, ... 1 50

Sigourney's New Volume of Poems.

The Western Home, and other Poems. By Mrs. L. H. Sigourney. In one handsome volume, 12mo., cloth, ... 1 25

Cloth, extra, ... 1 50

Read's Illustrated Poems.

Poems, by T. Buchanan Read. A new and enlarged edition. Beautifully illustrated with designs by eminent artists, and finely engraved on steel. Cloth, extra gilt edge, ... 3 50

Turkey morocco, ... 6 00

Read's Poems.

Poems, by T. Buchanan Read. A new edition. In one volume, 12mo., cloth, ... 1 00

"Strongly imbued with poetic genius."—*Eliza Cook's Journal.*

Anne Boleyn, by Boker.

Anne Boleyn, a Tragedy. By George H. Boker, author of "Calaynos," &c. Cloth. 75

The Podesta's Daughter.

The Podesta's Daughter, and other Miscellaneous Poems. By George H. Boker, author of "Calaynos," "Anne Boleyn," &c. Cloth, . 62

"Mr. Boker possesses the poetic faculty in a very high degree."—*Evening Bulletin.*

Poets and Poetry of America.

The Poets and Poetry of America; embracing Selections from the Poetical Literature of the United States, from the time of the Revolution. With a Preliminary Essay on the Progress and Condition of Poetry in this Country—and Biographical and Critical Notices of the most eminent Poets. By Rufus W. Griswold. *Twelfth edition.* In one volume, octavo, cloth, ... 3 00

Turkey morocco, ... 5 00

"A work entirely without a rival in its department, and for which there has for years existed a marked and increased necessity."—*National Intelligencer.*

"The best collection of American poetry that has been made."—*N. Y. Evening Post.*

The Prose Writers of America.

The Prose Writers of America. With a Survey of the Intellectual History, Condition, and Prospects of the Country. By Rufus Wilmot Griswold. Illustrated with Portraits from original artists. *New edition.* Complete in one volume, octavo, cloth, ... 3 00

Turkey morocco, extra, ... 5 00

"We deem this book by all odds the best of its kind that has ever been issued." —*N. Y. Courier and Enquirer.*

Washington's Administration.

Memoirs of the Administration of Washington and John Adams. Edited, from the Papers of Oliver Wolcott, Secretary of the Treasury, by George Gibbs. Two volumes, octavo, cloth, ... 5 00

Historical Sketches of the Statesmen of the times of George III.

To which are added Remarks on the French Revolution. By Henry Lord Brougham. The three Series complete in two volumes, 12mo., 2 50

Watson's Annals of Philadelphia.

Annals of Philadelphia and Pennsylvania in the Olden Time; being a Collection of Memoirs, Anecdotes, and Incidents of the City and its Inhabitants—and of the earliest Settlement of the inland part of Pennsylvania, from the days of the founders. Intended to preserve the Recollections of olden time, and to exhibit society in its changes of manners and customs, and the City and Country in their local changes and improvements. By John F. Watson, Member of the Historical Society of Pennsylvania, &c. &c. Two volumes, octavo, cloth, extra, 4 00

Heroic Women of the West.

Heroic Women of the West; comprising Thrilling Examples of Courage, Fortitude, Devotedness, and Self-sacrifice amongst the Pioneer Mothers of the Western Country. By John Frost, LL. D., author of "Pictorial History of the World," "History of the United States," &c. &c. One volume, 12mo., cloth, ... 1 25

Memoirs of Josephine.

Historical and Secret Memoirs of the Empress Josephine, first wife of Napoleon Bonaparte. By Mad'lle M. A. Le Normand. Translated from the French by Jacob M. Howard, Esq. In two volumes, 12mo., cloth, gilt. 2 00

"It affords a clearer insight into the private character of Napoleon than we can obtain through any other source."—*Baltimore American.*

Memoirs of Mary, Queen of Scots.

Memoirs of the Life of Mary, Queen of Scots; with Anecdotes of the Court of Henry II., during her residence in France. By Miss Benger, author of the "Memoirs of Anne Boleyn." Two volumes, 12mo., . 2 00

Memoirs of Queens of France.

Memoirs of the Queens of France. By Mrs. Forbes Bush. From the last London edition. In two volumes, 12mo., cloth, ... 2 00

"Full of sentiment and romance, rendered all the more touching from the graceful drapery in which they are adorned."—*Saturday Courier.*

Memoirs of Marie Antoinette.

Memoirs of the Court of Marie Antoinette, Queen of France. By Madame Campan, First Lady to the Bedchamber of the Queen. From the third London edition. With a Biographical Introduction from the "Heroic Women of the French Revolution," by M. De Lamartine, Member of the Executive Government of France. New edition, with three additional Chapters. In two volumes, cloth, extra, . . . 2 00

Memoirs of Anne Boleyn.

Memoirs of the Life of Anne Boleyn, Queen of Henry the Eighth. By Miss Benger, author of "Memoirs of Mrs. Elizabeth Hamilton." Second American, from the third London edition. With a Memoir of the Author, by Miss Aikin. One volume, cloth, ... 1 25

The Lady's Historical Library.

Containing the above five popular works, bound up in uniform style, in nine volumes, cloth, extra, ... 9 00

Lady Russell's Letters.

The Letters of Rachel Lady Russell. New edition. Containing many Letters never before published. Complete in one handsome volume, 12mo., ... 1 00

Howitt's Visits to Remarkable Places.

Visits to Remarkable Places; Old Halls, Battle Fields, and Scenes illustrative of striking passages in English History and Poetry. By William Howitt, author of "Rural Life of England," "Rural Life of Germany," "Book of the Seasons," &c. First Series. Third American edition. Two volumes, cloth, ... 2 00

"The most delightful book William Howitt ever wrote."—*Bulletin.*

Howitt's Rural Life of England.

The Rural Life of England. By William Howitt, author of "Visits to Remarkable Places," &c. &c. From the third London edition, corrected and revised. Two volumes, 12mo., cloth, ... 2 00

"The most unaffected writer since Goldsmith."

*

The History of the Bible.

The Book and its Story; a Narrative for the Young on the occasion of the Jubilee of the British and Foreign Bible Society. By D. N. R. With an Introductory Preface by the Rev. T. Phillips, Jubilee Secretary. Handsomely printed, in one volume, crown octavo, on fine paper, and illustrated with numerous wood-cuts. Cloth, . . . 1 00

Extract from the Preface.

"The 'Story' of THE BOOK, in all ages, countries, and languages, is told with simplicity and truthfulness. The work contains the 'Story' of the Bible from the first dawn of Revelation to the completion of the Sacred Canon, with the interesting tales of its translation and circulation, from the earliest efforts to the present time. To tell the Story of the Book in former days, a multitude of curious facts have been culled from works of difficult access; and its latter progress is illustrated by an abundant variety of statements drawn from numerous authentic sources."

Schwarz's Geography of Palestine.

A Descriptive Geography and Brief Historical Sketch of Palestine. By Rabbi Joseph Schwarz, for sixteen years a resident of the Holy Land. Translated by Isaac Luser. Illustrated with numerous maps and engravings. One volume, octavo, cloth, ... 2 50

Dufief's Nature Displayed.

Nature Displayed in the mode of Teaching Languages to Man; being a new and infallible method of acquiring Languages with rapidity, deduced from the Analysis of the Human Mind, and consequently suited to every capacity. Adapted to the French. To which is prefixed a development of the plan of tuition, so powerful in its operation, and so economical, that a liberal education can be afforded to the poorest of mankind. By N. G. Dufief. Twenty-first edition. In two volumes, 5 00

Onderdonk's Sermons.

Sermons and Episcopal Charges. By the Right Rev. Henry V. Onderdonk, D. D. In two volumes, octavo, cloth, ... 5 00

Salomon's Sermons.

Twelve Sermons delivered in the New Temple of the Israelites at Hamburg. By Gotthold Salomon. Translated from the German by Anna Maria Goldsmid, ... 1 00

CAREY'S POLITICAL ECONOMY.

Principles of Political Economy. Part I. On the Laws of the Production and Distribution of Wealth. Part II. On the Causes which retard the Increase in the Production of Wealth and Improvement in the Physical and Moral Condition of Man. Part III. On the Causes which retard the Increase in the Numbers of Man. Part IV. On the Causes which retard Improvement in the Political Condition of Man. By H. C. CAREY, author of "An Essay on the Rate of Wages." Three vols. 8vo., cloth, ... 6 50

CAREY'S PAST AND PRESENT.

The Past, the Present, and the Future. By H. C. CAREY, author of "Political Economy," &c. One volume, ... 2 00

CAREY ON SLAVE-TRADE.

Slave-Trade, Domestic and Foreign; Why it Exists, and How it may be Extinguished. By H. C. CAREY, author of "Principles of Political Economy," "Past, Present, and Future," &c. One volume, 12mo., cloth, ... 1 25

McCULLOCH'S COMMERCIAL DICTIONARY.

A Dictionary (Practical, Theoretical, and Historical) of Commerce and Commercial Navigation. By J. A. McCULLOCH, Esq. Edited by HENRY VETHAKE, LL.D., Professor in the University of Pennsylvania, &c. &c. With an Appendix, containing the New Tariff of 1846, together with the Tariff of 1842, reduced to ad valorem rates as far as practicable, &c. &c. In two volumes, 8vo. cloth, ... 7 50

Sheep, ... 8 00

MORFIT ON SOAP AND CANDLES.

Chemistry applied to the Manufacture of Soap and Candles. A thorough Exposition of the Principles and Practice of the Trade. By CAMPBELL MORFIT, Practical and Analytical Chemist. Illustrated with 170 Engravings on Wood. One volume, 8vo., ... 5 00

HINTS ON DAGUERREOTYPING.

Plain Directions for obtaining Photographic Pictures by the Calotype and Enengeal. Also, upon Albumenized Paper and Glass, by Collodion and Albumen, &c. &c. Including a Practical Treatise on Photography, &c. Also, Hints on the Daguerreotype. Illustrated with engravings, 1 00

"Every Daguerreotypist will find this Manual an essential guide in the practice of his art."—*N. Y. Commercial Advertiser.*

Brass and Iron Founder.

Practical Brass and Iron Founder's Guide. A Concise Treatise on the Art of Brass-founding, Moulding, &c. With numerous Practical Rules, Tablets, and Receipts for Gold, Silver, and Copper founding; Plumbers, Bronze and Bell founders; Jewellers, &c. By James Larkin. One volume, ... 1 00

"A gentleman admirably qualified for the task, which he has ably accomplished."—*Boston Evening Gazette.*

Miss Leslie's House Book.

Miss Leslie's Lady's House Book. Manual of Domestic Economy, containing improved Directions for Washing, Dress-making, Millinery, Dyeing, Cleaning, Quilting, Table Linen, Window-washing, Wood Fires, Straw Bonnets, Silk Stockings, Rag Carpets, Plated Ware, Porcelain, House-cleaning, Laundry, Wood and Coal Grate Fires, Evening Parties, &c. &c. Nineteenth edition, enlarged. With numerous additional Receipts for removing Stains from Silks, Woollens, Cottons, &c. Being a Companion to "Miss Leslie's Lady's New Receipt Book," and "Complete Cookery." One volume, ... 1 00

Turnbull on the Telegraph.

The Electro-Magnetic Telegraph. With an Historical Account of its Rise, Progress, and Present Condition. Also, Practical Suggestions in regard to Insulation and Protection from the Effects of Lightning. Together with an Appendix containing several important Telegraphic Decisions and Laws. By Laurence Turnbull, M.D., Lecturer on Technical Chemistry in the Franklin Institute of Pennsylvania. Second edition, revised and improved. Illustrated by numerous engravings. One volume, ... 2 00

Railroad Accidents.

Railroad Accidents, and the Means by which they may be Prevented by the Use of the Electro-Magnetic Safety Apparatus. With some useful Hints to Railway Travellers. By Laurence Turnbull, M. D., and William C. McRea. One volume, ... 25

Burnet on Painting.

Practical Hints on Composition in Painting. Illustrated by examples from the Great Masters of the Italian, Flemish, and Dutch schools. By John Burnet. One volume, quarto, half morocco, ... 3 00

BAUCHER ON HORSEMANSHIP.

A Method of Horsemanship, founded upon New Principles; including the Breaking and Training of Horses; with Instructions for obtaining a good Seat. By F. BAUCHER. One volume, 12mo., ... 1 25

ARABIAN NIGHTS' ENTERTAINMENTS.

Arabian Nights' Entertainments, embellished with nearly 100 engravings. A new edition, carefully revised and corrected. Complete in one volume, 8vo., cloth, ... 1 00

Scarlet cloth, ... 1 25

ROSE OF THE PARSONAGE.

An Idyll of our own Times. Translated from the German of ROBERT GISEKE, author of the Romance "Moderne Titanen." One volume, paper cover, ... 50

Cloth, ... 75

NOVELS AND TALES.

BY CAROLINE LEE HENTZ.

New Editions in nine volumes, 12mo., paper covers, ... 4 50

Cloth gilt, ... 6 50

I.

LINDA; OR, THE YOUNG PILOT OF THE BELLE CREOLE.

A Tale of Southern Life. Eighth edition. In one volume, 276 pages.

Paper covers, ... 50

Cloth gilt, ... 75

"This is no ordinary story; it exhibits the most useful phases of romance."

City Item.

II.

RENA; OR, THE SNOW BIRD.

A Tale of Real Life. Fifth edition. In one volume 273 pages. Paper covers, ... 50

Cloth gilt, ... 75

"It will be found to be the best story which Mrs. Hentz has ever given to the public."—*Saturday Courier.*

III.

MARCUS WARLAND; OR, THE LONG MOSS SPRING.

A Tale of the South. Sixth edition. In one volume, 287 pages. Paper covers, ... 50

Cloth gilt, ... 75

"Should follow in the wake of 'Uncle Tom's Cabin.'"—*Pennsylvanian.*

IV.

EOLINE; OR, MAGNOLIA VALE.

A Novel. Complete in one volume, 257 pages. Fifth Edition. Paper covers, ... 50
Cloth gilt, ... 75

"It is worthy to be pronounced a charming and delightful story."—*Southern Literary Gazette.*

V.

WILD JACK; OR, THE STOLEN CHILD.

A Sketch from Life. Together with Bell and Rose, &c. Third edition. Complete in one volume, 277 pages. Paper covers, ... 50
Cloth, gilt, ... 75

VI.

HELEN AND ARTHUR; OR, MISS THUSA'S SPINNING-WHEEL.

A Novel. Complete in one volume, 280 pages. Third edition. Paper covers, ... 50
Cloth gilt, ... 75

VII.

THE VICTIM OF EXCITEMENT, THE PARLOR SERPENT,

And other Nouvellettes. Second edition. Complete in one volume, 272 pages. Paper covers, ... 50
Cloth gilt, ... 75

VIII.

PLANTER'S NORTHERN BRIDE.

A Novel. Complete in two volumes, 12mo., 600 pages, with six illustrations. Paper covers, ... 1 00
Cloth gilt, ... 1 50

"It is unquestionably the most powerful and important, if not the most charming work that has yet flowed from her elegant pen; and though evidently founded upon the all-absorbing subjects of slavery and abolitionism, the genius and skill of the fair author have developed new views of golden argument, and flung around the whole such a halo of pathos, interest, and beauty as to render it every way worthy the author of 'Linda,' 'Rena,' 'Marcus Warland,' and the numerous other literary gems from the same author."—*American Courier.*

"We have seldom been more charmed by the perusal of a novel; and we desire to commend it to our readers in the strongest words of praise that our vocabulary affords. * * * The incidents are well varied; the scenes beautifully described; and the interest admirably kept up. But the *moral* of the book is its highest merit. * * * The '*Planter's Northern Bride*' should be as welcome as the dove of peace to every fireside in the Union. It cannot be read without a moistening of the eyes, a softening of the heart, and a mitigation of sectional and most unchristian prejudices."—*N. Y. Mirror.*

LORD BACON'S WORKS.

Price Reduced to $7 50.

In 3 Royal 8vo. Volumes, Cloth Gilt.

THE WORKS OF LORD BACON,

WITH A MEMOIR, AND A TRANSLATION OF HIS LATIN WRITINGS,

BY BASIL MONTAGU, ESQ.

In Three Volumes, Octavo.

The American edition of the works of Lord Bacon, now offered to the public, is reprinted from the most approved English edition, that of Basil Montagu, Esq., which has recently issued from the celebrated press of Pickering, (the modern Aldus,) in seventeen octavo volumes. It contains the complete works of the illustrious philosopher, *those in Latin being translated into English*. In order to render the publication cheap, and therefore attainable by all our public and social libraries, as well as by those general readers who study economy, the seventeen octavo volumes have been comprised in three volumes, imperial octavo. Being printed from the most accurate as well as complete English edition, and carefully revised, the American edition will possess greater advantages for the critical scholar as well as the general reader. In typography, paper and binding, it will be recognized as a brilliant specimen of the products of the American book trade.

"We may safely affirm, that, by giving the Inductive Philosophy to the world, Lord Bacon has proved one of its most signal benefactors, and has largely done his part towards promoting the final triumph of all truth, whether natural, or moral and intellectual, over all error; and towards bringing on that glorious crisis, destined, we doubt not, one day to arrive, when, according to the allegorical representation of that great poet, who was not only the Admirer of Bacon, but in some respects his kindred genius—TRUTH, though 'hewn like the mangled body of Osiris, into a thousand pieces, and scattered to the four winds, shall be gathered limb to limb, and moulded, with every joint and member, into an immortal feature of loveliness and perfection.'"

"We are more gratified than we can find words to express, to find a publishing house in this country, putting forth a publication like the Complete Works of Lord Bacon, in a form at once compact, elegant and economical."—*Brother Jonathan.*

WALTER SCOTT'S COMPLETE WORKS,

In 10 vols., Royal 8vo, Cloth gilt, for only $10!!

Including the Waverly Novels, Poetical and Prose Works, with the Author's latest Corrections.

Also, Full-bound Library Style. Price $12.50.

Price Reduced to $2 50.

THE WAVERLEY NOVELS.

COMPLETE.

3340 Pages for Two Dollars and a Half.

CAREY & HART, have recently published A NEW EDITION OF

THE WAVERLEY NOVELS,

BY SIR WALTER SCOTT,

With all the Author's latest Notes and Additions, Complete, without the slightest Abridgment.

In Five Royal 8vo. volumes, upwards of 650 Pages in each volume.

CONTENTS.

Waverley, Guy Mannering, Antiquary, Rob Roy, Black Dwarf, Old Mortality, Heart of Mid-Lothian, Bride of Lammermoor, Legend of Montrose, Ivanhoe, The Monastery, The Abbot, Kenilworth, The Pirate, Fortunes of Nigel, Peveril of the Peak, Quentin Durward, St Ronan's Well, Redgauntlet, The Betrothed, The Talisman, Woodstock, The Highland Widow, Two Drovers, My Aunt Margaret's Mirror, Tapestried Chamber, The Laird's Jock, Fair Maid of Perth, Anne of Gierstein, Count Robert of Paris, Castle Dangerous, The Surgeon's Daughter.

The object of the publishers in thus reducing the price of the Waverley Novels, is to endeavor to give them a greatly extended circulation, and they have, therefore, put them at a price which brings them within the reach of every family in the country. There is *now* no fireside that need be without a set of the most charming works of fiction ever issued from the press: for there is no one that can't afford two dollars and a half—TWO DOLLARS AND A HALF for twenty-five of Sir Walter Scott's Novels! ten cents for a complete Novel!! ten cents for "Ivanhoe," which was originally published at a guinea and a half!!! It seems impossible, and yet it is true. In no other way can the same amount of amusement and instruction be obtained for ten times the money, for the Waverley Novels alone form a Library.

The publishers wish it to be distinctly understood, that, while the price is so greatly reduced the work is in no way abridged, but is CAREFULLY PRINTED FROM, AND CONTAINS EVERY WORD IN THE LAST EDINBURGH EDITION, in forty-eight volumes, which sells for seventy-two dollars.

Now is the time to buy! Such an opportunity may never again occur. Let every one, then, who wants the *Waverley Novels for two dollars and a half, now purchase*, for if the publishers do not find the sale greatly increased, by the immense reduction in price, they will resume the old price of twenty-five cents for each Novel, which *was* considered wonderfully cheap.

CIRCULAR.

PARRY & McMILLAN (successors to A. Hart, late Carey & Hart,) respectfully announce to the Trade that they have succeeded Mr. Hart in the Publishing and General Bookselling Business, at the old stand, S. E. corner of Fourth and Chestnut Streets, having purchased his entire Miscellaneous Stock, together with a large portion of his Stereotype Plates, at the sale on the 8th inst., to which they purpose making such additions of Standard, Popular, and Scientific Works, as will secure the attention of the Trade. P. & McM. hope, by strict attention, to merit a continuance of that patronage and confidence so deservedly bestowed on their predecessor.

J. PARRY,
JAMES McMILLAN.

In retiring from business, I beg to return my sincere thanks to the Booksellers for their uniform courtesy and kindness extended to me during a period of twenty-five years, and take great pleasure in recommending my successors (Messrs. Parry & McMillan) to the confidence of the Trade, feeling satisfied that their transactions will be conducted with the strictest principles of honor and integrity. Mr. Parry has served me long and faithfully, having been in my employ for the last eighteen years, and of course is fully acquainted with the business. Mr. McMillan has also been long engaged in the Bookselling business, formerly in the West, and for the past nine years in St. John, N. B., where his name stands pre-eminent.

Both parties bring a sufficient amount of capital into the business, which is a guarantee for the faithful performance of their contracts.

A. HART, late Carey & Hart.

Philadelphia, *March* 9, 1854.

www.ingramcontent.com/pod-product-compliance
Lightning Source LLC
LaVergne TN
LVHW020059110826
845151LV00001B/28

* 9 7 8 1 4 2 5 5 4 4 6 3 8 *